POSTMODE RNIZATION

POSTMODERNIZATION

Change in Advanced Society

Stephen Crook
Jan Pakulski
Malcolm Waters

SAGE Publications
London ● Newbury Park ● New Delhi

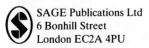

SAGE Publications Ltd
6 Bonhill Street
London EC2A 4PU

SAGE Publications Inc
2455 Teller Road
Newbury Park, California 91320

SAGE Publications India Pvt Ltd
32, M-Block Market
Greater Kailash – I
New Delhi 110 048

British Library Cataloguing in Publication data

Crook, Stephen
  Postmodernization: Change in Advanced
  Society
  I. Title   303.4

  ISBN 0–8039–8327–1
  ISBN 0–8039–8328–X

Library of Congress catalog card number 91-051149

Typeset by Ann Buchan (Typesetters), Middlesex
Printed in Great Britain by Dotesios Ltd,
   Trowbridge, Wiltshire

Contents

Preface   vii

1 Modernization and postmodernization   1

2 From culture to postculture   47

3 The shrinking state   79

4 Simulated inequality   106

5 Social movements and the new politics   136

6 Disalienation and debureaucratization   167

7 Science and technology: decomposition of the 'Grand Design'   197

8 The dialectics of postmodernization ·   220

References   241

Name index   257

Subject index   261

For Felicity,
for Peter and Magda,
and for Penny and Tom

Preface

On the face of it, Hobart is a strange place in which to write a book about postmodernization. It is the capital of Tasmania, the smallest, most southerly and only island state of Australia. It is situated on the estuary of the river Derwent, and we look down the estuary from our offices to the expanse of the Southern Ocean which extends, uninterrupted by land, to Antarctica. Tasmania's extreme geographical marginality often seems to be reflected in an extreme social conservatism. What are coyly referred to as 'homosexual acts' remain illegal in the state, and condom vending machines only recently ceased to be so. By contrast, guns (unlike fireworks) are readily available to anyone over the age of sixteen with the money to pay for them. But this is not the whole story about Tasmania. Hobart is indistinguishable in many respects from any other late modern, or early postmodern, city. Its suburbs nestle around airconditioned shopping malls; its urban landscape is dotted with the familiar icons of Kentucky Fried Chicken, McDonald's and Pizza Hut outlets; its radio and television stations transmit sounds and images which would be instantly recognized in Melbourne, Miami or Manchester. There are even senses in which Tasmania sets the pace of global change. The United Tasmania Group of the 1970s has a claim to be the world's first 'green' political party. Environmental issues have long been at the forefront of political debate, and the present state Labor administration holds office only with the support of a group of green parliamentarians. In short, 'marginality' is no longer an entirely self-evident category. We have found the paradoxical and volatile mix of past, present and possible futures which marks our state to be a suggestive background for our reflections on postmodernizing change, change which seems simultaneously to disrupt, accelerate and reverse the developmental logic of modernization.

In another, and more immediate, sense our teaching and research has formed the context from which the book has emerged. It became clear to us that our diverse interests in culture, state, inequality, social movements, organizations and science were converging on a concern with patterns of change in contemporary advanced societies. From this realization came the idea for a book in which a general account of postmodernizing change would be put to work in our individual areas of interest. While the book is conceived as much more than a series of unconnected essays, we have not attempted to apply the general account in a rigid, mechanistic, way. The reader will find that different dimensions of postmodernizing processes are emphasized in different chapters according to the peculiarities of the subject matter. The greater part of Chapter 1 was designed and written by

Waters, although Crook and Pakulski also contributed sections and proposed amendments to successive drafts. The other chapters have been subjected to a rather less exhaustive process of collective revision. Crook bears responsibility for Chapters 2, 7 and 8; Pakulski for Chapters 3 and 5; and Waters for Chapters 4 and 6.

We extend our thanks to colleagues and students in the department of sociology who have borne with us as we rehearsed the themes of the book in lectures and seminars. The department's research budget has carried the costs of the project. Finally, we are grateful to our families for putting up with our dereliction of domestic duties during the writing of the book.

Stephen Crook, Jan Pakulski and Malcolm Waters

1

Modernization and postmodernization

Long-run social change is at once the most fascinating and the most elusive of topics for general theorizing in sociology. The emergence of the modern era provided a nascent sociology with both its reason for theory and its topic to be theorized. However, even the most robust of sociological arguments about the emergence of modernity, those offered by Marx and by Weber, ultimately cannot be sustained. This is possibly because they seek to isolate a critical transition point, a great divide or transformation, which provides a watershed between a traditional and a modern era. In fact, general social transformations are quite unlike the general political transformations which are known as revolutions. Although such terms as the 'industrial revolution' or the 'bourgeois revolution' are in frequent use to describe such phase shifts the transformation signified involved some very long-term patterns which were uneven in their development both in terms of the aspects of societies which they affected and the geographical regions in which they occurred. Indeed many such patterns of development remain unresolved to this day. There are quite pronounced arenas of traditionalism, however one wishes to define it, in all societies, and there are societies which are less modernized than others.

Implicit in many arguments about modernization is the notion that its trends can be projected into an infinite future. This notion of a continuous qualitative progression of modernity now needs to be re-evaluated in the light of the direction of social change now being experienced in advanced society. So, this book offers an alternative view of whether a general long-term transformation is under way which is similar to the emergence of modern society. This process of postmodernization will give rise, we argue, to a form of society which is radically different from that given within modernity.

As is discussed later in this chapter, the observation that radical social change is in process is shared widely but there is considerable disagreement as to whether we are witnessing a simple extension, or development, of modernity, or whether we are entering a genuinely new historical configuration. The argument here tends to the latter view. Although the matter should be approached with considerable caution, the conclusion that radical change is occurring is inescapable. This is because change is now so widespread in its penetration of various social and cultural realms and because it reverses so many of the normal patterns of modernity.

From the range of possible alternatives, the adjective 'postmodern' best describes the emerging form of society.[1] This is not least because the social form emerges after modernity in a temporal sense. It is also because variants of the term have achieved currency in describing new and destylized forms of cultural expression and it is in the cultural arena that the sources of the the new social formation are located.[2] The argument below incorporates this element by suggesting that a defining outcome of postmodernization is an increased level of cultural effectivity.[3] However, the most convincing reason for the use of the term is that the emerging social form is still indeterminate and problematic: we have no firm knowledge of what it is but only that it is not modernity. Thus no claim is offered that the advanced industrial societies are postmodern in any remotely complete sense. Our insistence on this point sets us against several other observers. Bauman (1988a: 811), for example, has no doubt: '(p)ost modernity . . . is an aspect of a fully fledged, viable social system which has come to replace the "classical" modern capitalist society and thus needs to be theorised according to its own terms'. For us, this claim is radically premature.

The contemporary changes which concern us here are, we must stress, incremental in character, in the manner of what has been called the Industrial Revolution, rather than cataclysmic, in the manner of the French Revolution. Although at least one other observer has put a specific date of 1973 on the emergence of the postmodern condition (Harvey 1989: 141–72),[4] we can fully expect modernity and postmodernity to coexist until well into the twenty-first century. Therefore we concentrate on the processes of change which produce postmodern social forms, the processes of postmodernization, rather than a vision of the new society.

This rather long chapter has four components: an examination of some standard statements on modernization; a specification of the features of modernity which are centrally relevant to the the stance taken in this book; a review of theories of the transformation of modern society; and a preliminary argument about the emerging form of postmodernity.

Theories of Societal Transformation

There is nothing new about social change. However the common perception that change is endemic and enduring is relatively new. Until the emergence of modern industrial capitalism the general conception, in whatever type of society, was that things were about the same as they had always been. This was not because there was no change but because processes of change were very slow. The shock of modernization was that things were never going to be the same again but it at least offered the reassurance that the direction in which things were going to change was, at least in principle, perceptible. Social scientists, politicians and others could easily agree that modern societies would both grow and differentiate, even if some believed that there were finite, even cataclysmic, limits to such processes, and they could approach the future with some measure of certainty. As we shall we see, the shock of postmodernization is that directionality is totally unclear: the only certainty is continuing uncertainty.

We begin by identifying three theoretical approaches to societal change which have been associated with the Durkheimian, Marxian and Weberian traditions. These traditions specify the direction of modernization by identifying processes, respectively, of differentiation, commodification and rationalization. Individually or in combination these processes are the focus of many social scientific accounts of change.[5]

Perhaps the most common theme in accounts of the process of modernization is one or another of the variations of the notion of *differentiation*. Social structures are held to be more or less differentiated to the extent that the units of social structure are specialized relative to one another with respect to operation or function. The idea of differentiation emerged in the context of rapid modernization as nineteenth-century social theorists sought to understand the emergence of industrial capitalism, which had been experienced in the societies of Europe and North America. So, that rather complacent Victorian Englishman, Herbert Spencer (1972), invented the idea of differentiation in order to explain the superiority of his society over both its historical antecedents and other societies around the world unfortunate enough not to have developed in quite the same way. Spencer's notion of differentiation is a Darwinian evolutionary statement – a more differentiated society is a more advanced society, that is a society which is better adapted to its environment because it has competed with other societies and outlived if not absorbed them. An industrial society, defined by its high level of differentiation, accomplishes a natural internal harmony as its specialized components dovetail neatly with one another. Free trade and exchange is all that is needed to ensure peaceful mutuality, voluntary co-operation and relief from the oppressiveness of an overgrown state. Industrial society, with its natural pattern of integration, thus compares favourably with its predecessor, the undifferentiated 'militant society' which is oppressively state regulated and rigidly structured.

Durkheim (1964) was far less sanguine about the superiority of differentiated social formations and was particularly concerned about Spencer's assumption of natural harmony between the differentiated parts of a society. The critical aspect of differentiation on which Durkheim focusses is the division of labour, the extent to which work is subdivided into specialized tasks. Like Spencer, Durkheim sees growth as the cause of advances in the division of labour. Growth in population size increases 'moral density', the number of social relationships in which each individual must engage, which in turn forces each relationship between individuals to be narrower in its compass. Durkheim's initial approach to integration, the well known distinction between mechanical and organic solidarity, is much like Spencer's but he becomes increasingly concerned with the cultural effects of social differentiation. Durkheim's characterization of cultural aspects as the *conscience collective* leads him to a position in which the sharing of value-commitments becomes problematic in the modern context of heteronomous social membership. Modern society is therefore threat-ened by the disintegrative pattern known as *anomie* as rapid spurts and jumps in the differentiation process tear apart traditional ties and commit-ments. Integrative and regulative norms become outmoded by social practice.

Durkheim's warnings of the cultural dangers of differentiation were, however, submerged by the confident structural-functionalism which emerged in a post-Second World War America engorged on its own material and military successes. Just as Spencer had sought to celebrate the hegemony of Victorian Britain so Levy, Smelser and, above all, Parsons reasserted the notion that the most advanced society was that which was most differentiated, and the most differentiated was the most adaptively successful. Levy (1966) and Smelser (1968) offer virtual carbon copies of Spencer – they write of *structural* differentiation, a process in which functions held to be necessary for the maintenance of society are each increasingly performed by separate specialized institutions; for example the family does primary socialization, the school does secondary socializa-tion, etc. Smelser (1968: 138–40) 'solves' Durkheim's differentiation–integration paradox by speaking of the emergence of differentiated structural units which specialize in integration, including trade unions, political parties and state agencies. This formulation, of course, begs the question of how these new institutions are themselves integrated with others.

Parsons' approach is altogether more interesting and challenging. First, with the assistance of Bales (Parsons et al. 1953) and then Smelser (Parsons and Smelser 1984), he specifies the functional dimensions along which the lines of differentiation will occur within the famous AGIL quaternity of functional imperatives: adaptation, goal-attainment, integration and latency.[6] This provides theoretical purchase on several problematic issues, not least that of integration. He is able, for example, to make a distinction between two types of integration problem. The problem of orderly exchange between social units (what has become known as system integra-tion) is located in the I box, while the problem of shared commitment to societal value-orientations (social integration) is located in the L box. For Parsons, any system will by necessity devote energy to each of these activities in the same way as it must to issues of material survival (A and G).

Also, the notion of differentiation can now be understood as displaying two aspects. First a more differentiated system is one in which the subsystems which perform the four functions move apart, so to speak, so that the social distance between them is greater and the boundaries between them are more explicit. So in a modern society the distance and the boundaries between economy and family or between religion and politics are far more apparent than in a traditional society. Second, each differentiated subsystem itself undergoes internal differentiation along the AGIL dimensions. So in a highly modernized society, the economy (A subsystem) might be seen as subdividing into capitalization (A), production (G), organizational (I) and human relations (L) sub-subsystems and the polity (G subsystem) into administrative (A), executive (G), legislative (I) and juridico-constitutional (L) sub-subsystems. Each of these sub-subsystems is subject to further differentiation along AGIL lines. The driving force for this process is no longer unidimensional, material, adaptive upgrading but multidimensional upgrading on each of the functional dimensions.

Parsons also differs from other structural-functionalists in that whereas they offer continuous or dichotomous views of the process of differentiation his is an evolutionary view of a series of stages.[7] Once initiated the process of differentiation is more or less continuous but Parsons makes a distinction between what might be termed developmental processes and what might be termed phase-shift processes. The former consist in a continuous and incremental elaboration and separation of subsystems, which does not alter the general overall pattern of the society. By contrast, phase-shift processes are fundamental differentiation leaps or evolutionary breakthroughs, typically caused outside the social realm (e.g. in the realms of culture or personality) which reorient the social pattern.

Two principal phase transformations are identified by Parsons (1977). The first is the development of 'explicit cultural legitimation' (by means of writing) in the L box. Writing opens up new possibilities for transmitting social patterns through time especially in circumstances in which extreme inequalities need to be made legitimate. Explicit cultural legitimation enables the emergence of the centralizing inequalities found in ancient imperial and feudal societies, which Parsons calls 'intermediate' and which displace 'primitive' (forager and tribal) societies. The specific differentiation process which marks the emergence of modern societies is that which moves law from the G box (i.e. as subordinate to political action) to the I box (as an independent and abstract set of rules which governs political action as much as any other). Here once again there are shades of Spencer insofar as modernity is held to be marked by the reduction of the state and the emancipation of human action in civil society.

Differentiation is associated with functionalist theory, and here it is seen to offer evolutionary advantages. However, the process has also come to occupy a prominent place in Marxist scholarship although here it is seen as far more problematic and tension ridden. The originating statement is Marx's well-known fragment on alienated labour (1967: 77–87) but the idea was submerged in his later, more general and more powerful analysis of commodification. Only recently has differentiation in its own right become a central focus for Marxist analysis, particularly in Braverman's iconic statement of changes in the labour process (1974). Here differentiation is understood solely in terms of the division of labour. The division of labour is argued to take on two forms which might, after Durkheim, be

called normal and abnormal. Normal divisions of labour between occupations or jobs are held to be found in all known societies. Each occupation
has a sense of completeness and self-control and such a division is often
regarded as nonproblematic. This is seen to be the case even where there
might be a division of labour by gender between say domestic activity on
one hand and political or religious activity on the other. The distinguishing
and problematic feature of modern (capitalist) societies is an abnormal
division of labour in which occupations become fragmented into minimum
component tasks. Braverman traces extensions of this process through
manufacturing to clerical labour as elements of mechanization and automation progressively penetrate the modern workplace allowing employers to
control employees by splitting their work into components, each highly
circumscribed in the level of skill required.[8]

The common arguments which transcend these positions are: first, that
the direction of change is always towards increased differentiation;[9] second
that differentiation implies separation of units of social structure (e.g.
institutions, collectivities, occupations, people, positions, tasks) in time
and space; third that increased structural differentiation is matched by an
elaboration of the categories of social discourse so that the form of modern
thinking is to divide the world into such categories and to reify them;
fourth, that there must be generalized media of exchange to connect and
allow exchanges between highly differentiated units; fifth that the cement
which binds highly differentiated elements together is located at the level
of highly generalized ideas and values in the form of what has become
known as a 'dominant ideology' (Abercrombie et al. 1980) or common
value system;[10] and sixth, that the process takes an evolutionary direction
through a series of stages in which each successive stage is more positive
than the previous ones in terms of general material or social well-being.
Although many of these ideas are topics of vigorous debate in social
science, let us temporarily suspend disbelief and pursue the implications of
the idea of differentiation for the present argument. The proposition is that
modern society is highly differentiated relative to earlier forms.

Unlike the functionalist notion of continuous differentiation or the
Weberian vision of the relentless progress of rationalization (see below),
the Marxist view holds the process of commodification and its vessel, the
capitalist mode of production, to be temporary developments. Advances
on modernity require transcendence of the commodity form so that
production is geared to human needs in the form of use values rather than
to capital accumulation. This ultimate and revolutionary transformation,
which Marx does not analyse in detail, would resolve the contradictions of
capitalism and eliminate alienation and reverse commodification. Marx's
ambivalent view of capitalism as both a progressive system liberating
human creative potential and as imposing a new set of constraints is also
reflected in a parallel ambiguity about the pattern of capitalist development. Capitalism initially resolves the contradictions between a feudal
political system and contains a capitalized economic system by privatizing

property and contractualizing exchange relationships. However, other contradictions emerge,[11] so that commodification and capitalist relations of production must be reversed if human progress is to proceed.

Marx's analysis of capitalist industrialism focusses, then, on the commodity, that: ' very queer thing, abounding in metaphysical subtleties and theological niceties' (1954: 76). The peculiarity of the commodity form lies in its capacity to establish equivalence between the 'exchange values' of the most radically diverse 'use values', the medium of this transformation being money. So the products of human labour are transformed into commodities when bought and sold for money at a price established in a market with the intention of realizing profit. The metaphysical significance of the commodity lies in the fact that it externalizes the products of human labour from the labourer. Equally, its queerness lies in its 'unnatural' condition, its difference from a primordial state in which products were used by their own producers. Marx elaborates on this peculiarity in terms of the 'commodification' of human labour itself: commodity production is possible only where 'labour power' is bought and sold for a wage. For our purposes, and begging the complexities of Marx's labour theory of value, the process of *commodification* is one in which an increasing proportion of social objects are brought within the ambit of exchange relations, so that they are bought and sold for money in a market. As they thus become objects external to the self, commodities receive a significance previously given only to religious objects: they are treated with awe and reverence. Modern culture is thus, according to Marx, afflicted by commodity fetishism.

Two closely related processes contribute to the development of commodity fetishism: the creation of new 'use values' and the colonization of old ones. The former process treads familiar paths related to the use of advertising and the mass media to create demand by the manipulation of material preferences. In the latter process, the commodity form is extended to areas of cultural and personal life once considered as 'qualitatively' insulated from the taint of commerce: family life collapses into the rituals of mass consumption, and Great Art is prostituted in the market place.[12]

The most extreme statement of this commodification of culture thesis is given in the work of the Frankfurt School. Here commodification, and associated processes of rationalization which are discussed below, are argued to provide a phase shift within the development of capitalism, occurring between about 1920 and 1940. The new phase is marked precisely by a transfer of commodification from the economic sphere to the cultural-ideological sphere. This is interpreted as a general triumph of instrumental over emancipatory reason (Adorno and Horkheimer 1979; Horkheimer 1974). The ideological manifestation of this instrumental supremacy is the dominance of positivistic scientism and technicism which displaces the reasoning processes and value-commitment of everyday discourse and experience. Its cultural manifestation is the growth of a

homogenized, commercialized, and electronically mediated culture industry. As discussed in the sections on culture below, the creative, critical and
transcendental functions of art are lost as works of art are stripped of their
aura and become commodities which have the mere function of reconciling
a mass public with the status quo, circuses to match the commodified bread
of capitalist materialism. This culture industry takes over the socializing
functions of the invaded and collapsing family, promoting conformist and
authoritarian attitudes (see, for example, Adorno et al. 1975 and Marcuse
1964).

Paradoxically, although it is the market for commodities which originally
gives rise to commodification, the market eventually comes to be regarded
as inadequate to the preservation of the commodity form. The economy is
etatized and regulated by collusion between the state and oligopolistic
corporations.[13] So, much of what is accomplished by commodification in
the arenas of production and distribution is engulfed and frustrated by
rationalization but, strangely, it is the commodified culture which endures
and develops.

It is Weber who identifies the process of modernization with this
increasing formal *rationalization* of social action. 'Rational' here refers to
action which is calculable and impersonal,[14] and which contrasts, first of
all, with traditional, ad hoc and intuitive arrangements for customary
aquiescence. However, formal rationality not only displaces tradition: it
also progressively erodes any ethical basis of commitment to general or
substantive values. In modern societies the 'ethical rationality' of consistent moral principle is increasingly marginalized by an 'instrumental
rationality' which imposes a calculus of cost and benefit on all social action.
Worth, or value, thereby becomes increasingly instrumentalized, so that
the value of work is assessed according to the measurable criterion of a
wage, rather than the imponderable of creativity. Similarly, education
generates credentials rather than learning, while art, literature and
music become mere instruments of relaxation and leisure. In sum, rationalization involves: 'the depersonalization of social relationships, the refinement of techniques of calculation, the enhancement of the social
importance of specialized knowledge, and the extension of technically
rational control over both natural and social processes' (Brubaker
1984: 2).

Brubaker identifies three main unifying themes in Weber's analysis of
societal rationalization. The first of these is knowledge: to act rationally is
to act on the basis of knowledge (1984: 30–2). In modern society the
growth of positivistic scientific and technological knowledge systems
inflates the importance of knowledge as a basis for action almost to the
level of sanctification. Such forms of knowledge displace religious knowledge systems and in so doing intellectualize and demystify the world.
Paradoxically, the greater the level of factual knowledge of the world the
further the retreat of the possibility of discovering its meaning. Action
based on scientistic knowledge tends to be instrumental, focussing on

short-run calculations of self-interest rather than on long-term commitment.

The second unifying theme is impersonality (Brubaker 1984: 32–3). Traditional, personal expressions of power are displaced by abstract sources of authority in the economic and political realms. Economic power is understood to be the consequence of market forces, that 'hidden hand' which dictates the actions of both capitalist and worker. It controls them by the twin threats of bankruptcy and unemployment, which are defined as no person's fault but simply that of the 'system'. In the political realm, the governing system is constituted as a set of legal rules administered by ranks of ethically neutral bureaucrats. Individual attitudes develop in comformity with these impersonal systems as lives are increasingly evaluated in terms of material success and of doing one's duty rather than in terms of personal development or contribution to transcendentally valuable human achievements.

Last, rationalization involves extensions of control over natural and social objects (Brubaker 1984: 33–5). Here the central focus is the technical rationalization of social relationships, their reduction to aspects of scientific, industrial or administrative processes. Much as in Marx's formulation of the commodification of labour, human beings may be seen as being disciplined to conform with the instrumental needs of centrally organized industrial and administrative systems. Success in establishing control depends on calculability and specifically on the measurement and empirical analysis of the consequences of individual human action. In part control is accomplished by internal processes of commitment to materialistic values and to duty, that is by the development, among other things, of what Merton has called the 'bureaucratic personality' and of what Marx and Engels thought to be false consciousness. But it is also the systematic and intentional accomplishment of bureaucracy, formalistic law and, above all, industrial capitalism.

Thus, although Weber regards rationalization as all pervasive it is clear that he views the process as critical in the transformation of four social arenas: production, law, administration and ethics (Brubaker 1984: 10–29). The key development in the arena of production is industrial capitalism with its orientation to market relationships, monetary calculation of profit and loss, legal protections for property, stress on technical knowledge, and contractualizing orientation to labour. The law equally is characterized by an abstract formality and universality in which legal norms have no meaning (they are established without appeal to general principles of justice, for example) but merely serve to resolve disputes, protect property, and enforce contracts. Administration is subjected to the relentless rise of the bureaucratic administrative staff which is as impersonal and technically efficient as a machine. Last, worldly asceticism which derives from the Protestant ethic delivers labour and a commitment to duty but fails to deliver on the substantively rational criteria of truth, beauty and, above all, happiness.

Processes of Modernization

Differentiation, commodification and rationalization, then, define the transformation of premodern into modern systems as well as the central internal processes of modern societies. The three processes are closely related: modern social systems have a high or complex level of differentiation and are equally characterized by progressive commodification and rationalization. One further point might be made about the intersection of these processes. As Marx and Weber respectively make clear, commodification and rationalization are closely connected to the forms and distribution of power in society. The level of their development is an index of the extent to which commodity producers and 'rule producers' are able to extend their control over material and cultural objects and over other human beings. The concept of differentiation, by contrast, specifies a dimension of modernization which is in itself 'power neutral': it identifies the distributional arrangement of activities in social space, rather than the ways in which they are controlled or ordered. This, of course, is why functionalist theories which give priority to differentiation are able to construct modernization as a fundamentally benign process.

In concrete processes of modernization, the analytically distinct processes of differentiation, rationalization and commodification have been intertwined in the most intimate way. If the latter two processes are already implicated in power relations, each might be said to be factored against a second and common underlying dimension of change. This dimension is to do with the extent to which power is concentrated, that is, with the extent to which a society is centrally organized. We shall refer to it as the level of *organization* of the society and identify two significant reference points within it, a diffuse level of organization and a systematic level of organization.[15] A diffuse level of organization is one in which power is relatively dispersed and is intrinsically bound up with domestic arrangements. Typically the state will be nonexistent or weak and economic production units will be relatively small in scale, that is they are able to be comprehended and negotiated in a face-to-face way by participants without need for social relations to be conducted through steering media, such as money or power. Likewise military and ideological power will be highly circumscribed. By contrast, when there is a systematic level of organization, management (or 'steering' as some have it) is separated from the purely domestic level and concentrated in relatively few hands. Goal setting and goal attainment patterns for the society are intentional processes. The centres of power concentration which might include the state, production organizations, the army, or such ideologically oriented organizations as churches and political movements (Mann 1986), are highly developed and concentrated. Because of their social and spatial distance from domestic arrangements, social relations between these power centres and local spheres of action are highly mediated, taking the form of bureaucratic commands, monetary transfers, military orders or ideological

DIFFERENTIATION

	Simple	Complex	
	FORAGER–TRIBAL	**LIBERAL**	
	Collective foraging/horticulture	Mechanized manufacturing	*Critical economic feature*
ORGANIZATION Diffuse	Acephelous gerontocracy	Plutocratic nation state	*Political arrangements*
	Clan (lineage group)	City	*Significant community*
	Speech	Print	*Emergent cultural medium*
	FEUDAL	**ORGANIZED**	
ORGANIZATION Systematic	Collective agriculture	Mass production/services	*Critical economic feature*
	Monarchy & aristocracy	Democratic welfare state	*Political arrangements*
	Village/manor	Suburb	*Significant community*
	Writing	Electronic technology	*Emergent cultural medium*

Figure 1.1 *A scheme of societal types*

imperatives. We take the term modern to encompass both these levels of organization but identify the central process of change *within* modernity to be a move from a diffuse to a systematic level of organization principally in terms of the systematic concentration and extension of the powers of control of economic production (commodification) and of administrative regulation (rationalization).

The intersection between differentiation and organization is indicated in Figure 1.1. We have provided instances of only some exemplary types of premodern social structure but a brief review of these as stages of social change is possible, identifying their main features more or less in terms of the AGIL scheme.

Forager-tribal Society (Simple Differentiation/Diffuse Organization)

Economic Features   Production is typically collective in terms of property ownership, the organization of labour and the beneficial use of products. This is in part because technology is relatively simple, so for example the trapping of large animals or the cultivation of fields using simple horticultural methods requires co-operation and sharing. Divisions of labour usually occur in terms of age and sex, so typically women engage in production activities which are relatively close to the domestic arena while men range further afield.

Political Arrangements   Age, generational membership, and location in a kinship structure typically specify access to political power. In forager societies rulership resides with the collectivity of mature adults, i.e. the gerontocracy. Tribal societies are characterized by power differentiation between core and cadet lineages, the former being regarded as having special cultural significance as well as a capacity to appropriate and accumulate economic surplus produced by cadet lineages. The core lineages therefore assume political leadership in frequently elaborate hierarchies of chiefs and paramount chiefs.

Community   Kinship is the key integrating system for this type of society. The significant community is normally a kinship group which lives and works together. The form of interpersonal relations is also established in kinship terms and is fixed and non-negotiable.

Cultural Patterns   Collective co-operation is made possible by the emergence of language as a cultural medium. Knowledge and lore are transmitted through oral traditions which seek to provide meaning and explanation by reference to animistic, totemistic or, in the most advanced cases, polytheistic cosmologies. Representational art emerges but is a common practice only in the materially richest of such societies.

Feudal Society (Simple Differentiation/Systematic Organization)[16]

Economic Features   Production takes an agricultural as opposed to foraging or horticultural form. Agriculture is settled and thus typically involves the following: continuous habitation and cultivation of a given area of land; the application of animal power to cultivation along with such enabling technologies as the plough and the horse-collar; and, frequently, such simple methods of food processing and storage as milling, which also entail technological development. Much of the implied technology is relatively costly and if owned individually would be under-utilized so ownership is shared. However, land is the major means of production and feudal society is characterized by complex landholding arrangements in which tenancy is distributed hierarchically from the centre and reciprocated by service, especially by labour service at the margin. Nevertheless considerable autonomy applies to the production process carried out locally by the peasant farm family.

Political Arrangements   Feudalism typically emerges as mode of reintegration of residual tribal groups exposed by the breakdown of ancient imperial systems. That reintegration is military in character. It is a transformation in which a group which is technologically advantaged in military terms (e.g. by the stirrup in Europe and the long light sword in Japan) is able to dominate peasants, offering protection in return for service. The system is transformed and relatively centralized as a monarchical leadership emerges from this military ruling class and then becomes religiously legitimized. Nevertheless the significant power remains with the military aristocracy, which uses its monopoly of force to maximize its control over economic production.

Community   The significant focus of social relationships is the local community or manor. It is defined by the set of service relationships between the peasant and the local aristocratic knight, who himself holds the manor in tenancy from higher aristocratic orders. The manor is also conceived of at another level as a peasant collectivity in which the use of agricultural technology and draught animals is shared. There is only a minimum division of labour in such a community. Specialized occupations are typically restricted, perhaps to a miller who is compensated by a share of each job lot and a priest who will similarly accept a tithe.

Cultural Patterns   The single cultural and all-pervasive integrating theme is religion. Human society is conceived of as Christendom, the kingdom of Christ on earth, bound together by an intricate, hierarchical arrangement of spiritual leadership which transcends all political boundaries. Monarchs theoretically receive their kingdoms in tenancy from God and universal military campaigns, known as crusades, are fought by knights against rival religious systems, frequently independently of their own monarchs. Religious meanings unite cultural products and performances. All knowledge of the world and all representations of it must be religious in character and any that are not are stigmatized as heretical, with only the occasional madrigal or romantic ballad to provide relief from the theocratic cultural network. The combination of the significance of religion with technological limitations provides monasteries with wide-ranging fiduciary significance in preserving and transmitting religious knowledge. Within such a context writing manuscripts together with the building and decoration of great churches are the most developed artistic forms.

Liberal Society (Complex Differentiation/Diffuse Organization)

Economic Features   The defining process of differentiation is the separation of the production of commodities from domestic production in relation to immediate use. This transition is halting and nonrevolutionary but nonetheless radical in character. An important transitional stage is the putting out of jobs to domestic contexts but even this requires the transformation of use values into exchange values. There occurs the rapid development of a medium of economic exchange, money, and of insitutional contexts for its accomplishment, markets. Market competition is the hallmark of an economic system focussed on industrial capitalism. It forces the adoption of advanced technologies and thus capital intensification and from there mass marketing. It also forces a contractualization of labour services so that as few obligations as possible are owed to one's workers.

Political Arrangements   Christendom and the seamless political network of aristocracy differentiates into a nation-state system in which territorial boundaries are conceived of as complying with ethnicity and with shared goals. In genuinely liberal societies[17] the state's role is principally external, ensuring raw material supplies, foreign markets and, where necessary, immigrant labour to autonomous and secure production enterprises. The state's internal role is restricted to dispute resolution, the security of private property, and maintaining order in the labour force. Otherwise the state yields power to economic and religious centres. Fundamental class politics occurs in industrial arenas beyond the state whose leadership is itself clearly representative of but a single class.

Community   The differentiated centres of economic activity in industrial production systems and the differentiated state which controls the use of violence are defined as separate public arenas which are general and visible throughout the society. The residual household is defined as a private arena focussed on reproduction. The household also defines a minimum kinship unit, a conjugal nuclear family, in which kinship responsibility is held to extend only to spouse and children. The differentiation of family from work and its nuclear structure relative to kin endows households with a peculiar paradox – they are both isolated and concentrated. They are isolated by the differentiation of commodity production from reproduction and they are concentrated because they cluster around industrial production and its attendant services. Industrial cities are a particular feature of modern life in which people are crowded together in relatively tight spaces yet remain anonymous and socially indifferent to one another. At the household level this is achieved by the maintenance of precise spatial boundaries between domestic units in the form of doors, walls and fences. Thus modernist liberalism represents an eclipse of spatially located community identification.

Cultural Patterns   As social structure differentiates, religion loses its force as a thematic unifier although not as a specific legitimizer. The particular substantive change which exemplifies this process is the Reformation, which disunifies beliefs and opens the way for a proliferation of religious denominations. As is discussed in much more detail below, this liberates the value-spheres from their intimate link with the social and opens the possibility for abstracted and stylized art forms. So liberalism allows for a most intensive development of secular art, music, science, philosophy and literature. However the security of religious legitimation is now denied to them and they are available for colonization by commodifying and rationalizing interests. In the laissez-faire environment of liberal capitalism they can survive as elite expressions against the technologized assaults of popular music and literature in particular. But a differentiation of high and popular art forms is already entailed in the development of media of mass dissemination.

Organized Society (Complex Differentiation/Systematic Organization)[18]

Economic Features   Commodity production enterprises are large in scale and capital intensified. They tend to dominate their markets in terms of control of both supply and demand, the latter being accomplished by cultural manipulation through advertising. The economic system is integrated by connections through large-scale financial organizations and by state sponsorship and regulation. State enterprise is a common feature of an economy in which the market progressively disappears as an organizing principle. Large-scale organizational patterns ensure that a large proportion of nondomestic economic activity is devoted to the production of services rather than goods.

Political Arrangements   The state is highly developed and interventionist. It is a critical agent of social regulation which is accomplished by means of administrative action and economic redistribution. This has two principal consequences. First the state is organized along formal democratic lines with commitments typically channelled through mass parties which broadly represent the main interest groups of the society. Second the state liaises continuously with big business and with worker representative organizations to plan both economic development and reward distribution. The legitimation of this pattern typically involves an elaborate system of state social welfare provision. Thus described, corporatism is a central feature of organized society.

Community   The typical late modern arrangement for domesticity is the suburb, a collection of broadly similar nuclear family dwellings with a planned and organized location on the edge of an industrial city. Here women are isolated by the constraints of child care, at least for certain periods of their lives, and men are constrained by travel to work and by loans and mortgages which enable them to purchase major household assets (Connell 1987). Domestic isolation is reified by the privatization of domestic disorder behind a facade of precisely laid out streetscapes, concrete paths, clipped hedges and scrubbed automobiles. In city centres domesticity is almost completely excluded. Commercial and government buildings project domination by means of scale and height and express order by means of an increasingly uniform and geometric style. Teeming human life is denied in the artificial canyons of the central business district and only emerges, irrepressibly, in the slums and ghettos of the underclass which has been squeezed out of the modern complex. But community is elsewhere eclipsed by corporate planning and administrative penetration by state agencies.

Cultural Patterns   The predominant themes are massification, commodification and rationalization. The culture industry becomes well institutionalized. Its tentacles reach into the private domesticity of the single family dwelling, snaking through a dense network of electronic connections. For the most part these connections are unidirectional, serving as the medium for a uniform and disintellectualized fare of soap operas, spaghetti westerns and other pabulum. Meanwhile high culture retreats to the legitimacy of artistic lineages produced within liberal and earlier societies. It focusses on standard repertoires of classical music, or old masters, or great philosophers, or even classical sociological theorists, which become the benchmark against which popular culture is measured and found wanting. Culture thus becomes a vehicle for social differentiation rather than for the socially integrative provision of meaning.

What is essential in the above scheme is the notion that societies do not stop changing once they cross the divide into modernity. Importantly there is a specific change from a less organized to a more organized modern form in which the state and production organizations progressively acquire means of power and extend their control over both cultural and domestic arrangements. In the following sections we begin to lay the groundwork for this book by summarily tracing the transformations of modernization through the six substantive social arenas which it covers: culture, the state, inequality,the organization of work and production, politics, and science.[19]

The Value-Spheres of Culture

Cultural modernity was the outcome of processes of differentiation, rationalization and commodification which disrupted the peculiar unity of medieval culture. As Gurevich (1985: 8) notes: 'In the context of the middle ages, it is hardly possible to differentiate clearly between such spheres of intellectual activity as aesthetics, philosophy, history and economics.' For medieval culture, theology: 'provided a general semiolog- ical system in terms of which the members of medieval society appre- hended themselves and saw their world both motivated and explained' (Gurevich 1985: 9). The symbolic system of medieval culture is relentlessly hierarchical: every kind of person, or animal, or plant has a specific place in a cosmic 'chain of being' which links God with Creation. In an argument which closely parallels Gurevich's, Ferguson (1990) has stressed the complex intertwining of natural, social, cultural and spiritual hierarchies in the medieval period.

No doubt there is a danger in overemphasizing the unity and hierarchy of medieval culture. So, for example, medieval philosophy and theology are marked by fierce scholastic disputes and constant outbreaks of heresy (e.g. see Leff 1958). It has recently become fashionable to stress the inversion of hierarchy in the medieval 'carnival' considered as: 'the second life of the people, who for a time entered the utopian realm of community, freedom, equality and abundance' (Bakhtin 1984: 9).[20] Again, such studies as Ladurie's *Montaillou* (1978) have drawn attention to the distance between 'official' doctrine and hierarchy and the everyday practices of often isolated communities. However, in the broad sweep of a contrast between the medieval and the modern, what stands out is the extent to which disputing schoolmen, carnival revellers and the Albigensian peasants of Montaillou share the assumptions of what Gurevich terms the medieval 'world model' even as they contest some of its particulars.

Differentiation produces and defines cultural modernity in two senses. First, other subsystems (economy (A), polity (G) and societal community (I) in the Parsonsian scheme) extricate themselves from an all-embracing medieval culture. Economic activity, political strategy and social stratification gradually become independent and secular concerns.[21] Second, differentiation within the field of culture itself yields art, science and morality-law as the typical 'value-spheres' of cultural modernity which operate with increasingly heteronomous values. Within the medieval 'world model' the values of a painting, a contribution to knowledge and a judicial process derive from a single theological system. In cultural modernity beauty, truth and goodness-justice have become incommensurable.

Differentiation does not stop at the three 'value-spheres': literature is differentiated from music and the visual arts, while poetry is differentiated from drama and prose. It would be a mistake, however, to see differentiation as a one-way street. By the middle of the nineteenth century the loss of cultural unity is increasingly seen as a threat to any cultural value. The Romantic protest against the divorce between 'life' and 'art' and against the fragmentation of spheres within culture itself defines mature cultural modernity in a tension between differentiating and dedifferentiating forces.

The rationalization of culture is implicated in the differentiation of value-spheres. The 'splitting' between and within music, the visual arts and literature is legitimized as the working out of their endogenous principles of development. The task of the cultural expert is to push the formal potential inherent in, say, the string quartet, the portrait or the novel as far as it will go. However, an exclusively formal development of culture risks a complete separation from the concerns of nonexperts. This tension pervades the avant-gardism of the early twentieth century, giving it a paradoxical joint concern to work at the leading edge of cultural form and, at the same time, to protest against the gap between art and life.

The rationalization of techniques for the production and, critically, the reproduction of cultural objects plays a crucial role in the commodification of modern culture. This point clearly connects with the typically modern split between 'high' and 'mass' culture: technical innovations such as cinema, radio, television and sound recording are often taken to define the forms of mass culture. However, the connection is widely misrepresented. The commodification of culture is set in train, first, among the European aristocracy and bourgeoisie in the eighteenth century, driven by the phenomena of 'sensibility' and 'taste'.[22] Commodified forms of popular culture (e.g. the music hall, the 'penny dreadful') are often appropriations of the already commodified forms of bourgeois culture (the opera house, the newspaper).

The potent idea of high art unsullied by commerce would have been unfamiliar to medieval or early modern aristocrats for whom music, art and literature were diversions, frankly connected with wealth and power in the same way as sumptuous clothing or banquets. The peculiarly modern idea of 'Art' connects with the enlightenment demand for a 'universal' standard of taste, with the Romantic elevation of art into a substitute religion, and with tradition-mongering in which a lineage of 'old masters' is constructed for each sphere of culture. While 'Art' effaces its commodified character, and despises 'mass culture' as its commodified other, its practice is quite compatible with commodification. Mechanical and electronic reproduction of sound and image come to play a critical role in constructing the archives of modern museum culture. In the earlier phases of the recording industry, a decision to record, say, a Beethoven symphony conducted by Toscanini not only makes that performance available to the public but confirms the stature of Beethoven as a 'great composer' and Toscanini as a 'great conductor'.[23]

In summary, the terrain of mature modern culture is defined by a tension between cultural differentiation and dedifferentiation, by formal rationalization, and by a process of commodification which projects a disingenuous distinction between 'high' and 'mass' culture.

The Authoritative State

In certain important respects the economic changes we have come to associate with modernization were preceded by developments in the political arena and specifically in the institution of the nation-state. The feudal state had been, for all practical purposes, a federation of aristocratic holdings loosely integrated by idealized service relationships between baronial vassals and a monarch and legitimized by reference to a universal religion. In practice seigneurial power predominated. In Europe certainly and in Japan possibly this fragile coalition was disturbed by religious differentiation and intra-aristocratic civil war in the seventeenth century. As Kosselleck (1988) points out, the response was to strengthen and extend the central power of the monarch, in a word, the development of an absolutist state which could resolve conflicts by centralized domination. In an absolutist state the monarch is the sole source of secular law and governs with the aid of a bureaucracy and an army which is permanent, professional and dependent on the monarch (Mann 1986: 476). The monarch's power was thus rendered independent of religious or aristocratic control and was applied in an expedient and rationalized manner.

However, not all major European states followed the same absolutist path. England and Holland, particularly, stand apart. Kosselleck attributes this distinctiveness to rapid economic differentiation which allowed a fast emerging bourgeoisie to curtail monarchical power. For Anderson,

England under the Tudors and early Stuarts was among the earliest absolutist states, but its development was 'cut off by a bourgeois revolution' in the mid-seventeenth century (Anderson 1979: 142). Mann (1986: 478–9) also gives credence to the notion of an emerging capitalist class but attaches great significance to the fact that England and Holland's military power was primarily naval and thus could not be used to establish state power internally. However, whatever the differences between state systems their relationship to the modernization process is similar – that is, state practices were primarily military rather than economic in character. The state did not own property, it extracted its revenues on a fiscal basis and it was the co-ordinator of class action for military purposes rather than a usurper of class power (Mann 1986: 482–3).

The emergence of the modern industrial state in the late nineteenth century involved a set of related processes: the unification and centralization of power centres which overcame the resistance of formerly independent corporate bodies; the autonomization of state power, so that it rested on an internal principle of sovereignty rather than being derived from tradition or from 'external' sources; a broadening of the political community and popular support, achieved by an extension of suffrage and constitutional reform; the development of state-national symbols (flags, anthems, a national language, etc.) which increased the popular legitimacy of the state; and the activization of the state, so that the domain of its legitimate intervention extended beyond military and law and order functions, especially to fiscal reform.[24] These processes coincided with the rise of an industrial bourgeoisie which vigorously advocated principles of laissez-faire, yet also promoted the development of the sovereign, authoritative state. The progressive constitutionalization of absolutist states became the instrument by which this capitalist class achieved its own technical and economic goals, not least by using the state to establish external colonies and thus to affect international competition by seeking to control global flows of resources. This was part of a process of nationalizing the interests of the bourgeoisie. Thus in the early liberal state the principal activities of government involved 'defence' of the nation, the liberation of labour and property from ties to rural and aristocratic interests, and the maintenance of law and order over displaced rural vagrants and an emerging urban proletariat. So from the very outset the modern industrial state has been active, interventionist, purposive and instrumental relative to preceding forms, and its domain has been progressively separated from the realm of civil society (Poggi 1978: 95–7).

In the twentieth century there have been three main patterns of state development. The West European pattern is corporatist in character, stressing intervention, welfare, and above all mutual administrative arrangements with business and labour. The American state, by contrast, acts as a broker between competing and lobbying interest groups rather than as an active manager. In the Soviet Union, China and Eastern Europe the state reached its most centralized level of development. Here there has been an all pervasive and dominating party-state focussed on planning, command over the economy and civil society, and moral-ideological unity.

To summarize, the modern state has emerged as a complex, powerful and interventionist machine 'whose parts all mesh, a machine propelled by energy and directed by information flowing from a single centre in the service of a plurality of co-ordinated tasks' (Poggi 1978: 98). It is an organized and deliberate construct. Its goals are increasingly civilian and domestic so that the modern state becomes progressively introverted, moving its principal legitimizing functions away from external conquest and defence and toward internal organization and regulation. There is therefore a progressive increase in the extent of state surveillance (Giddens 1985). The object of state surveillance systems is both to minimize economic cost and to maximize compliant labour force participation. Thus state intervention is not only permissible, but essential in legitimizing its powers – the state is defined in teleological terms. Its core tasks are rational regulation, the reconciliation of interests, general welfare, and transcending regional, class, ethnic and religious particularisms. Their realization requires knowledge, control, objectivity and autonomy, all of which are maximized, internally through the relentless application of bureaucratic principles, externally through strengthening and defending state sovereignty.

The instrumental and interventionist character of the modern state and its differentiation from arenas of production and domesticity promotes its rationalization. It comprises a series of bureaucratically defined offices, that is occupational positions with legally limited and functionally specific powers, which are linked together in complex hierarchies. This is the mechanism by which government intervenes in the lives of citizens, and political contests focus on obtaining control of this bureaucratic machinery. Processes of direct command and crude coercion which characterized state interventions in the eighteenth and early nineteenth centuries give way to more subtle domination through surveillance and manipulation. State administrative power is exerted by control over the circumstances of an autonomous citizenry rather than by issuing orders. This is supported by persuasion, exerted through a tutelary system of state-controlled media and glossed in a rational-technocratic idiom.

Elaborate Inequalities

Medieval society is, at least ideally, fixed in terms of legal estates or statuses: nobility, peasantry, and clerisy. The emergence of industrial society is marked by the formation of a class system which gradually replaces social stratification on the basis of status group membership.[25] Early industrial society shows a tendency to polarization into two principal classes, industrial capitalists and industrial workers. Conflict between these classes is a major source of tension and change. In early capitalism, capitalists are defined by their ownership of the means of production and their capacity to exploit the labour of others.

However, organized society sees a rapid differentiation of this simple and economically generated pattern. First, capitalist enterprises reach such a scale that capital generation requirements prevent direct ownership. Ownership and control are separated. The capitalist class now comes to comprise both executive managers and large-scale shareholders. Second, large-scale enterprises and the highly elaborated state lead to the growth of a 'new middle class' of salaried employees, who interpose between capital and labour. Third, extensions of state activity into arenas of social reproduction tend towards the development of credentialized professional fragments of this new middle class. Fourth, the working class disintegrates into skilled, affluent semiskilled, and unskilled manual service fragments. Fifth, direct support by the state leads to the development of a dependent underclass which is fixed in poverty.

In summary, changes in patterns of class membership between early and late modernity trend away from a polarized dichotomy and towards an elaborated mosaic of class segments, each defined as much by their market-specified consumption capacity as by their place in the system of production. As all classes move in the direction of propertylessness the form of their reproduction becomes increasingly 'cultural' in character depending on closure by the application of such consumption standards as 'distinction' and 'taste' rather than on material inheritance (Bourdieu 1984).

Related transformations occur in the area of gender inequality. Under premodern conditions the situation of women is defined, as in many other eras, by their location in domestic production, the contours of which are given by Laslett and Brenner (1989: 386):

> In the pre-industrial economy based on household production, home and commerce, social reproduction and production, women and men, children and adults, were located in the same world of daily experience. As property-holders and legal representatives of their households, men directed household labour and monopolized political, religious, and domestic authority.

Under the pressure of industrial capitalism this pattern gives way to a differentiation of spheres of activity and radically altered arrangements for gender relations, although gender relations still turn on domestic arrangements. Although there are class and cultural variations, the domestic division of labour by gender typically assigns routine household chores, feeding responsibilities, child care, and emotional support functions to women. Men are defined as primary income earners for households and so their domestic responsibilities are confined to financial decision making and, where apposite, simple maintenance of household assets. The arena for men's labour is the dominating public sphere of production and societal power, for women the private arena of social reproduction. Sex differences are thus socially reified and reproduced as gender inequalities.

In the later stages of modernity the gender division of labour takes on an expanded form. This occurs as families are progressively defined by the state as inadequate to the task of the reproduction of labour power, especially where there is an economic premium on technical skills as well as labour compliance. The state takes over the social reproduction activity of the family in such arenas as education, health and social welfare. As it does so women are progressively released from domestic childrearing tasks and are increasingly employed in institutions of state reproduction as teachers, nurses, social workers, clerks, secretaries, librarians and so on by the welfare state. Within this development women's employment continues to be viewed as a component contribution to household income and women remain as primary child carers and domestic workers (Laslett and Brenner 1989; Brenner and Ramos 1984; Waters 1989b).

Interest Politics

Absolutist rule paved the way for a massive transformation of political institutions and a reorientation of political action. Six aspects of this change need to be emphasized:

- Differentiation and separation from religion, morality and tradition. Politics developed its own autonomous rules, principles and techniques. By the end of the nineteenth century, this process of autonomization had culminated in the emergence of the professional politician, living on and for politics, and treating political pursuits as a vocation .
- Under the impact of the bourgeois ethos, instrumentalism, sobriety and pragmatism. The goals of politics increasingly involved stability and prosperity, providing a framework for effective capital accumulation. This was achieved through pragmatic settlements between recognized sectional interests, particularly class and national ones. While passion continued to colour political declarations, and while moral principles were regularly evoked on ceremonial occasions so that appeals for legitimacy were coated in an ideological gloss, the pursuit of everyday political tasks was increasingly guided by pragmatic sober calculation rather than ideological, moral or religious conviction.
- Impersonality and objectivity. The modern: '*homo politicus*, as well as the *homo oeconomicus*, performs his duty best when he acts without regard to the person in question . . . without hatred and without love, without personal predilection and therefore without grace, but sheerly in accordance with the impersonal duty imposed by his calling' (Weber 1978: 600).
- Increasing technicism. Politics was no longer considered an art, an aristocratic pursuit or the leisure task of dilettante notables. The science of politics, involving increasingly differentiated and specialized fields of diplomacy, administration and social policy, became an area of academic pursuit, and technical political training became a standard channel of political recruitment.
- A control-orientation, transpiring in administration and legitimized in

terms of effective change achieved through administrative measures. Politics became a systematic, calculable and disciplined exercise of control over people. The increasingly complex bureaucratic machinery of the modern state, and the equally bureaucratized machineries of new mass milieu parties created an institutional framework for this power politics.

• A gradual extension of political participation. Premodern politics had involved few individuals, because political status was restricted and intimately linked with social status. For most subjects, contact with the state was made only through taxation and military service and participation meant either sporadic rebellion or more frequent pledges of allegiance. By contrast, the politics of the modern administrative state permeated most daily tasks and drew into its orbit all subject-citizens, regardless of social status. This broadening of the political community by extension of suffrage and representative institutions, accelerated in the nineteenth century in tandem with the widening scope of state intervention. In the twentieth century, modern politics became mass politics in the sense of involving all adult citizens, even though this involvement has been formalized and strictly regulated.

Patterns of modern political development mirror the transformations of the modern state. Western Europe has been dominated by the idiom of bureaucratic-corporatist politics in which mass parties represent sectional interests. American politics is more 'untidy', incorporating pressure group processes of lobbying, constitutional challenges and litigation, and parties which are loose federations of interest groups. The state socialist societies exhibited, by contrast, a politics of incorporation in which sectional interests were either certified and co-opted into the single party programme or vigorously suppressed or extinguished. Oppositional politics has developed outside the party system within such mass movements as Polish Solidarity which have recently effected a dramatic systemic change. While there are apparent differences between these three patterns their successful institutionalization has a common origin in the emancipation of emerging social forces from archaic or dictatorial political regimes (Bauman 1991). Even party-state politics, as Konrad and Szelenyi (1979) suggest, can be seen as an instance of such an assertion by a socially ascendant section of *burgerliche Gesellschaft*, the intelligentsia.

Capitalized Production

Marx, Weber and Durkheim each regard work as the focal point for an analysis of the emergence of modern society. The starting point for us is an analysis of the differentiation of economic activity, so that the production, distribution and exchange of commodified goods and services take place in nondomestic social arenas. The labour performed in these arenas is identified for the first time as a special form of activity known as work. Work activities are separated in time and space from other activities, they receive material compensation, and are organized into specialized work roles, that is, there is an increasingly complex division of labour. These work activities are explicitly organized on an economically rational basis, that is, so as to maximize revenue and to minimize cost. This process of organization is carried out by managers whose work is not directly oriented to the production or distribution of marketable commodities and services but to the rational co-ordination of those workers who are directly involved.

The initial, liberal phase of capitalist development is governed by the commodity form and the market. So during the nineteenth century capitalist enterprises were small to medium, post-artisanal, entrepreneurial or family firms in which owners did their own managing and there was a high level of interpersonal contact between owners and workers. This was changed by one of the processes indicated above: the reversal of commodification in the face of relentless rationalization. The effect of inter-firm competition for markets was to produce monopolies, and the state increased its management of the reproduction of capitalistic property ownership forms. So the major form of capitalist ownership in contemporary society is state sponsored and regulated corporate capitalism in which ownership rights are divided into shares which may then be owned by individual and corporate shareholders. Contemporary, large-scale corporations have thus undergone a separation of ownership from control. Here the organizing and exploiting functions of capital are performed by managers. Executive managers may be said only to 'possess' enterprises (Poulantzas 1982: 102), to have the capacity to put the means of production into operation.

Because managers seek continuously to reduce the cost of labour, one of the main rationalization aspects of industrialism is the increasing application of technology to production. Indeed Dobb (1964) argues that the emergence of industrialism in England itself was a response to costs imposed by shortages of labour artificially induced by rural aristocratic control of the labour supply. Textile manufacturers were compelled to be inventive in the application of mechanical tools and of inanimate sources of power to production.

The production of commodities therefore requires the organization of work in teams comprised of both people and machines but there is a progressive subordination of people to machines. The labour process undergoes continuous reconstruction so that work is progressively differentiated into 'manual' and 'mental' components in such a way that the former is progressively deskilled and the latter progressively enskilled. Progressive applications of 'scientific management' are a hallmark of change in the workplace under modern conditions.

We do not mean to suggest that the economic development of modern societies has been uniformly capitalist in character. In the USA for example production enterprise has been notably more privately owned and market oriented than elsewhere. Between this and the command economies of state socialism lie the mixed economies of Western Europe. However all exhibit the main modernization trends of differentiation and rationalization to an advanced degree.

Big Science

As much as any other value-sphere, modern science can also be understood as the product of differentiation, rationalization and commodification. Science offers the paradigm case of development through differentiation: once 'natural philosophy' has disentangled itself from theology and mutated into 'science', it begins to divide and redivide into disciplines, subdisciplines and research fronts. The gentleman amateur of the Royal Society in the seventeenth century could reasonably hope to keep abreast of all developments in natural philosophy. By contrast, the professional particle physicist of the mid-to-late twentieth century would not claim expertise outside the subdiscipline. This increasing specialization is kept in motion by the rapid, verging on exponential, 'growth' of science, a growth that can be measured in terms of funding, personnel or output. Modern science is 'big science' in all senses. In the midst of the 'science boom' of the 1960s in the USA de Solla Price (1963) made the famous calculation that 90 per cent of all scientists who had ever lived were currently alive and working, and that 90 per cent of all scientific knowledge had been discovered in the previous fifty years.

A further dimension of the differentiation of science is that of norms and values. The basic thesis that science should be understood as a specific 'value-sphere' is established in Weber's 'Science as a Vocation' (1970). The Weberian insight is developed and systematized in Merton's influential (1973) model of a science defined by its 'institutional imperatives', or norms, which place it in ambiguous relations of partial convergence with, and partial divergence from, the norms of the wider society.[26] The emphasis on the normative dimension of science links the process of differentiation to that of rationalization, and once more Merton's work has shaped the field. He borrows the argument-form of the 'Protestant Ethic' thesis to assert that the Puritan religious convictions of many early members of the Royal Society acted as a 'spur' to scientific enquiry. From this point, science can be regarded as undergoing a twin rationalization of professionalization and institutionalization (see Ben-David 1971) on one hand and increasing normative autonomy on the other.

The Mertonian-functionalist account offers a 'soft' rationalization thesis. A much 'harder' version stresses the extent to which modern science, as the leading edge of intellectual rationalization, has eroded other spheres of meaning and contributed to the 'iron cage' of modernity. For Adorno and Horkheimer (1979) rationalizing science is driven by an attempt to dominate nature and thereby to widen the sphere of human freedom. Its effect, rather, is to generalize domination in the social, as well as the natural, world. More recently, Habermas (1971) has argued that science and technology are a modern substitute for ideology, securing compliance with a depoliticized and administered social order by ministering to privatized 'needs'.

When the rationalization of science is considered from this rather gloomy perspective it converges with commodification. Habermas (1971: 104) is among those who make the point that modern science and technology have become, in combination, a 'leading productive force'. During the twentieth century an increasing proportion of professional scientists have come to be located in the research facilities of business corporations, and an increasing proportion of modern science has been developed with a view to commercial application. The commodification of science is intimately connected with its growth and rationalization: professionalized 'big science' costs the kind of money which only large corporations and the governments of large nations can afford. Sklair (1973) made the point in the early 1970s that big science had become a critical element in the inequitable international division of power and wealth.

The connections between science, commerce and the state (particularly the military) in the late modern period have been especially deep and intimate. Arguing from the British experience, Rothblatt (1985) has claimed that state and commercial sponsorship of science during the nineteenth century played a crucial role in its professionalization and institutionalization. This claim points to a more general tension within modern 'organized' science. Modern science is defined by differentiation and endogenous rationalization at the levels of content, values and institutions. It can be analysed as a 'system' built around the circulation of a specific (non-commercial) commodity. However, the very close relations which organized science establishes with state and commercial interests threaten that autonomy. In practice, the threat is held at bay in the modern period: the relations between science, state and commerce are relations between autonomous systems. However, as we argue below, this threat has now become a major disorganizing force.

Theories of the Current Transformation

Twentieth-century social theory, especially in its more critical and Marxist oriented forms, has precisely been concerned with the move from liberal capitalism to organized capitalism discussed above. For example mass society theories emphasize an increasing and radical differentiation between elite centres of power and a disorganized, culturally based mass which is vulnerable to manipulation through vulgar and commercialized mass media. Similar themes are to be found in the work of the critical theorists of the Frankfurt School who posit a new social configuration to follow liberal capitalism, a state-organized form of neocapitalism. Neocapitalism has two central characteristics: the displacement of the market by large-scale bureaucratic systems in the state and economic arenas; and an industrialization of culture through which docile consumerism is established as a basic stabilizing force.

The leading contemporary intellectual heir to these critical traditions is Habermas, who might be described as the last modern social theorist (e.g. see Crook 1991). Habermas argues forcefully that the concept of modernity retains its analytic and normative salience at the end of the twentieth century. His work is thus a focal point for debates about whether a full-scale phase shift is currently under way. During the 1970s Habermas can easily be located in relation to his Frankfurt School antecedents as he stresses the way in which contemporary capitalism needs to be understood in terms of the complex linkages between economy, state and culture (1976). Organized capitalism is seen as entering a series of related crises focussed on the ability of the state to deliver enough welfare to its constituent individuals to secure adequate legitimation for its activities in managing ('steering') the economic system. In the 1970s Habermas' critical theory remains a theory of 'crisis' to the extent that the severe steering problems of late capitalism retain a traceable connection to the fundamental 'system crisis' of commodity production.

However, by the 1980s Habermas is convinced that the crises experienced a decade earlier have been resolved in a new and more extreme form of neocapitalism which might be described as hyper-organized (1984; 1987a). This argument is located within a quasi-Parsonsian discussion of differentiation which is modulated by Marxian and communication-theoretic themes. Habermas accepts from Parsons the idea that modernization is fundamentally constituted as a process of differentiation and that, at the societal level, this differentiation produces four subsystems: the economy, the state or polity, a public societal community, and a private sphere of domesticity focussed on social and cultural reproduction. The fundamental uncoupling is between the former two subsystems and the latter two. The political and economic subsystems are normatively characterized by strategic action, that is participation within them is normally understood to occur on the basis of self-interest and will involve attempts to manipulate or to coerce others. They are known as the systematic or 'steering' subsystems because they manage and direct the society. By contrast, the community and domestic subsystems are normatively characterized by communicative action in which participants will normally seek to reach a level of agreement between themselves by the application of reason and argument. They are known, respectively, as the private and public subsystems of the lifeworld, the world of everyday lived experience.

From this point Habermas' treatment of Parsonsian themes becomes more critical and issues in his thesis that late capitalism is characterized by processes of 'internal colonization'. None of the four subsystems is independent – each is specialized in what it produces and relies on other subsystems for what it does not produce. The economy produces money, the state produces power, the public lifeworld influence, and the private lifeworld commitment, and these products are known collectively as media of exchange because they can, and indeed must, be traded between subsystems. Thus, for example, the economy relies on the state to establish such legal economic institutions as private property and contract, on the public lifeworld to influence consumption patterns, and on the private lifeworld to provide a committed labour force, and itself sends money into each other subsystem. However, the media are not equivalent in their instrumental capacity. The steering media, money and power, have superior effectivity relative to influence and commitment – that is power, for example, will always succeed over influence if they are applied in theoretically equal amounts.[27]

As system and lifeworld differentiate, relations between them must become increasingly mediated and as they do the steering media and thus the steering subsystems progressively dominate the lifeworld. In terms linked directly to the Weberian theme of rationalization and the Marxian theme of commodification, the lifeworld becomes colonized, that is increasingly state administered ('juridified') and commercialized. Possibilities for communicative action in the lifeworld become attenuated as social participation becomes hyper-rationalized in terms of immediate and instrumental returns. Participants encounter each other as legal entities and as parties to contracts rather than as thinking and acting subjects.

Late capitalist society is then a highly organized and steered society. While it is beset by pathologies, Habermas has moved further away from the notion that there is a way out of late capitalism via crisis.[28] The system crises that are displaced as lifeworld pathologies can now be managed by monetarization and bureaucratization. Change can come only through a reconstitution of the public sphere of the lifeworld, a prospect Habermas discusses in terms which his critics often regard as utopian. Whatever faint and 'unrealistic' hopes for emancipation there are must now reside in 'silent revolutions', youth subcultures and 'new politics' (see Chapter 4) which emerge from the communicative sphere of the lifeworld. For Habermas the more likely outcome appears to be an enduring, hyper-centralized and mediated system of economic and political power.[29]

Habermas' early collaborator, Offe (1985b) offers a diagnosis of late capitalism which is closer to an orthodox 'theory of crisis'. Whereas Habermas insists that crises can be displaced and overcome by hyper-organization, Offe provides a thesis of *disorganization* in which the crises, or 'contradictions' as he has it, lead to an unravelling of state management systems. Organized capitalism consists of a special relationship between the state and capitalist power distributions in which the former operates to maintain the latter. There are two central and independent contradictions which prevent this from occurring completely in any instance and which lead to disorder in advanced or welfare capitalism: the labour market contradiction and the administrative contradiction. The labour market contradiction lies in the fact that capitalist power relations rely on the treatment of labour as a commodity and the fact that absolute ownership of labour power is never possible. It is possible for workers to withdraw labour power from the market and to seek subsistence in other ways. The more the state seeks to reproduce labour power by providing nonmarket based assistance (as in the welfare state) the greater the extent to which labour power will be withdrawn and the greater the development of centres of possible alternative value positions to those given in capitalism. The administrative contradiction is between the Weberian standards of efficiency and effectiveness. The greater the extent to which bureaucratic administrations seek to deliver services, the greater will be the rationality requirement of value-neutral adherence to rules. The more that energy and resources are given over to the latter the less the former is possible. To the extent that bureaucracies fail to deliver services there is an increased possibility of a bureaucratic legitimation crisis.

While it is less a theory of disorganization than a description of it, the argument of Lash and Urry (1987) adds considerable flesh to Offe's thesis. Their description of disorganization is neatly summarized in a fourteen-point list (1987: 5–6), which is here condensed to a rather shorter version in which there are suggested to be five elements of disorganization:

- a disaggregation of capitalist organizations: the dismantling of cartels; flexible work organization; declining plant size
- a differentiation of classes and labour markets: the emergence of a service class of professionals and managers; a reduction in the size of the manufacturing working class; the decentralization of industrial relations; a decline in class voting
- the dismantling of the state: reduced national-political control over economic enterprises; challenges to the welfare state; emergence of social movement politics
- geographical dispersal: the globalization of markets; the spread of capitalism to the third world (and to formerly state socialist societies); industrial deconcentration; the decline of industrial cities; rural repopulation
- cultural postmodernism: cultural fragmentation; a reduction in time-space distantiation; the collapse of the high/popular culture separation.

By and large Lash and Urry insist on the independence of these elements. There is no unifying motor or axial principle which drives societies towards disorganization. Lash is particularly concerned to stress the autonomy of the development of postmodernist culture (1990: 3–4) relative to any change in society. Postmodernism is a cultural movement rather than a type of society or a social condition. It is not the product either of disorganization or of postindustrialism (see below) that is, of processes which operate at the socio-economic level. The most Lash and Urry are prepared to say is that postmodernism is compatible with disorganization and postindustrialism, in effect, that there is elective affinity between them.[30]

By contrast Harvey (1989) seeks explicitly to establish a determinate link between a disorganizing social structure and a dedifferentiating or postmodernist culture. He wants to connect the transformation of culture directly to long-run tendencies in capitalism first identified by Marx, principally those to over-accumulation. An earlier solution to over-accumulation was to extend capitalism into new markets, especially to the third world. The most recent solution provided by the capitalist system to such problems, he argues, is the rapid deployment of new and flexible organizational forms and technologies with a view to an acceleration of turnover time in production. This has imparted a new temporariness to commodities, and especially to the commodified cultural forms of the electronic mass media. Two developments are important: the generalization of fashion from elite to mass markets to create lifestyle fads; and increased marketing of services, especially entertainment services of an ephemeral character. Taken together these 'geographical' and 'temporal' solutions to accumulation problems have led to a new postmodern sensibility or consciousness in which time and space are compressed and in which the chief contents are those most ephemeral of products, referent-free images, which have now come to take precedence over narratives.

The thread which draws together the views of Habermas, Offe, Lash and Urry, and Harvey is a determination to save the analytic and normative salience of elements of the idea of modernity (frequently within some variant on Marxist themes). For these writers, whatever transformation is occurring, at a social level it ultimately cannot be postmodernization. If modernity is associated with the rise of industrial capitalism and the current transformation is merely a modification of capitalism which allows it to accommodate its own contradictions and crises then we are still, as Habermas and the others insist, merely in an advanced stage of modernity, specifically an advanced stage of capitalism.

An approach which ignores the issue of whether capitalism is central to modernity at all and indeed is generally much less cautious than the above approaches is Bell's thesis of the postindustrial society (1973). What distinguishes industrial from postindustrial societies is their form of production. Industrial societies, whether capitalist or state socialist, are goods manufacturing societies in which the ownership of physical capital is a critical though variable issue. Postindustrial societies are predominantly producers of human and technical services and concentrate most of their workers in these areas. The most senior of these service workers, the professional and technical class, become the ruling class of the new society. They rule because of their superior control and facility in relation to theoretical knowledge which is the focus for a new information storage and retrieval technology and an orientation to planning future development. Although Bell provides a critical neoconservative commentary on post-modernist culture (1976) he in no way links it to the idea of postindustrial society. Indeed he argues that postmodernist culture is a purely hedonistic orientation based on values of consumption which needs to be understood as an extreme development of modernism and which displaces traditional bourgeois values of thrift and sobriety. Presumably as modern industrial society disappears so too will postmodernist culture and human civilization will take a genuine neoconservative turn.

Notwithstanding Turner's hopeful claim of a resurgence of interest in Bell's concept of the postindustrial society (1990: 2–3) the critical reception the thesis received has more or less stuck (see especially the critiques by Frankel 1987 and Kumar 1978, 1988). Although it is relatively common to speak of postindustrialization as an aspect of the current change few use the term to mean anything more than the expansion of the service sector. An exception is the influential postmodernist philosopher, Lyotard (1984). As in all the arguments reviewed so far Lyotard analyses society and culture separately – society is moving into a postindustrial age, culture into a postmodern age but the two operate in tandem. Modern culture is unified (one might say 'organized') around 'grand-' or 'meta-narratives'. Ideas of Progress, or Emancipation, or Enlightenment convey a sense that the first-order narratives of the separate value-spheres are moving in the same direction, a direction that has intrinsic worth. These overarching stories-about-stories are losing their credibility, according to Lyotard. Postindustrial developments see the commodification of knowledge through the application of new technologies. Increasingly, 'performativity', the capacity to deliver outputs at the lowest cost, replaces truth as the yardstick of knowledge. In the wake of these developments incredulity towards modern meta-narratives increases. Cultural production dissolves into a series of localized and flexible networks of language games and since the cultural is the source of legitimation for the social, general social structures correspondingly lose their capacity to attract commitment.[31]

In identifying possible outcomes of the transformation, Lyotard (1984: 15) puts some distance between himself and the other French high priest of postmodernity, Baudrillard. Lyotard models a possible society in which, at best, flexible networks of language games provide localized capacity for resistance to performativity, and at worst Habermas' vision of a totally steered society becomes a reality by the mechanism of computerization. For Baudrillard (1981, 1983b, 1988) both these alternatives are expressions of a modernist 'nostalgia' based on a notion of the production of culture rather than its consumption in which knowledge can be centrally organized and controlled by its producers. Rather in postmodern society the producing and consuming subject is decentred and so relations of production and power no longer have force. The effectivity of culture is so increased that only the relations between its symbolic contents, its 'signs', have force. The postmodern experience consists in 'hypersimulation', a double counter-reflection in which life simulates the simulated contents of the mass media.[32] The social thus does not reference or mediate the signs, that is they have neither labour value nor use value but merely consumption value. Instead it is merely absorbed by them so that they become a 'hyper-reality' in which simulations are the only form of existence. What was once the social is described as a mass, a shapeless void.[33]

Processes of Postmodernization

The above summary conveys the flavour of the changes being analysed
here, changes which are radical, sweeping and general. The three most
promising theoretical statements about these changes, and the ones which
guide subsequent analysis in this chapter, are the ideas of postindustrialism, disorganization and postmodernist culture. However, each is incomplete relative to the others. The concept of postindustrialism remains
modernist in its insistence that society must be organized along some
central axial principle, in this case the development of theoretical knowledge, and that it must develop in a single utopian direction according to
that principle. We may well want to accept that society is entering a phase
which is 'after industrialism' but as it is framed postindustrialism is merely
another form of industrialism, a social structure determined by the
material relations of production, a kind of 'hyperindustrialism' as Kumar
(1988: 65) has it. Paradoxically while the idea of disorganization clings
explicitly to the notion that we are merely in a new and less centrally
managed region of industrial capitalism it offers a greater level of
substantive advice that a phase shift is in process by alerting us to
breakdowns in centralized steering. Taken to their extreme these breakdowns would indicate an unravelling of structural arrangements which had
been initiated as early as the beginning of the ancient imperial period, well
before industrialism – a more radical shift would be difficult to contem-
plate. By contrast, the limits of many recent discussions of cultural
postmodernity lie in their resistance to the notion that postmodernization
is a social as well as cultural phenomenon. Again, to make such a claim is
to insist on a level of differentiation between the cultural and the social
which is precisely modern in character. As Baudrillard suggests, an
argument about postmodernization must surely focus on the collapse of
this boundary, but unlike Baudrillard the argument offered here is that the
outcome is not beyond the reach of sociological reasoning.

We argue above that the form of society given in the advanced stage of
capitalism was the product of two main groups of processes. It is a highly
differentiated society exhibiting high levels of specialization and complexity which provide problems of integration; and it is also a highly organized
society exhibiting high levels of rationalization and commodification,
processes which provide for centralized management mediated through
bureaucratic power and money. Here we argue that the process of
postmodernization may be analysed as the consequence of the extension of
these two modernization processes to extreme levels.

The form of *differentiation* in advanced capitalist society is essentially
functional in character. Twentieth-century capitalist societies are made up
of a series of types of social unit, specialized by function. Social units
having a similar function are also similar in structure. So all production
units, for example, are broadly similar in structure – they have human–
machine teams, they separate ownership from control and employees from

managers, they orient to market domination by mass production, etc. Likewise families tend to be conjugal-nuclear and masculine dominated; states to be democratic and welfare oriented; schools to be compulsory and age-graded; churches to embrace universalistic and abstract theologies; political parties to espouse multiple issues and to seek mass appeal, and so on. However, in the contemporary period we are witnessing an extension of this process in which social units are differentiating at the level of structure as well as of function. So it is now far less possible to read off the structure of a social unit from its function. For example, in the case of production units, mass production systems may still be found but so also may market-niche producers, co-operatives, technocratic partnerships, segmented organizations, subcontractors, homeworkers, and so on. Patterns of economic production may be said to be hyperdifferentiating, providing a multiplicity of directions in the absence of a unifying structural principle. Such hyperdifferentiation of structure is, we argue, a generalized and widespread pattern.

The second major process of modernization identified above is an increasing level of centralized organization. To argue this is almost directly to reiterate Habermas' theory of modernity (1987a). Increasingly centralized organization may be viewed as an increase in the extent to which the state and economic units at the system level are able to use the media which they generate, power and money, to take control of the private (domestic) and public (mass media) domains of the lifeworld. This ability is given in the superior instrumental capacity of money and power relative to the communicative rationality of the lifeworld. In the argument offered here both the zenith and the nadir of modernization are simultaneously contained in the culmination of this process, in the virtual completion of what Habermas calls the colonization of the lifeworld. More analytically, the logical extension of the dimension of organization is a monocentric condition. Here lifeworld structures (family, community and culture) are subsumed completely within a centralized steering system.

The argument so far is summarized in Figure 1.2, which extends the scheme of societal types given in Figure 1.1 although itself makes no statement about the direction of social change.[34] It yields an additional set of five possible societal types, four of which – technocracy, pure corporatism, statism and absolutism – are suggested only by way of illustration. Our chief interest lies in the bottom, right-hand cell, an analytically possible intersection of hyperdifferentiation with monocentric organization. Our chief interest must lie in this cell because, as is indicated above, although the scheme offers a series of analytic possibilities the general thrust of change in concrete societies is towards increased differentiation and increased organization although with the clear possibility of frequent and widespread deviation from this general line of development.

It is at the point of this new and extreme possibility that the scheme takes on theoretical as opposed to purely analytical significance. If the intersection between monocentrism and hyperdifferentiation is viewed as a simple

DIFFERENTIATION

		Simple	Complex	Hyper
	Diffuse	FORAGER-TRIBAL	LIBERAL	TECHNOCRATIC
Systematic		FEUDAL	ORGANIZED	PURE CORPORATIST
Monocentric		ABSOLUTIST	STATIST	* * *

ORGANIZATION

Figure 1.2   *An extended scheme of societal types*

extension of the intersection between a complex level of differentiation and a systematic level of organization then there would be no justification for arguing for a phase shift. An argument in favour of a phase shift is only supportable at this conjunction because there is a critical measure of contradiction between hyperdifferentiation and monocentric organization such that they are not mutually sustainable in the long term. We now indicate the form of the contradiction and its general consequences in purely theoretical terms.

The contradiction between hyperdifferentiation and monocentric organization has three aspects: issues associated with the sources of the media of control; issues associated with the vulnerability of objects to control; and issues associated with the reduction of distance between social units.

- *Sources:* Under modernization, the capacity of some social units to control or colonize others is the consequence of a differentiated capacity to generate media of exchange – economic units are more able to generate money than are religious units, for example, and so on. Hyperdifferentiation implies that there is no longer a restricted range of types of social unit (economic, political, etc.) but rather a theoretically limitless range within which given units can generate mixtures of media types. So, for example, TV churches can generate money as well as value-commitments and influence, and businesses which professionalize their employees and offer them lifetime security can be a source of value-commitments as well as money. In other words there is no longer an oligopolistic set of sources for money and power and they thus lose their effectivity as sources of control.

- *Objects:* Hyperdifferentiation also reduces the vulnerability of social units as objects of control. Under a complex level of differentiation similarities of structure arise from similarities of function. Manipulation of a given dimension of structure will therefore produce a widespread and predictable effect across units of given type. Under postmodernization, hyperdifferentiation ensures that the consequences of a given piece of bureaucratic or economic manipulation cannot be foreseen. States become ungovernable, economies unmanageable, and lifeworlds anarchistic.

- *Distance:* Monocentric control is constituted as a process of dedifferentiation, a reduction to a minimum of the distance between the public (state and economy/system) and domestic (civil society/lifeworld) spheres. The intertwining of the public with the domestic negates hyperdifferentiation, reducing social units to an indeterminate mix. There are so many different types of social unit, so much individual distinctiveness that boundaries and distances collapse.

The effect of these contradictory aspects is not merely to render monocentric organization untenable but to release differentiating tendencies from underlying axial principles. The onset of postmodernization is genuinely explosive as liberated societal components diverge rapidly from the central direction of modernity. Postmodernization is characterized by an unprecedented level of unpredictability and apparent chaos. Action is divorced from underlying material constraints (or rather these constraints disappear) and enters the voluntaristic realm of taste, choice and preference. As it does so the boundaries between determined social groups disappear. So class, gender and ethnicity decline in social significance and so also do some of their characteristic forms of expression, including class-based political action and the distinction between high and popular culture. On a more abstract level the progressive differentiation of culture, society and personality characteristic of modernity involutes so that the very idea of an independent, purely social structural realm no longer makes sense. Rather, 'society' must be understood in terms of 'culture' as patterns of signs and symbols penetrate and erode structural boundaries. The power of the large-scale social phenomena of modernity including states, monopolistic economic organizations, ecclesia, military forces and scientific establishments is attenuated as cultural currents propagate and sweep the globe, intersecting in indeterminate ways.

The following six chapters of this book seek to show that the advanced societies of the contemporary world are poised on the cusp of this transformation, that the trends present in each of the arenas analysed

indicate that postmodernization is well under way and that the denoue-
ment of modernity is imminent. The trend is not irreversible – the
refeudalization of Russia in the seventeenth century is clear evidence that
change is not inevitable. However, in the face of the effectivity of action, a
reversal would involve a legitimation crisis of such massive proportions
that it would demand either cataclysmic economic decline or extreme
coercion, or both, on a global scale, a new and terrible 'dark age' .

In brief the arenas addressed and the main trends identified for each of
them are as follows.

Culture

Modern culture is best understood as a 'regional stability' generated by
processes of differentiation, commodification and rationalization working
at a particular stage of development and level of intensity. Postmodernization of culture is best understood as an extension and intensification of
differentiation, rationalization and commodification which dissolves the
regional stability of modern culture and reverses its priorities.

Value-spheres become hyperdifferentiated, that is, their internal boundaries multiply to the point of fragmentation. As the particular genre, or
style, becomes the unit of production and consumption, we orient ourselves to nostalgic classicism rather than 'Art', to heavy metal rather than
'Music' or to nineteenth-century women novelists rather than 'Literature'.
The eventual effect of hyperdifferentiation is to set loose cultural 'fragments' of intense symbolic power which transgress the boundaries between
value-spheres and between culture and other subsystems. In other words,
hyperdifferentiation produces just that effect of dedifferentiation which
Lash (1990) and others see as the mark of postmodernist culture.

Hyper-rationalization is responsible for the 'elitist splitting off' of expert
cultures which Habermas (1987) laments and the related 'crisis of the
avant-garde' which Bürger (1984) diagnoses. The work of cultural virtuosi
in elaborating the 'logic' of their discipline increasingly cuts them off from
nonexpert audiences: the music of Schönberg and his contemporaries is
still regarded as modern and 'difficult' by concert audiences, for example.
In Bürger's view, the radical, dedifferentiating, avant-garde response to
hyper-rationalization, epitomized in Dada, had exhausted itself by the
1920s. Cultural 'modernism', then, is the mark of a modern culture caught
in a terminal crisis of hyper-rationalization. Once the idea of a 'logic' of
cultural development, the meta-narrative of aesthetic 'progress', loses its
hold on producers and consumers then the modern conceptions of 'art' and
'culture' themselves are in decline. Postculture offers a flat archive of
'styles' which furnishes materials for pastiche and parody in the place of a
developing tradition.

Hypercommodification erodes the boundaries which modern culture
disingenuously erects between 'Art' and the commodified 'culture industry'. Hypercommodification is closely connected with the two processes

outlined above. Hyperdifferentiation, by freeing symbolic meaning from the constraints of value-spheres, contributes to a critical shift in which consumption becomes a dominant concern of postculture and cultural, or symbolic, value becomes a dominant concern of consumption (see, for example, the discussion of 'the Jeaning of America' in Fiske 1989). Hyper-rationalization or, rather, its exhaustion, opens the whole terrain of postculture for commodification through the modulation of hierarchical cultural tradition into a postcultural emporium of styles. The principle of taste, generalized and released from hierarchy, becomes the sole criterion for the consumer's selection.[35]

Postculture does, indeed, exhibit that semiotic promiscuity and preference for pastiche and parody which commentators widely associate with postmodernism. A television commercial sells cat food by setting the sales pitch to the music of a Mozart aria, Andrew Lloyd Webber writes a hugely successful pastiche of a late Romantic Requiem, the Kronos string quartet plays Hendrix. The argument here is that these frequently noted developments need to be explained by referring to general processes of change which are not only 'cultural'.

The State

The progressive postmodernization (dedifferentiation and disorganization) of social life is reflected in two general political processes: a *decentralization* of power, a general tendency for power to become multifaceted and so widely distributed across society that there is no precise set of power loci; and a *decoupling* of conflicts in which political confrontations are progressively separated from an economic basis (see the section on political processes below).

Within modernity, state political processes are primarily class and national processes. Given a decline of economic class differences, the growth of supra-national bodies and an increasingly global scope for cultural transactions, under postmodernization state political processes are of decreasing relevance. Under modernization the state regulates the capitalist system by the protection of physical property and the reproduction both of labour power and of the social relations of production but under postmodernization physical means of production, are no longer critical to the process of accumulation and the social relations of production are diverse in relation to market demand. Moreover the corporatist settlements of late modernity established under the aegis of the state are beginning to show evidence of considerable dysfunction.

More importantly, the three essential functions of the modern state, external defence, internal surveillance and the maintenance of citizenship rights, have been undermined. The ties of military establishments into the state have been weakened by a decentralization of economic decision making and increasing difficulties in legitimizing the commitment of vast resources for military purposes.[36] Moreover, the proliferation of nuclear weapons, and world-wide coverage of hostilities by the mass media, has made the use of violence a risky option, open to question by the public and by influential political groups.

The state's role as provider and guardian of citizenship rights and political freedoms has also been eroded. Most of these rights and freedoms have been depoliticized and thus defined as 'human rights' and 'individual freedoms' located above and beyond state control and guardianship. Publicity given to state violations of these rights has undermined the core elements of state legitimacy and paved the way for a devolution of state power. Although this may not result in an immediate 'withering away' the role of state apparatuses is in considerable decline.

There are four significant elements in this unravelling of the state: a horizontal redistribution of power and responsibility to autonomous corporate bodies; a vertical redistribution of power and responsibility to local councils, civic initiatives, and extra-state self-governing bodies; the marketization and privatization of previously state run enterprises; and an externalization of responsibility by shifting it to supra-state bodies.

Given a definition of the nation-state as the organization monopolizing the legitimate means of violence, it follows that the dissolution of political power is accompanied by a dissolution of military power. The ties of military establishments into the state are weakened by the disorganization of economic decision making. There ceases to be an industrial establishment which can relate symbiotically to the military. Moreover the absorption of the state into global economic and political networks delegitimizes the commitment of resources to military purposes. Military forces exist to protect the state against other states. Where the state is in decline we may expect a decentralization of military power to international policing and/or mercenary status.

Class and Gender Inequality

Changes in the distribution of economic power are given in the above statements on disorganization. Dispersed, diverse and small-scale economic organizations disallow massive capital accumulation and thus radically unequal distributions of economic power. Bureaucratic hierarchies dissolve as owners and workers work at the same desk or workstation. Moreover the power of owners is constrained by the possibility of workers withdrawing their skills and knowledge and transferring them to other organizations, or indeed of setting up new organizations of their own. Under these conditions the great industrial classes are beginning to merge rather than to polarize – a process specifically manifested in the decline of labour unionism. Economic power differences while continuing to be real are becoming more fluid and negotiated so that any given individual may have widely differing levels of economic potency in a lifetime.

Gender inequalities are also affected by processes of postmodernization. The central pattern is dedifferentiation at the boundary between the domestic sphere and the public arena. This has the important secondary consequence of a progressive dissolution of the categories of male and female. This is being accomplished within an extension of the standard processes of modernization. Masculine and feminine gender categories are subdividing into various masculinities and femininities. As this differentiation process accelerates to radical levels the binary differentiation will lose clarity and dissolve.

Domestic and economic production are therefore losing their power as arenas within which inequalities become established. The generation of inequality is progressively displaced into the arenas of consumption. In the later stages of modernity this is manifested as a return of status, especially in terms of the political action as disadvantaged status groups make claims for equal inclusion in general standards of consumption. With the onset of postmodernization these claims are realized and 'real' status groups dissolve to be replaced by identifications constructed in the electronic mass media but having the possibility of genuine political and economic force within market-democratic systems. Such communities, which might be called 'simulated power blocs', differentiate and proliferate, swamping and obscuring the old determinate divisions of class and gender.

Political Processes

The modernization of politics involved four related processes: the separation of political activities from other forms of activity; the concentration of authority within the executive apparatuses of the state; an extension of political participation; and the emergence of the bureaucratized idiom of 'power politics'. Current trends partly reverse the direction of change. First and foremost, political divisions and processes have been progressively decoupled from the socio-economic structure and from the market-shaped relations of production and exchange. This decoupling of political conflict from underlying material determinants is occurring in two contexts: political culture and political constituencies. The elements of political culture, including the dominant values, orientations and repertoires of political action change under the impact of new social movements. Political constituencies have been affected by changing political allegiances indicated by declines in union membership, declining class voting, and declining support for the major political parties. The new conflicts are more contingent and conjunctural. They tend to erupt around general values and lifestyles, and they involve status, situs[37] and generational categories rather than socio-economic groups. Under these conditions traditional, class-based 'milieu parties' lose ground and are displaced by 'third parties', as well as less permanent social movements. The latter represent more ephemeral and more global concerns, undermine the old political divisions, and transcend state boundaries. Although some elements of new politics, such as its informalism and public orientation, are likely to normalize, this change of format is unlikely to alter the substance of new politics, which is increasingly diverse and contingent.

Work and Production

The foundation of modernity is what may be called the industrial complex – the concentrated organization of the human system of production and consumption around a mechanical technology. A frequent theme in theories of the new society is that, during the third quarter of the twentieth century, mechanical technology is being displaced by electronic or information technology. Many such theories take a position of technological determinism, arguing that the new technology causes fundamental societal change.

The argument offered here is of a decoupling of organizational structures from technological determination. There is a widely documented growth in flexible and small-scale production organizations which concentrate on the production of components or of services and whose existence is a function of immediate demand rather than of planned expansions of capital investment. This in turn implies a dissolution of centralized authority systems and of collective bargaining between employers and employees in favour of relatively fluid circuits of fee-for-service, contractual and other directly 'market driven' commercial relationships.

This economic shift marks a transformation in the processes by which capital is accumulated. The transformation is widely described as a movement from 'Fordism' to 'flexible specialization' (see e.g. Harvey 1989: 121–201; Piore and Sabel 1984; Scott 1988: 7–10). In Fordist accumulation, named after the leading mass car producer Henry Ford, maximum accumulation possibilities are achieved by the application of two basic principles: first, the larger the scale of production the greater the return on investment; second the greater the extent to which human skills are replaced by technology, the greater the return. The giant industrial corporations which emerged were able to control their product and labour markets and, to a considerable extent, the states in which they operated as well. In flexible specialization maximum returns on investment are provided by a capacity to respond rapidly to changing market demand, a capacity which can better be provided by human rather than technological inputs. The Fordist industrial dinosaurs are giving way to a more complex range of economic creatures, each adaptable to its own niche.

Science

If modern science shares a structure with a wider modern culture, its postmodernization is similarly linked to wider social and cultural processes. Modern 'big science' is highly organized in the sense that it is financially and institutionally well integrated with the two archetypical forms of organized capitalism: the corporation and the state. Just as economic and social disorganization is related to the end of the postwar boom and a looming 'fiscal crisis of the state', so too is the 'disorganization' of science. As Barnes (1985:4) observes, the growth rate of science in the 1950s and 1960s, which would have seen its costs doubling every decade, was clearly unsustainable. Anyone who has worked in universities or research institutions in any advanced society since the mid-1970s will have become habituated to the constant attempts by governments to rein in the costs of science.

These attempts are no mere external irritant to modern science, whose 'regional stability' has depended on growth, on the pursuit of endogenous differentiation and rationalization. It is growth which has prevented the latent contradiction between institutional and normative autonomy on the one hand, and integration with the state and the corporation on the other, from flaring into crisis. As growth slows, so the autonomy of science comes increasingly into question and calls are heard for a 'hyper-organization' of science which would see its agenda set more explicitly by the state and the corporation. However, contemporary science is constituted in a degree of hyperdifferentiation and hyper-rationalization which will defy any attempt at centralized and nonexpert co-ordination. Far more plausible is the image of a decentred and transnational science in which the level of the nation-state becomes less and less relevant. Hyperdifferentiation corrodes the disciplinary structure that underpins modern science. As research fronts proliferate disciplines fragment, and for researchers in a particular field communication across disciplinary boundaries may become more important than communication within a discipline.[38]

If modern, rational, science is premised on a drive for domination and control of the natural world, that drive has come to seem increasingly paradoxical. First, scientific hyper-rationalization increasingly runs up against established normative constraints and fundamental values. An early example of ethical ambiguity is to be found in nuclear weapons research, a more recent one in genetics. Genetics is also in the forefront of hypercommodification, as organisms genetically engineered in the laboratories of universities and corporations are patented as private property. Second, the drive for control has come to seem self-defeating: induced climate change and environmental pollution are increasingly regarded as the consequences of a science and technology out of control. Surveys of public opinion on science find ambiguity and distrust: scientific and technological research is supported, but is seen as potentially threatening. The preference for a simpler way of life is widespread.[39]

Notes

1. The first use of the term to periodize history is probably Toynbee's: 'We think of the new chapter of Western history that opened at the turn of the fifteenth and sixteenth centuries as being "modern" *par excellence* because, for the next four centuries and more, until the opening of a "post-Modern Age" at the turn of the nineteenth and twentieth centuries, the middle class was in the saddle . . . the advent in the West of a post-Modern Age [is] marked by the rise of an industrial urban working class. . .' (1954: 338). Few contemporary

sociologists would accept that the twentieth century is anything other than modern and indeed that one of the hallmarks of modernity is a class system which includes both a middle class and an industrial working class. Possibly the earliest usage which corresponds with our own is provided by Mills in 1959: 'We are at the ending of what is called The Modern Age. Just as Antiquity was followed by several centuries of Oriental ascendancy, which westerners provincially call The Dark Ages, so now The Modern Age is being succeeded by a post-modern period. Perhaps we may call it: The Fourth Epoch' (1970: 184). Interestingly, Mills anticipates many current arguments which identify scepticism towards meta-narrative as the hallmark of the postmodern period, referring to the collapse of an acceptance that liberalism and socialism are adequate explanations of the world and ourselves as the signal for the onset of a fourth epoch.

2. Jameson (1984: 87) offers the strongest version of a Marxist appropriation of this argument, viewing postmodernism as the cultural counterpart of late capitalism. However, his own description of the transformation gives cause for doubt that there is much room left for material determination even in this formulation. There is, he argues, a 'prodigious expansion of culture throughout the social realm, to the point at which everything in our social life from economic value to state power and practices and to the very structure of the psyche itself – can be said to have become "cultural". . . .'.

3. We use the term effectivity, much after the fashion of Althusser, to mean the extent to which the arena is the source of causal determination. So here we are saying that culture as opposed to society or as opposed to material relationships is an expanding source of the causes of change in other arenas.

4. Lash and Urry (1987: 7) provide not a single date but different dates for each of the societies they analyse as experiencing 'disorganization', a structural process compatible with postmodernization: 'the crucial aspects of such disorganization are to be found in Britain and the USA from the 1960s, France from the late 1960s/early 1970s, Germany from the 1970s, and Sweden from the late 1970s/early 1980s.' Lyotard puts the date even earlier, suggesting that the transition to postindustiral society and postmodern culture has been under way since at least the 1950s (1984:3).

5. For arguments against the notion that change in social structure has taken a marked alteration in direction see Calhoun (1990), Habermas (1984, 1987a), Kumar (1988), and Offe (1985b).

6. This scheme of functional exigencies encompasses an earlier scheme known as the 'pattern variables', which in turn is an elaboration of Tönnies' familiar *Gemeinschaft–Gesellschaft* dichotomy. The four elements are, in common sociological parlance, referred to as 'boxes'. This is because in deriving the categories from the pattern variables Parsons needed to set up intersections between dichotomies in the form of a 'two-by-two' table. Each of the four exigencies, AGIL, is located in a box beginning with Adaptation in the top-left cell, with Goal attainment, Integration and Latency being distributed around the scheme in order in a clockwise fashion.

7. Against our position Alexander makes the surprising claim that: 'Parsons' theory lacked a developmental notion of particular phases. While he plausibly argued against the feudalism–capitalism–socialism trichotomy [sic] of Marx, he did not distinguish clearly coherent historical phases of his own' (1990: 8). In support of our position we may cite Rocher (1974: 71): 'Parsons distinguished three principal stages in social evolution: primitive societies, intermediate societies, and modern societies.' Also see Toby's introduction to Parsons' theory of evolution (Parsons 1977: 10–19).

8. For a detailed discussion of extreme task fragmentation within Taylorist and Fordist approaches to work organization see Chapter 6 below.

9. The grounds for such an argument vary. In conservative traditions more complex differentiation provides increased adaptive capacity for a society relative to its environments; in Marxist traditions higher differentiation provides increased capacity for control by the privileged over the disprivileged.

10. Alexander describes the substantive direction that modernization takes when driven by these processes: 'Institutions gradually become more specialized. Familial control over social

organization decreases. Political processes become less directed by the obligations and rewards of patriarchy, and the division of labour is organized more according to economic criteria than by reference simply to age and sex. Community membership can reach beyond ethnicity to territorial and political criteria. Religion becomes more generalized and abstract, more institutionally separated from and in tension with other spheres. Eventually cultural generalization breaks the bonds of religion altogether. Natural laws are recognized in the moral and physical worlds and, in the process, religion surrenders not only its hierarchical control over cultural life but its institutional prominence as well' (1990: 1).

11. The central and increasingly extreme contradiction is that between the social relations of production (who owns the means of production) and the forces of production (who contributes the labour power which gives value to products) (see Marx 1977: 388–92).

12. As this parody implies, great care is needed if arguments about colonization are not to resolve into misleading nostalgia. However, if a core of good sense is conceded to the colonization thesis, a connection with the first process can be made. Consider the commodification of home-based musical entertainment. In a simple form, this begins with the manufacture and sale of pianos and sheet music. It takes off in the ages of 'mechanical' and then 'electronic' reproduction, so that the consumer is faced with choices between a bewildering variety of technologies (radio, tape, DAT, vinyl disc, compact disc) and recordings. Some of the complexities and paradoxes of commodification will be considered in subsequent chapters.

13. Offe and Ronge (1984) discuss in considerable detail the way in which, in seeking to protect the commodity form, the state in fact negates it by protecting capitalist enterprises from the vagaries of the market and by socializing the costs of the reproduction of labour power. Habermas (1976: 53–4) offers a similar argument about the reproduction of the social relations of production in the advanced stages of capitalism.

14. This is a simplification of Weber's definition of rationality. Brubaker (1984: 2) indicates that some sixteen meanings of the term can be extracted from Weber's analyses: 'deliberate, systematic, calculable, impersonal, instrumental, exact, quantitative, rule-governed, predictable, methodical, purposeful, sober, scrupulous, efficacious, intelligible and consistent'.

15. This formulation is transparently related to Habermas' reification of the well-used functionalist terminology of 'social' and 'system' integration (1987a).

16. Some of the statements made here about feudal societies also apply to some aspects of the ancient empires from which they emerged. However, such ancient societies might be regarded as early forms of absolutism as described in Figure 1.2. Generally, however, the discussion here refers principally to classical European feudalism.

17. The principal examples are nineteenth-century England, Holland and the USA.

18. We include only western capitalist societies within this category. In a subsequent development of this typology in this chapter we introduce the category 'statist society' to indicate instances of the intersection of complex differentiation with an extremely high or 'monocentric' level of organization. Statist society shares characteristics with organized society but takes them to an extreme level. So the commodity form disappears entirely and the economy becomes a controlled and planned or 'command' system of production and distribution run by the party-state which also envelops and directs community and culture, rendering them common and uniform. Interestingly, post-Stalinist Soviet societies moved some distance towards the organized category by developing a corporatist pattern of interest integration but remained resolutely statist in terms of their totalitarian institutional framework.

19. We restrict our analysis of economic modernity here to capitalist modernity, largely because capitalism was the originating form but also because state socialist industrialism, always arguably and now apparently, is incorporated within the capitalist orbit (see Wallerstein 1974). Soviet-type society may be considered as a variant of industrial or modern society which co-exists with western capitalism. However, it differs from the western form in many important respects: it has an etatized command economy rather than a market economy; private ownership of capital is restricted; and the economy, politics and culture are

managed centrally by an ideologically unified partocratic elite. We pay less attention to this form of society because it has a less central historical status, a status which is becoming increasingly apparent in current circumstances. The Soviet system is undergoing a transition which, if continued, may place it in a trajectory similar to the one experienced in the West. Some aspects of these convergent trends are discussed in Chapters 3 and 4.

20. Ferguson (1990) turns the spirit of carnival into the template for that 'fun' which (with the official quest for 'happiness') is displaced by bourgeois 'pleasure', while Fiske (1987, 1989) makes of it the source of a modern popular culture of resistance.

21. The Weber thesis, if nothing else, should guard us from the temptation to make too much of 'secularization' in the early modern period. Secularization is better seen as an outcome of differentiation, rationalization and commodification than as an independent force for change.

22. The argument here owes a good deal to Campbell's suggestive (1987) account of the rise of consumerism.

23. This approach to the 'auratic' character of modern art and its connection with 'mechanical reproduction' implies a critique of Benjamin's influential account (1973a).

24. These developments have been discussed in the European context by Carr (1968), Poggi (1978), and Grew (1984).

25. A class may be defined as a group of people whose recognizably common and bounded access to material welfare and to power is contingent upon their common location (or the location of someone upon whom they are materially dependent) in the system of production and its reproduction.

26. The norms are held to be: universalism, communism, disinterestedness and organized scepticism. Merton argues that these norms 'fit' with those of the USA particularly well, although not perfectly. There are tensions between the communal 'ownership' of intellectual property and the capitalist market, and between organized scepticism and religious faith, for example.

27. Indeed, Habermas concedes that it is not really appropriate to persist in regarding the public and private spheres of the lifeworld as 'systems' because influence and value commitment cannot, in the end, sensibly be regarded as 'media'. The lifeworld is structured by patterns of generalized communication through ordinary language which cannot be 'technicized'.

28. However, shades of the idea of 'contradiction' linger in Habermas' (1987a) conviction that 'mediatization' becomes self-defeating as it erodes the communicative basis of normative order and socialization.

29. Habermas (1981a, 1987a: 396) regards postmodern*ism* as a neoconservative turn which argues for the abandonment of the emancipatory enlightenment project of modernity.

30. Lash offers two arguments which contradict this position. First, he locates the development and reception of postmodernist culture in terms of alterations in the class structure (1990: 18–30, 263; Lash and Urry 1987: 292–6). Postmodernist culture is used by an emerging postindustrial new ('yuppified') middle class to identify and legitimize itself against traditional bourgeois definitions. The pattern becomes generalized as working-class unity dissolves and its culture fragments and occludes with consumption-centred yuppie culture. So the origin of postmodernist culture is located clearly at the level of the social. Second, quite properly, the principal characteristic of postmodernist culture is held to be dedifferentiation (see Chapters 2 and 8 below) one aspect of which is its increasingly nonauratic character. If a principal characteristic of postmodernist culture is that 'it is no longer systematically separated from the social' (Lash 1990: 11) it would be impossible to understand postmodern-ism simply as a purely cultural movement. Lash argues then that postmodernism is a development with social origins which eventually turns upon its origins and subsumes the social, yet he also wishes to argue for its confinement to the cultural sphere.

31. Here Lyotard mentions nation-states, parties, professions, institutions, and historical traditions (1984: 14).

32. Nowhere are Baudrillard's reflections on postmodern culture quite so convincing as in the area of spectacles, mass participation entertainment events. A description of the 'city' of

Orlando, Florida in the popular press might have been written for his benefit (*Time* 27 May 1991: 44–51). The story is written under the headline: 'Fantasy's Reality. Orlando, the boomtown of the U.S. South, is growing on the model of Disney World: a community that imitates an imitation of a community.' In Orlando, Disney's 'Main Street, USA' becomes reality: the streets are vacuumed each night; everyone is middle class and white; and when you pay your money to go into Disney World you can't spot the difference.

33. In describing this emerging configuration Baudrillard's language becomes physicalist in its metaphor: 'The social void is scattered with interstitial objects and crystalline clusters which spin around and coalesce in a cerebral chiaroscuro. So is the mass, an *in vacuo* aggregation of individual particles, refuse of the social and of media impulses: an opaque nebula whose growing density absorbs all the surrounding energy and light rays, to collapse finally under its own weight. A black hole which engulfs the social' (1983b: 3–4).

34. Although Figure 1.2 is far from being a model of social change, to be acceptable it must at least be consistent with known patterns of historical evolution. If we were pressed to argue a general direction for social change it would be along the diagonal from top left to bottom right. Deviations from this route are possible, typically in the direction of bottom left. However, moves off the diagonal may be regarded as unsustainable in the long term. That is, all concrete societies must pass through the forager/tribal cell and the organized capitalism cell but the other cells are, as it were, optional. Further, we are fairly certain that any passage from one cell to another must be by a vertically, laterally or diagonally contiguous route. It is not possible, for example, to jump directly from the feudal to the technocratic cell. Finally, reversal of the general diagonal direction of change is possible but unusual.

Three examples of evolutionary routes through the figure may be offered, each of which begins with a move from forager/tribal to feudal. The first is indicated by what Kosselleck calls 'the exceptional position of England' (1988: 15) that is, a situation in which trends towards monocentric organization were undermined by early differentiation. In England a differentiated economic structure enabled a rising bourgeoisie to pre-empt the growing power of the state, to constitutionalize it and thus to force a move to liberal capitalism. Nowhere was this move more pronounced than in what was at that time a subsociety of Britain, the USA. In the Anglo-Saxon example (which includes Australia, Canada and New Zealand) organized capitalism emerges from the reproductive failures of liberal capitalism.

The second example is indicated by the case of France. Here the absolutist state was well institutionalized but disrupted by the extreme instability of the revolution – the annihilation of absolutism itself required an absolutist response. Thus throughout the nineteenth century France experienced wild swings between various forms of Bonapartist and monarchist absolutism on one hand and various constitutional, republican and even socialist formations on the other. Still, it could not avoid some measure of systematic organization at the centre and eventually settled down quite early in the central cell. The Scandinavian societies also moved directly from absolutism to a highly organized form of capitalism.

Absolutism survived much longer in the continental imperial states pressed by the contingencies of ethnic, linguistic and religious diversity. The collapse of absolutism in these cases was succeeded by an equally monocentric organizational form, statism. In Russia, statism became so well entrenched that only in the 1990s does it appear to be giving way to organized capitalism. In the formerly nationalistic statist societies, Germany and Japan, organized capitalism has been institutionalized since the middle of the twentieth century.

Two other empirical instances need to be discussed. The first is that of the formerly colonial societies of the third world. The colonial situation is itself an absolutist one. Not surprisingly, therefore, third world societies tend to be either statist or organized rather than liberal. The other, more difficult, example is that of ancient societies (Greece and Rome), which originate in tribalism and exhibit at various times feudal, liberal and organized attributes before undergoing reversal.

35. This case requires a critical reworking of Bourdieu's well-known (1984) discussion of taste as the principle of 'distinction'.

36. Although a controversial matter, the 'Gulf War' of 1990–1 might be seen as the first postmodernized war. It could not be fought in terms of the interests of a particular state but

was legitimated in terms of the interests of the entire global community of states, with only a few minor ones standing against it, that is, by claims to a 'new world order'. The majority commitment of US forces could only be accomplished under UN sponsorship and if bankrolled by the Arab oil-states and Japan – that is, only if detached from their own nation-state. Moreover, the war was a live-to-air mass mediated event in which much of the entire global community participated vicariously. It was therefore immediate, brief and available in every home with a TV set, a prime example of the reduction of time-space distances.

37. Situs refers to a position in the 'horizontal' dimension of the division of labour (e.g. sector of the economy).

38. A contrast may illustrate the point. The relationship between biological sciences and neo-Darwinian evolutionary theory is modern and differentiated: the theory serves as a 'paradigm' which unifies a disciplinary field and differentiates it from others. The impact of the ideas usually referred to as 'chaos,' by contrast, has been hyperdifferentiated and postmodernizing: chaos grew at the boundaries of a range of disciplines from mathematics to meteorology through the co-operation of marginalized research teams. Chaos illustrates the dedifferentiating potential of hyperdifferentiation in science, as in culture more generally.

39. For Australian data in support of this argument see Eckersley 1987.

2

From culture to postculture

Three theses on postmodernization have emerged from Chapter 1. First, its dynamic principles (differentiation, rationalization and commodification) are the same as those of modernization. Second, postmodernization is not simply an accentuation of modernization. The tension between these two theses generates the third: 'hyper' differentiation, rationalization or commodification produces outcomes which look very much like 'de' differentiation, rationalization or commodification. These theses point towards a conception of postmodernization which can be crystallized in the image of a 'dialectic of differentiation'. Beyond a certain point of development, differentiation produces ironic dedifferentiating reversals.[1] The present chapter considers the modernization and postmodernization of culture in the light of these theses. Because postmodernization is to be understood as an extension-cum-reversal of cultural modernity, it is important to be clear about the forces which shape the latter. To this end, nearly half of the chapter is given to an account of cultural modernity. Processes of differentiation, rationalization and commodification serve as foci for three subsections in each of two sections concerned with modernization and postmodernization respectively.

Cultural Modernization and Cultural Modernity

Differentiation

'Differentiation' has long been the key concept of functionalist theories of change, from Spencer through Durkheim and Parsons to contemporary neo-functionalism.[2] A major focus of interest is the modernizing dynamic through which the 'subsystems' of economy, polity, societal community and culture become differentiated and functionally interdependent. Sociological functionalism does not have a monopoly of concern with cultural differentiation, however. For a tradition whose members include Weber, Adorno and Habermas, Kant's division of his philosophical enterprise into three distinct 'critiques' (of pure reason, practical reason and judgement) articulates and legitimates the historical emergence of science, morality-law and art as differentiated and autonomous domains of activity, experience and value.

Two key concepts here are 'legitimacy' and 'autonomy'. When Lash (1990: 5–8) specifies modernization of culture as 'a process of cultural differentiation' he draws on the Weberian identification of cultural modernity with the 'autonomy' or 'self-legislation' of differentiated spheres of value. Science, morality-law and art are *legitimate* spheres to the extent that each turns on a specific 'value': truth, goodness, justice and beauty. They are *autonomous* spheres to the extent that none of these values can be defined in terms of the others. This model connects with the crucial idea, to be considered in the next subsection, that each of the autonomous spheres of modern culture is driven forward by the rationalization of its endogenous principles.

There is one divergence between Kant and Weber which is consequential for the fate of cultural modernity. For Kant, differentiation is compatible with a configurational and *rational* unity of culture. The three spheres exercise different 'faculties': understanding for science, judgement for art and reason for morality-law,[3] but the faculty of reason is privileged in relation to the others.

> To every faculty of the mind an interest can be ascribed, i.e., a principle which contains the condition under which alone its exercise is advanced. Reason, as the faculty of principles, determines the interest of all the powers of the mind and its own. (Kant 1956: 124)

Notoriously, the Weberian doctrine of 'value-spheres' has abandoned this enlightenment rationalism, and optimism.[4] The values operative in different spheres have become radically incommensurable: 'the value-spheres of the world stand in irreconcilable conflict with each other' (Weber 1970: 147). Disenchantment and incommensurability of values must be faced as the 'fate of the times' which calls for an heroic decision in favour of some value.

> Life as a whole, if it is not to be permitted to run on as an event in nature but instead is to be consciously guided, is a series of ultimate decisions through which the soul – as in Plato – chooses its own fate. (Weber 1949: 18)

Such decisions can be followed though in a consistent and coherent way, but they are not rationally accountable: one can be 'rational' within science but the commitment to the 'values' of science is not itself rational.

While the internal differentiation of culture is central to both these conceptions it is regarded either as not absolute (in Kant) or as deeply problematic (in Weber). Cultural modernization renders differentiation increasingly problematic as faith in an underlying 'rational' unity becomes progressively less tenable. While differentiation is a fundamental transformative principle within culture, it does not follow that cultural modernity is exhausted by the affirmation of differentiation. Rather, the field of cultural modernity is determined as a series of *tensions* between differentiation and dedifferentiation. This point will be taken up again shortly.[5]

The differentiating modernization of culture takes place through related processes of institutional and occupational differentiation. Throughout the modern period various forms of patronage have supported actors, playwrights, composers, musicians, painters, sculptors and others in a variety of ways,[6] and thereby facilitated the 'autonomy' of drama, music and visual and plastic arts. If patronage has been indispensable to the development of the differentiated artistic 'career', so has the later institutionalization of artistic training in art schools, musical conservatories, academies of dramatic art and the like. As artistic culture shifted its primary site from the private sphere of the aristocratic court into the bourgeois public sphere, an array of institutions specifically given to the arts emerged, such as art galleries, opera houses, concert halls, publishers and theatres. In turn, these institutions support a range of 'second order' occupations of managers, impresarios and specialized critics connected to the differentiated arts. Institutional and occupational differentiation is implicated in that hierarchical differentiation which is so much a mark of modern culture: the opening up of new markets for cultural goods among the lower middle and working classes of Europe and the USA also turned on the establishment of new institutions and associated occupations, from the popular newspaper to the music hall, the charabanc and the holiday resort. The popular culture of the turn of the nineteenth century is no premodern folk-culture: its differentiated, institutionalized and commodified forms are constitutive elements in cultural modernity.

A notable paradox is connected with the process of occupational and institutional differentiation of culture. The emergence of modern 'artistic' professions is accompanied, from the late eighteenth century on, by the emergence of a series of *de*-differentiating aesthetic movements. In Romanticism, which sets the pattern in many respects:

> we find a subjective approach to reality which is assumed to lie first in the particular, then in oneself; we find respect for the organic, often incalculable, in opposition to the planned that is reducible to rational formulae . . . We also find the passionate and uneasy discomfort or anguish, the causeless melancholy, the vague aspirations, the search for something one does not quite know what, that the Germans call *Sehnsucht* – longing. (E. Weber 1960: 13)

Romanticism is many-sided: sometimes radical and sometimes reactionary, sometimes vigorously engaged in the world and sometimes withdrawn and aestheticized. A connecting thread is a perception that the rational differentiation of enlightenment culture tears asunder that unity of experience which gives culture its value. This is as true for the aestheticism of a Gautier, which subordinates 'life' to 'art', as it is of the activism of a Byron, which subordinates 'art' to 'life'. Refusal of the internal differentiation of culture finds an exemplary expression in Wagner's reunification of music, drama, poetry and the visual arts in the *Gesamtkunstwerk*, of which more in the next subsection. In the aftermath of enlightenment rationalism, Romanticism defines the central problem of cultural modernity as a *tension* between differentiation and dedifferentiation. The resolutions which are rehearsed in Romanticism, from aestheticism to activism, provide the template for later developments.

It is instructive to reconsider Weber's version of a differentiated cultural modernity in the light of this argument. Weber demands an heroic dedifferentiation to be accomplished through will and commitment. The 'Romanticism' of this stand was noted by Gouldner (1975: 324).[7]

> Weber's theory of plural perspectives, of plural values and plural ideal types, comes down to the Romantic assumption that each man makes his own world and fights for it. . . . The unity of the world is, in characteristic Romantic style, not vouchsafed by anything external to the individual but is created, rather, in his own personal and passionate commitment.

That is to say, Weber may well be the 'paradigmatic theorist of the modern' (Lash 1990: 11), but he fights against the alienating differentiation that fragments modern culture.

Rationalization

The Weberian 'rationalization' theme suggests that culture is transformed by the modernizing drive for consistency and calculability. One aspect of this transformation is the 'endogenous' development of the formal possibilities inherent in different spheres of culture. So, Weber (1958) argues that western music has achieved a remarkable degree of harmonic rationalization based on mathematically integrated relations between musical intervals, a rationalization achieved in no other culture. However, he insists that the rationalization of culture must remain incomplete. It is doubly so in the case of music: within harmony itself, the interval of the 7th defies integration, and more generally 'chordal rationalization lives in a continuous tension with melodicism which it can never completely devour' (Weber 1958: 10). An entirely formalized and calculable culture would be devoid of the value which only a tension between the rational and the nonrational can impart. A second dimension of cultural rationalization is the 'technicization' of instruments of production and re-production. Weber (1958: 123) notes the impact of the 'technology' of the piano, for example. The piano prefigures the phonograph and the radio as an instrument of 'reproduction'. Piano transcriptions of orchestral works begin the process, whose latest phase is represented in the compact disc player, by which technical innovation shifts cultural consumption from the public to the domestic sphere.[8] Adorno draws on the idea of a 'technical' rationalization of culture in his critique of Wagner's *Gesamtkunstwerk* which re-unites poetry, drama, music and the visual arts. The bad faith at the heart of this conception is that while Wagner

> plays off the mythic unity of poet, singer and mime against the division of labour, and acts as if the *Gesamtkunstwerk* were capable of achieving that unity itself, the division of labour is in fact intensified rather than abolished by his techniques. (Adorno 1981: 108)

Wagnerian music-drama is a highly rationalized production. Its phantasmagoric settings depend upon advanced stagecraft, the link between character and musical motif atomizes the music and mechanizes its composition, the musical 'colour' depends on a fragmentation and reintegration of the parts of specific instruments to produce a single, 'thing like' sound.

> The greater the progress in the technicization of the work of art, the rational planning of its methods and hence of its effects, the more anxiously is Wagner intent upon making his music appear spontaneous, immediate and natural and upon concealing the controlling will. (Adorno 1981: 50)

If modern culture cannot be wholly rationalized, neither can it evade rationality: rational technique underpins even the protest against rationalization and differentiation.

The avant-garde movements of the early twentieth century are a critical nexus between rationalization and differentiation of culture, opposition to rationalization and differentiation, and the limits of cultural modernity. In one of the most effective of avant-garde gestures, Marcel Duchamp exhibited a urinal in the 1917 New York salon under the title 'Fountain'. The artist was given as 'R. Mutt', the sanitary engineer responsible. Duchamp was the best-known member of the Dadaist movement, one of a number of 'oppositional cultural formations'[9] such as constructivism, futurism and surrealism which prospered in the early twentieth century. Avant-garde movements take up the Romantic 'dedifferentiating' protest against the splitting of 'art' and 'life': Duchamp inserts the most everyday of objects into an aesthetic field, challenging conceptions of both the aesthetic and the everyday. The failure of avant-garde movements is indexed by their reabsorption within the aesthetic field they set out to challenge. As Bürger notes (1984: 72), '(t)he intention to revolutionize life by returning art to its praxis turns into a revolutionizing of art'. Photographs of 'Fountain' find their place in coffee-table art histories.

Modernist movements in art, literature and music pursue endogenous rationalization with particular single-mindedness. Convinced that realist art and literature or harmonic music have exhausted their potential, modernists take a 'problem-solving' approach in which 'the working out of the possibilities in the aesthetic material is the problem to be solved' (Lash 1990: 14). As a result of this self-referential and accelerating rationalization Schönberg's music, Joyce's writing, Picasso's art, become increasingly impenetrable to even an educated bourgeois audience.[10] For the avant-garde this 'elitist splitting off of expert cultures', in Habermas' (1987a: 330) phrase, extends, rather than resolves, the pathologies of modern culture. Their *intention* is to reverse it. But, as the case of Duchamp shows, the avant-garde cannot break with aesthetic 'problem solving' and its *effect* is to further the endogenous rationalization of art.[11] If, as Bürger puts it (1984: 22), the avant-garde represents the self-criticism of the subsystem of art, the failure of the avant-garde to reverse that split between art and life which is the defining problem of developed cultural modernity also marks the *limits* of cultural modernity. Aesthetic modernism reaches the limit of endogenous rationalization and differentiation of value-spheres, while the avant-garde reaches the limit of a rational dedifferentiation.

Huyssen (1986: ch. 1) has noted the 'hidden dialectic' linking the avant-garde to technology and mass culture. Duchamp's 'Fountain' and his various exercises with hat-stands are examples of the fascination that mass-produced objects held for the avant-garde. Benjamin articulates this fascination, arguing that 'mechanical reproduction' erodes the authenticity, aura and traditionalism of art objects which promote a 'reactionary' individualized and contemplative reception of art (Benjamin 1973b: 222–3, 236–7). He endorses the Dadaist attempt to 'shock' the audience out of a 'contemplative immersion' in art, and adds that 'the film has taken the physical shock effect out of the wrappers in which Dadaism had, as it were, kept it inside the moral shock effect' (1973b: 240). Benjamin's vision is of an emancipatory, anti-auratic, convergence between the radical avant-garde and popular culture, a convergence accomplished by new technologies of reproduction and communication.[12]

Benjamin's error concerns the allegedly anti-auratic effects of technical rationalization. The case can equally well be made that technologies of reproduction have played a crucial part in the solidification of cultural tradition. Reproductions of 'great paintings' are packaged in books that make tradition palpable by the placing of pictures in an historical sequence accompanied by a respectful linking narrative. Similarly, the mechanical reproduction of 'classical' music in the mid-twentieth century was hardly anti-auratic in its impact. It reinforced, rather than subverted, the ideas of a 'great composer', 'great performer' and 'great performance'. This manufacture of an 'aura' which is not simply the echo of a premodern cultic value sits comfortably with commodification: the great conductor sells the record, and the promotion and success of the record underlines the conductor's greatness.

A more general point connects with this critique of Benjamin: the active 'invention' of tradition is a dominant concern of art, literature and music in the twentieth century: the 'high' culture of late modernity is overwhelmingly a museum culture.[13] The cultural objects of earlier phases of cultural modernization, the paintings of Rembrandt, the plays of Shakespeare, the symphonies of Beethoven, have a massive authoritative presence.[14] In the late nineteenth century contemporary works in art, literature and music were at the centre of the concerns of bourgeois culture. The audience for a Brahms symphony could receive the work as a contemporary manifestation of a musical tradition going back through Beethoven to Bach. The twentieth-century advent of modernism, particularly in music, was associated with inaccessibilty to even an 'educated' audience and the standard repertoire became more and more oriented to the past.[15]

The burgeoning institutions of late modern culture – university departments, academies, critical journals and the rest – engage in a massive work of classifying and cataloguing the cultural objects of the past and relating them to those of the present. It is here that the invention of cultural tradition takes place, so that, for example, the newly established university departments of English literature could invent a tradition which links

Beowulf to the plays of Shakespeare and the poems of Eliot. This work then shapes the display of cultural objects by publishers, galleries and concert promoters. The museum culture is quite compatible with a sense of novelty and dynamism. First, there is the novelty of performance in which new actors, theatrical directors, or orchestral conductors present new interpretations of classic works. This novelty is brought to the visual arts through blockbusting exhibitions which can re-present and reinterpret established works. A second accommodation between novelty and museum culture is the constant modification of tradition. The explosion of interest in Baroque, and pre-Baroque, music which began in the 1960s introduced a host of 'new' works to the repertoire, and established a 'new' type of musical ensemble committed to authenticity in performance. This example is instructive because, in a different way to modernism and avant-gardism, it brings the rationalization of culture close to its limits. Beyond a certain point, the absorption of ever more cultural producers of the past, and ever more historical periods into the museum culture erodes the organizing figure of a 'tradition', and the museum becomes a data base to be accessed on the basis of any or no criteria.

Commodification

From the viewpoint of a differentiated modern culture, commodification can appear as a colonization in which commerce erases aesthetic value. This viewpoint dominates those theories of 'mass culture' in which themes from the conservative critique of enlightenment find echoes in the Marxist critique of capitalism.[16] In an influential and nuanced variant, Adorno and Horkheimer (1979) drew an analogy between the Nazi manipulation of mass media in Europe and the commercial manipulation of media in the United States. In late capitalism, cultural production and consumption are absorbed into the system of capitalist production so that culture becomes 'commodified'. As cultural production is industrialized, the differences between cultural products become a matter of mere 'image' or 'style', no more significant than those between a Chrysler and a General Motors automobile (Adorno and Horkheimer 1979: 123). In this erosion of difference and triumph of style lies the convergence between the 'culture industry' and totalitarianism. 'In the culture industry . . . imitation finally becomes absolute. Having ceased to be anything but style, it reveals the latter's secret: obedience to the social hierarchy' (1979: 131). Culture loses its capacity to function as a site at which mature individuals can critically reflect upon their society and their own lives. Drawing on Freudian themes, Adorno and Horkheimer assert that the net effect of the culture industry is a real regression of individuality. The imitative, or 'mimetic', attitudes and behaviours it fosters arrest individual development at a stage which is still infantile.

From this darkest of perspectives, then, commodification converges with totalitarian manipulation in the destruction of all cultural value, the promotion of conformism and the retardation of individual development. 'High' culture is not exempted from the critique, and many of the processes which prepare culture for commodification originate in 'high' art (see, e.g. Adorno's analysis of Wagner, noted above). Adorno and Horkheimer often focus precisely on the erosion and transgression of boundaries between high and mass culture, as in their remarks on Benny Goodman's collaboration with the Budapest Quartet (Adorno and Horkheimer 1979: 136). To this extent they are early analysts of cultural *post*modernization, and their pessimism can serve as a corrective to more celebratory accounts.

However, there are limits to an analysis of cultural commodification cast solely in terms of the working out of an inner logic of capitalism and its disastrous effects. Notably, it displaces attention from the complex ways in which the institutional differentiation and endogenous rationalization of culture are intertwined with a commodification of relations of cultural production. Market relations, as Marx and Weber both recognized, are relentlessly anti-traditional, tending to subvert premodern patterns of action based on custom and status. If the bourgeois culture of the early modern period takes on a critical and subversive stance in relation to the authority of Crown and Altar, its commodified character is in part responsible. The idea and reality of a 'market' in cultural goods constantly subverts attempts to subordinate cultural production, distribution and exchange to the requirements of religious orthodoxy or monarchical authority.[17] Successful operation in a market for cultural goods offers a vivid icon of cultural autonomy, however rarely it is achieved in practice.

Very many cultural institutions, and individual cultural producers, throughout the modern period subsist through a combination of some form of patronage, adapted to modern conditions (see note 11) and market activity. Williams (1981: 107) argues that the balance between patronage (particularly state subsidy) and market mechanisms is caught in 'asymmetries' between the idea of a 'necessary' high culture and threats to it from profit-driven market forces, and between pluralistic and market-oriented conceptions of cultural diversity. The sense that commodification is the debased and colonizing 'other' of cultural value hovers around these tensions. The institutions and practices associated with bourgeois 'high' culture are commodified to a considerable degree while not surviving exclusively through market mechanisms: late-modern culture is shaped by a constitutive tension commodifying and decommodifying pressures. The question arises in the next section of whether the shifting balance between the two is implicated in postmodernization.

It is clear that there is no line between the commodified and the noncommodified which can legitimize a distinction between 'high' and 'mass' culture. While the massive commodification of 'popular' pleasures and entertainments has been one of the most notable outcomes of cultural modernization, this process must be placed in analytic and historical context. It is easy enough to understand the 'supply side' of cultural commodification in terms of capitalist dynamics: the creation of new use values (as in the case of tourism, perhaps) and the colonization of old ones (singing, eating, drinking) are basic to economic growth. However, problems arise when accounts at this level are also taken to explain the 'demand side' of commodification. When consumption is perceived as mere passivity, with no productivity of its own, it is an easy step to mass culture theories in which consumers are the victims of 'false needs' created by capital. If such elisions are to be avoided, the question of the historical productivity of consumer demand must be addressed. One route, which has the virtue of reintegrating the histories of 'high' and 'mass' culture, is through a consideration of the peculiarly modern phenomenon of 'taste'.

Taste is definitively modern in that premodern cultures do not present their members with the degree of choice in consumption which is necessary for the exercise of taste. Campbell's (1987) distinction between 'traditional' and 'modern' hedonism adds a further dimension. Traditional hedonism is oriented to basic 'needs' (for food, drink, sex and not much more) whose repeated indulgence tends to blunt the appetite. While there are possibilities for recreating the want–satisfaction cycle and for an epicurean titillation of the senses, the scope for a differentiation, rationalization or commodification of traditional pleasures is limited. Campbell (1987: 69) argues that 'the key to the development of modern hedonism lies in the shift of primary concern from sensations to emotions'. The development of 'modern autonomous imaginative hedonism' in the early modern period is critical to the linked phenomena of consumerism and taste. Consumerism requires an 'endless wanting' on the part of consumers, who will 'not so much seek satisfaction from products, as pleasure from the self-illusory experiences which they construct from their associated meanings' (Campbell 1987: 89). On this basis, '"taste", regarded as the typical pattern of a person's preferences, is largely a function of day-dreaming' (1987: 93).

If the trajectory of cultural commodification is closely related to that of the phenomenon of taste, it is consequential that different social strata are drawn into the field of taste in different periods. The phenomenon of taste 'trickles down' the social hierarchy during the modern period, the pace and scope of this trickle-down being contingent on the changing social and economic circumstances of different strata.[18] Taste emerges as a specific problem in the seventeenth century, and especially in France (see Moriarty 1988), in connection with monarchical and aristocratic opulence. For contemporary authorities such as the Chevalier de Méré, *le bon goût* was the exclusive mark of an aristocratic, court-based, elite. The eighteenth century saw the emergence of an enlightenment conception of taste, attuned to the growing economic power of bourgeois and professional groups. For David Hume the basis of taste lay in those 'common sentiments of human nature' which were universally distributed but which produced the capacities of 'a true judge of the finer arts' only in the rarest and most favourable of circumstances (see Hume 1964: 170–9). Bourgeois consumption enters, and transforms, the field of taste. The phenomenon of working-class taste began to emerge in the late nineteenth century and exploded in the mid-twentieth.[19] As Tomlinson and Walker (1990: 221) write of Britain in the 1930s,

> the average real price of entertainment and recreation fell. Regularly employed working people had no problem finding the cost of a cinema, theatre or music hall seat, a dance hall or excursion ticket. Hire purchase was also available for new commodities such as bicycles.

Tomlinson cites J.B. Priestley to make the point that in this period 'through forms of mass consumption, previously deferential social groups were throwing off the shackles of subordination' (Tomlinson 1990: 14).

Suspicion and outright hostility has marked the response of intellectuals to the spread of consumerism to the working class. The quality of cultural and material goods consumed is lamented or ridiculed, the degree of choice open to the consumer is denounced as limited or simply illusory, and many millions of dollars are spent on research into the deleterious effects of cultural products favoured by working-class consumers. A straightforward way of understanding the phenomenon is as the continuation and development of a process which was set in train at the outset of modernization and had previously transformed the cultural practices of other social strata. Commodification reaches working-class practices some time after aristocratic and bourgeois cultures have been commodified and merged.

There is no great divide between a noncommodified high art and a commodified mass culture. The *plausibility* of such a divide rests on a conjunction of circumstances in a specific phase of commodification. It requires, first, that the nobility and the bourgeoisie have withrawn from any identification with popular culture, a process which Burke (1978: 270) suggests was complete by 1800 in most of Europe. This withdrawal generates the early modern distinction between a field of taste or elite culture, and the non-taste, non-culture of popular practices. The distinction mutates into the critique of mass culture in the period during which commodification and taste trickle down to the practices of subordinate classes, transforming (from the point of view of elite cultures) the nullity of non-taste into the threat of bad or degenerate taste. High–mass culture distinctions appear plausible when divisions between recognizable 'taste cultures' are aligned with those between social strata. Once taste cultures merge, or proliferate in ways which cross boundaries between strata, the high mass distinction has no more than a nostalgic force.

Retrospect: The Syndrome of Cultural Modernity

Processes of differentiation, rationalization and commodification work on the practices of premodern culture to produce the syndrome of cultural modernity. The term 'syndrome' (used by Mowlana and Wilson 1990) suggests the concurrence of a number of characteristics which may be interrelated in a number of ways but which do not form a 'unity' or 'totality' centred on some single principle. The syndrome in question is a regional stability which arises from the interaction of the three processes over a range of values for the scope and intensity of each. That is to say, before differentiation, rationalization and commodification attain a certain scope and intensity, they do not generate the syndrome. Once they operate *beyond* a certain scope and intensity, they move beyond the syndrome of cultural modernity in processes of postmodernization. It is this postmodernization of cultural modernity which is to be considered in the next section. Here, it may be useful to summarize the main features of the syndrome.

First, cultural modernity is determined by a particular level and intensity of *differentiation*. It requires, in its early stages, the differentiation of cultural from other practices and, in its mature form, the autonomy of different 'spheres' of culture. The question of autonomy, in turn, positions cultural modernity in a series of ineradicable tensions between differentiating and dedifferentiating moments. A differentiated cultural modernity reaches its limit when 'hyperdifferentiation' leads to a proliferation of divisions which effectively erodes the significance of distinctions between autonomous spheres. *Rationalization* of culture proceeds on two distinct but related dimensions: the endogenous development of the 'inner logics' of value-spheres and the development of techniques of production and reproduction. Rationalization, too, generates a series of tensions which form historical and thematic limits to modernity. Modernism takes the principle of endogenous rationalization to a limit which is both 'logical' and, through disconnection from an audience, social. It stands in a complex relationship with its dedifferentiating avant-garde critique and with the increasing turn towards a 'museum culture'. The exhaustion of modernism, the failure of the avant-garde and the erosion of 'tradition' are the limits of a rationalized cultural modernity. Cultural modernity is marked from the outset by a *commodification* which is frequently denied and displaced. While different regions of mature cultural modernity are commodified to different degrees, no region is immune. On the 'demand side', the bearer of commodification is the phenomenon of taste, and early cultural modernity is marked by the spread of taste among dominant social groups. The regional stability of mature modernity arises from the spread of taste to subordinate groups in a way which legitimates an 'ideological' distinction between a noncommodified 'high culture' and a commodified 'mass culture'. Commodification sets limits to cultural modernity which are breached as its scope and intensity become more even between regions, and as the proliferation of 'taste cultures' erodes the 'high'–'mass' distinction.

Towards a Postculture

It was argued in the previous chapter that the advanced societies are 'poised on the cusp' of a postmodernizing transformation which is increas-

ingly unlikely to be arrested or reversed. Cultural transformation has a
particular importance in this process, since a postmodernized culture itself
becomes a potent agent of social postmodernization. The limitation which
we face (and which is discussed in Chapter 8) is that we are positioned
within processes of postmodernization. We are granted a 'point of view'
from which the horizons of the syndromes of social and cultural modernity
stand out with a certain clarity. However, such horizons as the syndrome of
postmodernity may have lie in the future, and our map of the syndrome is
of necessity less precise. Attempting to make a virtue of this necessity, our
objective here is not to offer yet another point-by-point differentiation of
postmodern from modern culture (see Hassan 1985 and Lash and Urry
1987: 287 for two such attempts). The more restricted objective is to show
how the processes of differentiation, rationalization and commodification
which generated the syndrome of cultural modernity are themselves
responsible for its fragmentation and transformation as they operate at a
'hyper' level.

Hypercommodification, Taste and Style

There is a line of development within the mainstream of cultural production which is common to other sectors of the economy. Until, say, the early
1970s the major trend is towards the 'organization' of cultural production.
Standardized production forces the pace in film, television, newspapers
and popular music. Ownership concentrates in large conglomerates, and
the tendency towards globalization can be traced back to the beginning of
the century.[20] A recent shift to 'niche marketing' is indexed by the triumph
of video, the development of pay television and the proliferation of
specialized radio stations. Accelerating globalization has been assisted by
satellite and other 'new media technologies'.

The production of cultural commodities also shares in some of the
paradoxes of the general trend. The challenge for modern culture is to
maintain both a distinction and a compatibility between aesthetic and
commodity value. The philistinism which recognizes only cash value and
the aestheticism which entirely refuses it are opposite limits of modern
culture. Williams' (1981) account of the tensions between market and
subsidy suggests that 'in our own period' these tensions have been resolved
in practice by a division in which 'the market [is] dominant in the new
reproductive technologies and subsidy most evident in the older live forms'
(1981: 107). Recent data on arts funding suggest that subsidies work
towards what Offe (1984: ch. 4) terms 'recommodification'. Recommodification is a response to that de-commodification brought about through
either a failure to find a market at a viable price, or through a transformation of a commodity into a welfare service free (or very cheap) at the point
of delivery.

In 1984–5 British museums and galleries received 10 per cent of their
income from sales, 82 per cent from public contributions and 8 per cent

from private contributions, in something very close to a 'welfare' pattern. 'Mechanical performances', by contrast, were largely market driven, receiving 71 per cent of their income from sales and only 29 per cent (mainly through licence fees) from public contributions. Theatres and concerts occupied an intermediate position, relying on sales for 53 per cent of their income, public contributions for 43 per cent and private contributions for 4 per cent (Rodgers 1989: 37). It is this pattern which suggests 'recommodification'. In the United States, Ford Foundation figures on funding for theatres and symphony orchestras in the period 1973–4 show 53 per cent of income coming from commercial activity (ticket sales, recording etc.), a proportion identical to that in the equivalent British category in the subsequent decade. However, the division between state and private patronage is inverted: in the American data only 14 per cent of income is provided by the state, while 33 per cent comes from private sources (Netzer 1978: 101).[21]

For the quintessential performance arts of modern 'high' culture the commodity form is preserved. Ticket sales match supply to demand, but subsidy is crucial to the preservation of a balance without which prices would rise, or income would fall, to a degree that would threaten viability. The equivalence of level and function between private sponsorship in the USA and state sponsorship in Britain and Australia suggests that subsidy of the arts does not challenge commodification but is a moment in its hyperdevelopment: subsidy works to preserve the compatibility of aesthetic and commodity value.

The syndrome of cultural modernity generates taste cultures whose boundaries can be mapped onto social strata. Gans (1975) identifies five such in the United States whose 'taste publics' can be defined by social variables (occupation, education, urban–rural etc.). Bourdieu (1984) treats class difference as the 'real' foundation for cultural difference, while even Lash's account of postmodernism searches for, and finds, a class-basis for the phenomenon. 'It is [the] newer, post industrial middle classes, with their bases in the media, higher education, finance, advertising, merchandising, and international exchanges that provide the audience for postmodern culture' (Lash 1990: 20). The argument here will be that the proliferation of taste progressively undermines the typically modern co-ordination between taste culture and social stratum as taste or 'style' itself becomes an active principle of proliferating divisions.

Analyses of contemporary consumerism frequently suggest that a shift has taken place from a consumption of goods and services to a consumption of cultural meanings. As Slater (1987: 457) puts it, 'the greater part of consumption is the consumption of signs'. Fiske (1989: 26–32) takes the example of television to show how the 'culture industry' is located within a financial and a cultural economy: in the former, television audiences are a commodity on sale to advertisers, in the latter they are producers of 'meanings and pleasures' in relation to television texts. Considerable attention has focussed on the 'style' through which individuals and groups are held to mark out their identity and difference in consumer societies:[22] armies of social researchers and marketing experts seek to map and exploit differences of 'lifestyle'.

Some purchase on 'style' can be gained by re-placing it within the history of taste. Taste arises in the early modern period in a conjunction between the possibility for choice in consumption and the absence of authoritative standards by which choice might be guided. Campbell (1987: 158) perceptively remarks that while this problem of the 'standard of taste' which agitated the seventeenth and eighteenth centuries defied all attempts at a formal solution, it found a de facto solution in fashion. A further dimension of the 'solution' which Campbell does not consider is that invention of authoritative cultural tradition which is the concern of the institutions of 'high' culture in mature modernity. Fashion and cultural tradition both solve the problem of taste by subordinating it to an institutional authority which will typically articulate with social standing. Style follows the erosion of institutionalized cultural authority, just as taste precedes its establishment. The symmetry is apparent in Ewan's (1990: 43) account of the threefold centrality of style to consumerism. 'Style has become a critical factor in definitions of self . . . style has a major impact on the way we understand society . . . style has come to comprise a basic form of information within our society.' The same claims could be made about taste in seventeenth-century France or eighteenth-century England.

There is nothing specifically postmodernizing about the commodification of meaning as such. As Campbell (1987: ch. 5) argues, that modern hedonism which is essential to consumerism and which turns on images and daydreams emerges in the early modern period. The difference between commodification and hypercommodification of meaning relates to the scope of the commodity form. Until the early years of the twentieth century in most advanced societies family, class and community ties and religious affiliation were basic to identity-formation and were relatively noncommodified. In such circumstances a wide variety of goods, from clothing and furniture to books and sheet-music, can be sold in association with their 'images'. The limiting condition is that the images must engage with conceptions of self rooted in noncommodified relations. Notoriously, mature modernity sees the erosion of 'traditional' community, family and religion, with social class not far behind.

To take a crucial example, family life is transformed into the major sphere of consumption (see the useful brief discussion in Windschuttle 1988: ch. 7). The 'meanings' of family-based activities, from eating to cleaning to leisure pursuits, are increasingly marketized and refracted through images drawn from advertising. The process is under way in the United States during the 1920s with the marketing of consumer durables from automobiles to radios. Its contemporary manifestations include the proliferation of pre-packaged and 'fast' foods. Now, even a 'refusal' of commodification, a preference for fresh over prepared foods, for example, is subject to packaging and commodification as a 'lifestyle' choice.

Hypercommodification is the spread of the commodity form into all spheres of life, negating the distinction between commodified and non-commodified regions. In consequence, the images and daydreams which link commodities with identity no longer need to orient themselves to a non-commodified region of meaning. In hypercommodification, commod-ified meanings become self-referential.

'Style' and 'lifestyle' are products of hypercommodification in this sense, just as 'taste' is a product of an earlier phase of commodification. The variability of taste is limited in two ways: in principle by formal canons of aesthetic value and in practice by the mores of different social strata.[23] Style, by contrast, operates within a self-referential universe of commodi-fied meaning, and is not subject to external constraint in quite the same way. The kind of 'order' that style brings to cultural practices is illuminated by McCracken's (1988: 72) account of the 'consumption rituals' which enact a relationship between a commodity, a consumer and the 'culturally constituted world'.[24] These questions of order and constraint connect with those of conformity and resistance in a hypercommodified culture.

On one side can be heard echoes of Adorno and Horkheimer's critique of style as a veneer over the commodified sameness of mass culture. Tomlinson (1990: 6) fears that 'if popular culture can be reduced to a set of apparent choices based on personal taste then we will see the triumph of the fragmented self, a constant lust for the new and authentic among a population of consumer clones'. Fiske's elision of the production of popular style with carnivalesque resistance to cultural authority is an extreme version of another response. Popular style 'is essentially liberat-ing, acting as an empowering language for the subordinate. Its similarities to carnival lie in its insistence on the materiality of the signifier, its excessiveness, its ability to offend good taste (bourgeois taste)' (Fiske 1987: 249). Commodification can be appropriated and turned against itself: teenagers appropriate the strategic 'places' of a powerful consumerism such as the shopping mall as their own 'spaces', becoming 'shopping mall guerrillas' (Fiske 1989: 32). The discussion of 'hyperdifferentiation' below will suggest that neither this account of style-as-resistance nor pessimistic views of style-as-conformism are adequate to the effects of postmoderniza-tion.

Hyper-rationalization and Postculture

The importance of rationalization in the syndrome of cultural modernity is nicely caught in the idea of artistic 'progress' within an unfolding tradition. The discussion of rationalization above indicated that this idea of progress reaches something of a crisis in the phenomena of modernism and the avant-garde. In modernism, aesthetic rationalization turns in on itself and accelerates through its problematization of artistic representation (see Lash 1990: 13). Avant-garde movements are paradoxical attempts to reverse the 'elitist splitting off' of modernist aesthetics while remaining within the ambit of the 'problem' of art. Modernist and avant-garde movements embody the constitutive tensions of a faltering cultural modernity which has reached a phase of hyper-rationalization. Far from articulating the maturity of the syndrome of cultural modernity, modernism and avant-gardism herald its inevitable exhaustion and eclipse.

Two strands in the debates over modernity and postmodernity now appear in a rather different light. First, attempts to defend modern*ism* by eliding it with the modern*ity* of enlightenment have not taken the measure of the qualitatively different effects of rationalization and hyper-rationalization. This is so when Adorno (1984: 429) defends an hermetic modernism by appealing to Kant's concept of 'disinterested' aesthetic appreciation, and when Habermas (1981a:4) suggests that aesthetic modernity (as part of the 'uncompleted project') 'reached its climax in the Café Voltaire of the Dadaists, and in Surrealism'. Second, a grain of sense can be found in what Jencks (1987: 36) regards as Lyotard's 'crazy idea' that postmodernism is present in the early phases of modernism. Once the distinction between modern*ity* and modern*ism* is understood, it can be argued that a hyper-rationalizing modernism leads to the exhaustion of cultural modernity. The avant-garde is post-modern*ist* to the extent that it foresees and protests against that exhaustion.[25] However, this is precisely not to regard the avant-garde as an historically retrojected element in a syndrome of cultural postmodern*ity*.

There is no place for the avant-garde outside cultural modernity, a circumstance that sheds some light on the postmodernizing aftermath of a hyper-rationalizing modernism. In Bürger's (1984) view, the prewar avant-garde is absorbed into the logic of aesthetic progress which it sets out to contest. For what he terms the 'neo-avant-gardes' of the postwar period such as Pop Art, would-be sublations of the gap between art and life are promulgated as art objects. For Huyssen (1986: 9), the failure of the avant-garde opened the way for 'false sublations' of the art–life dichotomy in the aestheticized politics of Fascism, in commercial mass culture and in the claims of 'socialist realism'.

Bürger's diagnosis points to a postmodernist, post-avant-garde expansion of 'the aesthetic' coupled with the fragmentation of any idea of 'progress'. For example, Oldenburg's 'Soft Toilet' of 1966 invites comparison with Duchamp's 'Fountain'. While Duchamp takes a mass-produced object to challenge conceptions of the aesthetic, Oldenberg's vinyl toilet and cistern offers a joke-aestheticization of the everyday object which decontextualizes it from both 'art' and the 'everyday'. 'Fountain' gains its point only in the context of the gallery (and, by extension, the institution of Art): placed on a building site it is one more urinal. Huyssen's point can be extended to suggest that in a hypercommodified, hyper-rationalized, hyperdifferentiated postmodernity 'art' no longer exists as a unified and autonomous sphere of value. It has no logic which can 'progress', and it cannot be held over and against 'life'. Such circumstances abolish the basic preconditions for modernism and the avant-garde.

If hyper-rationalization sets in during the terminal phases of cultural modernity, should postmodernization not be regarded as post-, or even anti-, rational? This interpretation converges with a number of perspectives on social change. Bell's account of what he still terms 'modern' culture argues that 'modernism is exhausted. There is no tension. The creative impulses have gone slack. It is an empty vessel' (Bell 1976: 20). In its place is left what Bell might, but does not, call a 'postculture', absorbed in self, lifestyle and hedonism, which erodes the moral and rational foundations of economic, social and political modernity.[26] Elias' celebrated (1978, 1982) account of the 'civilizing process' points to the importance for a stable modernity of the processes (from state formation to the development of table manners) which produce self-restraint and foresight in modern individuals. On this view, the possibility arises that cultural postmodernization produces 'de-civilizing' phenomena such as moral permissiveness and increasing violence (see the sceptical discussion in Mennell 1990). Of course, an irrationalist postmodernization need not be seen as a road to ruin. Elaborating on Parsonsian themes, Lechner (1990) argues that the differentiation, rationalization and value-generalization of cultural modernization can have anomic consequences as pattern-maintenance is stretched. 'Irrational' dedifferentiating movements (Lechner's major example is religious fundamentalism) can be understood as cases of a socio-cultural 'revitalization' which modernity has always required (see the discussion of Romanticism above, for example).

However, the opposition between a 'rational' modernization and an 'irrational' postmodernization cannot be maintained. The notorious and frequently pronounced 'death of modern architecture' can help to make the point. Architectural modernism insists on the closest relation between form, material (particularly the 'new' materials of steel and concrete) and (social) function. In this sense Corbusier, van der Rohe and others share many of the concerns of avant-garde movements.[27] As Harris and Lipman (1986: 849) put it in their defence of a 'socialist' modernism, 'prominent modernists sought a new architecture for a new society; for, that is, their socialist utopias'. In Jencks' (1987: 27) rather more sceptical terms, architectural modernism was 'a Protestant Reformation putting faith in the liberating aspects of industrialism and mass-democracy'.

While the heyday of modernist architectural theory was (as for other modernisms) the inter-war period, the heyday of its practice came in the postwar period with the drive for reconstruction and later booms in commercial property. The 'social failure' (Jencks 1987: 15) of modernism is evident in both desolate and alienating housing developments and city centres devastated by 'reconstruction'. Jencks (1987: 16) suggests two dates for the 'death' of architectural modernism: the collapse of the Ronan Point tower housing block in England in 1968, and the blowing up of the Pruitt-Igoe development in St Louis in 1972. Against this failed modernism, architectural postmodernism is held to offer a more humane scale, a less bleakly functional line, a greater diversity of spaces. At its core is the idea that 'the architect must design for different "taste cultures" ' (1987: 20).

An immediate difficulty arises since, *ex hypothesi*, postmodernism is highly diverse. The term has been used promiscuously of the hi-tech, of classical revivalism and other historical pastiche, of neo-vernacular housing developments and of every mediocre office block with a portico and pediment or an atrium. While the friends of postmodernism celebrate such diversity as the abolition of a totalizing modernist rationality, enemies such as Harris and Lipman (1986) echo Jameson's (1984) view of a more general cultural postmodernism as the 'cultural logic of late capitalism'. Postmodern architecture appropriates populist and classicist themes to repress social content and defend consumerism. Bourassa (1989) draws on Foster's (1983) distinction between postmodernisms of 'resistance' and 'reaction', assigning historical pastiche and Venturi-influenced commercialism to the latter, while allowing a 'critical regionalism' attuned to the creation of noncommercial urban places into the former.

The debates noted above often run together two kinds of distinction which need to be separated. The first is a distinction between the field of cultural modernity at a late stage of its trajectory (or some corner of it such as architecture) and the emerging field of cultural postmodernity. The second is a distinction between different styles or schools. 'Modernism' is (just about) a precise enough term to denote a style or school, but 'postmodernism' is not. Despite its popularity, the term is unhelpful because it straddles the two types of distinction. When used (as it often is) to designate a field (cultural postmodernity), it implies that fields can be defined by dominant themes in the same way as styles. When used to designate a style, it is too imprecise. This point reconnects with hyper-rationalization and postmodernization. If the aesthetic and social rationalism of architectural modernism is contrasted with an indeterminate postmodernism which is part-field and part-style, the latter must appear to be ir-, non- or anti- rational, hence many of the modernist responses to the postmodern.

If modernism is more appropriately contrasted with neo-classicism, with hi-tech, with neo-vernacular a different picture emerges in which rationality is not negated but detotalized. Each postmodern style elaborates its theme in a methodical, 'rationalized', way: even the most exorbitant pastiche or parody (from Portmerrion to Disneyland) explores as it exploits the limits of simulation. Hi-tech continues the modernist discourse on the relation between form and material, critical regionalism continues an argument about social function, and a variety of neo-classicisms take up 'rationalities' of decoration and proportion effaced by modernism. This view connects with Claygill's (1990: 284) concern that postmodernism in architecture simply recapitulates (and only appears to reverse) the modern opposition between the avant-garde and the popular.

In the field of late modernity, modernism has a hegemonic presence, but even in architecture it does not exhaust the field: various forms of vernacular and pastiche have a continuing presence in domestic building, for example. Further, the field must include the existing building stocks and urban environments which are transformed by modernist projects and in relation to which modernism acquires at least part of its meaning. That modern*ism* can persist into postmodern*ity* is the unstated condition which underpins Jencks' (1987: ch. 4) persuasive argument that what Foster, Lyotard and many others regard as 'postmodernist' (Pompidou Centre, Lloyds Building, Hong Kong Shanghai Bank) should be understood as 'late modernist' (see also Jameson's 'preface' to Lyotard 1984). To twist Jencks' argument a little, the mistake arises from the confusion between 'field' and 'style' noted above: anything present in a field designated 'postmodern' must be 'postmodernist'. Jencks is surely correct to see hi-tech essays in the 'tradition of the new' as a continuation of modernism, and as very different from those postmodernisms proper which are sensitive to context and the vernacular. However, the pluralistic field of an emergent postmodernity alters the 'meaning' of modernism, whose rationality of form and function is no longer hegemonic. Late modernism does not evade its context of multiple rationalities, of course: the grain of sense in the confusion which Jencks corrects is that in late modernist buildings the unity of material, function and form can become 'decorative' as the flat surface is abandoned.

Architecture can yield one more insight into the effects of a hyper-rationalizing postmodernization. On a superficial view modernism appears as the negation of architectural tradition by technique and function, while a number of postmodern styles appear to revive, and indeed celebrate, traditional forms and practices. However, this misses the point Bürger makes of the avant-garde, that its critique is defined by, and helps to define, aesthetic tradition. The point of modernist architecture within cultural modernity is entirely lost without a potent sense of its relation to an unfolding tradition of materials, forms and functions: modernism is conceived as the culmination and radical reorientation of tradition. Hyper-rationalization explodes the plausibility of a single, totalizing and unfolding 'reason'. Once this is gone, that sense of developing tradition which is such a peculiarly modern invention goes with it. In the formula used earlier, the museum of culture ceases to be a guardian of the integrity of tradition and becomes an archive of styles whose geographical and historical dispersal is a matter of contingent fact.

The transformation of tradition into archive is a critical element in that 'depthlessness' which many commentators (Jameson 1984, for example) ascribe to the postmodern. The archive can be drawn on in an eclectic and often parodic bricolage of elements (brightly coloured 'toytown' pillars and pediments), or in a 'nostalgic' re-creation of a valued past (Prince of Wales populist and neo-classicism). In either case, the depth and rationality of the modern idea of tradition is lost. Turning away from architecture, the rediscovery of 'early music' and the cult of the 'authentic' performance have already been cited as linked cases of the hyper-rationalizing erosion of tradition. Once again, the case argued here is counter-intuitive: surely an archaeological extension of the musical past and a concern with authenticity must deepen and enrich tradition.

When Glen Gould played Bach on the piano, or when Karajan and the Berlin Philharmonic performed a Mozart symphony, the effect was entirely inauthentic. The rationale in each case was that the resources of the piano or the modern symphony orchestra served to express, or interpret, the 'inner meaning' of the music. Modern, invented, traditions discern such 'meanings' and place them in an unfolding logic of development. Tradition in this sense is quite compatible with musicological studies of styles of performance, of course. When the cult of authenticity takes popular hold, however, it encourages a postmodernizing depthlessness in which the 'meaning' of the work is no more than the performance surface of colour and tempo. The 'authentic' performance can only be a simulation which effaces historical distance and meaningful tradition.

The expansion of the repertoire into pre-classical music is corrosive of tradition because it moves outside a mature cultural modernity into fields in which aesthetic autonomy is not established. In the early modern period music serves as an accompaniment to a variety of 'everyday' activities and moves in an economy of taste rather than under the legitimate authority of tradition. Contemporary uses of recordings of early music often mimic this early modern pattern, undermining the peculiarly modern aura of Great Art and its Tradition.

What was termed 'technical' rationalization in an earlier section also produces postmodernizing outcomes at its 'hyper' level of development. First, technologies of mechanical and electronic reproduction tend towards the domestication, or privatization, of cultural consumption. Cinema and disco are virtually the only examples of *public* cultural spaces created by modern technologies.[28] The overwhelming tendency is towards the displacement of public cultural events into a private sphere of consumption, as television and recorded music replace theatres, music halls and opera houses. This is not to say that 'live' events and traditional spaces disappear: considerable financial subsidies, state and private, are devoted to their survival. But this very fact, which brackets 'live' culture with the 'heritage' values of national parks and historic buildings, indexes a shift of significance. For all but a very few of the 'professional devotees' of the arts (Jencks 1987: 10) living in major centres of cultural production, live performances are an occasional supplement to a regular diet of radio, television, video and sound recording.[29]

The supplementarity of the live, public, performance receives a consequential twist when the performance becomes a simulation of the products of electronic media. From the quite early days of recorded music, popular performers have been known primarily through recordings, and audiences attend live shows to see, as well as hear favourite numbers. The phenomenon received a further twist in the late 1960s when the recorded 'album' was produced as an integrated unit (rather than a concatenation of individual songs), and became the matrix for the live simulation (the Who's *Tommy* is exemplary here). In another field, the British television comedy *'Allo 'Allo* has toured internationally in a stage version, taking further the established practice of using television 'stars' as a draw for popular plays and pantomimes.

Up to a certain point, 'the family' of mum, dad and 2.4 children is the primary unit of this privatized cultural consumption. Morley (1987) is among those who have argued that television use requires to be understood in a constitutive relation with family organization and interaction, intertwining with variables such as age, gender and class. Over recent years, however, the decreasing costs of radios, televisions, cassette players and the like have combined with developments such as multi-channel pay television and time-lapse viewing on video to increasingly individualize a domesticated cultural consumption. In many affluent homes, at any given time, each member of the family may be using a different medium or channel. The icon of the extension-cum-reversal of this domestication of culture is the Walkman, which allows the most individualized consumption to be reinserted in a 'public' space. Its ambiguous and transgressive other is the 'ghetto blaster', which refuses a quiet accommodation and can be heard, according to temper, as a carnivalesque subversion of the public–private split, or as an absolutist assertion of ego.

Implicit or explicit models of technical rationalization and hyper-rationalization underpin a number of utopian and dystopian diagnoses of modern culture: witness the divergence between Adorno and Benjamin.[30] The same is true of a number of influential accounts of postmodernization, from which McLuhan can be taken to stand for the utopian and Baudrillard for the dystopian strains. The slogans of McLuhan's culture theory, 'the medium is the message', 'hot and cool media', 'the global village' have such an air of 1960s cliché that it is easy to overlook the extent to which they prefigure later and more fashionable themes.[31] McLuhan's main significance lies in his insistence that media 'forms' are far more consequential for culture than are their incidental 'contents'. 'The "content" of a medium is like the juicy piece of meat carried by the burglar to distract the watchdog of the mind' (McLuhan 1967b: 26). New media offer new extensions, or externalizations, of self which introduce a new scale into social relationships (1967b: 15). Electric media turn such 'extensions' into information systems, so that the person becomes an 'organism that now wears its brain outside its skull and its nerves outside its hide' (1967b: 57). For Kroker and Cook (1988: 74) this passage 'perfectly describes postmodern experience as a ceaseless "outering" of the senses' and links McLuhan with Baudrillard.

Among electric media, radio and cinema are 'hot', 'extend[ing] one single sense in "high definition"' (McLuhan 1967b: 31). Television, by contrast is 'cool', and McLuhan prefigures the theme of a 'distracted' postmodern audience when he argues that television discourages intense, linear involvement. Television re-integrates the senses and establishes a

regime of experience which is mosaic rather than linear, iconographic
rather than perspectival. McLuhan's displaced and refracted Leavisite
quest for wholeness links the new wholeness of experience to a world-
community in the idea of a 'global village' in which electric communication
overcomes social and geographical distance. He projects a postmodernity
in which the alienating fragmentation of modern culture is healed precisely
by the hyperextension of modern technical rationality.

McLuhan's benign vision takes on a nightmare quality in Baudrillard, for
whom (1988: 183n.) '"the medium is the message"is the very slogan of the
political economy of the sign when it enters into the third-order simulation', an order in which the image 'masks the *absence* of a basic reality'
(Baudrillard 1988: 170). Media technologies become complicit in the
erosion of distinctions between representation and reality, surface and
depth, leaving 'an immanent surface where operations unfold – a smooth
operational surface of communication' (Baudrillard 1983a: 127). No
'resistance', in any traditional sense, is offered to this simulated, operational universe. 'The masses' do not counter one code of meaning with
another but resort to silence and invisibility, 'redirect[ing] everything *en
bloc* to the spectacular, without requiring any other code' (Baudrillard
1983b: 43).

The fourth and final 'phase of the image' is that in which it 'becomes its
own pure simulacrum' (Baudrillard 1988: 170). Loss of the real induces a
'panic' reaction, in which nostalgia blooms, cults of authenticity arise and
the (post-)culture abandons itself to the 'panic-stricken production of the
real' (1988: 171). Baudrillard argues that the secret of Disneyland is that it
has to be presented as 'imaginary' to preserve the fiction that America is
'real' (1988: 172). Kroker and Cook (1988: 268) apply these themes to
television, so that 'Television is, in a very literal sense, the real world . . .
of postmodern culture, society and economy'. Just as the effaced hyper-
reality of Disneyland is necessary to preserve the 'reality principle' of
America, so a variety of ideologies and practices efface the circumstance
that 'it's not TV as a mirror of society but just the reverse: *it's society as the
mirror of television*'. Television enacts the postmodern 'precession of
simulacra' in which 'it is the map that engenders the territory' (Baudrillard
1988: 166).

Hyperdifferentiation and Dedifferentiation

To friends like Lyotard postmodernization sets in place a cultural universe
of incommensurable genres, pluralizing the singular and capitalized Reason, History, Value and Language of modernity (see the 'Preface' to
Lyotard 1988). In postmodernization, a thousand flowers bloom. For
critics, a superficial pluralism and diversity hides a latent and regressive
syncretism which converges with the premodern. Wolin (1984: 27) is
typical here, pointing to the danger of a regression 'behind' the modern
differentiation of value-spheres which can promote dubious movements

such as religious fundamentalism. Most notably, Habermas has polemi-
cized against critiques of modernity and enlightenment which must be
either overtly or covertly conservative (see Habermas 1981a, 1985, 1987b).
In short, the question of differentiation and dedifferentiation is pivotal in
contemporary debates on postmodernization.

Lash's work is particularly important in this context, moving beyond
polemic to offer a reasoned account of 'dedifferentiation' as the basic
principle of postmodernism. Lash distinguishes between four components
of a 'cultural paradigm' (of which modernism and postmodernism are
examples): the relations between different cultural objects, the relations
between culture and society, the cultural economy, and the mode of
signification (Lash 1990: 11). In each case, postmodernism is dedifferentiated. First, the three spheres of value identified by Kant (aesthetic, moral
and cognitive) lose their autonomy. Second, culture loses its 'aura' (in
Benjamin's sense) and becomes 'immanent' in the social. Third, distinctions between author and reader, performer and audience, artist and critic
are eroded. Fourth, distinctions between signifier, signified and referent
become problematic (1990: 11–12).

While it is possible to argue with the detail of this case,[32] the overall
model is quite persuasive. The more fundamental problem concerns the
way postmodernization is to be explained. Why should a process of
differentiation which has been in train for hundreds of years suddenly
reverse itself, and turn into dedifferentiation? Lash is not so persuasive
here. He suggests that the increasing penetration of experience by media
representations may have something to do with it, and then suggests that a
'sociological grounding' is called for (1990: 15). He finds that grounding in
four 'properly sociological explanations' which link modernity and postmodernity to questions of 'bourgeois identity', the fate of the working class,
the built environment and the 'political economy' of culture. The details of
Lash's arguments are of considerable interest, and justice cannot be done
to them here.

The overall strategy runs on well-worn tracks, however and Lash
converges with a series of more-or-less-Marxist attempts such as Anderson's (1984), Jameson's (1984) and Harvey's (1989) to tame postmodernity
and postmodernism by simply reasserting the priorities of modernist social
theory. Chief among these, of course, is the priority of 'social' over
'cultural' processes, so that in neo-Marxist variants postmodern culture
'articulates with' the latest phase of capitalism. For Lash, just as aesthetic
modernism has an ambiguous relation 'sometimes of compatibility, sometimes of incompatibility' with organized capitalism, so has postmodernism
with disorganized capitalism (Lash 1990: 18). In consequence, Lash is
drawn into the quintessentially modern game, played by Foster (1983)
among others, of drawing the line between postmodernisms which support
and postmodernisms which resist 'a regime of capital accumulation' (Lash
1990: 37–8).

Lash's sociology of postmodernism has two related and major defects as an account of the postmodernization of culture. First, it begs the question of whether postmodernization in 'culture' and 'society' may not have so altered the structures of, and relations between, the two as to render anachronistic modernist ('properly sociological') explanatory strategies. This question is taken up in a more general way in the final chapter. Second, while Lash can explore the ramifications of the reversal of differentiation into dedifferentiation, and comment on its 'articulation' with capitalist development, he cannot, finally, explain it.

An alternative approach has some of the same counter-intuitive quality noted in the discussions of hypercommodification and hyper-rationalization above. The effect of cultural dedifferentiation is to be explained not as a reversal, but as a hyperextension of differentiation. It is a corollary of this claim that a postmodernizing dedifferentiation can be equated with neither an undifferentiated premodern culture, nor those dedifferentiating movements of the modern period (from Romanticism to the avant-garde) which resist the separation of 'art' and 'life'. The remainder of this subsection rehearses the general argument and then relates it to debates about popular culture and 'resistance' and to the phenomenon of 'style'.

The value-spheres of modern culture are not squeezed back holus-bolus into a premodern unity. The key to the transgression of boundaries between spheres is the proliferation of boundaries within them. The most striking example of this phenomenon is the development of the natural sciences (considered in Chapter 7), where differentiation produces and hyperdifferentiation erodes firm disciplinary boundaries. A similar logic can be seen at work in the postmodernization of architecture, where the splitting of a modernist unity of form, function and material leads to a dazzling profusion of styles (in Jencks' [1987: 23] 'evolutionary tree' six main traditions ramify and intertwine). Each style establishes its own relations with other arts, with theoretical knowledges and with the practical imperatives of economic, social and political life. The boundaries between the spheres of culture, and between culture and 'life' are much more permeable to the fragment than to the structured whole. Dedifferen-tiation occurs as boundaries are eroded by fragments which fuse together in new conglomerates.

This process can also be seen at work in popular music from the 1960s on. The emergence and eclipse of 'progressive' rock music is a speeded-up re-run of the trajectory of the avant-garde. Popular bands of the mid-1960s, from the Beatles and the Who to the Beach Boys and the Byrds, began to take themselves altogether more seriously later in the decade. Taking their cue from 'underground' bands with a more restricted cult following, they self-consciously aimed at the artistic 'development' of their music, and came to see that development as linked to the programmes of 1960s and 1970s 'alternative' politics. The serious practitioner of, or enthusiast for, progressive music in the early 1970s would locate Led Zeppelin, or Janis Joplin or Fairport Convention in a complex and developing tradition, growing out of blues, jazz and folk as well as commercial popular music. By the mid-1970s progressive rock had become so over-developed and portentous that it was ripe for the savage, Dada-like, avant-garde critique of punk.

The aftermath of punk has seen the postmodernization of popular music. While the mainstream reverted to a commercialism reminiscent of the 1950s, a variety of musical styles have prospered in niche markets served by specialist radio stations and retail outlets. Popular music has also absorbed its past into the present in a graphic example of the mutation of tradition into archive. The 1960s live on, not as a phase in the unfolding of tradition but as a series of styles which can be repackaged and resold to new generations of consumers. Nostalgia is a potent force in popular music not so much in a longing for some golden 'lost time' as by a transformation of the past which can erase history and stylize the present. For the producers, mediators and consumers of popular music, engagement is with the specific style rather than with a wider field of popular music. The musical style, in turn, crosses boundaries to congeal into 'lifestyles' with styles of dress, speech, politics, personal relationships and what you will.

The same effect of dedifferentiation induced by hyperdifferentiation is evident in the blurring of boundaries between 'high' and 'popular' culture. Once an image, or a musical theme, or a format has been decontextualized through hyperdifferentiation, it can be recontextualized in any number of ways. Recorded albums with titles such as 'Mozart's Greatest Hits' package together decontextualized fragments. The 'meanings' of such musical fragments in a postculture are available for appropriations as background music in film, television drama or advertising.[33] Popular music can appropriate the formats of a 'museum' culture, witness many 'rock operas' or the Lloyd Webber 'Requiem', while 'serious' music and performers can penetrate television formats from chat shows to quizzes.

The promiscuous openness of the fragmentary materials of postculture to an apparently endless variety of appropriations connects with questions of power and resistance in culture which were raised in the discussion of hypercommodification above. The resistant tactical appropriations of the 'places' of cultural power as 'spaces' for the subordinate (see Fiske 1987, 1989) presuppose a postculture of fragmentation and bricolage. The possibility Fiske does not explore is that the cultural power of the powerful is no longer primarily 'strategic', that it too articulates itself through an ever-moving logic of the tactical appropriation of meaning. Chambers is another who takes an optimistic view of the postmodernization of popular culture, arguing that in the 'mobile collage' of contemporary urban life 'a democracy of aesthetic and cultural populism becomes possible' (Chambers 1986: 194).

Two considerations suggest that this view may be utopian. First, it is a fundamental insight of the sociology of culture that the formation of individual and collective identity is exclusive as it is inclusive: I am not you, we are not them. A disconnection of divisions between cultural identities of lifestyle from premodern and modern divisions of ethnicity, gender and class may mean the proliferation, not the end, of cultural conflict. Further, Chambers and Fiske are more attentive to style as a challenge to 'macro' social hierarchies than to the 'micro' hierarchies which style itself establishes.[34] When style becomes a principle of identity, identity is contingent upon stylistic performance, as judged by acknowledged virtuosi. The vision of cultural postmodernization as an endless proliferation of internally hierarchical 'styles' which move in shifting patterns of accommodation and conflict is at least as plausible as the benign utopia of democracy and populism.

Fiske's account of popular culture has much in common with the Marxian 'cultural studies' which were so influential in Britain in the 1970s. Cultural diversity is to be recognized, even celebrated, but it must 'articulate' with the class-based struggle for cultural hegemony. This project understands effects of cultural postmodernization (the hypercommodification of 'youth', the hyperdifferentiation of popular culture) through the analytic grid of a stable social and cultural modernity. In one of the best-known examples, Hall and Jefferson (1975) collect a series of sophisticated attempts to understand the diversity of 'youth subcultures' in class terms. Jefferson discusses teddy boys, Hebdige analyses mods and Clarke considers skinheads in terms of their 'imaginary relation' to material conditions and their 'double articulation' with parent and dominant cultures. Fiske's image of 'resistance' as an almost metaphysical principle, an embodiment of the physical 'presence' of popular forces, is a nostalgic extension of the 1970s project after its analytic grid has collapsed. The critical point is not that style cannot resist, clearly it can in many registers, but contests between resistance and conformity do not conform to a single line between the hegemonic and the subordinate.

These issues lead back to the wider question of the effects of hyperdifferentiation on 'taste cultures'. As Lewis (1981: 205) argues, most studies of taste cultures 'assume some sort of correlative linkage between the social and cultural structures of society'. Against this trend, Lewis (1981: 206) notes that since the Second World War, in the United States at least, there has been little empirical evidence of close ties between taste and class position.[35] There are other grounds for doubting whether 'taste culture' is an appropriate term in the analysis of postmodernization. The concept retains too much of the idea of culture as a way of life, as something one lives within. The same is true of the concept of subculture, at least as it is deployed in the British tradition considered above.

Hyperdifferentiating postmodernization produces a postculture by eroding the sense of culture as a lived unity of experience. It is not simply the replacement of a few fully integrated cultural unities by many, but the erosion of the fully integrated cultural unity as such. Taken to its conclusion, this process would result in each person facing an agonizing existential dilemma at every point in his or her life: choices of clothing, music, automobiles or political viewpoints would need to be made anew and unguided on every occasion. Of course, this outcome is 'impossible': no person or society could work that way. The moot point concerns the way in which the impossible outcome is avoided.

In premodern societies the question does not arise because levels of economic and cultural development require little 'choice', and that which there is can be guided by habit and custom. The early modern problem of taste bears witness to the uncertainties induced by the expansion of choice coupled with the erosion of tradition. Mature modernity resolves these to a degree in the alignment of taste cultures with social classes and through the authority of fashion and cultural tradition. This modern solution is, in effect, a differentiated remodelling of the traditional cultural 'unity' of material conditions and experiential response. Postmodernization and the rise of style disrupt this solution, eroding traditon and fracturing cultural unity. This is why an analogy between the early modern problem of 'taste' and the postmodernizing problem of 'style' has been suggested.

If hyperdifferentiation, hypercommodification and hyper-rationalization of culture re-enact the dilemma of a profusion of choice and an erosion of authority, they also make available a range of definitively postmodernizing solutions. In different ways they all operate in the registers of simulation and hypersimulation, in Baudrillard's terms. One extreme possibility is an entirely commodified repackaging of cultural fragments into 'lifestyle'. McLuhan's emphasis on a mosaic, iconic, structure of experience which finds an echo in Lash's (1990: 175) conception of a figural postmodernity is to the point here. A short television commercial (a family eating cereal together for breakfast, perhaps) can draw together in iconic form a complex and powerful array of 'meanings' about age, gender, domesticity, employment and their connection with deportment, clothing, furniture, interior decoration, music. Commodified icons of identity such as this, which do not need to conform to either the authenticity of a tradition or the logic of a discourse, can serve as the principles of a simulated 'unity' of experience. It is notable that market researchers and advertising professionals who use such icons to address their audiences have begun to move away from models of differentiated markets cast in social, or demographic, terms (social class, age group, etc.) towards models based on 'lifestyle' factors. In Australia the SCAN (segmenting change and new values) project associated with the George Patterson agency and the Ogilvy and Mather-Roy Morgan VAL (value and lifestyle) programme have become increasingly influential (see Thompson 1989).

If the hypercommodified simulation of culture in an iconic 'lifestyle' lies at one end of a continuum of postmodernizing possibilities, the hypersimulated 'panic' or 'nostalgic' production of cultural reality lies at the other. Neo-conservative politics and religious fundamentalism can be understood as responses to the uncertainties of postmodernization which have affinities with some historicist tendencies in postmodern aesthetics and architecture. They offer a 'return' to traditional values which can only be hypersimulated. The strident assertion of the veracity of the Book of

Genesis in contemporary Australia, Britain or the United States is no more
an expression of 'tradition' than is a neo-vernacular shopping centre or a
theme park. Clarke's (1975) study of skinheads can be given a twist to
illustrate the point. Clarke understands skinhead 'style' in dress, territori-
ality, sexism, homophobia, racism and aggression as a 'symbolic' recovery
of the values of disappearing working-class community. Skinhead excesses
are explained by the absence of any 'material and organizational' community base (1975: 102).

Seen through the lens of postmodernization, Clarke's skinheads enter
the register of the hyperreal, where the iconic juxtaposition of cultural
fragments offers the reassurances of the real. Not only 'conservative'
cultural phenomena can be understood in this way: new age consciousness
and deep ecology, for example, are hypersimulated solutions to the
postmodern problem of 'reality' as much as religious fundamentalism. In
solutions of this kind, individuals and groups believe that they have access
to a deep reality around which a unity of experience, a real culture, can be
rebuilt. It is one of the most singular features of postculture that these two
apparently opposed solutions, hypercommodified lifestyle and hypersimulated reality, can intermingle. The concerns of the latter, tradition,
community, environment and the rest can be appropriated and commodified, so that consumption of string bags, recycled lavatory paper or rather
ineffective cleaning agents becomes a ritual, an act of dedication to 'The
Environment'. Equally, the iconic techniques of hypercommodification
sell environment, or heritage, or religion. Indeed, the icon or style defines
the reality: style and reality merge into a single dimension on the 'flat
surface' of postculture.

Retrospect: an Emerging Syndrome of Cultural Postmodernity?

Jencks (1987: 10) characterizes postmodernism in art and architecture as
'that paradoxical dualism, or double coding, which its hybrid name entails:
the continuation of Modernism and its transcendence'. Cultural postmodernization is also caught in a 'double coding' as the extension and the
reversal of the principles which shaped cultural modernity. The figures of
'hyper' commodification, rationalization and differentiation have
attempted to capture this paradox. It is anachronistic in a number of senses
to portray the outcomes of postmodernization, at least as they are
presently visible, as a 'fully fledged, viable social system' as Bauman
(1988a: 811) wishes to do. Nevertheless, the postculture which is emerging
from cultural modernity appears to be possessed of its own kind of 'unity'
and effectivity, brought about by the processes considered above.

Hypercommodification finally erodes the distinction between commodified and noncommodified regions and gives a twist to the commodification
of meaning. Institutionalized distinctions between cultural 'levels' give way
to the proliferation of style and its packaging as lifestyle. *Hyper-
rationalization* within modernity yields the 'elitist splitting-off' which seals

the fate of high modernism. In the aftermath of modernism and the failure of its avant-garde critique, aesthetic rationality becomes fragmented, and authoritative tradition mutates into an archive. Technical developments promote the privatization of cultural consumption and its reintegration within a global postculture of hypersimulation. *Hyperdifferentiation* produces the effect of dedifferentiation, the capacity of fragments of cultural meaning to transgress boundaries between the spheres of modern culture, and between culture and society. The iconography of style and the panic-production of the real become the principles of 'unity' in an increasingly fragmented postculture.

Two important lessons can be drawn from this account. First, the emerging postculture is not a structure, or a system, or even a syndrome, in quite the way of cultural modernity. It lacks clearly demarcated regions, its boundaries with economy, polity and society are blurred, its hierarchies are multiple and constantly shifting, and it registers no 'depth', no distinction between surface and reality. Second, and in consequence, the effectivity of postculture is of a very different order to that of modern culture. For a Marx or a Parsons, 'culture' is effective as a system which articulates with other systems, subordinated to the logic of class domination, or the need for pattern maintenance. The effectivity of postculture is that of the highly charged particle of meaning, free to move anywhere in socio-cultural space and to enter promiscuously into relations with almost any other fragment. It no longer makes sense to ask in general, structural, terms whether culture is a moulder or a mirror of social processes because 'culture' has so pervaded 'society' that the distinction between the two is becoming obsolete.

The question which remains, but which cannot be answered with confidence because the answer lies in the future, is whether the triumph of postculture is final and irreversible. The precedent of the institutionalization of cultural authority in mature modernity as a 'solution' to the uncertainties of the modern period holds out an in-principle possibility for some kind of restructuring of postculture. But for the present it is difficult to see where the resources for such a restructuring might be found. For all the emphasis on democracy and consensus in modernists such as Habermas, it is difficult to see how a remodernization of culture could be accomplished other than by some kind of force. However, the modernist nightmare of a wholesale reversion to the premodern is almost equally implausible. As Enzensberger (1976: 23–5) has pointed out, contemporary technologies of communication make 'total control' virtually unachievable, and without that control the promiscuity of the elements of postculture could never be subordinated to a single hierarchy of cultural value.

Notes

1. The analogy between such a 'dialectic of differentiation' and the 'dialectic of enlightenment' lamented by Adorno and Horkheimer (1979), and its implications for a sociology of

postmodernity, are considered in more detail in Chapter 8.

2. For examples of the growing confidence (and importance) of the latter, see the papers collected in Alexander and Colomy (eds) (1990).

3. The *Critique of Judgement* (Kant 1952: II I IX) sets out the 'principles' and 'faculties' at play in the three spheres. In science, the principle of subordination to law applies to nature and falls under the faculty of understanding. In aesthetics, the principle of purpose applies to art and falls under the faculty of judgement. In morality, the principle of ultimate ends applies to human freedom and falls under the faculty of reason.

4. For an excellent book-length treatment of Weber's value-theory and the debates it provoked, see Turner and Factor (1984). The best brief treatment of the conflict between 'value-spheres' can be found in Brubaker (1984: ch. 3). Crook (1991: ch. 2) expands upon the interpretation adopted without debate here.

5. This implies that to identify all dedifferentiating movements of the twentieth century as 'postmodernist', as does Lash (1990: 11–15), is to risk a misunderstanding of the tensions of cultural modernity (and, it will be argued shortly, of postmodernity).

6. Williams (1981: 38–44) differentiates five types of patronage. The first, and earliest, included the artist as an integral part of a household. The second, stretching from the Middle Ages well into the modern period, saw the artist as a paid retainer, often with an official title ('Master of the King's Music', for example) or as a professional commissioned for a particular project (the patronage of the renaissance papacy). In the third, a patron extended protection and support to artists who gained their income on the open market (royal patronage of the Elizabethan and Jacobean theatre). The fourth type shades from the relations of the third into those 'subscriptions' for the publication of books, or for series of concerts, which became so important in the eighteenth century. In the fifth type, typical of late modernity, public bodies funded from taxation continue many of the social relations of patronage. Clearly, the development of patronage is closely related to forms of the 'commodification' of cultural production.

7. It is notable that Gouldner understands Romanticism as a 're-vitalizing' social movement, rather than a merely aesthetic 'style' (Gouldner 1975: 326). On Lechner's recent neo-Parsonian analysis, revitalization requires to be understood as a dedifferentiating response to the 'tensions' of modernization (Lechner 1990: 101).

8. The references to phonographs and CD players are not Weber's. Weber also notes here how the piano repertoire moves between the public and the domestic scale. The piano can also be directed to the development of a performer's technique, or can serve as a tool in the work of composition itself.

9. In Raymond Williams' (1981: 70) formula. Williams' definition of such formations in terms of their 'opposition to the established institutions, or more generally to the conditions within which these exist' is unhelpfully one-dimensional.

10. Weber's sense that music offers the paradigm case of cultural rationalization finds some confirmation in the observation that it is music which becomes the least penetrable of modernist arts. A non-expert has at least some point of contact with a painting, which can be looked at first one way and then another as a visual field. Without quite high-grade skills in music (a capacity to read the score, a basic knowledge of traditional harmony) a twelve-tone composition is simply noise.

11. Lash argues that a modernism–postmodernism distinction can be drawn between different types of aesthetic 'problem': 'modernism conceives of representations as being problematic whereas postmodernism problematizes reality' (Lash 1990: 13). In his view, this means that surrealism, for example, was 'in part' postmodernist, although it emerged in the 'heyday' of modernism. The interest here is not so much in identifying modernism and postmodernism within particular works, but in identifying cultural modernity and postmodernity as differently ordered fields. From this perspective, surrealism and other avant-garde movements are active within the problematic field of late modernity.

12. Huyssen, with rather pessimistic hindsight, places Benjamin at the end rather than the beginning of this hope. He stresses the triumph of 'conformism' in the post-war depoliticization of the avant-garde (Huyssen 1986: 1, 7–9, 15).

13. Even the avant-garde is implicated to the extent that the critique of institutionalized art plays a role in defining its object. As Bürger (1984: 19) argues, it is from the 'standpoint' of the avant-garde that preceding phases in the development of art can be understood *as* phases in the development of art.

14. The availability of an authoritative canon of modern works distinguishes late from early modernity. The 'problem of taste' arose in the seventeenth century, in important part, because of the opposition between 'tradition', as embodied in antiquity, and a modernity which had not yet developed authoritative standards.

15. An important supplementary issue here is the role of composers who continued to write well into the twentieth century, but who were very little influenced by modernism: Elgar, Puccini, Rachmaninov, Sibelius, Strauss and their like.

16. There is no space to explore these complexities here. Giner (1976) offers a thorough historical exploration of the phenomenon, while Swingewood (1977) develops a more polemical critique of its Marxist variants.

17. So, Williams (1981: 101) refers to the 'complex asymmetry between the older established institutions of cultural and social reproduction (Church and State) and the new institutions and forces both of the market and of professional and cultural independence'.

18. To assert that the *phenomenon* of taste, the necessity for choice and discrimination in cultural consumption, trickles down from one class to another is not to adopt a Veblenesque view on which particular tastes in lower-status groups are an imitation of those of higher-status groups. The content of taste does not 'trickle down'.

19. As a counterweight to this over-simplification, see for example Burke's argument that increased prosperity enriched the material cultures of subordinate groups at much earlier periods: in Britain and regions such as Alsace during the late sixteenth and early seventeenth centuries, and in many other areas of Europe during the eighteenth. This development is closely linked to commodification. Standardization and specialization of production in Staffordshire pottery, or Dutch tiles, or Manchester linen makes consumer goods widely and cheaply available, while eroding local peculiarities (Burke 1978: 244–50).

20. Tunstall (1983: 180) suggests that the development of international news agencies and the later phenomenon of Hollywood were important steps towards globalization.

21. Given the political trajectories of the United States and Britain between the mid-1970s and the mid-1980s it is unlikely that the degree of state patronage in either case would have been higher in the later period than the earlier. Rather less comprehensive data from Australia in the late 1980s suggest a pattern which is closer to the British than the American model. In 1989 Australia's five leading opera companies obtained 54 per cent of their income from commercial activity, 12 per cent from private patronage and 34 per cent from government grants. Annual reports of leading arts venues in major capital cities for 1987–8 suggest a breakdown of 39 per cent box office, 37 per cent government grant and 22 per cent private patronage (Cultural Ministers Council, Statistical Advisory Group 1990: 86, 92).

22. This point was already well taken in a tradition of sociological research into (youth) 'subcultures' which extends from American work from the 1940s, 1950s and 1960s to British concerns in the 1970s with the 'articulation' between subculture and class (see Hall and Jefferson 1975).

23. On the former, for example, it is self-evident to Hume (1964: 269) that the refined Addison is a superior writer to the earlier and unrefined Bunyan. On the latter, the pretensions of (particularly) the middle classes to a taste above their station have been satirized mercilessly throughout the modern period.

24. McCracken (1988) distinguishes between rituals of possession, exchange, grooming and divestment which relate to different aspects and stages of the commodity's trajectory. A limitation of the analysis is that McCracken works with an overly-integrated conception of 'culture' as the unitary medium of consumption.

25. Paradoxes about the chronology of the postmodern must inevitably arise if a definition of it is required which is 'both historical and theoretical' (Hassan 1985: 122). The two lines of division cannot plausibly be made to coincide.

26. Of course, Bell is no friend of modernism itself, which represents a doomed 'effort to

find excitement and meaning in literature and art as a substitute for religion' (Bell 1976: 29).

27. The unity of form, material and function on the grand scale is not always carried through to points of detail, hence some of the unpopularity of modernist buildings. As Harvey (1989: 36) notes, Corbusier refused to allow blinds to be fitted to the windows of his Pavillon Suisse thereby causing extreme discomfort in summer heat.

28. It is arguable that Benjamin's enthusiasm for cinema leads him to take it as the paradigm of mechanical reproduction and to overestimate the emancipatory potential of the latter.

29. The geographical concentration of 'live culture' in Britain is starkly obvious from 1987–8 Arts Council data which show 52.6 performances of opera and dance per million population for Greater London and 16 for Scotland, the next best served region. In most other regions the number is well below 10 (see Feist and Hutchison 1990: 44).

30. Despite frequent references to the 'pessimism' of the Frankfurt School in the cultural studies literature (see Bennett 1986: 14), the 'optimistic' strain, deriving from Benjamin, has been much more influential. Witness Enzensberger (1976) and the prominence of Benjamin in Habermas' concerns of the 1980s.

31. It is arguable, for example, that McLuhan's *The Mechanical Bride* of 1951 is a far more innovative, amusing and insightful excursion into the 'whirling phantasmagoria' (1967a: v) of a commodified popular culture than is Barthes' very similar *Mythologies* of 1957. However, Barthes drapes his essays in the swagging of the structuralism which became so dominant in radical culture theory. Baudrillard, however, often cites McLuhan and pays credit to the 'true revolution which he brought about in media analysis' (Baudrillard 1988: 208).

32. So, the 'three spheres' lose their *rational* autonomy (as Weber noted) earlier than Lash implies, Benjamin's account of 'aura' cannot be taken at face value, while subversions of the modernist 'cultural economy' may be as old as cultural modernity (particularly in popular culture).

33. The appropriation can then be used to repackage and sell the original: recordings of the Mozart K467 Piano Concerto bill it as the 'Theme from Elvira Madigan', while collections of Baroque Concerti are sold as 'soundtrack albums' from *Kramer vs. Kramer*. Of course, some caution is required here in that such developments are not entirely 'new'. Adorno and Horkheimer complained about the mingling of popular and serious music, while many operatic performers of the early part of the century also recorded music hall songs.

34. When Fiske (1987: 249) elides 'style' with the functions of a resistant 'carnival' he defines away the connections between 'style' and 'taste', which for Fiske as for Bourdieu is essentially hegemonic. Once style is rendered as an anti-aesthetic anti-taste questions about conflict and hierarchy in connection with style need not be posed.

35. This runs against the very precise alignments which Bourdieu (1984) identifies, and the difference no doubt reflects differences of class structure, culture and sociological tradition between France and the United States.

3
The shrinking state

An illustrator for a seventeenth-century edition of Hobbes' *Leviathan* represented the state as a Prince-warrior. There was no doubt about either the main tasks of the Prince or his gender. A twentieth-century illustrator would have considerable difficulty with such an allegory. The functions of the state have changed, it has became an administrator and provider rather than a warrior. Moreover, there are serious ambiguities about its gender. Some suggest that a motherly figure, as in the 'nanny state', would be a more appropriate representation, combining the characteristics of a breast-feeding mother with the firm and intrusive generosity of Mary Poppins. In the 1990s, the picture is complicated further because the nanny state has aged. Some still see her as a tyrannical figure, but her breasts are drying up and she shows some early signs of sclerosis. Her performance is suffering and there are suggestions of relieving her of some of her duties.

There is irony in the fact that processes of crisis and the devolution[1] of state powers coincide with a current rediscovery of the state as a major social agency and with calls to bring it back into the political analysis.[2] Perhaps this late flight of Minerva's owl, particularly among Marxist scholars, reflects the crossing of an important historical threshold which divides late modernity, with its characteristic etatist and corporatist trends, from a new period, marked by the palpable arrest and possible reversal of these trends. Caution is advisable in taking such a position because the process of state devolution is very new, the evidence of its occurrence is patchy, and its diagnosis is controversial. At present it is hard to judge how much of the observed devolution is due to a particular historical-political conjuncture and how much reflects a more general, global and lasting process. It is also true that the pace of devolution is uneven and is most rapid in conservative-ruled and ex-communist countries. On the other hand, the state is unlikely to be rolled back overnight, even by ascendant East European elites newly converted to market liberalism and preaching a radical disetatization[3] of hitherto state-socialist societies. Highly structured nation-states will doubtless remain as the most basic political entities, sources of identity and repositories of citizenship rights, both in the West and the East, for many generations.

However, both the functions of the state as a tool of social and economic regulation and reconstruction, and the scope of state power and responsibility, have started to diminish. This is partly the consequence of such external factors as the globalization of politics and the increasing strength of international agencies, and partly the result of internal processes prompted by crises of 'governability', 'fiscal' security and 'legitimation'. Some of these crisis processes are ideological in character, referring to a declining faith in the effectiveness of the state. Others refer to an actual reduction in the scope of state power and responsibility.

Four general aspects of this devolution may be discerned and these are addressed in the final section of this chapter: a 'horizontal' or 'functional' redistribution of powers shifting some of the state responsibility and authority 'sideways', that is, away from central governments and bureaucracies and towards trade unions, industrial federations, semi-independent corporations, and specialized agencies; a 'vertical' redistribution of state power by decentralization 'downwards', that is, towards self-governing bodies, local groups, and civic initiatives; privatization and marketization; and a globalization of politics which shifts some of state responsibilities and powers 'upwards' to various supra-state bodies.

These four processes converge, mutually reinforce and thus become global trends. They cut across cultural, ideological and party political divisions. They have been diagnosed in Britain, on the European continent, in Australia and New Zealand, and in the USA. They transcend party-political divisions: similar trends have been noted in Conservative-ruled UK and in Labor-ruled Australia. Moreover, they also transcend the old 'great divide' between the capitalist West and the ex-communist East. In fact, the most vigorous disetatization has occurred in newly democratized Eastern Europe. The economic, political and cultural aspects of this devolution converge on a single, postmodern 'disorganization complex'. The convergence of such trends, combined with a tidal wave of anti-etatist sentiments among elites and such strategically important social categories as the young, the educated and the urban, heralds more than a temporary retreat. The process increasingly appears to be a major reversal, part of a historical shift which closes the twentieth century and marks the end of its distinctive etatist project.

As part of a diagnosis of the current reversal of modern etatist trends they must be located within a broader perspective suggesting main causes and outlining patterns of devolution. This presupposes a discussion of the key processes of modernization and their product, the corporatist state, which has formed the principal political and administrative framework of almost all of the advanced societies of the twentieth century.[4]

The Rationalization of Politics and Bureaucratic Trends

The formation of corporatist bureaucracies in Europe must be seen as a part of a wider process of modernization which involved the progressive differentiation of political functions and their separation from religious, aesthetic and, generally, communal activities. This coincided with the emergence of political roles culminating in the rise of the professional politician and specialization within the sphere of politics resulting in the emergence of specialized experts with divided areas of competence. The process of political stratification increasingly divided decision-making elites from expert advisers, the interested public and the masses. Political participation has been extended via the increasingly formalized structures of parties and interest groups. A modern political idiom of 'power politics' arose, based on systematic and rational interest representation and mediation. Its advanced or late modern form was founded on an alignment between major societal forces with organized political groups and on systematic, instrumental, pragmatic, elite-controlled interest mediation. Finally political modernization involved a concentration of the means of administration in the centralized state machines, a process which was subsequently accelerated by centralization and concentration in the economy and the mass media, and extension of control over social processes. Thus, on the most general plane, the process of modernization involved differentiation of political functions, bureaucratization of organization, and the rationalization of political action.

The terms 'rationality' and 'bureaucracy' are inexorably linked with the Weberian tradition in social theory. The former refers to types of action, orientations and social arrangements which are calculable, deliberate, systematic and impersonal. The latter describes 'the purest form of legal-rational authority' and a form of administration incorporating formal–rational principles, bureaucracy. Bureaucracy is a hierarchical and rule-oriented system which in its pure form maximizes calculability, impersonality, ethical neutrality and cost-effectiveness. It is thus materially 'irresistible' and gradually permeates all organizational domains from churches, armies and economic enterprises to political parties and the administrative apparatuses of the state. Rationalization has the more general consequences of 'depersonalization of social relationships, the refinement of techniques of calculation, the enhancement of the social importance of specialized knowledge, and the extension of technically rational control over both natural and social processes' (Brubaker 1984:2). The world has thus become increasingly disenchanted, 'shaped by scientists, industrialists, and bureaucrats' with a high potential for 'political, social, educational, and propagandistic manipulation and domination of human beings' (Levine 1981: 5; Weber 1949: 35).

Formal rationalism, symbolized by centralized and rule-oriented bureaucratic organizations, increasingly permeates all spheres of life by eliminating social arrangements based on tradition, and by blocking the development of substantively oriented or value-guided patterns of action. It is engendered in the market form of production and exchange (of commodities), in legal formalism, in class division, and in modern political institutions, especially 'that rascal the state'. It was seen by Weber (1978: 111) as the 'specific and peculiar' feature of western modernity and 'one of the most important sources of all "social" problems'. Because it rests on purely formal maximization of calculability of means, regardless of the particular ends they may serve, formal rationality cannot be tied to any 'substantive' principle, say to charity, equality or justice.

Bureaucracy proved the best ally of the modern state.[5] Effective domination and territorial control, which are two distinctive features of the modern state, depended on a level of administrative efficiency which only bureaucracy could guarantee. The state, in turn, provided the best institutional habitat for the development of bureaucratic machineries, to such an extent that the latter became closely identified with state administration. Another reason for this affinity and symbiosis was an overall growth in living standards and the extension of state functions, especially in the areas of welfare provisions. Increasing bureaucratization, as Weber pointed out,

> is a function of the increasing possession of consumption goods, and of an increasingly sophisticated technique of fashioning of external life, a technique which corresponds to the opportunities provided by such wealth. This reacts upon the standard of living, and makes for an increasing subjective indispensability of public, interlocal, and thus bureaucratic provision for the varied wants which were previously either unknown or satisfied locally or by the private economy. (1978: 972)

Weber, it may be added, was ambivalent about the bureaucratic trends he identified. He applauded increasing liberation from traditionalism, but stressed the problematic nature of the new social order. Formal rationalization, according to him, threatens human values and all relationships based on love, compassion, friendship and loyalty. Bureaucratization facilitates the further expansion of state apparatuses, their increasing penetration into everyday life, and a concomitant erosion of value-oriented, ethically guided politics. It also heralds changes both in personnel and in the very way in which political questions are approached. Bureaucratic politics leads to the replacement of visionary 'goal setters' by 'organization men' and 'party hacks'. It translates questions of value into problems of appropriate rules and administrative procedures, and moulds a particular bureaucratic personality syndrome (Michels 1962; Mannheim 1952). The price of increased efficiency is an 'iron cage' of rationalism marked by impersonal 'market compulsion', legal formalism, and rule-orientation. Above all, bureaucratization affects politics by transforming it into power politics under the domination of party machines and a ubiquitous state administration.

Subsequent historical developments in the West, following Weber's untimely death in 1920, necessitate both a supplement and corrective to his vision. The supplement concerns the role of coercion as the ultimate basis, and authority as the principal form, of state power. They have been gradually displaced by more subtle mechanisms of persuasion and control whereby domination is exercised through manipulation of the circumstances under which people make decisions. This has coincided with an increasing involvement by the state in both the administration and the bureaucratic provision for welfare. The corrective concerns Weber's notions of continuity and of irresistibility of formally rational modern trends. Although the bureaucratic trends did continue throughout the twentieth century, culminating in the emergence of the centralistic and bureaucratized corporatist state, the current developments point to their reversal.[6]

From the Night Watchman State to the Corporate Manager

Theoretical responses to the ascendancy of the rationalized state apparatuses and their progressive differentiation from the civil society took three forms. Mainstream democratic theory saw the state as a neutral arena in which various societal interests freely competed; the state had no identity and no interests of its own; it was a bureaucratic facilitator rather than an agent. For reasons discussed in the next section, this view proved particularly attractive to students of North American politics. The Marxist perspective defined the state as the management committee of the ruling class, and the state's strength and legitimacy as a reflection of class domination and class struggle. Faced with the ascendancy of the interventionist state apparatuses, European Marxists, most notably the Frankfurt School thinkers, assigned to the state a much more prominent role, yet still subordinate to the logic of capital reproduction and class domination. Finally, Weberian theory located the state at the centre of political processes, but as an autonomous entity with interests of its own. This view, which also impressed many continental Marxists, found its most vocal supporters among analysts of the 'totalitarian state' and corporatist configurations in Western and Eastern Europe.

The concept of corporatism embraces many meanings. On one hand, it has been seen as a new social configuration, a new social form, which is transcending and succeeding both capitalism and socialism. According to Winkler (1976: 103), 'Corporatism is an economic system in which the state directs predominantly privately owned business according to four principles: unity, order, nationalism and success.' By contrast, such neo-Marxists as Jessop (1978) see it as a capitalist configuration, a form of the state in which, unlike in 'parliamentary capitalism', representation and intervention are fused. However, the best known and the most useful conceptualization of corporatism is that which views it as a political configuration combining centralism, etatism and a distinctive pattern of state-controlled interest mediation.[7]

At the core of the corporate configuration lies the executive arm of the state. The formation of the corporate state involves a shift of power away from representative bodies and its concentration in the bureaucratized executive. Its corollary is the extension of the depth and scope of state intervention. The corporate state becomes preoccupied with economic planning, central management and the overall co-ordination of social activities. This includes, above all, control over interest articulation and intermediation. Corporatism promotes forms of interest articulation which stress the centrality of functional rather than attitudinal interests and concerns. It relies on active involvement of the state in the creation and maintenance of functionally based 'interest pillars', licensing them to select, aggregate, and legitimize interests, and incorporating these 'processed' interests in the central policy-making system. Corporatist strategies combine domestic stimulation of economic expansion by supporting investment and industrial development with an international preoccupation with stability. This process is legitimized by an ideology which emphasizes consensus and economic growth.

Although different forms of modern corporatism have specific historical roots, and although these roots reach deep into the nineteenth century, there seems to be a consensus among students of corporatism that its mature form emerged in Europe under the impact of the civil and political strife accompanying the communist and Nazi revolutions, the world wars, and the Great Depression. In Western Europe, the deprivations of the Depression and the spectre of the revolution propelled welfare reforms, economic regulation, and defensive consensus-building on the national level. The world wars further strengthened these tendencies. They accelerated social reform, especially in the arenas of political and social rights. After the First World War, as Weber pointed out, it was impossible 'to relegate returning soldiers to second place in their electoral rights by comparison to those strata which were able to maintain or even improve their social position, their wealth and their market opportunities while others gave their blood in the trenches to protect them'.[8] Wars prompted the political consolidation of major social forces and the formation of their organized representation, the major parties, trade unions and employers' associations. War economies led to a fine tuning of state interventionist and regulatory apparatuses and increased tolerance for state regulation.

> In modern wars of total mobilisation, all capitalist societies are corporatist: the need to win the war creates an overwhelming moral unity and defines an external enemy so clearly that internal conflicts pale into insignificance; the state engages in a degree of propaganda and popular activation not normally seen. . . . [T]he degree of economic regulation in which the state engages increases massively . . . and the working class is taken into a highly corporatist relationship. (Crouch 1983: 322)

Ideological responses to these upheavals also reinforced corporatist trends. For Leftist sympathizers the turbulent years represented the crisis of the old capitalist order, highlighting the need for social reform. Liberals and conservatives saw it as a temporary malady, a threat to law and order prompting calls for tighter control and the reassertion of traditional values. The corporate configuration that emerged in Western Europe between 1910 and 1960 responded to both expectations and incorporated elements of both ideological visions. It constituted a sort of a 'middle solution', a state-sponsored and state-controlled Great Armistice.

Three aspects of this armistice are particularly important. First, it was an etatist armistice, achieved under the aegis of the state, and resulting in a dramatic extension of state intervening powers and regulatory functions, involving:

- internal stabilization by mediation and arbitration in industrial conflicts;
- economic regulation, co-ordination and harmonization of increasingly complex activities;
- facilitation, that is, the development of an economic infrastructure of transport, communication, etc. and the socialization of such noneconomic costs as education, training and research;
- the reparation of industrial side-effects including environmental damage, regional poverty and urban blight;
- legitimation: justifying and defending policies and mobilizing generalized normative support (mass and elite consensus);
- external stabilization and safeguarding of socio-political order through military-political bloc arrangements.

Second, the Grand Armistice strengthened the legitimacy of the state through state-sponsored extension of citizenship rights into the area of 'social rights'. This meant increased entitlements and boosted welfare provisions. Civil, political and social rights were thus defined as domains of state power and state responsibility. Fulfilment of this responsibility required, in turn, further concentration of legal and political authority and further build-up of bureaucratic apparatuses.

Third, the armistice involved a social and political enfranchisement of organized labour through its incorporation into the government-sponsored deals.[9] This incorporation was conditional on abandoning revolutionary programmes, respect for the 'rules of the game', and tempering demands. More importantly, the corporate state also subjected to regulations and control private corporations by the partial nationalization of strategic sectors and industries, control over credit and currencies, and legal regulation.

The entire social structure of advanced societies was affected by corporatist settlements. They promoted articulation of interests and divisions along major class lines thus enhancing the socio-political articulation of classes, the formation of class-based social milieux, and stable alignment between these milieux and the major parties. Paradoxically, they also blunted class conflict by promoting its articulation, institutionalization and organization. When systematically articulated through bureaucratic structures of mass 'milieu parties', class conflicts were transformed from revolutionary forces into pillars of the status quo.

The corporatist settlements, it must be stressed, also involved an external aspect, the formation of power politics and superpower-controlled political-military blocs. International stability was based on a balance of power and the recognition of so-called geopolitical realities. This was shaped by a series of strategic deals, most notably the Yalta and Vienna agreements, which defined 'spheres of influence' and formulated general international rules of the game. Like the internal deals, these interstate agreements paved the way for regulated conflict resolution, and allowed the state to focus on internal steering.

Everyone, it seemed, could have a stake in the corporatist settlements, the Left and the Right, the elites and the newly enfranchized masses. Corporatism responded to socialist hopes for curbing the exploitation of labour, of reducing 'anarchic and wasteful competition', and of promoting a peaceful socialization of the economy. But, it also helped to extinguish revolutionary sparks fanned by the Great Depression and Soviet influence, it safeguarded property rights, and strengthened a fragile socio-political order, thus pacifying conservative critics. Growing state power did not bother liberals much either, because the state promoted citizenship rights and it was seen as a countervailing force of reason against local particularisms.

Corporatism responded to mass demands for order, peace, justice and prosperity. Exhausted by the Depression and scarred by civil strife and warfare, the population of Europe was highly receptive to settlements, especially since the benefits seemed enormous and the costs incurred in curbing aspirations, taming and deferring demands and tolerating more control appeared to be moderate. What also made the corporatist deal attractive was the fact that it strengthened elite consensus and cemented elite unity. In the West, the settlements reinforced the liberal-democratic ethos which emerged ascendant from the confrontations with fascism and communism. It looked remarkably like a socio-political version of the philosopher's stone, a transideological panacea for all social ills. Generally, corporatist settlements were seen by their protagonists as a rational pragmatic, nonideological and reformist solution, achieved in the name of partnership, national consensus, class harmony, economic growth and prosperity.

The growing power of the liberal corporatist state was thus welcomed by both the leaders and the led. The Prince was not only strong and enlightened, but also benevolent and democratic. The governmental core of the state was subject to periodic tests of popularity, and it was open to relatively unconstrained criticism from the opposition and free mass media. It was also embraced by all important social forces, including the new and growing service class. This affinity had more than one dimension. Service workers endorsed the rationalistic and technocratic ideological vision promoted by the state apparatuses and they were also the main beneficiaries of the expansion of the public sector. They became in effect the 'state class' (Berger 1987; Kriesi 1989).

Etatist Projects and Forms of Corporatism

The origin of modern corporatism resembles a multiple birth. It arose in three different forms. The socialist/communist corporatism stressed as its main principle the etatization of a class as 'the workers' state'. Fascist corporatism professed the etatization of a racially 'purified' nation. A much more benign liberal-democratic-bureaucratic corporatism settled for a partial etatization of political articulation and decision making.[10]

In its Leninist–Stalinist version, the socialist project led to the development of powerful and totalitarian partocratic regimes. Their key features included: a centrally managed 'command economy'; the fusion of all the top party, state and industrial positions into a single 'monocratic' hierarchy controlling all aspects of society; the emergence of ideologically unified, single-party elite which ruled through mass persuasion, command and coercion; and mass mobilization exercised through a centrally and monopolistically controlled propaganda machine. East European corporatism was the subsequent product of the post-Stalinist reforms in these highly centralized regimes.

In the fascist project, the state was depicted as the tool of a racially homogeneous nation. It aimed at arresting change and reinforcing a collapsing social order within a politically and ideologically reconstructed *Volksgemeinschaft* (national community). It was as radical in its etatist, centralist and totalitarian aspirations as its socialist-communist precursor. The state was not merely to encompass but rather to replace other associations as a source of loyalty and regulation.[11]

The liberal form of corporatism which emerged in Western Europe between the 1910s and the 1960s has been more pluralistic and more modest in its etatist zeal. First, the liberal state has never aspired to total control of economy and society. It has operated within a market matrix and respected certain freedoms which underlay the functioning of civil society. Second, it is highly formalistic and legalistic – the state has never been considered as standing above the law. Third, the corporate deals include few but diverse interests. The statement of a single overriding and supreme interest which propelled the communist and fascist forms contrasts with the more pragmatic notion of a workable consensus that underlies liberal corporatism. Fourth, co-operation and co-ordination have generally been achieved by peaceful means, with minimum violence and wide tolerance for dissent.

In spite of these important differences, all three projects adopted a highly etatized corporatist form. On an ideological level, this reflected a widespread faith in the state's ability to provide the universal panacea for all social problems. This faith was not just the ideological residuum of the enlightenment. Modern corporatism, especially in its liberal form, did indeed provide an effective solution to conflict, strife and warfare which had plagued Europe during the first half of the century. The fascist solution proved the most costly and the least successful, but it must be remembered that before 1939 the fascist regimes did achieve some of their objectives of economic stabilization, social peace, and a reassertion of national pride. However, repulsive intolerance, totalitarian intrusion, expansionism and predilection for violence made fascist corporatism untenable in the long run. The socialist/communist project has been more successful, although ultimately it is equally costly and untenable. Soviet Russia did negotiate the first stage of industrialization, achieved stability, and modernized, although at enormous human cost. Moreover, it became a military superpower, and created a relatively stable 'empire' lasting for over half a century. The Soviet state-socialist model has been emulated, with rather moderate success, by some dozens of countries in the third world. Its crisis-ridden collapse in the 1990s marks an important historical watershed.

Our main focus, however, is on the third etatist project, the liberal one. Unlike the other two, which resulted in the development of highly ideologized partocratic administration, liberal corporatism has been highly bureaucratized, that is formally rational and rule-oriented.

Corporate bureaucracy is to some extent a pleonasm. Bureaucracy involves, by definition, legitimate domination and centralism. But it is not synonymous with state administration, and not all bureaucratized administrations embrace the corporatist mode of interest mediation. A bureaucratic-corporate structure resembles a pyramid with a multiple apex consisting of the 'tips' of functionally organized interest-pillars. The tips comprise institutionalized and bureaucratized elite positions occupied by leaders of the largest private corporations, union federations, top state officials and the representatives of major interest groups. They play the key role in a process of systematic and orderly interest mediation that involves filtering and funnelling of interests so as to transform them into manageable negotiable form. Corporate filtering occurs through selective licensing. Only organized groups which claim political status, have distinct interest-constituencies, and present demands in a manageable form, that is, as demands for resources and/or specific policies, are admitted to the process. Funnelling involves an aggregation of demands into negotiable and manageable packages. This leads to elimination of radical, immoderate and non-negotiable demands, as well as those demands which are articulated in a 'nonpolitical', that is, nonorganized form and language. Corporate filters and funnels thus structure the very form of political organization so as to stabilize the process of mediation. Competing demands can be easily settled through collective bargaining, arbitration and conciliation processes which are systematic, pragmatic and predictable.

An important role is played in this process by the major parties linked to stable social milieux. These conservative, liberal, socialist, and Roman Catholic milieux have become stable bases of political articulation. Milieu parties, also called 'people's parties' and 'parties of democratic integration', turned into major political stabilizers by anchoring the loyalties of large sections of population, and by stabilizing voting patterns. Preferences were transmitted through family traditions, thus assuring a very high level of continuity and stability. Party machines acquired high level of autonomy in policy formulation. Milieu parties helped in the process of filtering and funnelling by formulating consistent policy options and alternative programmes. They mobilized support by canvassing votes and they moulded corporate elites. They still act as communication systems for corporate executives and as muffling devices. By imposing discipline in governments and reducing radical dissent in parliamentary representations they further stabilize the process of interest mediation.

As is discussed in chapter five, bureaucratic corporatism has generated a specific form of corporate 'power politics' and 'political man' with the following characteristics:

- Power politics is an interest group politics, focussing on class or market generated interests and demands.
- It is an elite politics, conducted mainly through intra-elite deals and relying on a low degree of mass participation and involvement.
- Corporate politics is consensual, based on a tacit acceptance by all corporate players of the rules of the game.
- It is 'cool' and disethicized and thus sober, pragmatic and instrumental. It aims at workable deals, acceptable compromises and pragmatic settlements.
- The corporate politician is a bureaucratic climber-player (company man, party man or union man), educated and competent but, above all, moulded in the process of selection and socialization which occurs during the long climb through the bureaucratized corporate hierarchies.

The corporate solution worked well. Even the most ardent critics of liberal corporatism and 'state capitalism' acknowledge that, in relative terms, it was successful. Corporate settlements produced a period of peace and prosperity which was unprecedented in its length and scope. They promoted a complacent social cohesion, rapid if uneven economic growth, and the spread of citizenship rights. Throughout the postwar decades strike action declined and the standard of living improved. Corporate settlements paved the way for generous welfare provisions, including publicly funded mass education and health care. Above all, they prevented total warfare and the nuclear holocaust. This success was eclipsed neither by Cold War tension nor local wars, since the latter were limited in scope and fought mainly by proxies. Emerging problems were seen as either teething difficulties or technical ones, which required fine tuning of planning and management, better co-ordination, further rationalization of administration, improvement of control methods, and extending international understanding, co-operation and control.

This somewhat apologetic assessment needs to be qualified. As stressed above, it was only the liberal form of corporatism which worked well. More importantly, even liberal corporatism has started to experience various problems, contradictions and dysfunctions, prompting calls for a radical revamping of the corporate model. These problems are much more acute in Eastern than in Western Europe, and they are more frequently diagnosed in Europe than in the USA. In order to throw some light on this pattern of criticism, a short digression on the East European and North American cases is necessary.

Extreme Cases: the USA and Eastern Europe

While most of the West European societies embraced the bureaucratic corporatist solution, developments in the USA were quite different. Despite the concentration of executive power prompted by New Deal policies, wartime control over the economy and the military concentration during the Cold War period and Vietnam War, the North American configuration looks distinctly less corporatist than those of its West European counterparts. There is no peak association in the USA exercising quasi-monopolistic hegemony over the decision-making processes under state aegis. Particularly striking is the absence of organized labour and of a unified industrial lobby. Despite the concentration of power, the overall structure looks more plural, diverse and fragmented. This, according to Salisbury (1979: 219), reflects a political system based on

> federalism, the separation of powers, [and] legislators nominated from single-member districts. These elements interact to perpetuate a pattern in which groups have multiple access points and governmental officials find it extremely difficult to assemble enough authority to act on a comprehensive scale. At the same time, the continued existence of dispersed centres of authority provides opportunities for influence to interest groups which are also organized in a fragmented, geographically dispersed manner. Government authority, although having a centralized executive core, is fragmented to the extent that one can hardly talk about the monistic state. Public policies are disaggregated, and their effects seldom form a systematic pattern. An established tradition of legal challenges makes any attempt at monopolization of policies by any coalition risky and uncertain.

There are many reasons for these idiosyncrasies. As pointed out by students of American state, the conditions of its formation differed from West European circumstances. Unlike West European capitalism, the American socio-economic system was never under serious threat from conquest or indigenous social revolution. It scarcely needed a dominating centralist state and defensive corporatist settlements. It could always rely on national solidarity, direct executive intervention, and technocratic planning. The federal system has always been more diverse and plural than in Europe. Americans cherish individualism and have shown a deep suspicion of any political monopoly. Corporate pillars could hardly gain legitimacy, and their practices would be challenged in courts. This cultivated individualism, liberalism and popular anti-etatism, shared by both the Left and the Right, has posed formidable barriers to corporatist developments. American parties never developed into permanent bureaucratic machines. They have remained fragmented along regional lines, and have restricted their functions to vote canvassing on the eve of elections followed by a distribution of the spoils after successful campaigns. Finally, the corporatist developments have been hindered by the absence of organized control over information, effective antitrust laws, and extensive legal regulation of business and political deals.[12] The resulting weakness or absence of corporatism in the USA has important consequences. The process of devolution there has been less conspicuous, and the American political system faces less radical challenges from new politics than its European counterparts.

In this respect, the state socialist societies of Eastern Europe represented a reverse mirror image of the American situation. Corporatism there was amplified by specific historical circumstances, and it took a highly concentrated form. For the last century Eastern Europe was the front line and the battleground of conflicting armies and ideologies. Due to its economic backwardness, political fragility and ethnic, regional and religious fragmentation, it was particularly badly affected by economic downturns of the 1920s and 1930s. Civil strife was much more destructive and conflicts much sharper than in Western Europe. National aspirations were strong and liberal traditions weak. Altogether, the conditions were relatively conducive to the adoption of the corporate solution. After some experimentation with fascist models, and after the destructive Second World War, Eastern Europe was drawn into the Soviet sphere of influence and forced to adopt the Stalinist model.[13] With few exceptions, the imposition was smooth and encountered little resistance. The communists harnessed sentiments and longings similar to those widespread in the West. They promised and partly delivered peace, order and economic security. When legitimation failed, it was backed by coercion. Most of the communist regimes that emerged after the Second World War relied not so much on mass normative approval as on more robust motives of fear and helplessness.[14]

In Soviet-type societies the state played a much more central role than in the liberal West. The fusion of party activists, senior military officers and state officials led to the emergence of the powerful, ideologically unified and Soviet-sponsored partocratic elites. The nationalization of banks and large-scale property gave partocratic officials almost total control over the economy which, in turn, facilitated the centralization of management through national planning and the replacement of the market by a centralized command economy. After an initial flirtation with political pluralism, the opposition was banned and political dissent suppressed. MELS (Marx-Engels-Lenin-Stalin) became the official state ideology and the key element in the legitimizing formula. Centralized control was extended into institutions of education and cultural activity, each of which was subjected to censorship and strict guidance, and gradually transformed into a complacent agency of the partocratic state.

The goals, and the logic of operation of the partocratic state, were unmistakably modern: communism meant accelerated modernization – industrialization, rationalization, secularization, in Lenin's words, 'electrification plus soviet power'. It was to be a short-cut path to modernization,

imposed from above by ideologically and programmatically unified partocratic elites that controlled powerful state apparatuses. The planned
(command) economy, centralized administration, and the massive tutelary
system encompassing the mass media and educational institutions, were to
serve as the tools for the implementation of scientific socialism. The
market system and commodity production were rejected because they
were insufficiently rational. Co-ordinated national plans, and the quota
system of production, were to overcome the alleged unpredictability,
wastefulness and anarchy of the market. The aim was to control fully the
nature-like processes of investment and production, to reshape the social
structure, to create a new culture, and to reconstruct the psychological
makeup of the people (the 'Soviet man'). The major tool of this project,
which was unprecedented in its scope and depth, was the partocratic state.

The absence of market constraints, and the atrophy of civil society,
made the partocratic state an exceedingly powerful tool of social reconstruction. It also prevented corporatist inclusion. The early Stalinist
configuration was too monopolistic and too intrusive to be called corporatist. It relied on pragmatic tolerance rather than normative approval and on
exclusion and suppression of interests rather than their incorporation. The
recent corporate configuration emerged in Eastern Europe from the
post-Stalinist reforms of the late 1950s when Soviet control was relaxed and
many totalitarian features were eliminated. This coincided with incorporation into the partocratic elite of large sections of industrial management,
the intelligentsia and the skilled workers. Such incorporation, it must be
stressed, was not synonymous with democratization since political opposition was banned and mass participation was largely restricted to pledges of
allegiance. But incorporation strengthened elite control by allowing for a
limited use of nationalism, and marked the emergence of a more inclusive
partocratic 'nomenklatura'. Like their liberal counterparts in the West, the
post-Stalinist corporatist elites could claim credit for considerable success.
Throughout the 1960s and 1970s most of the state-socialist countries
managed healthy economic growth, introduced extensive welfare systems
and achieved political stability. These halcyon years prompted the subsequent crisis of the socialist corporatism by producing its gravediggers, a
post-Stalinist generation. The crisis was much deeper than the downturns
experienced in the West and resulted in a more radical quasi-revolutionary
process of restructuring.

Corporate Dysfunctions and the Crisis of Etatism

In the 1970s and 1980s corporatism started to show symptoms of institutional sclerosis. In many respects this was the result of its previous
successes, which boosted the size of corporate bureaucracies, entrenched
corporate structures, dogmatized corporate strategies and inflated popular
expectations. The controlling and interventionist powers of the state were

extended but at the cost of creating cumbersome and expensive bureaucracies, high taxation, persistent inflationary pressures and spiralling demands for entitlements and services. The corporate solution helped to harness major interests by ceding responsibility for their aggregation and reconciliation to state-sponsored bodies, thus implicitly empowering them to act as supreme guardians and arbiters in interest mediation. This had numerous side-effects: it led to an enormous concentration of power beyond, as many critics claimed, the controlling capacities of anaemic representative-democratic mechanisms; the collusion of interests between the corporate elites; and a separation of formal responsibilities, in the hands of the politicians, from actual decision-making powers which were in the hands of corporate executives.

While helping to institutionalize and domesticate interest conflicts, corporatism also increased a specific form of closure resulting from the filtering, funnelling and deflection of interests. Particularly important was the subtle form of exclusion which results from the operational definition of what constitutes and does not constitute legitimate political demands and legitimate political action. This exclusion proved to be particularly aggravating for the new postwar generation born and brought up in the halcyon years of the 1950s and 1960s. Their idealistic expectations and 'post-materialist' value orientations proved hard to transform into the 'input' format of bureaucratized corporate politics, thus leading to peripheralization and disenchantment with corporatist politics. Large sections of this generation became the principal constituency of anti-bureaucratic and anti-corporatist new politics. Its ascendancy coincided with growing criticism of the overgrowth and alienation of corporatist bureaucracies, the declining effectiveness of welfare provision, increasing taxation burdens, and the adverse effects of burgeoning state deficits.

The best way of summarizing these criticisms, formulated under such labels as 'governability crisis', 'fiscal crisis', 'legitimation crisis' and 'failure of state', is in the form of paradoxes and unintended consequences of corporatist solutions.[15] Corporatist and bureaucratic 'dysfunctions' and 'contradictions' have been linked not only with the internal logic of corporatist developments but also with broader processes of social change including class decomposition, the disintegration of communities and large social milieux, the educational revolution, especially the rapid expansion of tertiary education, and the informational revolution, the growth of the electronic mass media and means of communication.[16]

The enfranchisement of organized labour and the extension of citizenship rights were both defensive measures aimed at defusing class conflict and positive steps towards empowering politically and economically marginalized groups. These developments had three unanticipated consequences. First, they resulted in an escalation of demand caused partly by detachment of entitlements from market endowments and partly by facilitation of political articulation. The former meant that making demands was easy because it carried no direct costs to the claimants, and the latter resulted in the emergence of better educated, informed and organized claimants. This resulted in an increasing volume of demands, which threatened the economic capacity of the state and clogged the political process. The old class conflicts were thus gradually supplemented by new divisions and conflicts between producers and claimants, provision and entitlement.[17]

Second, the corporatist solution leads to the displacement of demands which are directed to the most visible actors, the representative bodies, while actual decision-making power resides increasingly in the hands of corporate executives who are less visible and insulated from public pressure. This leads, on one hand, to responsibility without power, to impotent politicians, and, on the other, to power without responsibility in the form of corporatist 'invisible governments'. Inflation of promises made by political parties and individual politicians in their bids for election further aggravates this problem.[18]

Third, the halcyon years of peace and prosperity, for which corporate leaders claim credit, have generated a well educated and idealistic generation with high economic and political expectations and aspirations. In the three postwar decades, the proportion of tertiary educated persons among college-age cohorts has grown to over 15 per cent in the UK, 20 per cent in France, 25 per cent in Germany and 40 per cent in the USA. The civic and political aspirations of these people, and the demands they give rise to, transcend the materialist values and aspirations of the war generation. They result, as Inglehart points out, in a shift towards postmaterialist aspirations and demands which are increasingly difficult to satisfy. These new aspirations concern freedom, personal development and the quality of life, and they prompt challenges to the principles of consensus and growth underlying the corporatist settlements. Moreover the new values and concerns are frequently articulated in a form and language which defy political incorporation. By entering the political arena as an agenda for the educated and politically active sections of the postwar generation these new demands destabilize the corporatist system.[19]

Another paradox concerns the effectiveness of the principal corporatist legitimizer and pacifier, the welfare system. State financed and controlled welfare services have partly supplemented and partly replaced the less effective private institutions. The cost of welfare, however, has grown proportionally not only to the scope of entitlements and the size of entitled categories, but also to the size of the administrative-redistributive bureaucracies. These bureaucratic machines, according to critics, have become the main consumers of welfare resources, thus undermining their purpose and legitimacy. Moreover, the marginal effectiveness of the services has declined due to an overall upward shift in standards and expectations. So the satisfaction of welfare needs starts to take on a spiral character as increased provisions boost expectations, which in turn provokes disenchantment. Also, as critics point out, welfare generates a dependency syndrome. Recipients of services learn powerlessness and form an increasingly state-dependent underclass.[20]

One of the most widely publicized problems of liberal corporatism has been linked to its reliance on state interventionism which is increasingly difficult to legitimize. The difficulty reflects a paradoxical relationship between the state and the market. The state operates in an 'artificial' and visible way, through centralized authoritative regulation and redistribution. The market adopts a quasi-natural form of exchange, so that its operations are decentralized and thus do not require explicit justification. These two modes of operation are incompatible. Increased corporatist interventions into the market-regulated processes of production and distribution which are, as Habermas and Offe point out, essential for corporatist success, destabilize the market and have unfortunate publicizing effects. The visible hand of the state increases the need for explicit justification which can only partly be satisfied, thus increasing the chronic legitimation deficit.

Criticisms of the state are as old as the state itself and there is also nothing new about the anti-corporatist arguments. They have been well rehearsed throughout the 1970s and early 1980s. What is new, is the intensity and scope of criticism, and the linkages between the corporatist and etatist dysfunctions. The central point in the new critiques is the declining social relevance of the corporatist deals and the etatist solution in general.[21] The main social forces that the corporatist state has represented and empowered have ceased to be the principal and coherent actors, while the new, potentially disruptive social forces cannot be incorporated in the old deals. The former point brings us to the issue of class decomposition and the progressive disintegration of the socio-political milieux which have stabilized political preferences throughout the postwar decades. This process of decomposition and its political consequences are discussed in Chapters 4 and 5. The new social forces have to a large extent been generated by corporatist deals themselves. The main one has been variously described as a 'welfare class', an 'underclass' or the 'outsiders' – people largely dependent on welfare. Social conflicts between these categories and the 'insiders' have been diagnosed by many as the principal new conflict in 'industrial society' (e.g. Dahrendorf 1988). The second 'new' formation includes what Offe (1985a) labelled 'peripheralized' social categories, such as students and pensioners, who are not fully integrated into the market economy. Finally, there has been an increasing articulation of various status groups and categories, including ethnic minorities and generational and lifestyle groups, whose identities and political aspirations have been shaped in the socio-cultural sphere of consumption and lifestyle rather than in production (see e.g. Turner 1988). None of these new forces could be effectively incorporated into the old corporatist deals. The increasing volume of these politically peripheralized categories make the deals increasingly unrealistic and internally irrelevant.

The corporatist-etatist solution has also lost much of its external relevance. The internationalization of markets has seriously limited the capacity of states to control their economic environments and destiny. The growing gap between what is promised (e.g. regulated wages, stable currencies and interest rates) and what can be delivered progressively erodes the illusion of 'national control'. This is not limited to economic matters. Protection against threats to internal stability, including the principal state function of securing 'law and order', has been seriously compromised by an inability to effectively prevent the operation of drug syndicates and international terrorist groups. Finally, and perhaps most importantly, the proliferation of nuclear and chemical weapons makes the conduct of a large-scale war difficult and risky. So most of the Princely functions which have traditionally served as justifications and legitimations of the state have been undermined.

Finally, the corporate solution has also generated international tensions which start to undermine its legitimacy. It involves national compacts which maximize national and regional advantages as well as international compacts in the form of regional military-political blocs. The two are closely related. National prosperity and stability underlie the stability of bloc politics. The latter is legitimized by external threats to prosperity, stability and the way of life. Three consequences of these arrangements have been highlighted by critics. First, the internal corporatist deals do not eliminate tensions but displace them. Dependency theorists have analysed the processes of displacement and the resulting disparities between the prosperous core and impoverished and dependent peripheries.[22] Second, success in maintaining compacts depends on effective policing and insulation of peripheral areas. This becomes increasingly problematic with the globalization of ecological problems, the spread of the 'soft target' terrorism, extension of contacts through travel, and the broadening of mass media coverage. Difficulties in containing ecological damage, the spread of AIDS and terrorist actions demonstrate difficulties in dealing with such problems on the national level and through bilateral national treaties. Third, the corporatist compacts rely on legitimacy which evokes and mobilizes symmetrically hostile perceptions. These have been undermined by improved communications, contacts and, above all, the inter-bloc détente which followed the reforms in the Soviet Union.

A specific version of this crisis can be observed in Eastern Europe. While the corporate solution there has been (with few exceptions) tolerated by people who had experienced the Great Depression, the world wars and the Stalinist terror, the post-Stalinist generation has challenged the paternalistic and exclusionary policies of state socialism. Their participatory aspirations and demands have produced a particularly intense overload, legitimation crisis, and ungovernability crisis, proportional to the level of exclusion and rigidity of the Soviet-type corporatism. The challenge to partocratic corporatism is therefore more thorough and radical and results in what Ash (1990) terms 'refolutions'. These are sudden and revolutionary in their scope but reformist in their form. They are resulting in the dismantling of the old corporatist system and its international 'superstructure', the Soviet bloc.

Etatism and corporatism have fused as a result of the postwar developments to the extent that the crisis of corporatism started to undermine the very power of the state. This is no longer just an issue in academic debates. The past decade has witnessed the convergence of anti-corporatist measures in most advanced societies. To these measures, and their convergence, we now turn our attention.

Responses to Crisis: Dismantling Corporatism and Rolling Back the State

The devolution of state powers and responsibilities is difficult to diagnose because of the variety of forms it takes. In nations with traditionally authoritarian but noninterventionist states, like Spain and Portugal, it mainly takes the form of 'horizontal' or functional deconcentration and a 'vertical', mostly territorial, redistribution of authority. The latter takes the two forms of devolution 'from above' and appropriation 'from below' by various grass-roots civil initiatives and social movements. In more liberal regimes, especially those with a traditionally strong public sector, like Britain, the devolution occurs mainly through the change of control pattern, from political-administrative to market. This is associated with the most radical form of political-administrative decentralization and devolution: privatization, marketization and deregulation.[23] Finally, devolution through shifting some of the powers and responsibilities 'upwards' is more advanced in continental Western Europe, and in countries ruled by social democratic governments which are more committed to principles of international co-operation.

Decentralization

This involves shifting governmental powers and responsibilities from a single centre to multiple smaller units: territorial (federal, local, municipal, etc.) or to specialized functional bodies. A 'horizontal' decentralization involves shifts of power away from the central state executive towards some specialized and relatively autonomous quasi- and nongovernmental bodies, including trade unions, specialized agencies and public corporations. The growth of such increasingly autonomous bodies, as well as semi-autonomous quasi-governmental organizations, has been well documented in the 1970s and 1980s. The reforms in Britain involved setting up semi-autonomous agencies to take over most functions of centralized Civil Service departments. By the end of 1990, 34 such agencies had been created, and a further 28 departments were candidates for agency status. The reforms foreshadowed by the 'Next Step' initiatives detached over half a million civil servants into free-standing executive agencies.[24]

Vertical decentralization involves the redistribution of power and responsibility downwards to the lower territorial levels, localities and self-governing bodies. It takes the form of 'devolution proper', a process of orderly institutional redistribution, as well as less orderly and semi-institutional appropriations in the form of various civil initiatives and social movements. The autonomization of regions in Spain and the autonomization of municipalities in Portugal are the best examples of the territorial devolution from above but these are also occurring, though in a less conspicuous way, in France and Italy.[25]

Devolution is not limited to territorial units. A form of devolution of a partly vertical and partly horizontal nature has been diagnosed within the trade unions. Baglioni (1990) discerned three interrelated current processes in European industrial relations: declining union legitimacy and membership; decentralization of union structure with a shift towards functionally specialized unions; and decentralization of collective bargaining with a shift to the local (company) level bargaining and deals. This rejection of the peak union organizations and national compromises has often been associated with toughening of the legal restrictions of union action (UK) and increasing financial responsibilities and stakes of the unions (Scandinavia). Generally the changes mark the end of incorporation period, the disappearance of national co-ordination and a decline in industry-wide collective bargaining.

The horizontal shift of powers and responsibilities changes the corporatist configuration by making it more pluralistic, fragmented and polycentric. 'New corporatism' is a label often applied to this new pattern based on partnership and loose co-ordination rather than centralistic domination. The decentralization of trade unions, the growing independence of business corporations, and the multiplication of semi-autonomous quangos mark the weakening of the old, centralistic corporatism. By loosening central controls and shedding troublesome responsibilities the state sacrifices its ability to preserve corporatist consensus and maintain corporatist deals. This is a self-defeating strategy because the loosening of corporatist settlements undermines the central rationale for corporatist deals and this results, in turn, in a further autonomization of new arenas of politics. The new corporatism means collapsing corporatism and disetatization.

Civic Initiatives and Social Movements

These prompt vertical redistribution of powers and responsibilities, and are often analysed as a process of revival of civil society. Unlike horizontal decentralization, which is usually instituted from above, vertical decentralization is usually the outcome of uncontrolled and anti-corporatist pressures from below. This is the core element of European 'new politics'. The renaissance of grass-roots civic initiatives, self-organized actions and self-governing bodies, and, above all, the rise of new social movements which channel and partly unify these diverse pressures mark another challenge to corporatist settlements.

This challenge from below, discussed in detail in Chapter 5, has increased in recent years. 'Citizen politics' involves an increase in direct political involvement, a rapid growth of political participation, and rising demands for political representation from various politically peripheralized categories. All these grass-roots initiatives, amplified by mass media coverage, signal the decline of corporatist politics and seriously challenge the old political idiom. Not all these pressures, it must be stressed, are unconventional and antisystemic. Many of them are channelled through conventional parties in the form of organized demands, lobbying, petitioning, etc. The success of such civic initiatives, especially in the areas of restricting government secrecy, curbing surveillance and widening freedom of information, has been mainly due to its accommodation within conventional politics. All these activities, however, limit the autonomy of the state and restrict its regulative capacity, and these restrictions run against the functional aspirations of the corporatist state.

Privatization, Marketization and Deregulation

These constitute the most radical challenge to corporatist etatism. Selling nationalized property, adopting market-oriented criteria of operation, and withdrawing centralized administrative regulations, which have restricted the operation of many government-controlled agencies, become the pillars of a new political orthodoxy. This is synonymous with a change in the general socio-economic idiom: from the 'visible hand' of politics to the 'invisible hand' of the market; from administrative-political redistribution to market-regulated provision; from authoritative commands to less obtrusive control; from centralized regulation to polycentric and consumer-oriented competition; from entitlements to provisions.

This idiomatic shift has many aspects. The privatization of state-owned corporations is perhaps the most central and spectacular of all. What makes it spectacular is its almost universal acceptance by governments and parties, regardless of ideological shade. The privatization principle has been embraced by the British Conservatives as well as the Australian and New Zealand Laborites; it has been followed in over 100 countries, most vigorously in those with a traditionally strong public sector.

Privatization and marketization are most pronounced in Britain, but they have also affected Germany, Austria and the Scandinavian countries.[26] However, the British developments are particularly striking. In the last decade over 40 per cent of the state sector has been transformed into private enterprise; more than one million public housing tenants have become homeowners; the proportion of share owners grew from 6 per cent to over 22 per cent; more than 600,000 government employees have been transferred to the private sector. West European governments, including

Germany (especially after reunification), Austria and Scandinavia, show a similar trend. The privatization drive also becomes the key element of the Republican administrations in the USA.[27] Even more spectacular is the privatization drive in Eastern Europe where the postcommunist governments plan to privatize between 50 and 80 per cent of state-owned enterprises. With privatization goes a relaxation or removal of state control over production, prices, wages and salaries.

Privatization of state-owned enterprises is only one of the whole gamut of disetatizing measures. Others include selling public housing, extending private initiatives in schooling, reducing the level of state-controlled health care, private contracting of services, and various cost-recovery schemes. An increasing proportion of previously state-delivered services are provided by private firms and associations, as well as public–private partnerships. Even when delivery and control is still in the non-private hands of co-operatives, trusts, nonprofit organizations, and voluntary and charitable bodies, they are, nevertheless, removed from the control of centralized state bureaucracies. This is associated with the growing scope of management reforms, which aim to achieve greater market efficiency by increasing the representativeness and accountability of these bodies to their publics. In this way marketization, understood as a general shift from direct delivery by government to the use of regulatory environments, becomes an aspect of the overall decentralization.

Privatization also means a reduction in state-provided welfare and an overall shift from the 'welfare philosophy' to 'workfare principle'. Nationalized health services are increasingly supplemented by those financed by private insurance; state pensions are managed by private or mixed superannuation funds; community controlled welfare replaces state controlled services; uniform services give way to specialized and 'needs tailored' ones controlled by specialized agencies. All of this marks the overall shift to what Bennett (1990:12) labels a 'post-welfare paradigm'.

Finally, the logic of this disetatization involves reduction in state protectionism, one of the central pillars of the post-war corporatist deals. Despite some political setbacks, most notably in the areas of agriculture, state protectionism is decreasing. Abolishing subsidies and reduction of tariffs are on the agendas of all governments, regardless of their partisan colouring.

This shift carries high social costs and associated political risks. The withdrawal of the state from economic regulation and the trimming of welfare are bound to increase both inequality and 'market dysfunctions'. But the advantages it promises of reducing costs, easing inflationary pressures, cutting state deficits, and curbing bureaucratic inefficiency are politically irresistible. Calls for a minimal state and cuts in bureaucracy bring together traditional conservatives, liberally minded people, and also some democratic socialists. For the conservatives and liberals, it means the affirmation of freedom of choice; for socialists, it means bringing power closer to the people. Both seem to agree that decentralized structures are the best medium for translating increasingly diverse interests into effective pressures and actions.

Globalization

Globalization has usually been analysed with reference to economic integration, the international division of labour and transnational corporations. Since the 1950s there has been a shift in attention so that economic studies have been supplemented by analyses of the growing international nonstate regulative agencies.

> Among the changes of the last two or three decades [writes Luard] perhaps the most striking is the rapid increase in interdependence among nations. The world energy crisis, the world food shortage, the population explosion, the problem of hijacking, the traffic in drugs, the protection of the world's environment, the use of deep sea resources, commodity prices, the policing of the frequency spectrum, the regulation of multinational corporations – these are only a few among the many problems which can only be dealt with effectively on an international basis. . . . This has brought a considerable transformation to international politics. Many important agreements today are not bilateral treaties, as in earlier times, but those which are reached, almost unnoticed, behind the scenes at the International Energy Agency, the International Monetary Fund or elsewhere in a growing network of world agencies. This is the quiet revolution of our generation. (1977: i)

The agents of this quiet revolution are not state agencies. In fact nation-states seem to be the principal losers as far as power distribution is concerned. Their power is shifting to a variety of such extra- and supra-state actors as UN bodies, political-military blocs (NATO), regulative agencies, supra-national integrative organizations (EC), cartels (OPEC), and even transnational social movements (Greenpeace). International security networks impose restrictions on state autonomy which result in what has been described as 'qualified sovereignty' in the areas of defence, arms production and foreign policy. Similar restrictions are imposed in the areas of transport, communication and environmental protection. An increasing number of UN sponsored initiatives impinge upon vast areas of state responsibility and authority. The scope of these activities is hard to quantify. Even harder is to assess the shift of power this proliferation causes. One indicator of the scope of the shift is the number of agencies and the amount of resources they consume. Between 1950 and the late 1980s the number of intergovernment organizations increased 3.5 times to about 400; the number of international nongovernment organizations grew 6 times to about 5000. UN agencies alone grew from about five in the late 1940s to fifteen in the late 1980s. The number of employees has increased to over 50,000. The annual budgets of specialized agencies exceed $1 billion. More importantly, the range of problems tackled by the UN agencies has also grown and they have started to encompass some quasi-judicial and quasi-military functions (for example, International Law Commission, International Court of Justice).[28] These functions, as the response to the Iraqi invasion of Kuwait shows, cannot be dismissed as merely symbolic.

Some qualifications need to be made. By accepting international regulations, states do not relinquish their powers but rather limit and circumscribe them. All regulations are still policed by states and all measures are mediated by state bodies. Without such mediation and voluntary compliance international regulations would be little more than symbolic. But they do limit the scope and the depth of state autonomy both directly, by imposing codes, standards and regulations, and indirectly, by publicizing violations and noncompliance, and by stimulating the formation of international public opinion. International actions attract public attention, raise concern and influence strategic state actors.

There is a subtle trade-off involved in these power shifts. States and their corporate executives do not readily surrender their authority. What they gain in exchange for restricting their power is relief from pressures. This brings us back to the problems of overloads. Because pressures and demands are so heavily concentrated in 'visible governments', in the 'visible hand' of the interventionist state, and because they involve areas where the administrative interventions have become either ineffectual or have backfired, the redistribution, especially 'upwards', proves to be an effective solution. It is not only the powers, but also the responsibilities of the state that are shifted 'upwards'.

Conclusion: Toward the Minimal State

In the process of modernization the state became the main container of power, albeit power which was less coercive, more rational, more benign and more paternalistic or perhaps maternalistic than its absolutist predecessors, but which was also increasingly centralized and pervasive. The current devolution reverses these centralizing and interventionist trends and raises the question of the direction of future developments.

The power of the state rests on legal and military control over territory. This territorial sovereignty, combined with the legitimate use of coercion, is being undermined by current developments. The notion of territorial sovereignty has been undermined by the globalization and internationalization of economy and polity. The defensive role of the state, still crucial in self-legitimizing claims, is also undermined by the development of nuclear weapons, which renders confrontations highly costly, by anti-terrorist measures and, generally, by the increasing ability of small peripheral states and nonstate actors to disrupt the power bloc arrangements.

More importantly the key area of state responsibility, the institution of citizenship, has been undergoing subtle but important change. One of the central processes of modernization has been the progressive social extension of citizenship and the widening of citizenship rights. Civil revolutions, followed by political and social revolutions, have made the state the principal creator and guardian of citizenship rights to the extent that these rights presuppose the state. Their scope has been proportional to state power and resources, and their maintenance has reflected the state's willingness and ability to uphold them. This central position of the state as the guarantor of civil rights is starting to wane. The key rights associated with citizenship, especially civil and political rights, are gradually becoming detached from state guardianship. Many are being redefined as 'universal rights', 'human rights' or 'individual rights', and their guardianship is increasingly located above and beyond the state, either in supra-state agencies (for example, the UN Commission for Human Rights) or in the general notion of 'human status' incorporated into international laws and conventions. Moreover, the publicity given to violations of these rights by the states changes public perceptions of the relationship between civil rights and the state. An increasing number of people believe that rights have to be safeguarded against the state. This growing realization that the state cannot make people free, safe or equal just as it cannot make people beautiful or happy, is perhaps the best symptom of the exhaustion of the etatist-corporatist project.

Few people would lament the dismantling of corporatist deals. The dominant mood in Eastern and Western Europe seems to be strongly anti-etatist. But this mood, most vigorous among the young and educated sections of the 'service classes', is likely to be moderated. The shrinking state creates power vacuums which may be filled by many different institutions, from private corporations to civic initiatives. The outcome of the devolution may be either democratization or new forms of domination by forces less controllable than the liberal-democratic state.[29]

Whatever the outcome of these processes, the general direction of change can be charted with moderate accuracy. It involves a general shift away from corporatist centralism and towards a more decentralized and fragmented minimal state. More specifically, the vector of change involves shifts from centralized to decentralized state apparatuses, and from authoritative to manipulative forms of control.[30] This may prove to be the best temporary survival strategy for the state. The state may salvage some of its integrity by restricting its functions, moderating its aspirations and opening its political realm to new social forces and demands. But the Left's expectations of rebuilding an interventionist edifice are as unrealistic as are Conservative hopes for a return of the authoritative Prince. Both appear to belong to the past.

All these processes are difficult to square with popular scenarios of change. Modernization and postindustrial theories see the role of the state as increasing, especially in the areas of social and economic regulation. Neither is the current change consistent with either pessimistic (corporatist state capitalism) and optimistic ('withering away') scenarios constructed by Marxist thinkers. The current process of devolution seems to follow the logic of ironic reversals charted in Chapter 1: differentiation and centralization give way to fragmentation of domains, each with fuzzy boundaries and unspecific functions. What look like commodification processes – marketization, privatization and deregulation – in fact blur the very distinction between the commodity and noncommodity form, a process analogous to the 'blurring' in contemporary service economies facing the problems posed by intellectual property and copyrights of software. The very notion of 'the state' as a separate and autonomous institutional entity, intimately linked with the notion of 'politics' and 'public sphere' and clearly separated from the domains of economy, societal community and culture, is increasingly problematic. It is as problematic as the other elements of the modern vocabulary: social class, power politics, science and bureaucracy.

Notes

1. The term is used in a generic sense to embrace all aspects of shifts in state power and responsibility, territorial and functional decentralization, as well as privatization, marketization, deregulation and internationalization.

2. See, for example, Miliband (1973), Poulantzas (1978), Evans et al. (1985), Held (1989), McEachern (1990).

3. Reducing the scope of state power and the depth of state intervention.

4. The focus of this chapter will be on the ascendancy and the symptoms of a subsequent demise of the corporate state. The following chapters analyse in more detail the decomposition of the major industrial classes and the rise of 'new politics'. See the section below for a discussion of the 'North American exceptionality'.

5. See Poggi (1978, 1990) for an account of the state formation in Europe and the symbiosis of the state and modern bureaucracy.

6. Weber underestimated the likelihood of resistance to the modern trends. He saw centralization of authority as inescapable, and he largely ignored the dialectical link between growing formalism and substantive longings. He saw 'substantive breaches' as mere interludes in the irresistible progress of rationalization. In the long run, however, such breaches, marked by charismatic movements both religious and secular, could not compete with the bureaucratic machines. They were either routinized into bureaucracies or regressed into traditionalism.

7. See Schmitter (1974), Lehmbruch (1977), Schmitter and Lehmbruch (1979), Lehmbruch and Schmitter (1982).

8. Quoted in Dahrendorf (1988: 50). For a discussion of the impact of the wars on the formation of 'corporate bias' see Middlemas (1979) and Schmitter and Lehmbruch (1979).

9. This was most conspicuous in the liberal form of corporatism, though both the communist and fascist states claimed to represent workers. The former subordinated workers' claims to 'objective class interests'; the latter restricted them in terms of 'national interests'.

10. Lehmbruch makes an analogous distinction between 'authoritarian' and 'liberal' corporatism. For similar distinctions between 'state' and 'societal' corporatism, see Schmitter (1974). Different levels of corporatism (macro, meso and micro) are discussed by Cawson (1986).

11. For a review of European fascism, see Woolf (1968). The dramatic collapse of the fascist project in Europe did not eliminate fascist corporatism. Quasi-fascist corporatist regimes have been formed in South America (e.g. Argentina under Peron) and the Middle East (e.g. Iraq under Saddam Hussein).

12. See Salisbury (1979) and Wilson (1982).

13. For a review of East European variations on fascism see Woolf (1968) and Mosse

(1979). The Central European regimes were arguably less violent and authoritarian than the German Nazi version. It also has to be stressed that the communist movement in Yugoslavia was highly effective, and the resulting communist regime there was more indigenous than in other East European countries.

14. For more details see Pakulski (1986).

15. See O'Connor (1973), Wilensky (1981), Crouch (1977, 1983), Beer (1982), Habermas (1973), Birch (1984).

16. See Dalton et al. (1984a, 1984b), Inglehart (1977), Cotgrove (1982), and Dalton (1988).

17. For a good account of these new divisions and conflicts see Dahrendorf (1988).

18. See Crozier et al. (1975) and S. Berger (1979).

19. See the Chapter 5 below for an argument about the idiom of this 'new politics' and difficulties with incorporation. New values and orientations are discussed by Inglehart (1977, 1990), Veen (1989) and Dalton (1988).

20. See Hadley and Hatch (1981), Jasnay (1985).

21. See in particular Janicke (1990) and Poggi (1990).

22. See, for example, Wallerstein (1974), Amin (1976) and Frank (1975).

23. Forms of power distribution are discussed by Cornford (1975: 7–9) and Bennett (1990: 11–12). Bennett (1989, 1990) treats privatization and marketization as a form of radical decentralization in which power and responsibilities are shifted to economically enfranchised consumers.

24. See *Progress in the Next Step Initiatives*, HMSO, November 1990.

25. The decentralization of state authority has been occurring concurrently with similar changes in the economy. It is also motivated by similar concerns and takes similar forms. Low effectiveness of centralized administration, especially in responding to local demands and providing customized services, combined with the escalation of costs and political pork-barrelling, is one factor prompting decentralization. Declining support, and danger of delegitimation, is another. By shifting powers, the state sheds responsibilities, thus easing the overload and avoiding the blame for failures.

26. For a general review of decentralization in Western Europe and the US see the volumes edited by Bennett (1990) and Cornford (1975).

27. The radical programme of reform adopted at the end of 1990 by the Soviet government has the same aims of privatization and reduction of state control. Reforms in China, although slowed down after the Tienanmen massacre, tend in a similar direction. For a review of this general decentralization and disetatization drive, see Bennett (1989, 1990), Naisbitt and Aburdene (1990).

28. For a general review of these international institutions and their functions see Luard (1977, 1990a, 1990b).

29. Those enthusiastically embracing the current devolution often ignore the very restricted social basis of 'citizen politics' and undemocratic practices inherent in movement action. The devolution of the state may not necessarily bring the democratic and emancipatory outcomes many of its advocates hope for.

30. These changes are likely to be most advanced in Western Europe. Despite some spectacular reforms by the Republican administrations in the USA, the process of devolution there looks less convincing, partly because etatization and corporatist centralization had been less advanced there in the first place. In Eastern Europe the process of devolution, although currently strong and vigorous, is likely to encounter serious obstacles. Economic difficulties combined with strong residues of protest movements there may result in political instability and the formation of quasi-corporatist 'governments of national unity'. This is not likely to arrest the processes of privatization and marketization, but is bound to increase pressures for a centralized and authoritative government, especially during socio-economic transition.

4

Simulated inequality

Two arenas have now been identified in which dedifferentiating and disorganizing trends may be witnessed. In the arena of culture, commodification achieves universal penetration, authoritative cultural traditions are attenuated, and cultural fragments tend increasingly to transgress the boundaries between cultural realms and even the boundary between culture and society. Within this transformation culture becomes more effective and begins to undermine such social structural arrangements as the state. The state – understood as that elaborate, interventionary and progressive and thus modern social unit, the welfare state – is a defining characteristic of twentieth-century organized capitalism: it is the state which performs many of the organizing tasks. Within contemporary developments the state is beginning to unravel. It is hyperdifferentiating as one looks downward to local initiatives and thus dedifferentiating as one looks up to the national and international levels.

Within its modern organizing function the state plays a central role in managing the distribution of rewards in society. The welfare state, in particular, seeks to manage such arenas of social reproduction as health, welfare, industrial relations, education, the mass media and the administration of justice with a view to the maintenance of capitalist production. However, as Offe and Ronge (1984), for example, point out, a contradictory process in fact occurs in which classical patterns of liberal capitalism are disrupted. These classical patterns focus on private as opposed to state property, on market forces rather than centralized command, and on contract as against status. As liberal capitalism becomes transformed into organized capitalism so the unequal divisions it establishes between classes and genders also tend to become obscured. Let us begin this analysis by outlining these divisions and their foundations.

Liberal capitalist society, as described in the opening thematic chapter, focusses on economic processes. This emphasis is greater than the mere control and transformation of the physical environment which is characteristic of human societies in general. Rather modern societies are characterized by the application of machine technology and instrumental rationality to the extraction of raw materials and to the elaborate reconstruction of them so that value or utility is added to them. Liberal capitalism is therefore oriented to growth in both the value and the quantity of goods produced. This means that the material condition of at least some if not all of its members is improved. An impressive characteristic of modernity is therefore an improving level of material comfort in the domestic arena.

These orientations are possible because modern society is marked by the institutionalization of the capitalist mode of production. Minimally this means that ownership of plant, equipment and technology is concentrated in the hands of relatively few people, capitalists, while most of the other members of society, workers, contribute their labour power to the production process. Certainly in the terms of Marxist theories of this relationship and possibly in other theories, capitalists exploit the labour contributions of workers. Capitalists do this by paying workers only what they need to support themselves and their families, and take the rest for their personal benefit in the form of profit. Whichever theory of capitalism one might choose, the capitalist mode of production in this pure and liberal form provides for radical differences in rewards and in power between capitalists and workers. Liberal capitalist societies are often marked by pronounced and bitter industrial and political struggles between the classes about the distribution of power and rewards.

The social categories and forms of inequality characteristic of capitalist modernity are defined then by processes entailed by the capitalist mode of production. Three central processes may be identified: production, accumulation, and social reproduction. First, the production system of modernity makes extensive use of machines driven by inanimate sources of energy. Typically the greater the use of machines the lower the amount and the lower the skill level of the labour that needs to be employed. So the greater the use of machines the lower is the overall cost of production and the greater are the returns to the capitalist. Second, because capitalism is a highly effective and productive economic system it allows for the generation of surplus economic value, that is for the production of commodities in excess of the minimum requirements for subsistence of the workforce. Wherever there is surplus there is typically a struggle over its distribution but in capitalism there is the additional possibility for given individuals to accumulate surplus and thus to increase their own power and material rewards. Last, where there is an unequal distribution of power and rewards in society which might be recognized by participants as illegitimate, commitment as well as know-how must constantly be regenerated. Workers fatigued by arduous labour need recreation, intimate sources of emotional gratification and provision for their physical well-being. Specific processes of social reproduction are required to meet these needs.

Each of these processes defines a social category. Production defines the (male) worker. Given the use of high-cost, technologically advanced machines, capitalist production requires the concentration of workers in time and space – that is workers are concentrated together in factories and for specific, contractually agreed periods of time. The use of machines ensures that their skills are low and that their position in the market for their labour is controlled by buyers. Moreover the machines effectively control the process of production in terms of both the pace of work and the amount of skill required. Workers engaged in factory production typically experience low levels of self-control and receive small reward. Typically a large proportion of the members of society share this similar disadvantaged condition in the collective circumstances of the factory and its attached community. So those who labour in modern society are a working class defined by the production process.

Accumulation defines the (male) capitalist. The returns which accrue to the acts of co-ordinating workers and applying technology are under the control of property-owning individuals who pay wages and technology rents. Their capacity to appropriate surplus depends on the higher levels of productivity that result from the application of technology and of rational modes of organization (and not, we hasten to say, from any relationship between labour value and exchange value as specified by Marx). However, the general tendency is for a process of capital accumulation or valorization. This is to say that those who own productive property are likely to increase their level of ownership by the reinvestment of surplus. A second significant social category of modernity is therefore a capitalist or bourgeois class.

Reproduction defines the unequal position of women. Concentration of production in time and space separates primarily economic activity from primarily domestic activity and thus provides an arrangement in which women are located as a separate social category. If we assume patriarchal structures to be universal, the particular form they take under capitalist modernity is one in which women become responsible for the reproduction of labour power. This involves not only the biological reproduction of workers and capitalists but also the care and nurturing of infants, primary socialization, as well as the emotional and social support and domestic care of male workers and capitalists. Men exclude women from public production and from political arenas.

The transition from liberal capitalism to organized capitalism encompasses four related processes which transform this simple and well-defined pattern of social categories, blurring the boundaries between them and interposing new ones in their interstices. These processes are: the emergence of corporate capitalism; the growth of the state; credentialization; and the reorganization of patriarchy.

The source for the emergence of corporate capitalism is price competition in the market for commodities counterposed by the threat of rising technology rents and labour costs. The larger the corporation the greater its capacity to effect economies of scale and to compete in the commodities market. Smaller enterprises can be driven out of the market or absorbed. As corporations become oligopolistic or monopolistic prices can then be raised to maximize returns but they can temporarily be lowered at any time at which a new competitive threat occurs. In order to raise the necessary amount of capital, ownership of such corporations needed to be divided into multiple shareholdings. So everyday control of them passed into the hands of salaried managers, directors and chief executive officers. Baran and Sweezy (1966: 15–16) describe management as a self-perpetuating group which establishes corporate career structures to promote and recruit new members independently of the influence of the legal owners. As they developed, such corporations accomplished financial independence by achieving such levels of market dominance that capital could be accumulated internally in very large amounts. No longer were they forced to rely on capital markets or banks and other financial institutions.

The consequences of these developments for particular class formations are discussed in detail below. They may generally be characterized as being focussed on the boundary between capital and labour. Whereas previously the ruling class could unambiguously be described as those owning the means of production, management has taken on some of the characteristics of labour in that its rewards too come on a contractual and waged basis. More importantly corporate capitalism implies increases in the scale and internal differentiation of production organizations which generate imperatives for co-ordination and, by extension, control. A key characteristic of corporations is their hierarchical and bureaucratic pattern of organization. Such a hierarchy mediates the relationship between capital and labour, which becomes an incremental chain of surveillance rather than a sharp division of power. As control of the technical division of labour is delegated down this hierarchy a stable basis emerges for the development of a managerial middle class interposed between capital and labour.

There are also consequences for the working class. Corporate capitalism implies a drive in the direction of technological rationalization as a way of reducing costs and remaining competitive. Highly technologized production offers increased possibilities for the control of labour in the workplace by means of deskilling and machine control and thus its alienation (see Chapter 6). Simultaneously the capacity for instrumental resistance on the part of workers is increased because under a capital-intensive regime the costs to a corporation of the withdrawal of labour are very high. The working class therefore turns pragmatically away from struggling over issues of control, which it cannot reasonably hope to affect, to issues of instrumental rewards. It is moderately successful in securing these through the agency of labour unions and political parties.

A second process which coincides with the emergence of organized capitalism is the growth and elaboration of the state. Following Offe (1984: 125) we can say that there are three ways in which the state impacts on economic behaviour and thereby on patterns of social inequality. First there are processes of state regulation, which establish rules of market competition and protect commodity producers from competitive threats. Second, there are patterns of state intervention, in which the state establishes an organizational infrastructure within which labour-power can be reproduced (education, health, welfare, etc.). Third, the state sponsors corporatist arrangements between labour and unions which minimize class conflict and modify reward distributions.

In so doing the state establishes new socio-economic categories. Three principal categories may be identified. The first consists of those who control state property (what might be called the state elite) which, because of its control, is able to provide itself with privilege and even to reproduce privilege across generations. The second is the army of managers and administrators in the middle levels, the public or civil servants who are able to insulate themselves from reward deprivation in the labour market by means of their access to state power. Last there is a larger army of state dependants which emerges as a by-product of interventionary activities of social reproduction.

An important aspect of the processes that transform economic production and the state is a progressive differentiation of mental from manual labour, between conceptualizing, controlling and administering on one hand and physical performance on the other. The arenas of mental labour therefore become highly concentrated and these labour market niches become susceptible to capture by the collective action of their participants. The object of capture is to monopolize skills and rights to practise with a view to forcing up the price of labour. These closure processes, as they are known, originally enter modern social configurations as the residuum of medieval guilds in the form of craft occupations. But their most marked development occurs with the legal establishment of professions and the progressive professionalization of other middle-level occupations, including administration and management. The particular mechanism by which closure is accomplished is the use of educational credentials. Examinations become a gate-keeping mechanism which protects markets for particular types of skilled labour. So credentialism also makes a contribution to the decomposition of the capitalist–worker dichotomy.

These changes are linked to the reorganization of a second and at least equally important dichotomous pattern of inequality, that between the genders. In the early phases of industrialization the gender division of labour presented a complex pattern. Domestic outwork systems often ensured a fusion of domestic with economic production and that the latter was shared between men and women; migrant, industrially labouring men might leave women behind to do agricultural labour; and in some industrial settings – coal mining and textile manufacture leap to mind – women were the preferred labourers. However, by the establishment of trade unions men were progressively able to exclude women from nondomestic production. An institutionalized gender division of labour of this sort also suited employers because it meant that women could concentrate on the reproduction of male labour power by bearing and raising children and by providing emotional, sexual and care and comfort services to male workers. Such activities could not be provided where women were also full-time paid workers (see Brenner and Ramos 1984).

An aspect of the transformation to organized capitalism was a reorganization of this pattern of masculine domination into a form discussed below as 'extended viriarchy' (Waters 1989b). The key sources of the transformation are the development of 'new middle class' occupations which required relatively high levels of educational preparation and extensions of political and social citizenship rights. Each of these demanded explicit processes of social reproduction that the family was typically held to be inadequate to provide. So part of the elaboration of the state was the development of health, education and welfare provision, which removed reproduction activities from the family or at least regulated them. A transfer of female labour from the domestic to the state arena was thus made possible. Under organized capitalism women increasingly work in paid occupations and, as we discuss below, the form of their subordination changes.

As we have said, the above description of three main social categories of power and rewards, male capitalists, male workers and women, is characteristic of the early and mature stages of modernity, say up to the First World War. The following sections describe the progressive decomposition of these social categories from the middle of the twentieth century onwards, within the period of organized capitalism, and their eventual decay under conditions of postmodernization. We subsequently argue that this decay is constituted as a submersion of the divisions of class and gender into more fluid cultural patterns of social differentiation in which social membership derives not from underlying material determinants or even from socially constructed groups but rather from symbolically specified associations which are simulated within mass information media.

The Service Sector and the Deconstruction of Capital

By the middle of the twentieth century it had become apparent that the Marxist prediction of class relations as a struggle about ownership of the means of production could find little empirical support. This realization was greatest in the heartland of western capitalism, the USA. Here Berle and Means (1967) showed that American capitalism was a deconcentrated structure of multiple shareholding distributed relatively widely across the population. Marx had anticipated this, indicating that the joint stock company was in some respects a forerunner of socialism, but he failed to anticipate one of its critical consequences. If there was no *grand bourgeoisie* then who was to perform the role of the capitalist? The answer was provided by the American Marxist, Burnham, who proclaimed the onset of a 'managerial revolution' (1941). The functions of capital, 'services' as they have come to be known, would increasingly be performed by managers, that is by salaried employees receiving relatively high returns for their labour in exchange for the self-directed pursuit of capitalist objectives. The managerial class comprised both administrative and technical expertise and transected the boundary between privately owned economic organizations and public employment.[1]

Burnham showed remarkable prescience. The hallmark of organized capitalism has been the growth of service sector employment performing the functions of capital: reproduction, that of ensuring a continuous and adequate supply of labour-power and of ensuring that workers accept the normality of the current social relations of production; control, ensuring that workers do the jobs demanded of them by capitalists; and conceptualization, the formulation of objectives and the organization of activities so as to achieve them (Abercrombie and Urry 1983: 123; Lash and Urry 1987: 162). As a consequence there has been considerable theoretical debate about the location of managerial, administrative and professional employees in the class structure. The standard Marxist account of polarization has been advanced most forcefully by Braverman (1974) but the resistance of service employees to deskilling has given rise to a series of other accounts of their class location. Poulantzas (1982), for example, has them as a 'new petty bourgeoisie' outside the capitalist mode of production; Mallet (1975) sees them as a proletarian vanguard, a 'new working class'; Wright (1978) puts them in the contradictory class location of 'semi-autonomous employees'; the Ehrenreichs (1979) argue that they are an entirely new 'professional-managerial class' interposed between labour and capital; and in similar vein Johnson (1977) views them simply as a 'new middle class'.

Each of these formulations is constructed with the explicit intention of rescuing Marxist accounts of the class structure from the failure of their prediction of polarization. Some neo-Weberian sociologists have gone further in arguing not only that service workers take over the functions of capital but indeed that they replace the capitalist class. They take their guidance from the Austro-Marxist, Renner, who first proposed the concept of a 'service class' (1978). The service class, he argues, is distinguishable from the working class because rather than receiving wages in return for a commitment of labour-power to commodity production, service workers receive salaries or commissions which are fractions of profits. There are three basic components of the service class: managers, social service workers and public service officials. The service class must therefore be distinguished from two other categories, service workers and white-collar workers. The category of service workers includes such manual service occupations as cleaner, driver, postal worker and cook, which are prevalent in all stages of capitalism and which are clearly working class; and white-collar workers include such routine occupations as clerk and secretary, which are also clearly wage-based and disadvantaged.

However, while it is clear that Renner sees the service class as subordinate to a continuing capitalist class he is somewhat equivocal about its relationship to the working class. At one point it is said to be 'alongside' the working class (1978: 250) but at another to be close enough to the rising working class that it tends to merge with that class at the boundary (1978: 251). This is at least partly because the working class has been transformed so that workers have a legal status similar to that of officials: 'the working class as it appears in Marx's *Capital* no longer exists' (Renner 1978: 252).

The service class as constructed by functionalist and neo-Weberian sociologists (Abercrombie and Urry 1983; Bell 1973; Goldthorpe 1980,

1982; Lash and Urry 1987) takes up an altogether different position in the class structure.[2] Whereas in Renner the service class interposes between capital and labour here the service class is argued actually to displace the capitalist ownership class. The service class becomes the ruling class. The basis for such arguments is a change in the locus of power in society from legal ownership of physical and financial property to control of knowledge. Property is useless as a form of power without the capacity to put it into operation, that is to use it for purposes of accumulation. The capacity to do so essentially consists in skills and information. Proponents of the service class see its pre-eminence as the consequence of a victory in a class struggle fought out inside large-scale organizations in which service workers have taken over 'possession' of these organizations, along with their property assets, by virtue of superior information control and skills. Rather than being concentrated, capital is dispersed between shareholders. Large-scale capitalist 'entrepreneurs' are viewed as elements of the service class because they only retain large capital holdings by virtue of entrepreneurial skills.

If we were to consider only the numerical growth of the service class this argument could indeed seem compelling. Bell estimates the proportion of professional, technical and administrative workers in the American work-force to be 26.3 per cent in 1980, up from 21.9 per cent in 1900 (1973: 134–5); Goldthorpe gives the proportions of adult male workers who are members of the service class at 31 per cent for England in 1972, 31 per cent for France in 1970, and 24 per cent for Sweden in 1974 (1982: 173). So the class structure is undoubtedly changing, but there is a critical question about the direction of change. Are we witnessing the emergence of a new ruling class, that is a class with enough power to exploit the labour of others and to accumulate the surplus of that labour for its own benefit; is the service class a class merely by virtue of the different conditions of work that apply to its members and the different form of the market in which they sell their labour; or are we seeing a process in which the emergence of the service sector does not merely deconstruct the traditional industrial capitalist class but deconstructs the class system itself by dismantling the boundaries between classes? We tend to the view that the process under inspection is the most radical of these possibilities. As Lash and Urry show, the service class emerged in the USA at the end of the nineteenth century and it has grown continuously in all industrial societies since then. The service class is characteristic of organized modernity – the process of postmodernization is the subsumption of the service class within more inclusive patterns of social membership.

We now seek to support this argument both theoretically and empiri-cally. Let us begin by examining the location of the service class in terms of six analytic dimensions by which classes have typically been differentiated from one another:

1 *Situation in the labour market* Professionals and managers typically have a relatively high level of control over who is to enter the occupation. Entry increasingly occurs on the basis of credentials, and credentializing is frequently carried out by members of the profession itself. Labour supply is controlled by an increasing upgrading of training and qualification requirements.

2 *Autonomy* Service class workers are frequently located either towards the apex of organizational hierarchies or in specialized niches, situations in which they are able to exercise a relatively high level of discretion in relation to the establishment of work practices and the sequencing of tasks. However, right of disposal of product does not lie in the hands of the worker. Workers are precisely at the service of other sectors of an organization and thus subject to overall policy objectives.

3 *Patterns of exploitation* In traditional Marxist terms because service workers are not commodity producers they are not able to be exploited by means of the expropriation of surplus value. However, we can take the wider view that service workers contribute indirectly to the production of surplus value by performing the functions of capital. Within this wider formulation, exploitation can be understood to be significantly resisted because the skills and knowledge of the service class are in short supply, that is because of their superior market situation.

4 *Direction of the labour of others* It is a primary function of the service class to control the labour of other workers. This is especially and obviously true of executive managerial and administrative workers but it is also true of middle managers and professional specialists. These personnel are frequently able to direct the activities of support staff including laboratory technicians, research assistants, administrative assistants and secretaries.

5 *Capital accumulation* Extreme levels of capital accumulation of the kind that characterizes the capitalist class is impossible for the service class. This is because the primary bases for the position of the service class are knowledge and skill and these can be neither monopolized nor invested in the way that physical capital can. Yet a measure of capital accumulation is possible in the form of career development and associated increases in organizational control. The labour of support staff can to some extent be appropriated to further one's own career. The more advanced one's career becomes the greater the extent to which control of organizational assets can be used to yield material rewards and comforts.

6 *Control of the means of production* Members of the service class do not actually own the means of production in a narrow legal sense. But even in contexts where there is no proletarian manual labour force under its direction the service class may be said to possess the means of production in the sense given in Poulantzas (1982), that is it has the capacity to put the means of production into operation. However, this capacity, is not absolute for any member of the service class as it is for individual members of the traditional bourgeoisie. Control of the means of

production is also tightly circumscribed by the extent to which the means of production in a particular context are informational rather than physical in character. Where there is a high informatic content control of the means of production is relatively dispersed among workers.

Let us assume acceptance of the arguments of Burnham, Renner, Bell, Goldthorpe and Abercrombie and Urry that under late capitalism the traditional bourgeois class is being eclipsed by a service class. The above analysis of the structural situation of the service class will lead us to a further conclusion. It suggests that the service class is different, in fundamental respects, from the *grand bourgeoisie*. On each of the dimensions service class employees move away from the bourgeois pole and towards the proletarian pole in the traditional Marxist dichotomy. On several of the dimensions, notably capacity for capital accumulation and ability to expropriate the labour of others, they are rather more like workers than like capitalists. In all, this means that while the service class *dis*places the capitalist class it does not precisely *re*place it. In the most simple of terms, the service class has a different structural location from the capitalist class. But because the capitalist class is indeed displaced (or at least absorbed) we need to speak not merely of the relocation of a ruling class to an interposed or contradictory location but of the reconstruction of the class system as a whole.

We may now examine the form of this reconstruction. The fundamental element of a class system is a pattern of boundaries and boundary maintenance. In the capitalist mode of production as described by Marx the boundary between the classes consists of a continuous struggle between owners and nonowners of the means of production about the expropriation of the products of the labour of nonowners. We argue that in late capitalism dispersion of capital ownership implies a reduction in the capacity for expropriation to a nonfundamental although significant level. The service class cannot appropriate surplus value. Thus differences of interest between superior and subordinate classes shift from control of economic production to control of political authority in organizations more generally. For Bell the new class structure is entirely political:

> First, the major class of the emerging new society is primarily a professional class, based on knowledge rather than on property. But second, the control system is lodged not in a successor-occupational class but in the political order, and the question of who manages the political order is an open one. (1973: 374)

Bell describes a four-element class structure: a professional class comprising four estates, the scientific, the administrative, the technological and the cultural; a technician and semiprofessional class; a clerical and sales class; and a class of craftsmen and semiskilled workers. Even such a committed Marxist scholar as Jessop finds a basis for broad agreement with this view:

> [I]t is essential to focus on the internal organisations of the state apparatus (e.g. bureaucracy, administrative law, financial controls), the complex relations between the state and the forces liable to state intervention, and the complex

relations between the state and non-functionaries involved in policy-making
and/or implementation. If we focus on the relations among political categories it
is possible to establish a 'people–officialdom' axis of determination parallel to
the class axis. (1982: 248)[3]

Under such circumstances the pattern of power exercised by one class
over another may no longer be understood as structurally determined but
must rather be seen as fluid and shifting as different classes and alliances of
class members compete for political and organizational resources. Class
boundaries are no longer determined by structurally given divisions of
interest but by the ability of such groupings to effect closure against
outsiders and thus to maximize the quality of their working conditions and
their capacity to extract rewards from the labour market. So classes are
currently defined by shared work and market situations rather than by a
common relationship to property ownership. The class structures of late
capitalism are altogether more Weberian than Marxist in flavour.

This being the case we should finally ask whether the service class can in
principle be treated as a class even in Weberian terms – the service class is
instrumental in the deconstruction of capital but is it also instrumental in its
own deconstruction and that of class in general? In other words we are
asking whether the so-called service class does constitute a closed set of
homogeneous work and market situations. Clearly the locations it incorporates are highly diverse, including, for example, corporate CEOs and
senior state officials on one hand and laboratory technicians, librarians and
direct supervisors on the other. Although the functions of capital are
subsumed within the service class, this subsumption is by no means
uniform and many occupational locations identified as professional, managerial and administrative receive small material return in the market and
experience high levels of subordination in the workplace. Any attempt to
place a boundary underneath the service class begs the question of whether
its lower members bear a greater resemblance to those at the top of a
working class (say skilled craftsmen) or to other more superior members of
their own class.

We may also address this question in terms of empirical findings on the
extent to which the service class is closed to outsiders. Data from
Australia, France, New Zealand, Sweden, the United Kingdom and the
USA (Erikson et al. 1982; Kerckhoff et al. 1985; Jones and Davis 1988)
indicate that if one divides the workforce into categories with supposed
shared work and market situations, the service class exhibits the highest
level of closure bar farmers. This is to say that men whose fathers are
members of the service class have a greater probability of remaining in that
class than the members of any other class, and that men who enter the
service class at the beginning of their careers have a lower probability of
leaving that class than men who begin their careers in any other class. For
example, about two-thirds of the sons of service class fathers re-enter the
service class (Goldthorpe 1982: 177).

These data are convincing at one level but we remain sceptical about the long term solidity of the service class. There are five reasons for doubt. First, we suspect that the degree of closure effected by the service class is considerably less than that imposed historically by the industrial bourgeoisie – organizational assets and credentials do not match the power of property ownership in excluding outsiders. Second and in confirmation of this point there remains significant minority downward mobility from the service class – about one-third are downwardly mobile – which indicates a substantial lack of closure. Third, closure is being measured at a particular historical moment, that at which the growth of the service class is at its most rapid. With the progressive expansion of positions, downward mobility might normally be expected to be low and to increase as the size of the service sector stabilizes. Fourth, one of the main mechanisms of service class closure is credentials. The supply of credentials is increasing, they are becoming applicable to widening sections of the labour force, and are thus becoming progressively devalued. We may therefore expect their capacity to effect closure to deteriorate. Fifth, almost all of the cited data apply to men only. One of the major characteristics of organized capitalism has been the increasing and disproportionate penetration of what might otherwise be called service class positions by women. If such positions are becoming accessible to a group reckoned previously to be highly disadvantaged then it is difficult to maintain arguments in favour of a high degree of closure in that class.

Perhaps the most convincing of arguments about the fragility of the service class is the one proposed by Lash (1990: 18–25). Here he seeks to explain the emergence of postmodern*ist* culture and the establishment of a new bourgeois identity in terms of their elective affinity for the service class. Because the class has its personal origins in, and indeed shares important class chararcteristics with, the working masses, it seeks to legitimize itself by an act of deligitimation of the the traditional bourgeoisie, that is by elevating elements of popular culture to elite status while simultaneously widening or massifying the audience for high culture. In so doing it attacks the modernist boundary between the two, rejecting avant-gardes and auratic expression and demanding a commitment to cultural heterogeneity. However, in so doing the service class undermines legitimation for its own separate status and status identity becomes susceptible to differentiation on an extreme scale. To the extent that there can be cultural heterogeneity there can also be status heterogeneity.

The predominance of the service class might best be regarded as a way-station in this process of social change, confined to the end stage of organized capitalism. The end of the growth of the service sector, the generalization of credentialism, and increasing entry of women into the service class will erode and undermine its special privileges of rewards and conditions. Moreover its cultural legitimacy is undermined by its own strategy of legitimation. The most significant developments likely to destabilize the advantages of the service class are those discussed in terms of the emergence of flexible accumulation (see Chapter 6). The success of the service class is rooted in its capacity to wed credentialism to the control of large-scale organizations. As transaction costs reduce the scale of organizations and as intellectual property gains greater ascendancy over physical property we may expect the level of fluidity in the upper reaches of the class system to become so great that the very existence of a class system will have to be called into question. As organizations become more market responsive they become more susceptible to failure and outflow will become the rule rather than the exception. Upper class membership will become as ephemeral as the ideas on which promotion to it will depend.

Consumerism and the Deconstruction of Labour

As Marx tells us, under conditions of modernization and particularly under capitalism, the meaning of human life is given in human labour – we are human because we work and we work because we are human. Human identity is objectified in the products of labour; the appropriation of products and the consequent commodification of labour alienate working humanity from its own identity. Modern industrial production systems have the greatest capacity to effect such appropriation and so there emerged an alienated and controlled working class, united in its negative response to the mode of production and with a latent capacity to transform society by taking control of the systems of production which represent the means of its impoverishment.

These classical conditions for the development of class struggle existed *par excellence* in the capitalist industrial societies of the nineteenth century. Social identities were located in the system of production and thus polarized. The working class engaged in its struggle for control of the system of production primarily by forming labour unions. Industrial struggle focussed primarily on the right of unions to control the supply of labour. While in many capitalist societies labour won that right it failed to reach any further objective. In particular unions had limited success in guaranteeing the material security of their members and even less in gaining control of the production process largely because bourgeois class elements had succeeded in gaining control of the state and thus of the organized means of violence. The working-class response was itself to engage in political action by forming social democratic, communist and other workers' parties. However, in so doing the working class took the first step in its own dissolution.

The key development in this process of the dissolution of the working class was the progressive inclusion of its members in wider societal structures of citizenship. The classic statement on the development of modern citizenship is given by Marshall (1973). Marshall links the idea of citizenship to the emergence of the modern nation-state and disassembles it into three components: civil rights, which comprise 'liberty of the person, freedom of speech, thought and faith, the right to own property and to conclude valid contracts, and the right to justice' (1973: 71); political rights to vote and to run for office; and social rights, 'the whole range from a modicum of economic welfare and security to the right to share to the full in the social heritage and to live the life of a civilized being according to the standards prevailing in the society' (1973: 72). The establishment of citizenship rights is evolutionary. Civil rights establishing equality before the law become the basis for arguments for political rights to equal participation in the construction of the law because only thus can legal treatment be universalistic. These combined de jure equalities become a springboard for the institutionalization of de facto social and economic equalities. In Britain, which was the focus of Marshall's analysis, the springboard had been established by the end of the nineteenth century thus providing the working class with a means for claims to social and economic equality (Waters 1990a).

Although there is a widespread view that Marshall's evolutionary scheme is inapplicable to societies other than Britain (Giddens 1981, 1985; Mann 1987) there is nevertheless general agreement about its relationship to the class struggle. The extension of citizenship rights is an outcome of that struggle but it is also a fundamentally egalitarian and increasingly effective attack on structures of class inequality. Marshall is quite clear that citizenship did not merely ameliorate the consequences of class inequality so as to increase its defensibility but, says that the effects of citizenship on class were 'bound to be profoundly disturbing and even destructive' (1973: 85). The precise form of these effects is threefold: compression of the income distribution at both ends; an increasingly common and universalistic culture; and the establishment of firm links between education and occupation which enriched the 'universal status of citizenship' and stabilized status on the basis of equality of opportunity (1973: 116).

The emergence of egalitarian citizenship as the direct outcome of the class struggle led to its own decline. As the working class took control of, or at least began to influence, the state so that it became transformed into a welfare state, workers placed themselves in a new position in the system of inequality. They no longer struggled to take control of the production system. Rather the working class established itself as a client of the state engaged in distributional competition with employers. In some instances – the Scandinavian examples are paramount – the working class became a full partner in decisions about distribution within corporatist structures. In others control of government rotated between parties representing workers and parties broadly representing employers and managers. The strategy was generally successful but in refocussing on the distribution of surplus as opposed to control of production the working class in effect denied the basis for its own separate existence. The extent to which such a refocussing has occurred is apparent in the fact that even in such early and highly institutionalized instances of state control of productive enterprise as Britain, France, New Zealand and, most especially, Eastern Europe a process of privatization of state enterprises is under way with the support of virtually the entire working class.

The significant basis for social membership becomes not one's relationship to the means of production but one's relationship to the means of distribution, to the state rather than to the economy. As indicated above, this relationship was essentially clientelist, that is the state in effect compensated workers in return for political support and vying political parties sought to purchase that support by delivering, or promising to deliver the means or the opportunity for an equal material existence. The state achieved this by regulating relationships between employers and employees and by redistributive systems involving taxation and social welfare payments.

A number of sociologists have interpreted the move from class struggle to citizenship claim as a move from class to status, which became the main basis for social inequality and differentiation (Marshall et al. 1985, 1987; Rose et al. 1984; Turner 1988). Within such arguments status is understood as a set of legal entitlements against the state to minimum social and economic conditions. These minimum conditions are realized as lifestyle, that is as conditions and patterns of consumption rather than as working conditions. In classical Weberian terms status is viewed as a constraint on a market whose principal effect would otherwise be to generate high levels of class inequality.

By the third quarter of the twentieth century, in most western societies equality of standards of consumption between families had been more or less achieved in at least two principal arenas. The first was housing, in which single family dwellings with separated functional spaces within them became the norm. This was achieved by an irregular mix, according to the society in which it occurred, of privately financed owner-occupation, the regulation of private tenancy, and direct provision of public housing. Indeed, in many societies which of these forms of housing a family occupied itself symbolized status. The second arena was personalized means of transportation. This is best argued in a critique by Moorehouse (1983) of analyses of American car workers. These traditional analyses argued workers to be so alienated from the process of production that they focussed their aspirations and fantasies on escape from it as independent, petty bourgeois producers. Moorehouse shows that, on the contrary, workers found an alternative source of self-expression in the ownership of the very objects they were engaged in producing. Car ownership became a key element in a material culture in which one's identity and indeed one's dreams were centred on what has come to be called consumption.[4] So progressively the pattern of workers' identification came to focus less on their participation in the process of production, that is on occupation or class, and more on the standard and style of life they could provide for their families.

During the 1960s and 1970s a number of sociological studies documented this new and growing 'instrumentalism' among affluent workers (see especially Goldthorpe et al. 1968) and a series of debates occurred about whether consumption was the 'real' form of social membership for workers. In the 1990s, outside the most deeply entrenched Marxist positions, there is relatively widespread agreement that social participation for most workers does indeed involve access to a complex of status items including home ownership, privatized transportation, electronically mediated mass entertainment, exotic vacations, technologized leisure equipment, high-quality health care, superannuation oriented to income maintenance, tertiary education for children, day care facilities, and so on. This means that the critical forms of social experience for what previously has been understood to be the working class, while different from those of the service class in terms of quantity, are little different in terms of quality. If there are class boundaries at all they are based on exclusionary practices which seek to monopolize consumption advantages rather than acts of exploitation and appropriation in order to maintain control of production (Waters 1990b).

This consumption-centredness on the part of the working class is the instrument for its own fragmentation. Two particular developments may be noted. The first is the separation of the traditional working class from an underclass category on the basis of the exclusion of the latter from extensive consumption. As manufacturing employment has declined the traditional working class has fortified itself within a unionized, masculine redoubt, distancing itself from those with whom in a previous era it might have experienced class solidarity and moving closer in orientation to those it might formerly have despised. Even as late as the 1970s an intense geographical concentration of a young and black underclass continued in the USA (as indeed it has in other societies). In that decade the poor population of the 50 largest cities rose by 12 per cent, with half of this population concentrated in New York, Chicago, Los Angeles, Philadelphia and Detroit (Wilson 1987: 46). The source of this exclusion was collusion between the traditional white working class and bourgeois interests to secure a highly segmented labour market in which the lower segment was disproportionately populated by blacks and Hispanics, female-headed households, and the young. Such jobs as are available in that secondary labour market are postindustrial in character but are located in the nonprofessional region of postindustrialism encompassing such manual service industries as retailing, catering, hospitality and cleaning services. Although it is difficult to agree with Gorz (1982) that the traditional proletariat has been displaced by a 'non-class' of 'non-proletarians', the effects of postindustrialization in dividing the working class are clear.

The emergence of an underclass defined in terms of age, gender, race and ethnicity is a significant indicator of the declining potency of production relations in determining class membership. A further indicator is suggested by Lash (1990: 26). As the traditional working class became more affluent it was able to confer on its youth in particular an increased capacity to consume. This led to an adolescent cultural challenge to traditional working-class values which destabilized its solidarity. Adolescence became established in the 1960s as a particular phase of existence organized around a culture of rock music, dislocated from material determinants and standing opposed to traditional working class commitments to social transformation.

A direct consequence of such developments has been a significant decline in the forms of social action that are normally understood to be aspects of class struggle. One of the elements of this process is a reduction in the level of industrial action. This is reflected in two empirical tendencies. First the level of unionization, the proportion of the labour force who are members of trade unions, is in decline in most western societies.[5] This is the consequence of several factors: the growth of the service sector, which places employees outside of traditional working-class situations; the increasing entry of women workers into the labour force and into the service sector, workers who are not party to traditional masculine bases of solidarity; the dissolution of traditional single industry complexes of homogeneous and solidary workers; and increasing automation, which may reduce the extent to which manufacturing workers experience subordination in the workplace. More significantly, the consumption-centred interests of workers have now been in large measure realized and, moreover, the maintenance of lifestyle is now increasingly viewed by them as contingent upon individual endeavour and on guarantees by a captive state in response to its citizen clients. So there is a second and consequent empirical tendency for the incidence of industrial disputes to decline (Waters 1982: 203–25). Even at the high point of unionization the chief value of unions to workers in the market was not the extraction of wages deals from employers but their representation within corporatist structures set up by the state. Action outside these structures has been increasingly viewed by governments, with major support from its client citizenry, as illegitimate. So governments have supported employers in concerted attacks on unionists conceived to be acting in an unfair way against the interests of the citizenry at large. There were landmark industrial disputes in the 1980s in which governments successfully sought to deny sectional or class interests in favour of national interests. Some of the most notable of these were the PATCO (air traffic controllers) dispute in the USA in 1982, the British coal mining dispute of 1984–5, and the Australian domestic airline pilots' strike of 1989–90. In each case the dispute was bitter and extended and the government strategy of dismissal and the re-employment of 'scab' labour was successful. In none of the three instances was there any basis for assuming widespread working-class or union support for the strikers, and this is why the strikes were lost. They mark a turning point because thereafter the possibilities for successful working-class industrial action has been severely circumscribed.

This was not the first time that working-class industrial action had failed. What makes it different is that in the past workers had always been able to turn to the alternative of political action and, as we have indicated, this was an altogether more successful strategy. In the circumstances of the 1980s working-class party-political solidarity also began to become undone at the seams. The so-called de-alignment of class politics in which class member-ship ceased to be much of a predictor of voting behaviour was a consequence of just this working-class political success. A focus on consumption decollectivizes the consciousness. Rightist political leaders were successfully able to appeal to individualized, consumption-centred interests and thus to disrupt the voting coalitions which previously had sustained Leftist political parties. Reagan Democrats and working-class Tories were subsequently rewarded by such initiatives as income tax reductions and the privatization of home ownership. Moreover, in seeking to retain their political potency, Leftist parties have been obliged to extend the scope of their representation beyond sectional class interests and to incorporate within their orbit other interests. These include both the interests of such materially disadvantaged groups as women, sexual minorities and ethnic and racial minorities and also those of social movements committed to more general value positions including the environmentalist and peace movements. As Leftist parties have become more like rainbow coalitions and less like red menaces this has further reduced their appeal to traditional constituencies because in many instances these values are directly counterposed to the material interests of manual workers.

This statement anticipates an argument that with the success and consequent disappearance of class action it is replaced by status group action (Turner 1988). The successful reforms associated with the institu-tionalization of citizenship applied principally to the core sector of the working class. In most Western societies this core sector comprises male workers who were members of the majority or charter ethnic group(s) and their conjugal nuclear families. Part of the citizenship process has been a general demand from members of categories outside this core to gain access to an equal standard of consumption. Turner gives a neat descrip-tion of this process:

> Equality of opportunity allows individuals to enter a race at the same point, but it does not guarantee equality of outcome; indeed it partly requires significant inequalities in terms of ultimate benefits. Social groups which experience major disadvantages will seek to achieve greater equality of conditions, which will compensate for differences in individual capacities. Employing the analogy of an athletic race, we can say that elderly participants within the games will seek some compensation (such as starting the race in advance of younger competitors). (1988: 44)

In the real status races of late modernity the groups claiming such compensation include not only the elderly but women, members of minority races and ethnic groups, indigenous peoples, people with minor-ity sexual preferences, people with reduced physical and mental ability, and residents of rural or outlying areas. These are indeed status formations

in the sense that they seek to induce the state to modify market effects in
their favour, that is to usurp the privileges of established status groups.
However, to employ a distinction made by Turner, they are not status
communities, solidary groupings engaged only in internal interaction.
Rather they are status blocs, temporary alliances of people with common
characteristics that transect class boundaries and that will dissolve at the
point at which their interests are realized. Thus the political agenda of late
modernity is not industrial action and working-class politics but social
movements and a disaligned politics of new, often single-issue parties and
issues of global, nonsectional concern. (This 'new politics' is discussed in
detail in Chapter 5.)

Action by status blocs is also the source of their own decomposition
because insofar as they are successful they reduce status group differentiation. This is at the heart of the move to a postmodern system of
stratification, the abolition of fixed status boundaries. In this we part
company with Turner. He argues that current patterns of class and status
division will be replaced by a set of virtual distinctions between the
employed and the unemployed, between primary and secondary sector
workers. The position taken here is that the (relatively) severe levels of
unemployment experienced in some western societies towards the end of
the twentieth century do not themselves represent the new form of society
but mark the transition into it: just as the transition from feudalism/
absolutism to capitalism (c. 1800–50) and the transition from liberal to
organized capitalism (c.1900–30) were marked by severe economic disruption at the personal level so also is the current transition. What is surprising
is that the current transition is marked by so little.[6]

Even though we do envision the end of differentiated class or status
groups which persist across generations we do not predict the onset of a
simple egalitarian society in which standards of consumption are identical.
We expect the whole process of stratification to be much more fluid and
apparently chaotic than it has previously been. Taken to its extreme,
stratification on the basis of consumption implies constant hierarchical
shifts as new lifestyles are found to be more desirable in a serial fashion.
Purchasing consumer goods becomes an investment in a status claim which
may or may not pay off. In any event the investment will not be long term
in character – a new item can be purchased and the old one consigned to
the garage or basement to be forgotten. As Baudrillard (1988: 29–56) tells
us, in the consumer society objects are not purchased to be used – their
objective character becomes subsumed in their character as signs, brand
name displaces both aesthetics and functional utility as the mark of quality.
There is no status (standing) without its signification through consumption:

> Within 'consumer society,' the notion of status, as the criterion which defines
> social being, tends increasingly to simplify and to coincide with the notion of
> 'social standing.' Yet 'social standing' is also measured in relation to power,
> authority and responsibility. But in fact: There is no real responsibility without a
> Rolex watch! Advertising refers explicitly to the object as a necessary criterion:

You will be judged on – An elegant woman is recognized by – etc. Undoubtedly objects have always constituted a system of recognition (*repérage*), but in conjunction, and often in addition to other systems (gestural, ritual, ceremonial, language, birth status, code of moral values, etc.). What is specific to our society is that other systems of recognition (*reconnaisance*) are progressively withdrawing, primarily to the advantage of the code of 'social standing'. (1988:19)

For Baudrillard the code is universal, binding (totalitarian), instantly perceptible and global, a code of recognition for the millions of strangers whose worlds are collapsed in time and space by technologies of transportation and communication and for whom there is no possibility of negotiating the meaning of the other. A consumer culture constituted as a *mélange* of signs and images does not admit of fixed social divisions marked by specific referents. So the triumph of status over class provides portage for the ascendancy of socio-cultural differentiation over socio-economic differentiation in general.

Public Domesticity and the Deconstruction of Patriarchy

Modern societies are characterized by pronounced structural and categorical differentiation at the level of gender. Moreover the gender system is masculine dominated, that is it involves the subordination of women by men. Although this is often treated as an undifferentiated structure of patriarchy we prefer to see the masculine gender system of modernization as a process of transformation between two phases, direct viriarchy and extended viriarchy (Waters 1989b), which are at least partly analogous to the transition from production class to consumption status. The common thread which runs through them is a reification of the categories male and female, work and consumption, production and reproduction, formal and informal, public and domestic in which gender differentiation and female subordination are conceived of as natural and justified.

The essential defining relationship for direct viriarchy is the form of gender relations in the domestic sphere rather than participation in the public sphere. The predominant gender relationship is the conjugal one in which men control women by virtue of being spouses. This control is direct in that men have the right of disposition over the labour, the bodies and the children of women, a right established both in fact and in law. The fact that men could freely direct the labour of conjugal partners as if it were chattel property combined with the constraints of biological reproduction entailed a systematic marginalization of female labour: 'Because factory production in particular and capitalist production in general, could not accommodate childbearing and early nurturing, married women were forced to seek more marginal, lower-paying kinds of work. Already in the 1830s and 1840s – few married women were working in anything but the most marginal forms of paid work' (Brenner and Ramos 1984: 58).

So participation by women in the male-defined public sphere was severely circumscribed. Participation in public political life was negligible in that women neither voted nor held office but were merely some of the objects of political action. Participation in nondomestic production, where it occurred, was equally subordinated, being unskilled or so defined, component wage labour and subject to the authority of men. Working-class women were employed as domestic servants or in routine factory jobs especially in the production of such items as textiles, clothing and food, and middle-class women were employed as governesses, teachers of young children, nurses and secretaries. Women were thus provided with public work which mirrored domestic work and placed them in rigidly segregated labour markets in which men determined the pattern of their lives through supervision.

The transition to extended viriarchy is described by Holter, although in different terms:

> One of the historical changes brought about by capitalist industrialism is a shift from direct, personal forms of dominance to indirect or 'structural' ruling of the weaker groups and classes. This is true of male oppression of women too and forms part of the *reorganized patriarchy*. . . The main feature[s] of male oppression today . . . are social arrangements indirectly securing men's interests, giving men market advantages before and above women, and hegemony in personal relations between the sexes. (1984: 19; original italics)

The new phase, characteristic of the period between the beginning and the middle of the twentieth century, involved the removal of legal restrictions on domestic gender relations and on female participation in the public sphere so that full freedom of individual contract was institutionalized and women achieved full citizenship rights. Among other developments, typical legal changes included the following: divorce became easier; women gained property rights in marriage; women gained full rights of political participation; equal pay for equal work was legislated; abortion was decriminalized; attempts were made to control domestic violence; and discrimination on grounds of gender was prohibited. However, men retained de facto control of the public sphere through a process of social reproduction. This process comprised three practices: first, control of the means of material subsistence by men in families was used by them to control the domestic labour of women and to constrain them within domestic roles; second, men used their control of cultural representations of gender in school curricula and the mass media to ensure that its idealized forms were functionally and hierarchically differentiated; and third, men practised covert forms of discrimination in public contexts.

The sources of this transformation lie in an increasing incorporation of female labour into the orbit of capitalist economic production especially during such periods of intense male labour shortage as wars. It must be stressed that the form of this incorporation has itself constituted a form of masculine domination. Production systems have been segmented into internal labour markets in which career structures are radically separated.

Paradoxically, female careers were nevertheless structured in terms of male characteristics, that is without arrangements for interruptions for childbirth and without provision of day-care facilities for children.

There has also been a parallel reconstruction of arrangements for biological and social reproduction at the primary level during the organized phase. Families were increasingly defined as inadequate to the reproduction of labour power appropriate to an advanced industrial economy. This socialization activity was increasingly acquired by the state, which in turn reinforced the pattern of segmented labour markets by providing jobs specifically oriented to women in 'caring' occupations. The state also increasingly regulated the process of biological reproduction. It did this through legal and medical agencies which offered technological opportunities for intervention in conception and gestation and also by means of taxation and family support policy. A normal part of family support policy is welfare provision for sole parents, which tends to confirm nonemployed women within domestic roles. Thus extended viriarchy in organized modernity is characterized by the movement of women from private to public dependency and the progressive deprivatization of the domestic sphere. (Brenner and Ramos 1984; Hernes 1984; Laslett and Brenner 1989; Waters 1989b).

As is noted at several points throughout this book, the general process of historical change is theorized by Habermas (1987a) as involving a progressive decoupling of lifeworld from system – steering mechanisms become more remote and uncontrollable by individual actors, the lifeworld more encapsulated and powerless. However, as this differentiation becomes extreme, under such conditions as those found in late modernity, the lifeworld can no longer adequately be protected against invasions from the system: there occurs a 'coloni(ali)zation of the life-world' as 'subsystems of the economy and the state intervene with monetary and bureaucratic means in the symbolic reproduction of the lifeworld' (1987a: 356). So the move to extended viriarchy can be understood as part of a general process of bureaucratization and commercialization and is ultimately not separable from the decomposition of capital and labour analysed above. The general pattern of the collapse of boundaries which we intermittently discuss is understood by Habermas not as an accidental process but as the direct outcome of strategic action which steers the society in the direction of the specific goal of the maintenance and expansion of its systemic form.

Habermas is clearly and explicitly a critical theorist and while the present substantive analysis of late modernity is consistent with his it is possible to take issue with the implication that all elements of the lifeworld are *ipso facto* value positive, while all aspects of steering are value negative.[7] Indeed, an alternative direction for social change may now be indicated. For the moment, however, let us consider some conceivably positive developments that arise in the area of gender differentiation and gender relations as the precise consequence of the process of internal colonization.

For the USA, these developments are summarized by Lengermann and Wallace (1985: 195–231):

- A widely ranging increase in female participation in the labour force, to a rate of over 50 per cent in 1980 and an estimated level of about 60 per cent in 1990.[8]
- A movement of women into traditionally male occupations at both working- and middle-class levels. Much female labour force participation is in service sector/caring occupations but this is principally in the public arena rather than the domestic arena. (Internal labour market segmentation between managers and secretaries is the most resistant form of occupational segmentation.)
- Women's increasing participation in formal political structures, through holding representative offices.
- An overall increase in the extent of educational participation and attainment by women although some fields of higher education (science and engineering) remain resolutely masculine.
- A trend towards reduced family size indicating an increased level of control by women over their own procreative capacities and reduced domestic chores.
- A redistribution of domestic duties in the family. One form of this redistribution is the increasingly prevalent single-parent family in which a single adult carries out all domestic duties. Another is redistribution between the genders in dual-income households, although the redistribution of housework towards men is very limited.
- Legislation affecting access to employment, relative rates of pay, and increased opportunity for men in divorce and child custody cases.
- The removal of explicitly sexist content in educational materials, governmental and legislative documents, and the mass media.
- The development of male liberation and masculine consciousness-raising groups.

It is rather too facile to dismiss such changes as mere superficial reform. To be sure, a fundamental disruption of viriarchal structures remains to be realized but such reforms as these make critical differences to the lives of those who experience them. The situation of women at the turn of the twenty-first century will represent a very real improvement over their condition at the turn of the twentieth. Centrally this will be an improvement in lifestyle but there will also be a not inconsiderable improvement in life-chances.

We now turn to a consideration of whether these changes are purely social or structural in character and whether there are also changes in culturally prescribed meanings – is there a movement from the dual masculine–feminine meaning system in the direction of androgyny? There are two ways of addressing such a question neither of which can satisfactorily answer it at the present time. The first is to ask whether masculine and feminine personality types are converging on a single androgynous type.

This question has been occupying psychologists for some twenty years (for a comprehensive review of the first ten years see Kelly and Worrell 1977). The key difficulty here is the scalar construction of each of the three types (androgynous, feminine, masculine) – even if it is clear, for example, that there is a single form of masculinity there is a very real problem in specifying core traits, especially traits which are independent of particular social contexts. In general, psychologists have therefore been obliged to concentrate on working out how to measure androgyny rather than actually measuring its extent.

The second route to assessing the emergence of androgyny is to engage in a developed analysis of culture. At its simplest and most impressionistic level this involves identifying popular figures in the mass media as examples of 'new men' or 'new women'. Lengermann and Wallace (1985: 222–3), for example, note the emergence of such 'nontraditional' men as the actor, Alan Alda, as heroes and also the popularity of such movies as *Kramer vs. Kramer*, which emphasizes emotional, nonauthoritarian father-hood and *Tootsie* which raises questions about gender by reversing roles. Likewise Connell (1987) makes occasional reference to such androgynous popular musicians as David Bowie, Boy George and Grace Jones. More convincing evidence that a cultural transformation is under way is to be found in the pages of behavioural science journals. The very fact that androgyny has become a scientific issue calls into question the previously taken for granted and reified meanings which attached to masculinity and femininity. Until 1969 sex-role research accounted for less than 1 per cent of the articles listed in *Sociological Abstracts*. By 1978 it accounted for almost 10 per cent (Carrigan et al. 1985: 558).

The transformation is analysed by many to take the form of a crisis in masculinity. For example:

> [A] good many men feel themselves to be involved in some kind of change having to do with gender, with sexual identity, with what it is to be a man. The 'androgyny' literature of the late 1970s spoke to this in one way, the literature about the importance of fathering another . . . [I]t seems clear enough that there have been recent changes in the constitution of masculinity in advanced capitalist countries, of at least two kinds: a deepening of tensions around relationships with women, and the crisis of a form of heterosexual masculinity that is increasingly felt to be obsolete. (Carrigan et al. 1985: 598)

Brittan (1989: 178–204) is more cautious about the existence of a crisis involving the breakdown of heterosexualism and the deconstruction of masculine power and authority in the public sphere. Rather he argues there to be a crisis in the legitimation of hegemonic masculinity, a crisis which is progressively defused by incorporating and mobilizing opposi-tional discourse. Brittan's example of a cultural product which confirms this pattern is the film, *Fatal Attraction*, in which an unmarried woman is portrayed as a violent threat to a traditional conjugal relationship after abrief affair with the ('guiltless') husband. Brittan is prepared to admit only to local crises of masculinity precipitated by unemployment, sexual inadequacy, encounters with gay men, failed marriages, wayward teenage children, and so on.

While at this stage caution would be well rewarded we must also recognize that a long-term change is taking its first faltering steps. The argument is in its fundamental terms a response to Habermas. The developments of late capitalism need to be understood not merely as a colonization of the lifeworld and the subordination of its communicative practices to strategic ones but as the absorption of the lifeworld into previously purely systemic arrangements, a dedifferentiation of lifeworld and system. This means the dilution of strategic practices in a series of ways: the reduction of economic organizations to a more domestic scale, their penetration by professional commitments which challenge managerialism, a political unwillingness to accept the direction of traditional parties and unions and far less the dictates of the state, and the decline of elitism in art and education. As does Habermas, we view information media to be critical in this regard. His own view of the mass media is instructive – the mass media are said to one-sidedly channel communication flows through a centralized network but in providing information and a focus for responses they also have an emancipatory potential. In an information-based society in which control of the means of generating information can be decentralized, this emancipatory potential, we would argue, has the capacity to become overwhelming. Domestically based information technologies capable of dynamic interaction between processors, video and communications may provide a talk-back and eventually a talk-to capacity on a wide scale. If colonization of the lifeworld is the key characteristic of late modernity, penetration of steering mechanisms at the level of communication may well be the hallmark of postmodernity.

Given that hegemonic masculinity is primarily constituted at the level of masculine power and authority in the public sphere the penetration of that sphere has the inevitable consequence of its deconstruction. More importantly, as production becomes demassified and accumulation becomes unpredictable participation in the public sphere itself becomes a declining component of identity. If Baudrillard's (and indeed Habermas') vision of a consumption society is correct what one does, whether that is operating a keyboard or caring for a child, indicates less about identity or standing than does lifestyle. If androgyny means anything under postmodernization it is that it is not the body which is reified but the Rolex which adorns it and that can be worn by a person of either gender.

However, this is not to argue for an imminent androgynous dissolution of gender differences. As in other parts of our general analysis, dedifferentiation is to be expected as an outcome of hyperdifferentiation. Feminists have long argued against the masculine notion that women have a singular gender identity, pointing to a range of feminine lifestyles. The deconstruction of the domestic/public distinction can only enhance such possibilities. But a far more important outcome is that the 'crisis of masculinity' provides for differentiation of that gender identity into a range of acceptable styles of self-expression based on choice, or what one observer describes as 'playful plurality' (Tijssen 1990: 162). Possibilities for gender dedifferentiation reside in multiple, overlapping and intersecting gender identity sets which can obscure the currently prevailing binary distinction.

Conclusion

We are now in a position to attempt to sketch the emerging pattern of social inequality within postmodernization. The starting point is consumption rather than production. Consumption emerged during the later stages of organized capitalism as a significant marker or denotator of class membership. There were three main vectors for this transformation. First the emerging service class sought to establish its legitimacy alongside the traditional bourgeoisie by establishing a specific cultural configuration of its own and thus asserting the authority of knowledge relative to economic power. Second, the state was made tractable by an organized working class which also asserted its right to consume. Third, the expansion of state activity into arenas of social reproduction incorporated women into the labour market and transformed them into independent consumers equivalent, in these terms, to men. Thus, as Bourdieu's work on contemporary patterns of inequality (1984) demonstrates, an order of cultural differentiation emerges which intersects with and challenges the older order of economic differentiation. Membership of classes and genders is signified by participation in a specific habitus, a complex of cultural consumption items employed as a means of closure against other classes – but which , it must be stressed, has the consequence of reproducing economic differentiation. Late modernity is characterized by at least four such class–habitus complexes: the old privileged masculine aristocracy and established bourgeoisie; the emerging postindustrial service class characterized by relatively egalitarian gender participation; a shrinking, traditional, masculine, primary-sector, manual working class; and an emerging underclass of manual service workers and state dependants disproportionately populated by women and members of ethnic and racial minorities.

To the extent that these class/gender positions are structured by consumption rather than production, further and more intensive differentiation becomes possible. Such differentiation is marked by a transformation in the form of consumption which is indicated in the work of Baudrillard. In Baudrillard's early work (1981) the consumption patterns of the middle class are analysed as weak status claims which fail in face of the undeniable material privilege of the upper class. This Bordieuvian analysis is consistent with the arguments offered above about developments in the later stages of organized capitalism: the new middle class stakes its claim relative to others on the basis of its specific 'taste'; and the traditional working class does so in terms of its sheer ability to consume in quantity. However, as we have seen, in Baudrillard's later work consumption takes on an altogether new and autonomous form. In the former type of consumption the habitus is broadly determined by socio-economic location, consumption items signifying material relationships. Within the emerging form of consumption the only reality is the signs themselves.[9] Consumption items, signs, are no longer representations but codes, shared systems of meaning found in fashion, advertising, media messages and information processing but which are without material foundation and have no terms of reference but their own. The simulations established by such codes become the form of reality, that is they become lived experience rather than representations of it.

Baudrillard's totalitarian code might itself however be understood as a modern and thus outmoded formulation. If there is a single code there must be a single axial structure which determines it or at least a single dominant value system which contains it. Our general argument has been that cultural forms are now being liberated from structural determinants and have the capacity for independent development. The development envisaged here is an extreme form of code multiplication which offers the possibility of hyperdifferentiation, a genuine decomposition of class and gender categories.

To put this another way, classes and genders themselves become hyper-reified, they become what Calhoun (1989: 15–22) drawing on Anderson (1983) describes as imagined communities. Anderson's original formulation applies to the development of national identity. The nation, he says, is an imagined political community. It is imagined because: 'the members of even the smallest nation will never know most of their fellow-members, meet them, or even hear of them, yet in the minds of each lives the image of communion' (1983: 15). In current circumstances the nation is disappearing as the significant political community but so also are classes, which might otherwise be proposed as real political communities. Instead political communities become hyperdifferentiated and hyper-reified through the mass media. People are led by mass media simulations to regard themselves as members of multiple communities characterized by common ascriptive characteristics, tastes, habits or concerns. Such simulations may even encourage a sense of fellowship, common interest and shared identity. But imagined communities do not depend on an actuality of shared situation, much less on dense interpersonal networks. They are categorical identities, to use Calhoun's term, or status blocs, to use Turner's. However, as Calhoun indicates, they are not arbitrarily imagined but are linked to specific power arenas of advantage and disadvantage. Moreover, advanced communications media offer enormous capacity for the simulation and mobilization of imagined communities with a genuine potential to affect social practice. Effects on social practice are accomplished by the generation of instrumental demand expressed either through the market or through the clientelist processes of political constituencies.

Imagined communities are not new and in the past have extended to such formations as nations, political parties, religions and even classes themselves. However in each such case the imagined community referred to a concrete and bounded system of relationships. In the current transformation, it must be stressed, no such referent is required. Imagined communities are *simulated* via mass mediated images, mass spectacles, and even quantitative (i.e. mass) social science. So cultural products which, for example, formulate alternative gender identities are critical in forming imagined alternative gender communities. Such formations might best be described as 'simulated power blocs' (SPBs). The most apparent consequences of SPBs may be recognized in the political actions of new social movements notable for their membership not by a given concrete *group* of people but by a specific (and simulated) *type* of person. It must be stressed that while given SPBs might consist of persons with elevated and indeed worthy commitments, say to peace or the environment, they also form on such diverse unifying themes as soccer, feminism, *Neighbours,* retirement, sociology, Placido Domingo, being gay, socialism, monarchism, *Star Trek* and astrology, although SPBs formed around some of these themes have greater potency than those formed around others. Significantly, in the context of a disetatized, mediated and global civilization, the multiple and transnational intersection of SPBs may be a source not only of socio-cultural differentiation but of general socio-cultural integration.

It remains to be said that while we do envision the progressive dissolution and eventual decomposition of boundaries between classes and between men and women we are far from arguing for an end to inequality. Rather, postmodernization involves a shift in patterns of differentiation from the social to the cultural sphere, from life-chances to lifestyles, from production to consumption. The pattern of inequality will become altogether more fluid than previously and will approximate a mosaic of multiple status identities rather than a small number of enclosed social capsules. Status will not depend on one's location in the society, especially its system of production and reproduction, but on one's status accomplishments in the sphere of consumption, one's access to codes. These will involve the products one uses, the places one goes, the leisure pursuits in which one engages, the clothes one wears. Social membership will be contingent on mass participation, display and profligacy rather than on work and ownership. Interestingly, such attributes cannot be accumulated, reproduced or inherited and while they may give rise to well recognized and sometimes oppressive inequalities they will not give rise to divisive or enduring ones. In terms of familiar theoretical motifs, Bourdieu's 'distinction' gives way to Derrida's 'différence' .

If under modernity unequal social categories are the basis for the formation of political communities, their hyperdifferentiation under postmodernization must lead in the direction of new forms of politics; if social categories have their origins in the cultural realm then so too must political commitments and their forms of expression; if social categories are more ephemeral then so too must be the political organizations which represent their interests; and if social categories are multiplying at a rapid rate then so too must their political forms. Such a development would constitute a radically new politics which transcended a politics of modernity firmly located in the state and seeking to affect the distribution of rewards on behalf of classes. The hyperdifferentiation-dedifferentiation motif which we have repeatedly stressed might be expressed in a multiplicity of political organizations focussing on single issues, each of which might be held by its proponents to have consequences for the whole of humanity. The next chapter addresses the question of whether just such a new form of politics is emerging.

Notes

1. One of the earliest explicitly sociological formulations of the decomposition of both capital and labour may be found in Dahrendorf (1959: 41–57). Dahrendorf's argument about the decomposition of capital is similar to the one offered here, focussing on the differentiation of ownership and control. However he fails to link this decomposition to the emergence of the new middle class, viewing that as a separate development. His argument about the decomposition of labour focusses on skill, that modern dimension of worker differentiation, rather than on the postmodern dimension of consumption.

2. It must be stressed that these sociologists disagree with Weber as well as with Marx on the shape of the class structure. Weber proposes a system of four classes but in these neo-Weberian analyses Weber's 'privileged class' has been displaced by his 'propertyless intelligentsia and specialists'.

3. In interpreting and responding to Foucault's knowledge/power couplet Poulantzas offers a broadly similar although structuralist observation: 'the discourse of [the] Scientist-State, of its apparatuses and agents, enjoys a permanent monopoly of knowledge, which also determines the functions of state organization and leadership. In fact these functions are centralized through their specific separation from the masses. In this way, intellectual labour (knowledge/power) is materialized in state apparatuses, while at the other pole, manual labour tends to be concentrated in the popular masses, who are separated and excluded from these organizational functions' (1978: 56).

4. The term consumption may be slightly misleading because many of the objects of consumption do in fact last for a relatively long time and thus are conventionally understood to be 'consumer durables'. The frequent aim of consumption is not to use things up but to possess and even display them so that they become symbols of one's identity and position.

5. The unionization rate reached 15 per cent in the United States and 35 per cent in Britain in the late 1980s (Turner 1988: 45).

6. In fact there has been a recent downturn in levels of unemployment in the most industrialized societies. The American rate fell from 9.7 per cent in 1982 to 5.3 per cent in 1990. Between 1986 and 1990 the British rate almost halved to 5.8 per cent. Throughout the 1970s and 1980s the Japanese rate remained resolutely low at under 3 per cent (*Economist*, 17–23 March 1990: 71).

7. In describing the empirical investigations of this process carried out at the Institute for Social Research Habermas says, *inter alia*: 'Institute co-workers investigated the structural change of the bourgeois family, which had led to a loss of function and a weakening of the authority of the father, and which had at the same time mediatized the familial haven and left coming generations more and more in the grip of extrafamilial forces' (1987a: 380). The value implications of such a development are far from indisputable.

8. The comparable participation rates in various EC countries were as follows: Denmark 58 per cent; Belgium 37; France 47; Italy 33; Britain 50; Germany (BRD) and Holland 44; Ireland 34. Interestingly, in the first four of these countries the participation rate for women

with infant children is higher than the rate for all women, at 85, 65, 62 and 48 per cent (*Economist*, 17 March 1989: 64).

9. Baudrillard's own periodization of this development is from production, the dominant scheme of the industrial era, to simulation, the predominant theme of the contemporary era (1988: 135).

5

Social movements and the new politics

Modern politics has blurred the difference between political-representative and administrative functions; running a political office has been not much different from running a large corporation. Both progressively rely on managerial skills and professionalism; both require instrumental orientation, pragmatism and organizational competence. Similar qualities characterize a modern citizen. Instrumentalism, rational calculation of interest and, above all, 'optimistic faith in the theoretical and practical rationalizability of reality' (Brubaker 1984:3) form the foundations of widening – though increasingly formalized – political participation. These trends have mirrored changes in the social structure – the process of formation of the major industrial classes and their political articulation via the class milieu – as well as the sphere of commodified culture. The mainstream modernization theories and their neo-Marxist counterparts have diagnosed these trends well; the issue of contention is not the overall nature of modern politics – here the consensus is considerable – but the nature of collective interests competing in the political arena and the outcomes of political conflicts.

The assertion of the homogeneity of modern politics needs to be qualified; in fact, one can distinguish at least three, quite distinct, models of modern power politics. The West European model involves progressive organization and bureaucratization of politics in the context of gradually articulated nation-states, industrial classes and their political representations, mainly the etatized mass milieu parties. Under the impact of these ascendant forces, the political process became progressively transformed into a pursuit of sectional interests: internally, principally class interests, externally, the interests of nation-states and geopolitical 'power blocs'. The initial success of these processes of structural articulation was reflected in the unprecedented 'hundred years peace', a period of political stability in Europe achieved at the outset of the Vienna Congress (1815). The collapse of the Vienna order was dramatic and costly: from 1914 till the late 1940s Europe was torn by conflicts and warfare on a scale surpassing the seventeenth century upheavals. The measures taken to contain these conflicts involved a series of corporatist settlements and set a model of politics in many ways parallel to the absolutist 'solution' at the end of the turbulent seventeenth century. First, the interests of the major power blocs – the industrial classes, the nation-states and 'superpower' coalitions – were explicitly acknowledged, organized and institutionally mediated. The status of citizens was strengthened by legal formalization of civil, political and welfare rights, but also circumscribed by both the formal procedures that regulated political participation and semi-formal norms and notions of what does – and does not – constitute legitimate political action. The interests of the major industrial classes, as well as other regional, occupational and religious categories, were incorporated into the political mechanism via union organizations, employer bodies, pressure groups and mass milieu parties. In a similar fashion, the interests of nation states have been recognized and incorporated into the international political processes together with their 'legitimate' external interests and geopolitical concerns. The Yalta agreement of 1945 paved the way for the regulated coexistence of hostile power blocs in a way analogous to the Vienna Congress that settled political 'superpower' conflicts over a century earlier.

Corporatist politics enhances interest representation by curtailing direct participation. It is an elite politics, relying on the bureaucratic mechanisms of orderly representation that are controlled by elites. It guarantees stability and broadens access but at the cost of restricting participation to few ritualized acts and insulating politics from unorganized pressures and fluctuations of popular opinion. Stability attained through such insulation, in turn, enhances predictability and increases the likelihood of economic success.

The idiom of bureaucratic-corporatist politics was as unheroic, sober and pragmatic as its content: bracketing ideological issues and moral concerns, focussing on stability, freedom, security and economic growth, stressing national solidarity, and translating value commitments into the language of sectional interest and appropriate administrative procedures. What became known as 'new politics' emerged in response to the form, content and idiom of the bureaucratic-corporatist politics, in particular in opposition to subtle constraints and restrictions coded into the political institutions and cultures of liberal corporatism.

American politics differs from the European configuration. It has been 'an untidy process', less bureaucratic and less corporatist than politics of its European counterparts (see Chapter 3). The links between the state and the civil society are more direct. The corollary of such a noncorporatist configuration has been a more open, if one prefers more pluralistic, politics of lobbying, constitutional challenges and litigation, perhaps less effective in enfranchising weaker interests of blue-collar workers and minorities, but more open for lobbying by all sorts of organized pressure groups. The main constraint on political action has been the resources necessary for effective lobbying: it becomes a highly technical task requiring money and specialized professional skills. It has been mediated more by the mass media than by the mass parties, and even this mass-media mediated politics still requires high technical skills.

Communist etatism generated its own version of modern politics, different in form and idiom from the politics of its European counterparts and the United States. The quasi-corporatist politics of the post-Stalinist partocracies was much more restrictive and much less effective in defusing conflicts and enfranchising major interest categories than the bureaucratic corporatism practised by the Western liberal states. While the diversity of interests was covertly acknowledged, it was officially denied. The Leninist principles of 'democratic centralism', which formed the central element of the ideological formulae unifying the partocratic elites and the core organizing principle of partocratic power politics, prevented such acknowledgment and restricted incorporation. All 'legitimate' interests had to be certified by, and mediated through, the centralistic structure of the party-state, operating under the constant scrutiny of the Soviet sponsors ever watchful of political deviations. The absence of institutional mechanisms of free interest articulation and mediation meant that the 'independent' (i.e. uncertified) interests often asserted themselves through crypto-political and informal channels. Most of them were, eventually, at least partly incorporated – a process labelled by Staniszkis (1982) as 'regulation through crises'. East European 'new politics', animated by idioms of human rights and civil freedoms and articulated in Solidarity-type protest movements, has changed this pattern.

Modern political revolutions, as pointed out by Bauman (1991), were predominantly non-systemic in the sense of restoring the balance between the dominant social forces and political institutions; they emancipated social forces from political constraints inherent in the archaic or dictatorial forms of political regimes. They reasserted the link between modern politics and its social bases: social agencies and a set of directional, structurally given interests which determined the overall character of the political process. Even the communist takeovers, as Konrad and Szelenyi (1979) suggested, could be seen as an instance of such an assertion of the socially ascendant intelligentsia. These structural roots, marking the modern pattern of politics, have been progressively eroded. With them, the very nature of political processes starts to change.

From Old Politics to New Politics

Since the late 1960s, the political complexion of advanced societies has been undergoing a change which has rendered problematic the core assumptions of the mainstream and neo-Marxist analyses of politics, especially those concerning the instrumental nature and the structural-class determination of political processes. The central processes identified by students of 'new politics' include an increasing fusion and interpenetration of political and cultural spheres, and the decoupling of political conflicts and cleavages from the old structural class divisions. The main symptoms of these changes are a progressive decline in class voting or political dealignment, an erosion of support for the major 'milieu parties', and the rise of new political forces, including the ecopax (ecological and peace), the civil, human and minority rights, and the feminist social movements.

While they are global in scope, these changes are subject to some interesting regional variations. The new politics in North America shows clear signs of accommodation and integration within mainstream political processes. In Western Europe (as well as in Australia and New Zealand) the movements are much less accommodating; they differ from and compete with conventional political units. In Eastern Europe the process has taken a most radical and anti-establishment turn with mass antipartocratic movements producing a series of 'self-limiting revolutions'. Here we focus our attention on Western developments, treating the East European new politics as a comparative point of reference.

The first empirical diagnoses of the weakening allegiances between major social classes and the major 'milieu parties' had already emerged by the late 1960s.[1] Studies of voting behaviour and political activism showed a steady decline in allegiance between the major classes or occupational categories on one hand and the major political parties on the other. The critical reference for these studies was the classical formulation in which the emergence of industrial welfare capitalism is said to coincide with the institutionalization of class conflict and the articulation of class divisions in the form of stable political cleavages. The working class, according to this thesis, was the natural constituency for social-democratic parties of the Left, while the ownership and white-collar classes were the main base of support for liberal-conservative parties of the Right (Lipset 1960, 1981). The 'class voting index' provided quantitative evidence of this 'most impressive fact', first in the English-speaking democracies, and later in all advanced western societies.

Since the late 1960s, however, the class voting index has been in steady decline. Four overlapping processes may be seen as lying behind this trend: the fragmentation of the major parties; declining consistency in voting; a declining identification with, and allegiance to, the major parties which traditionally represent class interests; and the decreasing polarization of the old class/party blocs (see, for example, Miller 1990; Dalton et al. 1984a, 1984b; Saarlvik and Crewe 1983; Dalton 1988). Taken together, they form the empirical foundation of the dealignment thesis postulating a progressive divorce between the main industrial classes and their organized political representation.

One correlate of dealignment has been a decline in party trust. Studies of political attitudes in the early 1970s revealed a growing cynicism about the major political parties. These findings were confirmed by Marxist (O'Connor 1973) and liberal scholars (Brittan 1975; Blondel 1978). Analyses of survey data, and studies of party organization, of voting patterns, and of new forms of 'citizen politics' all provided evidence of growing voter distrust and declining allegiance to the major parties, as well as an increasing volatility and diversity in voting patterns. Interestingly, this mistrust of the major parties did not lead to political alienation and apathy. On the contrary, the studies revealed an 'increasing sense of political obligation' and a preference for expressive participation among the young, educated white-collar categories. These were less clearly articulated through conventional repertoires of action, such as voting and lobbying, and were less frequently channelled through the major political parties.

Processes of class and partisan dealignment coincided with widening repertoires of political action and the increasing popularity of unconventional forms of political activism. Various forms of this activism – examined under such labels as 'new politics', 'citizen politics' and 'civil society' – involved ecological, feminist, peace and civil rights issues, encompassed new forms of association which were semi-institutionalized, and experimented with new modes of political expression which were unconventional and symbolic in their form. Its key collective carriers were the new social movements and movement-generated 'Left-libertarian' (Kitchelt 1990) or 'New Politics' (Müller-Rommel 1990) parties.

The new movements, which are the backbone of the emerging political configuration, differ from previous mass movements.[2] By contrast with the 'old' liberal-bourgeois and socialist-labour movements, they appear to be apartisan or even apolitical in the sense that they reject the conventional institutional idiom of politics; they aim not to capture the state but to ignore or even abolish it. Also, unlike the student revolts of the late 1960s, they have proved to be persistent, widespread and politically fertile. They cannot be treated as a residuum of conventional politics, or dismissed as transient outbursts of collective protest. Movement-generated new politics attracts the support of strategically important social categories, and sympathetic media coverage. Movement campaigns transcend national boundaries, and spawn scores of groups and organizations, including successful political parties. In Western Europe, Australia, New Zealand, and to a lesser extent in North America, the new movements have become an increasingly visible and important element in the socio-political landscape.

The more institutionalized representation of new social movements, the Left-libertarian parties, are difficult to locate within the traditional political spectrum between the liberal-conservative Right and social democratic Left.[3] They share with the traditional Left a suspicion of market mechanisms and of big business, and they are fiercely anti-centralist and anti-bureaucratic, an orientation which is kindred to libertarian concerns. Yet they reject the ideological commitments of the old Left, including the appeals to class interests, endorsement of egalitarian policies, and acceptance of revolutionary strategies. The differences are not only programmatic. As well as being vague in their programmes and ideological leanings and volatile in their political dealings, Left-libertarian parties also differ from the conventional parties in their organizational form, which is less centralized and bureaucratic, and their overall philosophy, which places stress on representation and consultation rather than on leadership and electoral competition. They also lack the stability that characterized electoral support of the old milieu parties. This is partly the result of a very high turnover in membership, partly the outcome of programmatic vagueness and openness which makes them the natural spokespersons for many marginalized groups, and partly a reflection of weak leadership and discipline. All these features set new political associations apart from the old parties and promote a general change in the pattern of interest intermediation associated with the ascent of new politics (see Kitchelt 1990; Müller-Rommel 1990; Müller-Rommel and Poguntke 1989).

Assessments of strength of the new social movements in Europe and North America vary widely. This partly reflects differences in defining movement boundaries and gauging movement support. In terms of general public concern with such movement-publicized issues as peace, nuclear disarmament, ecological care and equal rights, this support exceeds 60 per cent of the population (Inglehart 1990). But this is an inflated indicator, since a concern about these rather uncontroversial issues is not necessarily synonymous with an endorsement of the solutions proposed by the movement organizations.[4] In terms of *declared* support for movement actions, the strength of the West European movements has been gauged at about 20 per cent of the adult population (Müller-Rommel 1990). Tangible support for movement actions, which includes participation in marches, rallies and demonstrations, and voting in national elections for the new parties, varies widely from less than 1 per cent in Britain to nearly 15 per cent in Northern Europe (Kriesi 1989). This, however, is not a good estimate of overall support either, because much of support for new movements is manifested in activities which are less tangible than voting and less spectacular than marches or rallies. Out of scores of movement groups in Europe, for example, only about 70 formed parties on the national level, and less than two dozen have won seats in national parliaments (Parkin 1989). Finally, in terms of formal membership, all these Green/Left-libertarian groups are small. Generally, their size does not exceed 2 per cent of voters; the largest of them, the German Green Party, has about 40,000 members (Kitchelt 1990; Pakulski 1991).[5]

Despite their political salience, the new politics, and the new movements in particular, are puzzling from a theoretical point of view. They do not fit the accepted pattern of political modernization and the dominant image of modern politics which are supposed to be pragmatic, technocratic, instrumental, value-neutral, and increasingly autonomous.[6] Nor do they fit the alternative image of class conflict provided by Marxist scholars. Established analytical categories of Right and Left, radicalism and conservatism, reform and revolution, socialism and liberalism, fail when applied in the analysis of new politics. Movements stimulate socio-cultural, as well as socio-political change; they follow a cyclical pattern of generational mobilization; and they grow by means of cultural diffusion (see Minkenberg and Inglehart 1989; Brand 1990).

In order to explain the ascendancy of new politics and the distinctive features of the new social movements, it is necessary to locate them in the broader socio-political and historical context involving a postmodern shift in economic and social organization and culture.[7] Two aspects of this change are highlighted here. First, progressive social differentiation has resulted in class decomposition and the weakening of stable socio-political milieux which were the 'natural' constituencies of traditional parties. This erosion of the social bases of the old politics coincided with the formation of the generationally specific but occupationally diverse social constituencies of the new movements. Second, the specific orientations and styles of new politics, especially those articulated by the new social movements and Left-libertarian parties, have to be seen as a hostile response to established corporatist structures and bureaucratized power politics. They are an attempt to resolve a tension between increasingly diverse social groupings seeking social articulation and political recognition, on one hand, and the bureaucratic rigidity and corporatist bias inherent in the old party system, on the other.

Class Decomposition and the Rise of New Politics

Class is, principally, a structural concept. In the classic formulations of Marx and Weber it refers to causal mechanisms which are rooted in ownership and market relations. In the process of socio-cultural and socio-political articulation, that is, the formation of class cultures and class-related political organizations, class becomes socially and politically salient: it shapes social relations, determines life-chances and structures political conflicts. This should culminate, according to Marx, in widespread class consciousness and class-propelled action. Marx's expectations were only partly fulfilled. Socio-political and socio-cultural articulation of the working class in particular occurred in a form which defied Marx's predictions of polarization and revolution. Class divisions and identities coexisted with, and were weakened by, national, ethnic, religious and regional cleavages, and successful working-class parties opted for reformist rather than revolutionary programmes. Although class-related (as well as religion- and region-related) milieux did form in industralized Europe, and although their political representations, the large milieu parties, did dominate politics throughout the postwar decades, most of these class-representing bodies proved reformist and tame. Class politics evolved into orderly and routinized processes cemented by formal rules and less formalized corporatist deals. Within this framework, the class/interest conflict transformed into a support of the socio-political status quo.[8] Opposed interests were articulated in the form of bureaucratically framed and negotiable policy demands which were aggregated within corporate blocs and systematically resolved through bargaining, arbitration and conciliation. The dominant role in these processes was played by bureaucratized elites, and the level of grass-roots involvement was low. Class milieux were the reference points rather than participants in political processes. They contributed to stabilization and routinization of politics by generating family traditions which, in turn, helped to cement class-based political alliances and transmit them across generations.

This continuity and stability has been eroded in two ways: by deep changes in the social structure and by cultural transformations related to the postwar generational transition. The former processes, outlined in Chapter 4 , have blurred the old class divisions, weakened class identities, and undermined the political cohesion of class milieux. The decomposition of classes has, in turn, been reflected in the decomposition of class politics in its bureaucratic-corporatist form.

The decomposition thesis predates the studies of new politics. We owe its classical formulation to Ralf Dahrendorf (1959) who highlights some major transformations in what he terms 'industrial society'. These include: the decomposition of the ownership class as a consequence of the differentiation of bourgeoisie, principally between owners and managers; a parallel decomposition of the working class, due mainly to increasing stratification (skilled vs. unskilled), regional and religious fragmentation, embourgeoisement, and a growing diversity of lifestyles and consumption patterns; the growth of the heterogeneous middle classes of state employees and professional and technical workers; increasing social mobility prompting the erosion of class boundaries, class identification and class consciousness; the gradual spread and extension of citizenship rights, covering socio-economic entitlements; and the institutionalization and 'domestication' of class conflict by processes of systematic arbitration and conciliation.

The widespread endorsement of the decomposition thesis led to a renaissance in stratification and mobility studies which largely confirmed Dahrendorf's propositions. Two ramifications of these studies are particularly important here. First, the decomposition thesis inspired studies of socio-political dealignment, the disintegration of stable class-based social milieux and declining support for the traditional parties. Second, it provided a springboard for theorizing about socio-political cleavages underlying the new politics.

The key aspects and symptoms of dealignment have already been discussed: declining class voting, declining identification with the major parties, growing cynicism about party machines, volatility in voting patterns, and widening repertoires of political action, including unconventional forms of activism typical of the new social movements. While there has been a growing consensus that these new forms defy the old concepts and cannot be linked with the old industrial class bases, there is little agreement on what new social forces and what aspect of social structure, if any, they reflect. The problems of the social bases of new politics and the nature of social constituencies of the new social movements has been propelled to the status of a major controversy in political sociology.

Three views on this issue, which vary in the extent to which they depart from the old paradigm of class-interest politics, are especially important. They are the 'radical decoupling' thesis; the milieu, status group and age group interpretation; and the 'middle class radicalism' interpretation which suggests only minor modifications to the traditional theories.

The radical decoupling thesis questions the very rationale for linking political-cultural phenomena, including unconventional politics of the new social movements, with any fixed social referents, be it classes, status groups or occupational categories. Featherstone (1987: 55–6) for example writes:

> We are moving towards a society without fixed status groups in which the adoption of styles of life . . . which are fixed to specific groups have been surpassed. This apparent movement towards a post-modern consumer culture . . . would further suggest the irrelevance of social division and ultimately the end of the social as a significant referent point.

This radical view also reverberates in Dalton et al.'s analyses of new politics. New social movements, they insist:

> signify a shift from group-based political cleavages to value- and issue-based cleavages that identify only communities of like-minded people. The lack of a firm and well defined social base also means that membership in new social movements tends to be very fluid, with participants joining and then disengaging as the political context and their personal circumstances change. (1990:12)

In the middle of the interpretive spectrum we find mass, status group and age group accounts of the new politics. Mass accounts partly resemble the decoupling arguments in that they see social movements as a result of 'destructuration', that is, of the collapse of classes and intermediate bodies. But they also follow a well established, if rather dated, line of argument which depicts movement constituencies as marginal, atomized and alienated, and link this alleged marginalization with semi-rational and extremist orientations and action.[9] Status accounts, depicting movement supporters as 'radical intellectuals', 'humanistic intelligentsia' or as a culturally defined 'class', are much more popular.[10] Some link movement activism with lifestyles and socio-cultural divisions in general (e.g. Turner 1988) while others link it with high intellectual or educational status, especially in the areas of humanities and social sciences (e.g. Eckersley 1989). Such explanations often allude to the frustrations or unfulfilled aspirations of intellectual dissenters which are consequent on a peripheral position in a market economy. Bürklin (1985), for example, characterizes supporters of the new movements as members of a 'new educated class' whose mobility opportunities are reduced by economic downturns (see also Cotgrove and Duff 1981). Age group accounts link movement activism with 'youth radicalism'. They have a long history, but empirical support for the view that age correlates negatively with political liberalism, social radicalism and environmental concerns has been produced relatively recently.[11]

Finally, on the traditional end of the interpretive spectrum we find an interesting 'new milieu' account and a whole gamut of class interpretations that link movement activism either with some sections of the (new) middle class or with an altogether new social class.[12] Veen (1989), for example, explores the connections with the green movement and Green Party in

Germany and a new 'left-alternative milieu'. This milieu:

> cannot be defined in socioeconomic terms, nor is its behaviour determined by economic interests. . . . [T]he values of the milieu . . . are devoid of a teleological framework in the sense of a religious or pseudo-religious ideology. The strongly developed ('postmaterialist') emphasis placed on freedom and personal development is not an ideology of this kind but of a more limited scope; it is an essentially secular and even egocentric orientation. (1989: 35)

A similar line is taken by scholars who link movement activism with socio-cultural rather than socio-economic aspects of class, that is with norms, styles, outlooks and values (e.g. Parkin 1968; Offe 1985a; Cotgrove 1982).[13] Despite the considerable difficulties posed by the attribution of such cultural traits to class(es), these accounts fare much better than more orthodox interpretations which attempt to link new politics with some economically defined 'class interests'. The latter vary immensely. Touraine (1985), for example, assumes a generic link between class and any form of large-scale collective dissent. Within such an interpretation, any serious challenge to the status quo, especially a socio-cultural challenge, is by definition 'class related', regardless of its objectives and the occupational profile of the participants. Other accounts treat class character as synonymous with social composition and focus on the occupational backgrounds of movement supporters, ignoring the problem of theoretical linkages between social composition, interests and cultural traits.

There are some obvious problems with accounts located at the extremes of the interpretive spectrum.[14] The radical decoupling arguments clearly overstate the case. Although the class and status backgrounds of movement participants and supporters of various Left-libertarian parties are diverse, they are neither random nor unstable. Involvement in new politics is far from episodic, and some social characteristics of movement supporters form a consistent, stable and distinctive pattern, which is discussed in more detail below. This pattern, however, defies class categories and makes class accounts, especially the more orthodox ones, difficult to sustain. They all have difficulty in demonstrating consistent and distinctive class (i.e. ownership/market) characteristics of movement participants, in attributing consistent attitudinal or structurally determined (objective, socio-economic) class interests to such 'classes', and in linking such interests and orientations with movement issues, styles and symbols.[15]

The most useful argument about the social base of the new politics may be found in the work of Offe (1985a), Inglehart (1981, 1984, 1990) and Veen (1989). The new movements/'New Left' alliance, according to Offe, represents the 'new middle classes' in coalition with such economically marginalized categories as welfare recipients and students, and focusses on specific situses in the public sector. The goals and issues of the movements are not related to the economic interests of classes and the groups that support them. Rather, they are more general and universalistic and reflect problems arising from bureaucratic and etatist dysfunctions. Veen and Inglehart each see the movements as reflecting specific orientations, that is as value- rather than class-based. Inglehart's studies reveal a generational shift in value orientations in all major western societies. This value shift or, more precisely, changed hierarchy of preferences, has resulted from both increasing affluence and historical changes in formative experiences. The ascendancy of new postmaterialist values represents an ascendancy of new, 'higher' ethical and aesthetic needs among the post-Second World War birth cohorts which grew up during a period of economic prosperity, political stability and peace. The new generation rearranges value priorities by stressing the importance of freedom of speech, participatory democracy and quality of life. Their value priorities are, in turn, reflected in the new politics, especially in the 'participatory revolution'[16] and the rise of new social movements. Assertion of these values leads, in turn, to a political reaction by the 'New Right', which seeks to defend the old materialist values.

These interpretations offer invaluable leads. First, the new politics, and new social movements in particular, mobilize not social classes or sections of classes, but specific *generational* segments of a population, which are characterized by specific occupational *situses*, as well as social characteristics reflecting certain lifestyles and social and geographical mobility experiences. Movements, in other words, do have distinct social bases, but these social bases are contingent rather than structurally determined, they are socio-cultural rather than socio-economic, and they are related to consumption and lifestyle rather than to production.

Generational orientations are the products of shared formative experiences. The particular character of each generation, and the boundaries between generations, reflect historical watersheds: wars, crises and natural catastrophies. In Western Europe these characteristics were established under the impact of the cataclysmic world wars and the Great Depression. One can therefore distinguish two dominant contemporary generations: the Great Depression and Second World War generation and the postwar generation. The latter includes birth cohorts which experienced a period of sustained economic growth, political stability, social reform and an 'educational revolution' during the 1950s and 1960s. This halcyon period generated high expectations and idealistic orientations, but it ended with a series of economic downturns and political turbulence during the late 1970s and 1980s. Such a historical sequence, reminiscent of Davies' (1962) 'J-curve', had radicalizing effects, especially among those sections of the postwar generation which had benefited from educational expansion but whose skills, mainly in the areas of humanities and social science, were less marketable under conditions of economic contraction. Most of these people found employment in the public sector, which was badly affected by economic downturns and contracting opportunities. Reduced career prospects, combined with low market power, made these categories more receptive to social criticism, especially criticism adopting an idealistic, anti-corporatist idiom of value-rationality.

The availability of members of this generation for movement mobilization has also been affected by two other factors: high autonomy, especially in the area of work, and freedom from community control. The former is correlated with public sector, especially professional, situses; the latter is highest among the socially and geographically mobile. Severing religious ties is a part of this mobility process.

Such an account is consistent with the results of empirical studies of social characteristics of participants and supporters of the new movements. Age appears to be the most powerful predictor of participation in movement protests and the highest correlate of movement-specific values. The primacy of generational effects has also been confirmed by studies of unconventional politics.[17] Most of the participants share generational experiences, high levels of education and high autonomy due to occupational locations mainly in the public sector and especially in the teaching profession. These characteristics are in many respects similar to the profiles of the post-Stalinist generation in Eastern Europe which gave impetus to Polish Solidarity and other reform movements (Pakulski 1991).

The orientations of the postwar generation, especially of its radicalized and educated sections, did not fit the conventional institutional framework with its high degree of bureaucratization and its relationship to corporatist deals. This incompatibility resulted in a 'bypassing' effect in which the outlooks and aspirations blocked and marginalized by conventional institutions found an outlet in the new movements. The type of political conflict that marked this process differed in its character and intensity from the institutionalized interest-conflicts which formed the 'content' of conventional power politics. The old conflicts focussed on sectional interests; they were specific, that is easily translatable into conflicting policy demands, negotiable and 'cool'. By contrast, the value-conflicts that new social movements articulate are fundamental and 'hot'. They are defined as matters of principle, and therefore generate a high level of commitment. Moreover, such conflicts do not focus on class or any other sectional interests linked with property or market position. In fact, they reject the very notion of sectional interests as the basis of political action, so the social matrix of the new politics has only a tenuous link with economically structured classes and class interests, and actors in the new politics cannot adequately be characterized in terms of class position.

This leads us to a second important point. New politics reflects not only a new social basis, but also new orientations. It is a politics of vigorous anti-bureaucratism.

New Social Movements: New Orientations and New Styles

What is new about the new movements is neither the issues they raise, nor the values they reassert, nor even their particular social form of recurrent, semi-institutionalized and value-laden protest. After all, the beginning of the civil rights, ecological, peace and feminist campaigns can be traced back to the turn of the century. Similarly, mass mobilizations resembling the current ones shook Europe in the nineteenth century and throughout the 1920s and 1930s, and these 'old' movements, including the fascist and communist-socialist ones, were semi-institutionalized, strenuously value laden and unconventional. The new elements in the contemporary movements are their *specific orientations* combined with international *mass media exposure*, especially by the new medium of television. The orientations are not only value laden and universalistic, but also vigorously anti-centralist, anti-formalist and anti-etatist, critical of the corporatist-bureaucratic model[18] – characteristics which are best encapsulated in the term 'anti-bureaucratic'. The symbiotic relationship with the mass media, and the heavy reliance on the amplification and dissemination of movement symbols, icons and appeals through the media, result in a partheno-genetic pattern of growth through diffusion which gives the new movements a specific exhibitionist and didactic character. The mass media not only disseminate and amplify movement messages but also create new forms of political discourse.

Five features of the new orientation, style and idiom of new movement politics may be identified. First, movement politics is driven by universalistic moral concerns rather than by instrumental considerations. This characteristic is encapsulated in such labels as 'antipolitics', 'counterpolitics', 'symbolic and lifestyle politics', and 'politics of the moral protest'.[19] Second, the new politics is not based on centralized and bureaucratized intermediation of interests through the 'pillars' of corporatism. Instead it relies on self-organization, and utilizes semi-institutionalized forms of pressure. Third, the key activists are openly suspicious of the established elites and centralized state apparatuses, whose effectiveness, rationality, and ability to represent collective good are all doubted. This is expressed in movement symbols and action repertoires, which are public- rather than elite-oriented and which rely on semi-institutionalized self-organized action. These features often analysed under the label of 'citizens' politics' and 'civil society' (see, for example, Misztal 1985; Melucci 1988; Dalton 1988; Schmitt 1989). Fourth, the new politics spills over into and fuses with the socio-cultural arena. The new movements defy the conventional forms and repertoires of the 'old' politics as protests combine with leisure activities and merge into a total countercultural *Gestalt*. Fifth, the new politics is highly dependent on the mass media. It constitutes a mass spectacle in which appeals combine with symbols and icons, where images rather than discursive arguments determine outcomes, where captivating drama may be more effective and more important than systematic analysis, and where anxiety may overshadow calculation as a spur to collective action.

The new politics coexists, and to some extent mixes, with 'old' politics. This coexistence extends to the very core of the new movements which always contains organized groups, proto-parties, and bandwagons of 'affiliated' lobbies representing sectional interests and operating in a conventional fashion. None of these conventional groups and activities, however, set the tone of movement politics, and they seldom represent more than a small part of a complex and 'fuzzy' movement constellation. No single organization controls the movement, no membership criteria encompass more than a small fraction of active participants, and no single ideological vision, world-view, strategy or programme attracts the support of the majority of supporters. Movements are polycephalous, polymorphous, inclusive, ideologically plural and programmatically incoherent. This is the source of both their strength and their weakness. It allows them to attract wide support unrestricted by any membership requirements and ideological or partisan commitments but leaves them unable, and unwilling, to form coherent strategies and to enter lasting intra-elite deals and compromises. Their uneasy coexistence with the conventional parties conveys a continuing impression of extremism and marginality.

Dominant Orientations

The new politics can be seen as a reaction to highly organized, instrumentalized and class-based 'power politics' and its institutional correlate, the bureaucratic-corporatist state. Power politics is based on the organized representation of interests by the major market categories and the systematic reconciliation of these interests through bargaining and compromise. The key actors are the leaders of bureaucratically organized interests, the corporate elites, and the entire political process is oriented towards influencing these elites. The idiom of power politics is instrumental, conventionalized and pragmatic. The bureaucratic-corporatist state that provides the institutional framework for power politics is characterized by centralization of executive power, a high degree of interventionism, the functional articulation of interests, and a characteristic pattern of state-sponsored licensing of access to power combined with filtering and funnelling of demands through the key corporate pillars. The dominant ideology of the corporatist state stresses economic growth and political consensus.[20]

Corporatism provided an effective solution to the economic depressions, class conflicts, the ideological warfare and the civil strife in the first decades of this century. Wartime regulation, especially the tripartite agreements pioneered during the First World War, and Keynesian anti-Depression measures first applied in the 1930s and 1940s, stabilized the socio-political order by enfranchising all major interest blocs and boosting the state's regulative capacities. The emerging corporatist structure provided a framework for lasting peace and stability and helped to democratize internal politics by developing a mechanism of effective political representation by all organized, market-generated interests, including unionized workers. Internationally, corporatism provided a framework for collective security arrangements based on laws, conventions and, above all, the recognition of 'geopolitical realities' of political-military blocs.[21]

From the 1950s on the corporate state became increasingly introverted, shifting its interventionist focus from the international defensive-expansionist activities to internal reforms and settlements.

In the long run, however, the bureaucratic-corporatist solution generated tensions. Three such tensions are particularly relevant here: a tension between corporate mediation of interests (including filtering, funnelling and muffling) and corporate closure; between participatory aspirations and political peripheralization of non-incorporated social categories; and between political legitimation in terms of general values and principles, on one hand, and actual political pragmatism and instrumentalism on the other.

While helping to institutionalize and domesticate interest conflict, corporatist politics increases a specific form of closure resulting from the the filtering, funnelling and muffling of interests. Particularly important here is that most subtle form of closure and exclusion which results from the operational definition of what constitutes and does not constitute the legitimate political domain and legitimate political action. As Offe (1990: 247) points out, there are absolute limits to the use of such conventional political means as legal regulation and surveillance, the manipulation of fiscal resources and persuasion. They fail when the social actors subject to corporatist regulations are capable of obstructing them, when they defy utility-maximizing calculation, and when they make excessive demands. Such conditions of failure, according to many critics, marked the end of the period of social peace and stability around 1970.

The success of corporatist-bureaucratic politics also depends on a high level of elite autonomy and a low level of public involvement which in turn establishes an unresponsive leadership on one hand and an apathetic public on the other. It also results in the reduction of societal power to market-political power concentrated in the hands of those social categories which are able to translate market position into an organized political lobby within corporatist structures. This closure has also been effected by the ascent of bureaucratized and milieu-based mass parties. While most of them originated in mass movements and therefore stressed representativeness and relied on substantive ideological appeals, during the twentieth century they were gradually transformed into vote catchers and highly centralized managerial apparatuses which became tightly integrated with state executive organs. Initially, this helped to open up the political system and guaranteed political success by means of electoral victories and consequent influence on policy making. Ultimately, however, bureaucratization weakened the substantive appeals of the parties and made them vulnerable to legitimation crisis. Weber's exhortations against lack-lustre bureaucratic politics and Michels' warning about 'the iron law of oligarchy' were increasingly hailed as prophetic by critics of political establishments in Europe.

The new movements can be seen as a response to these tensions and an attempt at their resolution.[22] They promote involvement, participation, self-organization and group autonomy, and reject the legitimacy of sectional interests as the basis of political demands. Moreover, they challenge the corporatist-bureaucratic model of intermediation in the highly charged language of general social values and universal human rights. This, it must be stressed, does not make the new politics reactionary or irrational. Rather the new social movements vindicate *value-rationality*, a mode of orientation which directly uses general value standards and moral principles as the yardsticks against which political organizations and outcomes are measured. The values that movement actions vindicate and reassert are not novel, they are at the core of the modern value repertoires.[23] What is new and distinct is not so much the value content, *as the way in which values are deployed*. They are presented as threatened, neglected and/or corrupted by the very institutional practices which are formally legitimized by reference to such standards. This is conducive to the development of an uncompromised value-laden stance whereby general values serve as direct standard of assessment and condemnation of bureaucratized institutions and policies. Such a stance makes new movements radical in the socio-cultural (but not necessarily political-programmatic) sense. They pose a challenge to old politics which is particularly damaging and difficult to neutralize.

This general diagnosis is consistent with more specific interpretations of the new western movements as manifestations of 'civil society', 'challenging the boundaries of institutional politics', manifestations of a 'new political paradigm', symptoms of resistance against bureaucratized mass parties, and protests against the displacement of representative bodies by administrative apparatuses (see Berger 1979; Offe 1985a; Melucci 1985; Misztal 1985). As is noted by some commentators, the new movements transcend the traditional Leftist idiom of opposition. They contain:

> [A] critique of industrial growth and waste which goes far beyond the traditional socialist critique of capitalism. They are sceptical of modern technological progress. They oppose not only the rule of capital but also patriarchy and the hierarchic division of labour. Oriented towards the life principle, they are fundamentally opposed to violence. They reject big statebureaucracies in favour of state self-determination, decentralization, self-initiative, individuality and manageable groups. (Hülsberg 1988: 109)

Despite this predominantly negative character, they imply, albeit in embryonic form, a new model of politics which is radically different from the old one. The novelty rests not only in the value-laden, anti-centralist orientation the new movements engender, but also in a new organizational form, and a specific counter-culture they generate.

Anti-parties: the Structure of New Movements

The Left-libertarian parties and the various movement-generated political groups form only the tip of the iceberg of the new politics. Its full scope is difficult to assess because it involves formalized groups as well as semi-formal and informal circles and networks. The social movements around which the new politics is centred defy attempts to draw their boundaries clearly. They are fuzzy, open, polymorphous and polycephalous. Their structure has been described as segmented, reticulate (web-like), polycephalous (many-headed), and cellular (see Gerlach and Hine 1970; Gunderlach 1984). The dominant groups and organizations have been seen as representing a 'new paradigm' (Offe 1985a), a 'participatory-democratic type' (Rothschild-Whitt 1979), typical of the 'new sector' (Levitt 1973) and a 'new mode' (Holloway 1990).

This fuzziness and openness makes it difficult to draw movement boundaries, both in time and space. It is unclear who is in and who is out, when they start and when they finish. There are no membership criteria to restrict participation in movement events. Activists, supporters and sympathizers do not need to share the programmatic consensus that unifies party supporters. Ideological demands placed on supporters are minimal, and they are not codified into doctrinal blueprints, platforms or strategies. Even though particular groups and organizations within the movements do construct programmes and formulate membership criteria, these pronouncements seldom restrict movement actions and they affect only a small minority of participants. The parliamentary wings, various Left-libertarian and Green parties, find enormous difficulty in maintaining enough cohesion and discipline to form stable coalitions and to propose viable alternative programmes. They are under constant pressures from internal factions and extra-parliamentary groups which they are seldom able or willing to resist. This tempers their political aspirations, produces characteristic 'electoral cycles', and makes the green groups natural 'opposition' and 'critical' parties.

Even the most formalized movement-generated parties reject the bureaucratic format of conventional mass parties and pressure groups. Their anti-systemic edge transpires in the very structure and forms of their activism. They reject centralism, discipline and preoccupation with winning votes which makes them 'floating', 'transfunctional', and detached from group interests. Despite this detachment they often graft themselves onto a variety of organizations including conventional parties, trade unions and professional associations and partly utilize their resources. Such transfunctionalism and parasitism makes them difficult to locate and confront politically. Groups opposed to new movements face a hazy and ubiquitous opponent with no clear institutional locus, plural organizational bases, weak leadership, and no clear programme.

The organizational structure of movement bodies is a mirror image of the corporatist-bureaucratic model. Typically, they:

> do not rely, in contrast to traditional forms of political organisation, on the organisational principle of differentiation, whether in the horizontal (insider vs. outsider) or in the vertical (leaders vs. rank-and-file members). To the contrary, there seems to be a strong reliance upon de-differentiation, that is the fusion of

public and private roles, instrumental and expressive behaviour, community and organisation, and in particular the poor and at best transient demarcation between the roles of 'members' and formal 'leaders'. (Offe 1985a: 829)

This is also reflected in movement polycephaly. Authority is decentralized and fragmented along issue lines, territorial lines and ideological-political lines. In fact, the very notion of authority, which implies legitimate, regular and institutionalized patterns of subordination, is ill suited to analysing movement power structures. Organizational leaders, with some vestiges of authority, coexist with activists and agitators who often temporarily usurp leadership functions for the duration of a manifestation. Other charismatic leaders act as spokespersons who represent movement causes in the mass media, as well as becoming exemplary figures, heroes and martyrs who symbolize the movement ethos. However, the power of exemplary figures is not exercised through commands and decision making. They become a focus of movement activities without necessarily being involved in movement events. Indeed, their direct involvement is often discouraged because it may compromise their stance and weaken the purity of purpose they symbolize. All these diverse forms of power, it must be stressed, are not clearly articulated and functionally divided and they seldom converge into a unified authority structure. Movement politics militates against such functional differentiation, specialization and convergence. Polycephaly is cultivated as an important part of the anti-centralist, anti-bureaucratic idiom.

New movements also experiment with a broad variety of forms. These include formal organizations, informal groups, loose social circles, and periodically activated networks of contacts and co-operation. At the core of the movements are usually organized and formalized bodies and 'ethos groups'. The former operate partly as conventional pressure groups by lobbying, making submissions and campaigning in elections, and partly in the new mode by organizing media campaigns and direct protest action. Ethos groups articulate and represent the principles the movements are set up to vindicate and reassert and they usually include symbolic exemplary figures. The 'fringes' encompass loose webs of semi-formal and informal groups, circles and friendship networks, as well as a whole gamut of loosely affiliated 'affinity groups', bandwagons of organized supporters (minor parties, interest groups, unions, associations, etc.) and, finally, non-affiliated supporters and sympathizers. The latter always form the large majority of participants in movement events.

In the process of consolidation, new movements draw into their orbit a wide variety of diverse protest streams. The ecopax movements in the West attract civil rights campaigners, feminist supporters, animal-liberationists and a host of other groups. This convergence occurs in the form of co-ordination of protests, marches and rallies, get-togethers, organizational hybrids (such as Women for Peace and Greenpeace) and theoretical fusions (such as eco-feminist analysis). The convergence is of a

horizontal nature and it seldom leads to organizational takeovers or
vertical co-ordination. As a result, the boundaries between particular
sub-movements and protest streams are increasingly hard to draw. Movements form broad 'industries' and 'sectors' covering a whole host of causes,
concerns, forms and events. They spill into the area of cultural contest and
blur the division between political action, social activism and general
lifestyle.

Repertoires of action include conventional lobbying, as well as less
conventional mass rallies and protest marches, and unconventional, often
eccentric and scandalizing, direct action. The latter aims to attract maximum media attention and it is often staged in such a way as to achieve this.
By harnessing the mass media to their causes the movements shift politics
onto new ground. They move into a public arena where images, slogans
and icons, and the value-laden appeals they engender, have more impact
than the discursive programmes and platforms of conventional parties and
interest groups. This high visibility and media exposure imposes a specific
logic of action. The new movements rely both on recurrent intense
campaigns, usually triggered by crisis events, and on less visible, 'subterra-
nean' activities aiming at cultivating networks of contacts, friendship and
co-operation (leaflet writing, informal gatherings, etc.).

Movement Counter-culture and the Mass Media

Movement actions are seldom directly political. They implicitly challenge
the notion of politics as a specialized arena of action by refusing to limit
their concerns to political matters, by adopting a moral idiom of criticism
and presenting ethical postulates which cannot be satisfied by concrete
administrative decisions. The critical edge of movement action is always
broad and fundamental and is articulated through general symbols, icons
and appeals. By means of such symbolic language, as Melucci (1985: 813)
points out, movements challenge the dominant cultural codes embodied in
institutionalized power relations. The symbolic-iconic sphere also performs
another important function: that of providing a degree of cohesion and
unity to extremely heterogeneous issues, concerns and strategies. In the
absence of unifying ideology, interests and/or programmes, movements
rely on this unity of symbolic-iconic, mostly negative, references.[24]

The distinctive features of symbolic-iconic language can be summarized
in five points:

- It is critical and expressed in an adversarial mode of opposition,
  rejection and protest. Appeals use such expressions as 'stop' and 'ban';
  symbols make use of proscriptive signs; icons stress danger (of war,
  nuclear radiation, etc.). The adversarial mode forms a broad 'common
  denominator' facilitating a coalescence within the new movements of
  many diverse protest streams. Such shared opposition constitutes a
  much broader basis of co-operation than a common ideology or
  programme.

- It is symbolic and therefore general and unspecific. Symbols are always ambiguous, multivocal and open to new interpretation. They resonate among many meanings and are open to connections with other symbolic universes. Symbolic language suits the ideological and programmatic vagueness of social movements and it is suitable for articulating general value concerns. At the same time it merges well with such other symbolic elements as mode of dress, behaviour, aesthetic taste and dietary habits into a recognizable and distinctive counter-cultural lifestyle. These lifestyles are not difficult to imitate, and they cross-cut class, age group, regional and ethnic divisions.
- Movement symbols are simple, syncretic, visible and didactic. They draw from popular repertoires including road signs, folk traditions and national symbols, and from different historical and socio-cultural contexts. Symbols and icons are often simplified so that they can be easily utilized in graffiti, banners and chants, and they are infused with purposeful spirit.
- The language of the new movements is compact. It relies on highly condensed symbols, slogans and appeals which form easily recognizable images. Such an economical form of presentation facilitates dissemination and is highly suitable for mass media (especially TV) consumption and amplification.
- The distinction between the form and content of movement events is blurred. The media become messages. Protest marches, rallies and sit-ins, as well as less conventional festivals, music concerts, street performances and happenings appeal through their very form, which is unorthodox, informal and, above all, critical and value-infused.

The general anti-bureaucratic character of movement symbols and repertoires of action is highly apparent. The symbols are antitheses of discursive platforms and programmes. Action which stresses grass-roots involvement, commitment, spontaneity and unselfish dedication contrasts sharply with a formalized corporatist-bureaucratic idiom. Movement initiatives are demonstratively informal, a feature which is expressed in the very mode of organization, behaviour, language and style of dress. Participants include families, often with children; programmes are 'open' and frequently inconsistent; and statements include spontaneous appeals, political declarations, plays, jokes, songs and personal confessions. The partial participation of passers-by is regarded as normal. Hierarchy and rank are demonstratively disregarded or even mocked. Speakers neither wear formal dress nor adhere to the conventional speech formats. Those who try can count on little sympathy or attention. This informality extends to the arenas of presentation. So movement messages appear on banners, car stickers, graffiti, tree hangings, on balloons, and even on the finger-painted faces of children. The conventional media of printed programme, platform and newspaper ads are seldom employed.

This highly non-discursive form fits well the format of the mass media, especially television, and makes movement events newsworthy, interesting and unusual. It is impossible to judge whether the language of protests has been tailored for media consumption, or whether it is the mass media which influence movement forms. Perhaps there has been a mutual convergence resulting in a symbiotic relationship. The media need movement events because, especially when they are unorthodox and eccentric, they are newsworthy. The movements need media attention to amplify and disseminate their appeals. They thrive on widespread concerns and, given the scarcity of resources and the unavailability of institutionalized channels of communication and dissemination, they rely heavily on voluntary (rather than commercial) coverage. Movement events are often planned by activists in a way that maximizes media access and facilitates coverage. For movement activists this is an effort aimed at informing, educating, converting and mobilizing. Mass media serve this purpose and they fit a form of protest which inhabits public space and leisure time.

The way in which movement issues are publicized and transformed into mass concerns also betrays the influence of the mass media. They are always contextualized, and linked with the global issues and general values, often in the form of such doom scenarios as nuclear holocaust and greenhouse disaster. This dramatizes them, adds a sense of urgency, and generates mass anxiety which proves to be an exceptionally potent propellant for action. Issues are combined with events into stories, often with dramatized plots, allowing for easy identification of heroes and villains. Such narratives not only make movement messages more attractive to the media, but also give them a currency similiar to folk tales. Movement activists often have a highly developed ability to frame, elaborate, dramatize and package movement appeals and this gives them the status and appearance of pop-stars.

The language, the media of expression, and the repertoires of action are more important than the issue content of movement appeals. Issues are diverse, and they change, both during campaigns and even within a single movement event.[25] A typical march, rally or demonstration will include a broad gamut of groups, slogans and appeals, including the religious and the secular, the radical and the conservative. To an outside observer, it is frequently difficult to discover which of them constitute a 'mainstream' and which belong to affiliated fringes and bandwagons. Some issues survive longer than the movements which propel them and some fade, giving way to new issues. These frequent switches from issue to issue do not seem to affect movement vitality. The gradual fading of peace issues within the western movements and their fusion with ecological and feminist concerns is a good example of this process.

Not only the iconic-symbolic language of the new movements, but also the very pattern of their mobilization has been influenced by the mass media. Much of movement development occurs 'parthenogenetically', that is, through diffusion of symbols and slogans and the emulation of lifestyles within generational and status categories. Because of this pattern of diffusion movements should be seen not only as responses to local conditions but also as elements of new lifestyles disseminated via the mass media, contact networks, and processes of geographical mobility. The pattern of dissemination is similar to that followed by fashions, fads and cultural innovations. Ideas flow along national and international circuits of contact as well as via the mass media. Just as merchant chains and monasteries formed the transmission belts for the modernization process, so these networks, aided by the electronic mass media, form the channels of diffusion of the symbols and lifestyles of the new politics.

New Politics in Eastern Europe and the USA

Before we examine the consequences of the new movement politics, a brief digression is necessary on the two 'special cases' of Eastern Europe and the USA.

While western developments followed an evolutionary path, the East European communist regimes entered an 'alternative route to modernity' which, according to the leaders of the revolution, was to be a shortcut. The principal tool of accelerated modernization was a monocentric party-state and the strategy combined ideological appeals, mass exhortations, and centralized control by the party-state elite which was totalitarian in its scope. The wide scope of central control and an initial ability to generate a high degree of commitment to ideological goals helped Soviet Russia to accomplish the first stage of industrialization, win a great war, and impose Soviet domination throughout Eastern Europe, albeit at enormous human cost.

In the process of post-Stalinist 'normalization' in the late 1950s and 1960s some totalitarian features of the Soviet partocracy were gradually toned down and diluted, especially in the East European satellites. In the 1970s the Soviet state and its East European counterparts acquired several corporatist features by incorporating some sectional 'interest blocs' especially regional-ethnic and functional ones, but they remained much more monocentric and all-inclusive than the liberal corporate systems in Western Europe.

In the 1970s and 1980s, all Soviet-type societies started to experience a series of crises marked by falling production, shortages of goods, rising absenteeism, alcoholism, rising crime rates, declining welfare services, increasing mortality and a 'leadership drift'. This provoked occasional protests and, eventually, mass social movements which were strongly anti-partocratic in character, first in Poland and subsequently throughout Eastern Europe. The scope of these movements was much broader than those in the West and, after an initial period during which Solidarity was suppressed, East European new politics has rapidly displaced the old corporatist-partocratic idiom in the series of spectacular 'refolutionary' transformations.[26]

Partocratic corporatism, in its totalitarian Soviet version, has constituted the negative frame of reference for the East European movements and 'self-limiting revolutions'. The movements are mirror images of partocracies. They are vigorously anti-centralist and anti-totalitarian. More importantly, the longstanding Soviet sponsorship of the communist East European regimes gave the anti-partocratic movements a characteristic anti-Soviet colouring. Their slogans, like those of the American Revolution, combined postulates of socio-political reform with demands for political autonomy and national sovereignty. This combination proved extremely potent, resulting in mass mobilizations, and it contributed to swift socio-political change.

Just as in western new movements, the dominant constituency of the anti-partocratic movements was the post-Stalinist generation which grew up after 1956 under conditions of relative stability and economic growth. Its members were better informed, better educated, less fearful of repression and, above all, had much higher political aspirations than the previous generation. The most educated section, known as the 'socialist new middle class', played a dominant role in the organization of the movements. Leaders and activists were often recruited from the ranks of the humanistic intelligentsia.

The East European movements illustrate the parthenogenetic character of mobilizations even better than their western counterparts. The symbols (like the V-sign), icons (like national flags with the removed communist logo) and protest repertoires (like mass rallies) spread throughout Eastern Europe in a domino-like pattern. Underground publications, radio, and above all TV played a crucial role as media of this diffusion. Movement activists, in turn, utilized the reformed media to spread their messages in the 'unconquered' territories. This symbiosis proved extremely effective as the protests spread with unprecedented swiftness and swept away weakened communist establishments. To paraphrase Ash (1990), what took Poland ten years, happened in Hungary in ten months, in ten weeks in East Germany, and in ten days in Czechoslovakia. It was the TV transmission of the reburial of Imre Nagy that mobilized the Hungarian public; it was the TV coverage of mid-November protests in Prague that derailed the Czechoslovak communist authorities; fighting in Romania focussed on the TV studio in Bucharest, and its takeover sealed the fate of the Ceausescu regime.

Despite some differences in the dominant orientations, the Western and the East European movements share many general features, so can be explained in a similar way.[27] Both mark the advent of a new politics which heralds changes that are potentially revolutionary in scope. Such changes will not be as dramatic in the West as they have been in Eastern Europe. Partial accommodation within the bureaucratic system blunts the anti-systemic edge of the western movements. The East European movements, in turn, will also have to partly demobilize and 'normalize' to give way to post-revolutionary administrations. This may lead to further convergence, especially if the direction of change in Eastern Europe remains as pro-western as it is at present.

The North American case is almost a reverse image of Eastern Europe. Unlike Eastern Europe, the USA has not experienced a sudden and radical resurgence of new politics. The American movements are also less radical and less anti-systemic than their West-European counterparts. There are well established movements there covering ecological, civil rights, feminist and pacifist issues. Many such movements in fact originated in North America and were later transplanted to Europe, Australia and New Zealand. But despite their thematic similarity, they are more organized and integrated with mainstream political institutions and processes. They form organized lobbies which are often more effective than the European counterparts in influencing state policy. This difference seems to reflect the idiosyncrasies of the American political system, which were discussed in more detail in the previous chapter. The USA has a fragmented federalist state with strong regional units of representation and powerful specialized Congressional committees. There are no bureaucratized, programmatic, ideologically legitimized mass parties. American party organizations already partially resemble social movements. They are mobilized for the short periods of electoral campaigns, do not serve as bases of corporatist intermediation, and they have traditionally relied on spoils rather than interest-representation and ideological appeals.[28] American corporatism, when it is diagnosed as such,[29] is more technocratic and more open due to reduced centralization. But formal legalism, a preoccupation with constitutionalism and procedural accuracy, are more pronounced in American than in European politics. America has been strongly affected, even if only in popular expectations rather than reality, by residual ideological blueprints of the mass parties. In a word, American politics is less etatist, less corporatist, and it focusses on constitutional interpretation and litigation.

One may argue that this weakness or absence of corporatism in the USA is the main reason for the weakness of radical anti-etatist challenges in the form of new politics. American mass movements resemble weakly disciplined interest groups rather than European protest mobilizations. They are more adaptive and interest-oriented than their European counterparts. Most of them promptly transform into interest groups, thus supporting the arguments of resource mobilization theory which is the dominant stream in American studies of movements. The anti-systemic edge is decisively weaker than in European new politics.

Transient Protests or a New Configuration?

At the most general level, the upsurge of new politics illustrates a paradox or, if one prefers, a dialectic, of modernity. The new movements can be seen as responses to, and extensions of, processes of political modernization. They are also the product of the stability, prosperity and consensus which the bureaucratized and corporatist welfare states have provided. Yet, this very genesis makes them critical and contesting. They challenge the very trends which indirectly prompted their formation, attacking bureaucratic apparatuses, criticizing corporatist closure and rejecting consensual deals.

One of the most contentious issues in current political debates concerns the effectiveness of new politics, its impact on conventional parties and electoral processes, and future trajectories for the new movements. Some observers, mostly in Europe, see the new movements as a part of a global transition which is permanent and revolutionary in its impact. Others see them as transient and marginal, as a residuum of institutionalized power-politics and/or as a stage of organizational evolution which may lead to new conventional political parties and pressure groups. Such views are particularly popular among 'resource mobilization' theorists in the USA.

These different assessments have two sources. They undoubtedly reflect the different configurations on each side of the Atlantic. The American configuration is characterized by a highly formalized but relatively open, noncorporatist politics, which generates movements that are more political and adaptive and less anti-systemic than their European counterparts. The West European (as well as Australian and New Zealand) movements respond to political configurations characterized by a higher degree of corporatist closure and rigidity, and they tend to be more contesting and more radical in their anti-bureaucratic, anti-corporatist orientations. Finally, the rigidity of the East European state-socialist regimes has sparked the most radical, vigorously anti-partocratic protest movements, which pave the way for revolutionary reconstruction. Although a character of the referent regime appears to be a key determinant of the nature and strength of movements, it is not the sole determinant. The vitality of new politics depends also on conditions of mobilization, the political opportunity structure, the strength of the social constituencies and the availability of the mass media carriers (see, for example, Kitchelt 1986, 1990; Wilson 1990; Kaase 1990).

Differences in assessment also reflect different criteria of judgement. If gauged in terms of group membership, mustered votes, number of parliamentary seats and direct impact on policy decisions, the new movements and their political representations appear rather weak. Such an assessment, however, is incomplete. It ignores the fact that, even if ultimately waning, the new movements speed up the process of dealignment and erode corporatist closure. One aspect of this process is the collapse of bipolar divisions and the rise of third parties. Still another is the formation of new channels of political recruitment and the rise of new movement-based elites.

The most conspicuous symptom of this process is the rise of movement-generated Left-libertarian parties which include such left-wing parties as the Danish Socialist People's Party, Green/Ecological parties such as the German Greens, and various independent, civil rights and minority groups. Over 70 such groups have competed in European national elections since the late 1970s although less than two dozen maintain seats in national parliaments. Together they form a broad family of new politics parties which are increasingly visible in national parliaments and local governing bodies.[30]

This has a number of important consequences for the existing political groups. The new politics parties compete mainly with the old social democratic parties, weakening their support, undermining their legitimacy and provoking internal schisms. The threat comes both from within as activists undermine organizational coherence and discipline, and from outside in the form of declining popularity and electoral support. In defence, the old parties open up their programmes, making pre-emptive bids for movement-publicized issues and seeking to accommodate movement leaders. The effectiveness of these defensive measures should not be underestimated. A large number of movement-generated groups are gradually being co-opted and absorbed into conventional politics. However, this absorption causes loosening of corporatist deals and adds flexibility to the process of interest articulation (see also Kitchelt 1990; Papadakis 1989).

The ascendancy of the new movements brings about a crisis for the old Marxist Left. The Communist parties either disappear, following the path of their East European counterparts, or join the bandwagon of the new politics by adopting the green and libertarian slogans and programmes. This political evolution of the Left is speeded up by an influx of old Left supporters into the ranks of Left-libertarian groups. The response on the opposite end of the political spectrum is equally significant. The movements provoke the mobilization of a New Right, thus escalating the shift from stable bipolar to shifting and cross-cutting divisions. Fears that such a change decreases political stability are justified although often exaggerated. Most electoral systems are protected against the destabilizing impact of smaller groups and thus encourage political normalization. Some new groups will undoubtedly be transformed into conventional parties, some will be co-opted and absorbed by the old social democratic parties, and some will fall victim to electoral cycles.

The new politics marks the ascendancy of new politicians propelled to elite positions by movement parties and organized groups. As individuals, they differ considerably from the old political man. An important difference is that the new figures are much more frequently 'political women'. In clear contrast to old conventional parties, the new political groups attract, and promote to leadership positions, almost equal proportions of men and women. Perhaps more importantly, the new politicians represent social categories which differ sharply from the old bureaucratic elite in their functions and orientations. They include conscience politicians, populist spokespersons, minority champions and internationalists. Their ascent, which is often meteoric, marks not only an important generational transition in the elite but also the opening of new, nonbureaucratic channels of recruitment likely to outlive the parties which established them.

These highly visible changes do not exhaust the impact of the new politics. The influence of new movements extends outside the sphere of institutional politics by changing political outlooks and attitudes of the politically active. The new movements disseminate universalistic value-concerns; they mobilize to much greater extent symbolic-iconic language and the mass media channels of political communication; they increase the openness of the political system, not only by incorporating new issues and broadening political agendas, but also by innovation in repertoires of political action; they promote the further globalization of politics; and increase the awareness of connections between various issues and problems, thus undermining national parochialism. These influences apply independently of the fate of particular political groups and parties generated by the movements.

Are these changes directional and permanent, or are they merely an aspect of generational, electoral and protest cycles? In fact, both assessments may be true. As far as the *substance* of politics, that is, the general socio-cultural basis, is concerned, the new politics marks a permanent shift away from structurally determined class politics. The new configuration is more contingent and conjunctural reflecting socio-cultural processes related to generational outlooks, value orientations and lifestyles, rather than economically structured interests. The general vector of this shift appears to be quite consistent:

- from structurally determined to more contingent, generationally specific divisions;
- from economically determined to socio-culturally (consumption and lifestyle) related;
- from interest politics to the politics of universalistic concerns (see Figure 5.1a).

Yet not all aspects of the changes analysed may be equally permanent. The *format* of the movement-propelled new politics is likely to normalize, that is, to adopt a more institutionalized, conventional and stable party-elite form. The crisis in the conflict- and faction-ridden Green Party in Germany, and its heavy losses in the 1990 elections, are likely to strengthen a normalizing drive not only among the German party but also among their European and Australian counterparts. Similarly, the collapse of the Green-Labor accord in Tasmania, seen as a model of coexistence between the new and conventional political bodies, leads to a critical reassessment of movement strategies. As these developments suggest, the semi- and non-institutionalized initiatives, circles and networks are likely to be routinized, and the contempt for elite deals and compromises is likely to be moderated, making the new politics more stable and consistent.

Four processes are instrumental in this normalizing shift. First, there is a

a) Substance

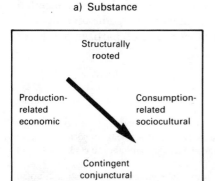

b) Format

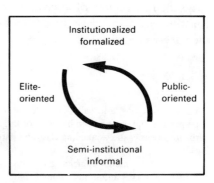

Figure 5.1   *Aspects of political transformation in Europe: the main vectors of change*

factor of exhaustion. Non- and semi-institutionalized movement initiatives, unlike the routine activities of parties and pressure groups, are heavy consumers of social energy. The high commitment and voluntary effort on which they rely is difficult to sustain. Hence the cyclical pattern of movement mobilization followed by periods of apathy, and hence the initial volatility of electoral support for Left-libertarian parties. Second, the process of institutionalization, organization, and even bureaucratization is likely to continue in response to internally generated pressures from new elites and in response to external pressures coming from disgruntled coalition partners and the state. Third, the new political groups and parties generated by the new movements are likely to experience what Kitchelt (1990) describes as electoral cycles. These cycles start with high popularity, which leads to electoral victories and temporary alliances and then to tensions, the breakdown of coalitions and subsiding support. Fourth, the movement format is likely to be affected by long-term generational shifts. Movement constituencies are already ageing, and they are likely to carry the radical anti-bureaucratic protest into older age groups and, ultimately, to its natural exit. Some elements of the new political ethos will undoubtedly remain, and they may even, as suggested by Veen (1989), become a part of a new stable milieu. But the appeal of new politics to the new (post-postwar) generation is much less, thus blunting the anti-systemic edge of political initiatives. A combination of these four factors is likely to produce a political format which is increasingly more institutionalized and more elite-oriented (see Figure 5.1b).

New politics marks both a substantive and permanent change in the political complexion of advanced societies, and a generational/political cycle. Its substantive novelty lies principally in the increased *diversity* of political processes – more open organizational structures, more diverse elites, more fluid and fragmented alliances and loyalties, and more complex networks of communication. Even if the inevitable normalization strips the new politics of some of its formal idiosyncrasies, the diversity that constitutes a major departure from the class-structured partisan politics of the past will persist.

Notes

1. Milieu parties, also called 'people parties' and 'parties of democratic integration', are mass parties representing the interests of large-scale structural segments of society. For the early diagnoses of the weakening class and party allegiances see Goldthorpe et al. (1968) and Parkin (1968).

2. These movements coincide and converge with other streams of protest: anti-urban development, local autonomy, animal rights, educational reform and pro-third world. The 'new politics' they generate has been analysed by Baker et al. (1981), Offe (1985a), Dalton et al. (1984a, 1984b), Dalton (1988), Schmitt (1989), Dalton et al. (1990) and Pakulski (1991).

3. Other important changes included a weakening of the corporatist deals and the exhaustion of the welfare state. These processes (discussed in Chapter 3) involve increasingly educated electorates and increases in 'sociotropic voting'. See Dalton (1988), Inglehart and Flanagan (1989) and Barnes and Kaase (1979).

4. In fact, most of the issues raised by the movements have also been adopted by conventional parties and interest groups. Movement-generated parties, in turn, extend their agendas by covering some of the 'conventional' issues. This process is discussed by Papadakis (1989).

5. The strength of the East European new politics is even more difficult to gauge. Poland apart, movement mobilization there has been sudden and followed by quick institutionalization. Political restrictions, as well as scarcity of resources, have prevented sociological research, and consequently assessments of participation are often impressionistic and vary widely. It has been estimated that at the peak of mobilization between 40 and 60 per cent of the adult populations participated in movement events.

6. See, for example, Huntington (1973: 170). He defines political modernization as involving rationalization of authority, including its centralization within bureaucratized state apparatuses; differentiation of political functions; and extension of participation through formalized political structures (parties, interest groups, etc.).

7. Some analysts add to this list a 'postmaterialist' change in dominant values. For an outline of the overall pattern of change see other chapters in this book and also Bell (1973), Lash and Urry (1987), Lash (1990) and Turner (1989).

8. The process of incorporation of the unions, and their transformation from a movement to 'distribution and security machines' has been analysed by Touraine (1986) and Schmitter and Lehmbruch (1979).

9. Mass accounts are the residue of mass society explanations of social movements, especially of totalitarian movements (fascist and communist). See Arendt (1966) and Kornhauser (1959) for general outlines.

10. The classic account can be found in Gouldner (1979). More recent versions have been referred to by Brym (1980), Cotgrove (1982) and Kriesi (1989). A most interesting status interpretation in terms of 'status categories' is offered by Turner (1988).

11. See Van Liere and Dunlap (1980) and Dalton (1988). Similar conclusions have been drawn by some students of feminist movement and Polish Solidarity (Pakulski 1991).

12. For general discussion of the issue of class and movements see Pakulski (1990).

13. There is little consensus on who belongs to the new classes and how new they are. According to Berger (1987: 67): 'Contemporary Western societies are characterized by a protracted conflict between two classes, the old middle class (occupied in the production and distribution of material goods and services) and a new middle class (occupied in the production and distribution of symbolic knowledge).' Other scholars (like Bell, 1973) and

Cotgrove, 1982) see the new class as a more recent product, a result of postindustrial changes. Conservative thinkers, like Kristol (1979) perceive it as a major threat to liberties; radical critics, like Gouldner (1979), see it as a potentially emancipatory counter-class which challenges the domination of technocrats, owners and managers. Most interpretations link the new class directly or indirectly with the new politics and social movements.

14. A more detailed criticism of all these accounts can be found elsewhere: see Pakulski (1990, 1991, ch.1,3).

15. Aware of these difficulties, Kriesi (1989) opts for a label 'state class' (and 'specialists in the social and cultural services'), while Offe (1985a) concludes that the new movements represent the politics 'of a class' (peripheralized section of the new middle class) but not 'on behalf of a class', that is, not promoting any sectional class interests. Behind these interpretive difficulties there is obviously a problem with the concept of class, which is one of the most vague, abused and 'stretched' of all sociological conceptual concepts. The notion of 'middle class' in particular has been applied indiscriminately to almost any socio-occupational and socio-cultural category. It is not this vagueness, though, which makes class analyses inadequate. The problem is more fundamental. Most class interpretations assume that, because of the capitalist nature of the societal context, all important social conflicts in the West have to have a structural socio-economic class basis, and that the identification of such a basis is an essential proof of a movement's reality and importance. This assumption needs to be critically re-examined.

16. This participatory revolution has been analysed by Barnes and Kaase (1979) and Kaase (1984) in a context of changing forms of involvement and repertoires of political action. Like most students of the new politics, Barnes and Kaase have linked the participatory revolution with economic growth, the spread of education, the widening of public tolerance, and the extension of citizenship rights. The revolution involves not only the intensification of participatory involvement, but also increasingly diverse forms of participation, including 'unconventional' forms 'which do not correspond to the norms of law and custom that regulate political participation under a particular regime' (1979: 41). The spread of these unconventional forms has been associated with political activization of young people and the use of the mass media.

17. Results of such studies are reported by Dalton (1988, esp. 65–9, 88). See Barnes and Kaase (1979: 524) for the discussion of generational effects. Summaries of research results are also in Cotgrove (1982), Offe (1985a), Morrison and Dunlap (1986) and Kitchelt (1990). Reviews of the social composition of the new movements can be found in Papadakis (1984: 120–2, 139–41), Hülsberg (1988: 70–85), Veen (1989), Kriesi (1989) and Pakulski (1991).

18. The point that movements represent a collective response to historically shaped state structures and actions of state officials has been forcefully made by Tilly (1978, 1988). Links with state actions and political regimes have been particularly well explored by Offe (1985a), Kitchelt (1986, 1990) and Wilson (1990). Similar observations on the 'anti-interest' orientations in student protests in Europe are made by S. Berger (1979, 1981).

19. See Berger (1979), Offe (1985a), Gibbins (1989), Rootes (1980), Schmitt (1989) and Pakulski (1991). The term 'new politics' was first applied in analyses of fascist mobilizations ('politics of the street', 'politics of the piazza'). The orientations and ethos of the fascist movements, however, were very different from those of contemporary western social movements.

20. For a more detailed analysis see Chapter 3. For a general outline of 'power politics', see Offe (1985a) and Pakulski (1991). Links between the new movements and modernity are also explored by Lash and Urry (1987), Lash (1990) and Eder (1990). Corporatist politics are discussed by Schmitter and Lehmbruch (1979), Lehmbruch and Schmitter (1982) and Wilson (1990).

21. International conflicts were highly conventionalized and localized. If open wars erupted, as in Korea and Vietnam, they were fought largely by proxy, did not involve the total warfare, and did not provoke direct and full-blown (nuclear) confrontation between the superpowers.

22. See Schmitter (1974), Pizzorno (1981), Kitchelt (1990) and Wilson (1990) on the link between the new movements and corporatism.

23. For critical assessment of the 'new values' interpretation see Lowe and Rudig (1986) and Offe (1985a: 849–50), Reimer (1989) and Pakulski (1991: ch. 2).

24. The importance of the symbolic-iconic sphere in the new movements has been stressed by Feher and Heller (1983). The importance of the negative references as a 'common denominator' in movement concerns has been analysed in more detail elsewhere (Pakulski 1991).

25. See, for example, comments by Parkin (1968) and the results of Schmitt's (1989) study.

26. The economic difficulties are analysed by Brus and Laski (1990), and the 'leadership drift' has been analysed in the 1989 issues of *Studies in Comparative Communism*. The concept of 'refolution' was introduced by Ash (1989, 1990).

27. In spite of some differences in orientations, issues and outcomes, and despite marked differences in the level of socio-economic development between advanced western and Soviet-type societies, the new movements in East and West are similar in their democratic ethos and anti-corporatist, anti-etatist orientation. This global scope of the new movements may result in an exaggerated view of their importance, especially when significant differences between the western and the East European movements are ignored.

28. For a classical formulation of the (North American) 'specificity thesis' see Huntington (1973). Interesting comparisons between the US and Europe can be found in Nettl (1968), Schefter (1977, 1979) and Skocpol (1985).

29. For the debate on corporatism in the US see Salisbury (1979) and F.L. Wilson (1990).

30. There is no agreement on which parties and groups are to be included within the new politics. Kitchelt's definition is more inclusive than those of Müller-Rommel and Parkin. See Müller-Rommel (1990), Müller-Rommel and Poguntke (1989), Kitchelt (1990), S. Parkin (1989).

6

Disalienation and debureaucratization

If the focus for this book had been processes of modernization then this chapter would probably have been placed somewhere towards the beginning rather than towards the end. Production is the key axial process of modern societies – the way it is organized might be held to determine, or at least to have serious consequences for, political, cultural and other developments. Indeed our early statements in Chapter 1 about the rationalization and commodification of social life under conditions of modernization are in essence statements about the pervasive influence of systems of production. It is no accident that we choose to begin with cultural matters and end with material ones. Postmodernization precisely involves a reversal of determinacy so that the fragments of a hyperdifferentiating culture impact upon, disrupt and deconstruct arenas of social structure which might previously have been thought impervious to change.

The particular vector for the impact of culture on production is the market. Paradoxically, under modern conditions especially those of organized capitalism the market is something of a myth. What are normally understood as open commodity markets are in fact typically dominated by mass producers able by the use of intensive advertising, predatory pricing practices, control of labour costs and government subsidy and protectionism to squeeze out competition and thus to develop something approximating a command relationship with consumers. As we shall discuss in detail below, so successful do they become in such practices that markets become saturated and consumers begin actually to exercise choice. Production systems are forced by the vagaries of consumer demand into structural change that allows flexible responses. Production systems themselves also begin to hyperdifferentiate and become choice-driven. The opening phases of the postmodernization of systems of production are, we shall see, very different from the opening phases of their modernization.

Gazing on the plight of workers experiencing the new forms of production organization of the early nineteenth century the young Karl Marx was in no doubt that modernization had reduced humanity to a new and terrible condition: 'the worker does not affirm himself in his work but denies himself, feels miserable and unhappy, develops no free physical and mental energy but mortifies his flesh and ruins his mind. The worker, therefore feels at ease only outside work, and during work he is outside himself. He is at home when he is not working and when he is working he is not at home' (1967: 292).

However, as Max Weber reminds us, it is not only labouring workers who experience a diminished level of humanity but also the industrial capitalists who exploit them, those: 'Specialists without spirit, sensualists without heart' (1978: 182). However, for Weber, the central process of modernization is rationalization, the progressive reduction of transcendent and enchanted commitment into goals which are short-run, instrumental and materialistic. Above all, this is accomplished in the form of organization which Weber calls the bureaucratic administrative staff, a rational, rule-bound, formal, hierarchical, impersonal, specialized, affectively neutral and instrumental form which is: ' "*Sine ira et studio*," without hatred or passion, and hence without affection or enthusiasm' (1978: 225 original italics). Marx and Weber both seek to convince us that modernization renders the organization both of production and of other aspects of social life unpleasant, unfamiliar, impersonal, threatening and thus dehumanizing, a consequence of the radical differentiation of economic activity and domestic activity.

The directions in which modern systems for the organization of production develop are given to us in the classical accounts. For Weber, as the above indicates, it is clear that this process is essentially one of bureaucratic rationalization, specifically in the arenas of state and commercial activity. As the scale of administrative tasks increases and as the tasks become more technical in character, the functional superiority of bureaucracy, its '[p]recision, speed, unambiguity, knowledge of the files, continuity, discretion, unity, strict subordination, reduction of friction and of material and personal costs' (1978: 973), ensures its rapid spread and growth at the expense of other organizational forms. In growing it disempowers all nonbureaucratic groups, with the singular exception of capitalist entrepreneurs, and displaces time-honoured value-commitments.

Marx, by contrast, shows us the way in which the power of the capitalist entrepreneur itself increases. The key problem for the capitalist is the tendency of market competition to reduce commodity prices and thus the long-run tendency of the rate of profit to decline. There are two possible solutions, either to monopolize markets and to mass-produce and so to maintain prices, or to develop the organization technologically, in order to reduce both the skill level of labour and the amount of labour required and thus to reduce wage costs. In practice both strategies are employed simultaneously and they indicate the general trend of modern capitalism. However, the second, known as the labour process, is the more critical because of its tendency to increase control by capitalists over workers and concomitantly to dehumanize and immiserate them.

We are thus provided with an analysis of the central sources of power in modern society, economic organizations and state organizations. In the advanced stages of modernity two further developments occur in relation to them. First, there is a general tendency for inter-organizational linkages to develop between the state and commercial organizations and also with such other organizational power bases as labour unions. This development, known as 'organized capitalism' (Hilferding 1981), arises partly out of the functional consequences the state and economic organizations have for each other and partly as a means of bypassing representative and participatory democratic controls which constrain their powers. A second general tendency is indicated in the recent work of Habermas (1984, 1987a). Habermas shows that bureaucratic and commercial power, 'strategic action', extend, under advanced capitalism not only to the internal practices of their respective arenas but also into domestic arenas of 'communicative action' previously deemed differentiated and sacrosanct. This is accomplished by the 'mediatization' of bureaucratic and commercial control ('steering', as Habermas has it) by means of informatic linkages, money, welfare provision, legal direction etc. into so-called lifeworld contexts. These developments provide the advanced stage of modernization with its special character of being centrally and pervasively organized.

Habermas takes his cue from Weber in being essentially pessimistic about the development of modern capitalism. By contrast, Marx is far from being so, celebrating capitalism as an extraordinary human achievement, the full flowering of history with enormous latent potential for human liberation and development. This potential is realizable within a postcapitalist organization of work, which comes about as the consequence of the technological implications of the labour process. As the labour process reaches its peak, and as labour becomes more and more subdivided into specific tasks, these tasks can themselves be replaced by the actions of machines (Marx 1971: 162–3). There appears then a final stage of capitalism, the stage of the *automatic system of machinery*, which is set in motion by an automaton which consists of 'a number of mechanical and intellectual organs, so that the workers themselves can be no more than the conscious limbs of the automaton' (1971: 154). In this system: 'The human factor is restricted to watching and supervising the production process. (This applies not only to machinery, but also to the combination of human activities and the development of human commerce)' (1971: 165). So the means of production become an integrated, tangible, enlarged whole which confronts workers with their own powerlessness. At last, confronted by the form of their own powerlessness, workers will take control of productive forces. At this point Marx envisions a reversal in which machines become the property of associated workers, continuing to be means of social production and contributing to a collapse of the boundary between production time and free time. A postcapitalist society is argued to be an automated society in which machines are tools of production owned and controlled by workers, who are thus disalienated.

We are not committed to an argument that society is entering such a postcapitalist phase but rather take the view that much of what Marx says finds clear parallels in the transformation of the organization of production which is part of the process of postmodernization. Indeed he showed remarkable prescience in anticipating not only advanced mechanical technologies but also intellectual technologies which would transform the nature of work and the scale of property ownership. Nor is the present argument as technologically determinist as Marx appears to be in these passages from the *Grundrisse*. Instead technology is a facilitating factor, a factor which creates several human possibilities but also limitations to them. In particular, informatic and automated technology allows for three possible sets of such changes in the organization of work which apply in contemporary society. First, it allows for an expansion of work organization in the service sector by reducing the amount of labour required for the production of commodities (postindustrialization); second, by reducing the capital costs of production it increases possibilities for self-employment in both the service and commodity sectors (petty entrepreneurialism); and third, it allows alternative forms of organization of commodity production itself (flexible manufacturing). Taken together these three developments constitute a differentiation of the production process so that a wide variety of arrangements is becoming possible for the organization of capital and labour.

The major part of the analysis in this chapter focusses on the third of these developments. This is because there is nothing uniquely new about the development of a petty bourgeoisie or of service industry. Indeed several critics (e.g. Frankel 1987; Kumar 1978) argue that all the service sector elements of so-called 'postindustrial society' are also integral components of industrialism. It is therefore also necessary to take issue with Lyotard's assumption that the postindustrialization of society is the simple counterpart of the postmodernization of culture (1984: 3). Instead it is possible to argue that taken together the complete development of all three organizational possibilities in principle would allow for the reintegration of work into culturally ordered lifeworlds, for a form of emancipation of the type envisioned by Marx. However, before engaging in an analysis of these postmodern developments the shape of modern work organizations must be indicated.

Taylorism and Fordism

The descriptions given by Marx and Weber of the modern workplace are so widely accepted that they structure not only academic accounts but also management practices. In an alienating workplace the key problem is control: ensuring that workers exert maximum effort in performing tasks assigned to them by management. Under craft production, which is an important point of reference for many analysts, control lies in the hands of workers to a significant extent. This is because the production process is contingent on the application of skills that are possessed by workers. However, under mechanized factory production skill is progressively reduced so that workers' control is also diminished and the context progressivley dehumanized so that workers will seek to resist control by managers. The problem for managers, then, is to overcome patterns of worker action stereotyped as work-shy, mendacious, rebellious, disruptive or pilferous.

As Marx tells us, the solution to the problem is contained in the labour process involving both mechanization and the increasing subdivision of tasks. The cognitive and ideological basis for such a process is encapsulated in a set of principles of 'scientific management' constructed by F.W.Taylor (1971). Taylor offered a scientific, that is an experimental and empirical, method of management in which labour was treated as an ordinary factor of production to be manipulated in the way that raw material supplies and machinery are manipulated. There are four steps in the process: first, management must appropriate the traditional knowledge held by workers; second, managers must scientifically select and develop workers suited to the task; third, they must carefully put their own knowledge together with the labour of their workers; and fourth, there must be a new division of work between conception and execution but with constant and intimate co-operation of management and workers. The aim was to arrive at the 'one best way' of achieving organizational goals, which normally involved breaking work down into its component elements so that each could be accomplished by the application of minimum skill and then engaging in detailed measurement of levels of production in relation to effort. Taylorism found a ready audience among the engineer-managers of American enterprises at around the time of the First World War (Lash and Urry 1987) and found its way into the main British corporations in the form of the Bedaux system between the world wars (Mathews 1989: 23).

The key weakness in Taylorism is the need for close supervision in the context of a capacity for informal resistance on the part of workers. This problem was solved by the car manufacturer Henry Ford, who used the technology of the moving assembly line to replace the supervisor. Ford's key organizational breakthrough was to move from a situation in which specialized workers travelled from partly assembled vehicle to partly assembled vehicle to one in which the vehicle being assembled was moved from worker to worker. Each worker's task was highly specialized and repetitive but more importantly the pace of work and thus the effort applied was controlled by the pace of the assembly line. In summary, assembly line systems of production have the following four characteristics (Hirschhorn 1986: 8–14):

- *Standardization* – the level of capital investment is such that assembly line production implies a minimum of product variety. Moreover assembly line economies are enhanced where standard components can be assembled within a range of products.
- *Continuity* – the multiplicity of machine operations implies maximum return on capital where there is continuous production by the transmission of power from a single (usually electrical) source.
- *Constraint* – relations between tasks must be precisely timed and managed and workers must meet the guidelines.

- *Task simplicity* – work is deprived of value or interest and worker commitment is thus reduced.

Ford elaborated his organizational idea into a general social philosophy. The key element in Fordist philosophy is mass production. Mass production offers the efficient manufacture of cheap commodities but to be successfully institutionalized it must be married to mass markets. Ford played his own part in the development of mass markets by a celebrated increase in workers' wages in 1914, the eight-hour, five-dollar day. But this increase also had the second purpose of securing the commitment of Ford workers by offering them increased compensation. Ford plants had a very high labour turnover – 53,000 hirings per annum to maintain a labour force of 14,000. The assembly line allowed Ford to bribe his alienated workforce – it had increased productivity on the Model T more than tenfold (Jones 1965: 214). But in the final analysis high wages in assembly line production were alone insufficient to ensure either the development of a mass market or a stable workforce. After all pure assembly line production has never accounted for more than about 10 per cent of manufacturing labour even in the USA (Hirschhorn 1986: 7).[1] Ford was obliged to employ social workers to ensure that labourers and their families met the rigidly conformist moral standards he prescribed for them, but in the post-Second World War period this particular function in the reproduction of labour power has largely been taken on by the state. During this recent period the state has educated workers to docile obedience, provided minimum standards of living for mass consumers, incorporated potentially troublesome labour unions into centralized decision making, and regulated the economy to even out business cycles and thus to provide continuity of demand. As Harvey (1989: 135) indicates: 'Postwar Fordism has to be seen . . . less as a mere system of mass production and more as a total way of life. Mass production meant standardization of product as well as mass consumption; and that meant a whole new aesthetic and a commodification of culture.'

As the market for mass produced goods is not infinitely expandable, eventually the imperatives of Marxist economics were inevitably to apply to the Fordist pattern of capital accumulation. There is, after all, a limit to the number of standardized cars that a person might wish to own. An initial solution is what has come to be known as neo-Fordism (Mathews 1989: 31–3; Piore and Sabel 1984: 195–204), a term which encompasses a wide range of strategies employed by large-scale corporations to deal with the crisis of demand including:

- *Diversification* – expansion into or merging with companies in adjacent product markets or the cultivation of new product markets. The outcome is even larger-scale, conglomerate companies with equally saturated markets.
- *Internationalization* – extension of economies of scale by expansion beyond the domestic market. (However, global markets also have their limits.)

● *Intensification* – the intensive application of technology, especially 'hard' automated technology of the type discussed by Marx, to reduce costs.[2] (However, demand for standardized consumer durables tends to be inelastic at low price levels.)

There is widespread agreement across the ideological spectrum that even neo-Fordism met the limits of a saturated global market around 1970. The long-run tendencies of capitalist development about which Marx had forewarned appeared to be coming to fruition. For example, Gershuny and Pahl (1979: 21) give data indicating the extent by which productivity began to outstrip demand: between 1960 and 1975 British productivity grew by 3.6 per cent while demand grew by 2.2; American productivity also grew by 3.6 per cent but demand grew by 2.5; and German productivity grew by 4.9 per cent and demand by 3.5. Harvey (1989: 141–2), by contrast, stresses the inherent contradictions of capitalism, the inability of Keynesian welfare states to promote revenues from exports which would keep displaced manufacturing workers working and prevent them bankrupting the public purse. Mathews (1989: 31) sees the problem as multidimensional, encompassing increasing governmental environmental regulation, increasing levels of product obsolescence, and above all overproduction, while Piore and Sabel (1984: 3) see all these events culminating in a series of economic crises of unemployment and slow growth, which have become chronic rather than episodic.

Whatever disagreement there is about emphasis the main elements of the 'crisis' are widely agreed to be as follows. The intensive application of technology in manufacturing has finally both saturated demand for mass-produced consumer goods and reduced employment. The crisis achieves self-generating 'circularity' by virtue of the failure of businesses because of slack demand, which further increases unemployment, which in turn depresses demand, and so on. Moreover, increased intervention by the state on behalf of the democratized masses leads to increased cost, reduced profitability, and thus an acceleration of the cycle. As a consequence, throughout the industrialized world the 1970s and 1980s have been a troubled period of industrial and organizational realignment. This is part of a general pattern of organizational rationalization which aims at reduced stockholding, throughput times and labour costs by downscaling from mass production to batch production and by emphasizing labour skills rather than authoritarian control of labour (Sorge and Streeck 1988: 26–7). We now address the three forms of realignment indicated above: postindustrialism, renewed entrepreneurialism and flexible specialization.[3]

Postindustrialization

As Offe indicates, service or postindustrial labour is frequently defined by negatives, that is as labour which is nonmanual, produces nonmaterial outcomes, is noncommodity producing, and noncontrollable because its productivity is nonmeasurable (1985b: 104–5). Most importantly it is frequently defined as non- or postindustrial. An alternative and preferable form of definition is one which specifies the functions of service labour. Here we conform with the definition of service labour offered by Abercrombie, Lash and Urry in terms of the functions of conceptualization of goals and means, the reproduction of labour power, and social control.[4]

Offe provides a survey of four possible explanations for the expansion of the service sector as industrial capitalism reaches its highest stage of development. Two of these are demand accounts – the service sector is said to increase either because structural complexity leads to an increased need for control or because demand for commodities is saturated at the domestic level and switches to demand for services. Supply side accounts feature either the need to absorb surplus labour thrown off by the manufacturing sector or usurpationary expansionism on the part of service workers themselves. The theoretical account of the leading exponent of the postindustrial society thesis, Bell (1973: 44), locates itself clearly in the camp of structurally induced demand. The source of service growth is a change in the character of knowledge in terms of scale, complexity and codification. Service labour expands to meet the demands imposed by the increasing application of knowledge to technical and social problems.

Bell's empirical argument about the expansion of the service sector has two strands. First, there has been a sectoral redistribution of the labour force away from the primary (agricultural) and secondary (manufacturing) sectors and towards the tertiary (services) sector. At the time Bell wrote he was able to say that the USA had the first service economy because more than half of its labour force was employed in the tertiary sector, but now most western capitalist societies have crossed a similar threshold. As Kumar (1978: 200–4) indicates, taken by itself this finding is widely accepted but theoretically insignificant. Industrial societies have always had a minority of their labour force, about one-third, employed in manufacturing – the significant decline has been in the proportion employed in the primary sector which in most advanced societies is now 10 per cent or less . Moreover the term industrial cannot simply be confined to manufacturing industry – it is as possible for agricultural or white-collar work to be organized along industrial lines as it is for manufacturing work to be organized in craft guilds. It is in the second strand of Bell's empirical account that the possibility for a new social order lies. Alongside the sectoral redistribution has been an occupational redistribution. This has meant an increase in the number of white-collar workers but more importantly a recent and very rapid expansion of the proportion of workers in professional, technical and managerial occupations. If we take the data on the service class given in Chapter 4 as an indicator of the scale of this occupational group it now approaches one-third of the labour force in most western capitalist societies. Even if we accept Kumar's argument (1978: 216) that most of this growth has been at what he calls the 'lower' or semiprofessional end of the professional spectrum, we must also accept that in terms of autonomy, status, pay and working conditions it is clear that even lower professional occupations have definite advantages over semiskilled manual workers on these dimensions.[5]

The idea of duality between a routine and a professional service sector is also taken up by other writers. Halal (1986: 54–5) divides the postindustrial era into two stages: the service society and the knowledge society (information age), in which the professional service sector comes to the fore. The service society focusses on what is elsewhere called the reproduction of labour-power but the white-collar occupations that constitute this sector, he argues, are now themselves becoming 'automated' and being replaced by occupations focussing on information technology. Jones (1983: 6–8) goes further in arguing for a postservice society in which service automation will reach such a level that relatively few workers will *need* to be employed at all. Society will be divided between the 'information-rich', the professional and technical sector, and the 'information-poor' for whom new kinds of work will have to be devised to keep them occupied.

Such speculative and unduly optimistic predictions should be resisted because standard capitalist patterns of the organization of labour still have a long way to go. It is indisputable, however, that a knowledge-based sector is growing and that it is growing very rapidly in all western societies. The question remains as to whether the organization of work in this sector is or will be fundamentally different from that found in modern, Fordist work contexts. Offe (1985b: 138–9) gives us two reasons for supposing that it is. First, because service work deals with heterogeneous cases, it is difficult to formulate control criteria for adequate performance. Second there can be no criterion of what constitutes worthwhile service work which is analogous to economic efficiency or profit; such work must be evaluated in terms of its social or economic utility in avoiding loss. Thus: 'In place of the faltering economic-strategic criteria of rationality, one finds calculations based on convention, political discretion or professional consensus' (1985b: 138). So in advanced or 'disorganized' capitalism professional service work sits as a 'foreign body' within economic rationality. It is still subject to external, technically rational constraints but is not internally structured by them.

The organization of professional work therefore has the capacity to take on a different structure from that outlined by Weber in his discussion of the bureaucratic administrative staff, a structural form which institutionalizes norms of 'interactive competence, consciousness of responsibility, empathy and acquired practical experience' (Offe 1985b: 138). Such an organizational form may be described as a collegial structure, one in which 'there is a dominant orientation to a consensus achieved between the members of a body of experts who are theoretically equal in their levels of expertise but who are specialized by area of expertise' (Waters 1989a: 956). Its main features as set out by Waters (1989a: 956–9) are as follows:

• *Theoretical knowledge.* Knowledge is the main means of production.

The knowledge is complex and nonroutinizable and requires continuous maintenance and development.

- *Professional career*. Work is carried out in terms of a set of vocational commitments to supra-personal norms. Typical careers involve a relatively long period of professional socialization to these norms. Job tenure is independent of short-term economic performance.
- *Formal egalitarianism*. Professional experts are not ranked hierarchically in terms of authority although they may be differentiated in prestige terms.
- *Formal autonomy*. Professionals are subject to internal self-regulation rather than external bureaucratic regulation of individual performance.
- *Scrutiny of product*. Products, especially information products, are available for peer review.
- *Collective decision making*. There are institutionalized committee forums for exchanging views and for achieving consensus-based decisions.

It must be stressed that none of the above elements is fully institutionalized in any professional context. Most professional workers are employed and will continue to be employed in heteronomous or intermediate professional contexts in which they work alongside managerial and/or manual workers. Nevertheless any extent to which it is institutionalized represents a reduction of bureaucratic rationalism. Increases in professional employment therefore mark a significant potential decline in bureaucratism.

It should not therefore be assumed that an increase in the development of collegial structures produces an absolute measure of equality. Burris (1989) warns that technocratic structures give rise to the development of dual internal labour markets. There is, to be sure, she says, a flattening of the organizational hierarchy but there is a corresponding polarization into expert and nonexpert sectors. In the expert sector there are good wages and working conditions, flexible, collegial forms of work organization in the typical form of autonomous project teams, and an emphasis on externally established credentials as the basis for organizational status. At the nonexpert level work remains routinized, subject to control and direction by professional 'superiors', poorly rewarded, and insecure.

Finally there is the question of whether an increasing level of professional service labour has wider social consequences. Offe (1985b: 139–40) is in little doubt that it does because the 'new middle class' has the task of consciously addressing the totality of social systems and processes. For these groups rational and instrumental criteria are subordinated to substantive, qualititative and humane value standards. The dissemination of such values to the wider society including manual work contexts is accepted by such popular commentators as Halal (1986: 67) and Toffler (1980) but Kumar (1978: 214), for example, is far more sceptical, wondering why the growth of professional ethics has not been directly reflected in everyday ethics and conflicts. However our analysis of the new politics in Chapter 5 above confirms that what Offe calls postmaterialist conflicts are increasingly finding their way to the centre of political action in the contemporary period.

Petty Entrepreneurialism

One of Marx's predictions about the long-term development of capitalism is the progressive polarization of the petty bourgeoisie of self-employers and small employers into the two great historic classes. Until the 1970s this prediction appeared to be supported by empirical data. For example Steinmetz and Wright (1989: 975–6) report a 'virtual monotonic decline' in the rate of self-employment in the USA between 1940 and 1973 from about 20 per cent to under 10 per cent. In Germany the percentage of the labour force in self-employment fell from 29 in 1939 to 17 in 1970 and in France from 38 in 1946 to 21 in 1970 (Steinmetz and Wright 1989: 984–5). In Britain also there must have been a decline in the *rate* of self-employment because the absolute number of self-employed people remained constant between 1949 and 1979 at between 1.8 and 2 million (Hakim 1988a: 426).

Since 1970, in the Anglo-Saxon capitalist societies in particular, there has been a perceptible growth in self-employment. In the USA the self-employment rate was stable during the early 1970s but since then there has been a small but steady annual increase so that by 1984 it had climbed by about 15–20 per cent relative to 10 years earlier (Steinmetz and Wright 1989: 975–6). In Britain the increase has been more dramatic, from about 7 per cent of the labour force in 1965 to 12 per cent in 1987. In the six-year period from 1981 to 1987 the number of self-employed workers increased by 740,000 or 34 per cent (Hakim 1988a: 426–7). Figures from the rest of Europe give general support but are somewhat less convincing. Between the mid-1970s and mid-1980s increases in nonagricultural self-employment were recorded in Belgium, Ireland and Italy but in Germany, France, the Netherlands and Denmark there was only a reduction in the rate of decline. However, in Europe as a whole the nonagricultural self-employment rate increased from 11.5 per cent in 1975 to 12.6 per cent in 1985 (Steinmetz and Wright 1989: 986).

Steinmetz and Wright suggest that there are three possible explanations for the growth in self-employment. The first of these is a supply side explanation suggesting that it is the simple consequence of rising unemployment and thus that while increased self-employment may be a consequence of the general pattern of economic change suggested in this chapter it is not an integral part of it (see Pollert 1988: 291). Steinmetz and Wright themselves find a countercyclical relationship between unemployment and self-employment in the USA but they also find that the strength of this relationship is declining (1989: 997–8). Similarly, Hakim (1988a: 431) reports that about three times as many British people transfer directly from employment to self-employment as from unemployment to self-employment. There is also a significant transfer from economic inactivity to self-employment, particularly among young people. Moreover the failure rate for the self-employed is far greater for those who have been unemployed. Taken together these data indicate that unemployment is not the central cause of rising self-employment. It may be a cause of the underlying structural base of self-employment but clearly something new is occurring in addition to this effect.

Steinmetz and Wright's second possible explanation is the postindustrialization process discussed above. They find some support for this argument. Business services and legal, engineering and professional services together account for over 55 per cent of the increase in self-employment in the USA (1989: 1006). Hakim (1988a: 428) also stresses increased demand for services. However, as Steinmetz and Wright argue, the contribution of postindustrial services to growth in self-employment is not the product of shifts of the labour force from employment to self-employment within the service sector. In fact there has been a shift in the other direction. Rather postindustrial services tend to be more self-employment oriented than does the manufacturing sector and so their absolute growth as a sector has provided a major impetus to self-employment.

Steinmetz and Wright's third possible explanation fits most closely with the general argument on flexible manufacturing offered below. They find positive growth in self-employment within what they call the transformative sector of the economy, the older traditional industrial sector, especially in construction, miscellaneous manufacturing, machinery and transportation but also in the chemical, textile and power industries (Steinmetz and Wright 1989: 1007). The generally though cautiously held view is that the growth of self-employment is in an important sense nongenuine, the product not of entrepreneurial motivation but of a tendency on the part of large-scale employers to subcontract tasks as a cost control measure (Hakim 1988a: 444–5; Pollert 1988: 289–91; Steinmetz and Wright 1989: 1007–8). Yet, no one examining the detailed evidence appears to wish totally to discount the possibility that the growth of the petty bourgeoisie is an expression of a more general process of disaggregation and downscaling in both the industrial and postindustrial sectors.

Flexible Manufacturing

The third response to market saturation is conceivably the most significant. Increases in service labour and entrepreneurship, while they may contribute to societal levels of disalienation and debureaucratization do not have the effect of dismantling the core industrial arrangements of modernity, those of Fordist manufacturing, within which alienation and bureaucratism are most entrenched. In this section we consider the embryonic development of a transformation which has the potential for just such an accomplishment. Fordists organized production so as to combine maximum specialization of workers with maximum standardization of product. The new flexible form of organization which is now widely agreed to be appearing seeks to generalize the skills of workers so that they can adapt to a wide range of tasks yet have the capacity to produce an expandable range of highly specialized products to meet rapidly changing market demand. Whereas Fordism concentrates on economies of scale, producing large numbers of standardized products in order to finance high levels of capital investment, flexible organization relies on so-called economies of scope, that is producing the widest possible range of commodities.

There are two main conceptual frameworks within which these changes are normally interpreted.[6] The first was developed in the USA by Piore and Sabel (1984) who are convinced that western societies have the potential to go through an industrial transformation of similar magnitude to the industrial revolution at the turn of the nineteenth century, a 'second industrial divide'. The outcome is 'flexible specialization'.

> Flexible specialization is a strategy of permanent innovation: accommodation to ceaseless change, rather than an effort to control it. This strategy is based on flexible – multi-use – equipment; skilled workers; and the creation, through politics, of an industrial community that restricts the forms of competition to those favoring innovation. For these reasons the spread of flexible specialization amounts to a revival of craft forms of production that were emarginated at the first industrial divide. (1984: 17)

The stress on the re-emergence of craft forms of production is the hallmark of the Piore–Sabel approach – flexible specialization is for them not the mere outcome of the application of flexible technology to industrial tasks but a revival of latent human talents which had been swamped by Fordism. In rejecting technological determinism of this sort the example to which they and many others consistently refer is the textile production system of the 'Third Italy', particularly the Emilia-Romagna district and Tuscany (1984: 213–16; also see Scott 1988: 43–59). This was an old textile-producing region in which large-scale integrated firms had been devastated by market saturation and Asian competition. The firms responded by selling off machinery and subcontracting to former workers. There developed a network of small plants, responding to market demand through commercial middlemen, transferring excess capacity between one another. Within these plants the workers are highly skilled and autonomous but still attempt to employ the newest technology, and skills and information are regularly exchanged in an informal way. The industry functions as a community of craftworkers much like a preindustrial guild. So the Piore–Sabel model is a geographical concentration of very small, petty bourgeois workshops responding to informatically mediated global market demands for high-quality products.[7]

A second and more convincing set of arguments emerges from a series of empirical industrial studies in the German Federal Republic under the direction of Kern and Schumann.[8] In the 1960s they had undertaken research on the labour process, documenting the spread of Taylorism in

German industry. During the late 1970s and 1980s they did some follow-up studies which suggested that the 1970s had been a period of quite significant transformation. This transformation was in part technological but focussed more cogently on a new set of policy orientations by management towards labour, from an orientation in which labour is an obstacle to be controlled to one in which labour skill can make a positive contribution to the success of an organization. They describe these emerging orientations as 'new production concepts':

> It sounds paradoxical: precisely at the historical moment in which technical possibilities for substituting human labour are explosively expanding, conscious-ness of the qualitative significance of human work performance, the appreciation of the special qualities of human labour, is at the same time increasing. For the creed of the new production concepts is:
> A. The attainment, by means of technification, of autonomy in the production process at the expense of living labour is not a value in itself. The greatest reduction of human labour does not per se produce the economic optimum.
> B. The restrictive grip on human labour places important limits on productiv-ity gains. In a comprehensive reorganization of tasks, there exist not dangers but opportunities. Qualifications and skilled proficiency of the workers are produc-tive strengths too, which should be more fully realized. (Kern and Schumann 1987: 160)

They note the spread of these concepts (which seem to accompany partial automation) in several leading-edge industries: in the car industry there is a reorientation of tasks into the occupation of 'production mechanic'; workers in the machine tool industry add computer programming and control to their existing skills and management encourages this develop-ment; the professionalization of production work in the chemical industry continues. By contrast with Piore and Sabel, Kern and Schumann's new form of work is not a craft revival but the absorption of manual labour into the professional-technical spectrum. Part of this process is multiskilling, especially the combination of maintenance and quality control tasks with production tasks. But a more important development is the assimilation of relatively high levels of theoretical knowledge of technical and organiza-tional procedures. As they stress, however, this reprofessionalization does not yet encompass the design and construction of these procedures.

Whatever the form of the transformation is argued to be there is relatively widespread agreement that it is market driven rather than technology driven (e.g. Harvey 1989: 156; Schumann 1987: 53–4). Produc-ers in the advanced societies can no longer compete with second-wave industrializers of the third world at the level of cost in mass producing commodities. Instead they must compete at the level of product variability, quality and customization. So there must be an acceleration in product innovation plus a capacity to search on a global scale for market niches. Harvey (1989: 56) estimates the half-life of each mass-produced item at five to seven years. In flexibly manufactured textiles the half-life is down to less than four while built-in obsolescence and faddism has reduced the half-life of video and computer software to less than one and a half years.

Success in the saturated global market place depends above all on a capacity to respond rapidly and precisely to unpredictable shifts in demand. As will have become apparent, the key organizational characteristic which manufacturing systems must have in order to accomplish this is flexibility. This flexibility is developing within three elements of the production process: an adaptable, reprogrammable technology; a dispersal of organizational authority and responsibility so that differentiated organizational segments are free to stay in contact with and respond to market developments; and workers with an expanded capacity and freedom to acquire skills and knowledge and to apply them in decisive ways in order to enhance productive capacity. Each of these elements is examined in detail in the following sections.

Flexible Technology

Although Marx used the term 'automaton' to describe the ultimate development in the mechanization of production it is unlikely that he could have envisaged the exact form of automation that is currently emerging. Marx's description fits most closely with what is now understood to be 'hard' automation, in which robotic machines merely displace human labour in fixed assembly systems. The current process of automation is 'soft' automation, in which installed machines are capable of producing a wide range of products because they can be given new sets of instructions (programs) about the work they are to perform. The significant development is the application of computers to control machine operations. The new technology is called CIM (computer-integrated manufacturing) or CAI (computer-aided industry)(Fix-Sterz and Lay 1987: 86).

CIM incorporates three sets of computer-aided technique, CAD (computer-aided design), CAP (computer-aided planning) and, most importantly, CAM (computer-aided manufacturing). To get the alphabet salad out of the way, it is worth noting that CAM includes numerically controlled (NC) and computer numerically controlled (CNC) machine tools, industrial robots (IR) and flexible manufacturing cells or islands (FMC). Applied in a piecemeal fashion they constitute CAI, in an integrated fashion around a centralized computer system CIM. (All technical information in this technology section is from Fix-Sterz and Lay 1987: 87–96 and Mathews 1989: 43–59.)

CAD means the use of information technology to assist in the design process, especially at the graphical or pictorial level. It is a system used by draughters in which data are entered into a computer by means of a keyboard, a touch-sensitive drawing board or light pen. The computer converts the data into three-dimensional geometric shapes which can be hard-copied into design drawings from any angle. CAD is the most successful and widespread of the new technologies because it is both versatile and inexpensive. CAD packages are available for both mainframes and PCs. In 1985 there were some 2000 CAD systems installed in the Federal Republic of Germany, for example, many of them assisted by government subsidy. At that time about 950 firms were engaged in extending or introducing CAD systems (Fix-Sterz and Lay 1987: 87–8). CAD is critical in maximizing flexibility of product.

CAP is a less specific term applied to a wide range of computer installations which control the flow of factors of production in time and space within a manufacturing plant, including flows of components, selecting machine operations, inventory levels, planning of production schedules to meet contracts, management of customers' orders, etc. Initial CAP systems involved centralized computer control of the entire production process but this neo-Fordist development has recently been softened in order to provide greater flexibility in accommodating rush demands or temporary supply shortages. The newer systems provide an overall framework of planning rules but allow detailed planning to be undertaken at the shop-floor level as the production process is monitored.

NC and CNC are systems which use different combinations of numbers to provide differing sets of instructions to machine tools. NC was developed as early as the 1950s with the principal purpose of automating metal cutting, drilling and grinding as part of a general Taylorist deskilling strategy. From an initial situation in which machines could be 'programmed' by the use of jigs or cams there was a gradual movement to machines programmed by means of a computer-generated magnetic tape. These early NCs were hard forms of automation. More complete flexibility was achieved in the early 1970s when CNCs were introduced which integrated the computer into the machine. CNC machines are continuously programmable as the operator monitors operations or responds to new orders. Expansion in the use of NC and CNC machines is exponential in character: in the FRG there were less than 2000 NC machines in 1972, by 1984 there were 15,000 NCs and 35,000 CNCs (Fix-Sterz and Lay 1987: 91); there were 10,500 NC/CNC machines in France in 1980 but by 1985 there were 35,000, about 5 per cent of the total number of machine tools, a similar proportion to that found in Japan and the USA (Magirier 1987: 121); and in 1985 there were about 27,000 CNC machines in use in Britain (Dodgson 1987: 261). The initial installations were in large-scale Fordist production enterprises but the most common application is now in small and medium-sized batch production engineering plants.

Already then the programmable (and reprogrammable) manufacture of components is a reality but the assembly of those components into complex manufactured products is a long way off. There has been some diffusion of IR machines which accomplish this but their application is limited and inflexible. There were 6600 IRs in Germany in 1984 (Fix-Sterz and Lay 1987: 93), only 828 in France in 1985 (Magirier 1987: 122), and 3200 in Britain in the same year (Dodgson 1987: 261). The principal uses for robots are parts handling and spot welding. The key limitation in the development of robotics to a programmable level appears to be the development of sensor technology.

A more likely prospect for immediate progress towards increased flexibility is the FMC. The FMC groups CNC machines, frequently alongside conventional machine tools and direct manual work. The FMC has two important characteristics: it manufactures a wide spectrum of components; and much of the transfer of components is automated. Frequently the FMC is centred on a microcomputer which carries out local CAP functions. The cell acts as a self-directed service centre responding to demands for parts from other centres in the plant as if they constituted its market. Typically FMCs are self-controlled in terms of organization and planning.

The complete development of CIM is known as a flexible manufacturing system (FMS). Here FMCs are linked together by a single control and transportation system. Control is exercised through a central computer and transport between cells is operated by automatic guided vehicles. Mathews gives the following first-hand account of a partial FMS in operation at the Volvo car engine plant at Skövde in Sweden:

> Each FMS [FMC], or 'line' as Volvo called it, produces an engine component, such as cylinder blocks, valves, or camshafts. Machining was carried out by CNC centres linked by Automatic Guided Vehicles (AGVs) and Volvo-designed overhead parts handling ('gantry robots') equipment. Under programmed control, the parts were moved from one machining centre to another, where different operations were performed. All programs were contained in discs or tapes resident in the machining centres: there was no separate, centralised 'control centre'. Different versions of components can be produced flexibly by change of program.
>
> Each FMS [FMC] is operated by a team of three or four highly skilled workers (a majority of whom were women, on the day I visited). The multi-skilled team members are in total control: they can at any time interrupt a programmed sequence, or reschedule operations, by typing commands into their consoles. They need never lay hands on an engine component. The whole plant, consisting of a series of independent FMSs [FMCs], was clean, quiet and busy. (1989: 50)

This 'factory of the future' as it is sometimes called is as yet a relatively rare development – Mathews says that there are 'several hundred' such systems operating in Japan, the USA and Europe (1989: 49) and Fix-Sterz and Lay find 278 instances of FMSs in 144 German companies (1987: 109). Nearly 70 per cent of the latter were in the machine tool industry.

The capital investment required for technological development of the scale of an FMS indicates that Piore and Sabel's vision of networks of artisans is at best only partially true. The German experience suggests that the early installations of flexible technology, particularly unintegrated CNCs, does indeed occur most frequently in firms with low output but wide product variability (Fix-Sterz and Lay 1987: 111–12). The key advantage for these firms is not flexibility, which is something they already have, but increased productivity and thus capacity to compete. FMSs tend to be installed in firms with medium ouput and moderate product variability. The genuine displacement of the assembly line is yet to occur but when it does, while it will produce some organizational downscaling, this is not likely to be extreme as Piore and Sabel suggest.

Flexible Organization

A second set of developments associated with flexible manufacturing surrounds the cultural globalization of the organizational practices of Japanese companies following their considerable market success towards the end of the modern period. Paradoxically that success, to use Dore's terminology (1989), comes from being primarily organization oriented rather than market oriented. Market-oriented companies are characteristic of the Fordist era and focus on immediately calculated issues of cost and revenue. So Fordist firms pay minimum wages to secure the immediate labour of employees and make the maximum mark-up to secure immediate profit. The key interest in the firm is that of the owners or shareholders and the managers act as their agents, manipulating workers in order to maximize returns on investment which are exported from the firm. Japanese style organization-oriented companies aim to secure the long-term position of the organization in the economy – the orientation is to asset building and market share rather than immediate return. The key reference group for the company is its employees, who include a far less differentiated managerial sector. Typically the company will prefer loan financing to equity capitalization because control is thus retained in the hands of employees and returns on investment can be reinvested rather than exported. In general the organization is conceived of as a community for whom shareholders are only clients.[9]

Some of the main features of Japanese style business management and associated practices are as follows.

Strategic Management   Strategic, as opposed to Fordist, tactical management practices aim to forecast and, if possible, to construct the future relationship between the organization and its environment, particularly supplier and customer markets. A typical example is the application of learning curve information to pricing policies (Swyngedouw 1987: 491–3). Continuous change in technologies, management practices, workers' skills, and the organization of work mean that the cost of production will be much higher early in the life-cycle of a product than at later stages. So it is possible to set prices at levels lower than the cost of production in the early stage in order to secure a market share of sufficient scale in the future to maximize not merely bottom-line profitability but overall gross profits. Another example is the practice of paying prices for raw materials at above current market-defined levels in order to secure long-term supply contracts. Strategic management involves a specific commitment to flexibility, not merely in securing a supply of labour which can be cut and rehired at will but in using a range of labour contracts and producing a range of products which can anticipate variations in market demand. Above all strategic management involves a capacity to anticipate and respond to variations in the market (Streeck 1987).

Just-in-Time (JIT)   Just as mass production was developed in relation to car manufacure, so also was the JIT or *kanban* system which was first introduced at Toyota by Ohno (Fix-Sterz and Lay 1987: 11–12; Mathews 1989: 79–81; Swyngedouw 1987: 494–6). The basic principle of JIT is to minimize inventory at each stage of the production process since surplus inventory represents unrealized value. The production process is divided into a number of stages each organized as a team of workers. Each stage uses components on a 'go and get' basis and produces its own components on the basis of demand from the succeeding assembly stage. This may be compared with the Fordist approach of maximizing the use of factors of production to push forward the supply of components and finished products. Although the key motivation for JIT is cost reduction and improved profitability it has several important side-effects. First it ensures responsiveness to markets by ramifying market effects in an immediate way throughout the production process even to the supply of raw materials. No worker produces anything which is not in demand. Second, control over workers must be established by alternative means to those given in the flow of an assembly line. In the Japanese case there are long-term incentives to continuous worker loyalty in the form of job security, promotion possibilities and family welfare. Third, there is an incentive to multiskilling so that surplus labour time can be employed. Fourth, JIT will only work if production stage teams are allowed to make their own decisions about which parts are required and about what to produce when. Fifth, supplies of components both from outside and inside the firm must be reliable in quantity and high in quality. Quality control is therefore of utmost importance and workers typically have the right to stop equipment where quality is under threat, something unheard of in assembly line production.

Quality Control   Under Fordist production quality control is accomplished by inspectors and checkers, usually as the assembled product emerges. The Japanese quality control system depends on all workers being involved in the maintenance of production standards. However, for workers to make judgements of quality they need information. Such information is supplied by statistical means. Workers are provided with charts and diagrams which identify systematic sources of quality failure. They are instructed to ignore fluctuations attributable to one-off causes (e.g. equipment breakdown, operator error) and to concentrate on the long-term effects of technological or organizational procedures, since the latter account for 85 per cent of error (Mathews 1989: 81–2). The information is studied and assessed in quality control circles (QCC). Typically these are informal meetings of the workers involved in a particular stage of production arranged on a theoretically voluntary basis outside working hours, although there are clear material incentives to participation. So successful have QCCs become that they have diffused rapidly throughout Japanese industry since the 1960s and are now spreading with similar rapidity in Europe and North America.[10]

Teamwork   Like many of the organizational patterns that first became fully institutionalized in the Japanese context, teamwork did not originate in Japan. The promotion of teamwork as an alternative to the dehumanizing and counterproductive aspects of Fordism in fact originated in a series of studies of autonomous work groups in the traditional British industries of coal mining, shipbuilding and textile weaving by the Tavistock Institute in the 1950s and 1960s. The Institute has long promoted the idea of semi-autonomous work groups, that is the adaptation of batch production organization to mass production. Teamwork involves the collectivizing and sharing of tasks by a small group of workers at a similar stage of the production process. In some instances tasks are mixed so that distinctions between skilled and unskilled work are broken down, in others workers maintain their individual skills but work together. The team is assigned responsibility for given levels and standards of production and will frequently be empowered to reorganize and/or rotate tasks and thus to multiskill (Mathews 1989: 101).

Teamwork (or group technology) was the subject of experiments in a number of mass production situations in the 1960s and 1970s, most famously at Volvo's Kalmar plant. Results were mixed and the experiment was abandoned in some plants, at the VW engine plant at Augsburg for example. However, teamwork is now experiencing a revival because it marries successfully with JIT and QCCs and also with flexible technologies, all of which demand local decisions on production rates, product quality and deployment of skills and labour. Teamwork appears to be the central element in organizational adaptation to meet Japanese competition in American car plants, the principal orientation of which is a change in the style of supervision and an orientation to improved quality. In older plants teamwork is merely manifested in the establishment of QCCs but General Motors' greenfield Saturn plant in Tennessee and Toyota's NUMMI plant in California are organized as team systems jointly designed by workers and managers (Wood 1988: 103–6).[11]

Managerial Decentralization   If the most successful organizations are those which respond rapidly to shifting markets, then centrally controlled, multilayered hierarchies are doomed to failure. By the end of the modern period many large-scale American corporations were beginning to flatten by instituting divisional structures, which differentiated the organization into separate cost/profit centres with only long-term reporting to the centre in relation to general policy matters.[12] However, as Halal (1986: 129–31) argues, this neo-Fordist strategy was only a transitional phase in the development of far looser networks of functional units engaged in quasi-market exchanges with one another within the organization. This represents a stark contrast to neo-Weberian analyses of industrial organization which stressed that 'goal displacement' or 'bifurcation of interests' in which organizational subunits accumulated resources and developed their own goals represented a threat to the overall goals of the organization. The postmodern organization has no centrally organized rational system of authority on which such spatial metaphors as 'hierarchy' can be placed. It becomes a shapeless and flowing matrix of shifting and flexible exchanges, a federation of organizational styles and practices each surviving on its capacity to respond to demand.[13] The extreme form of such a structure occurs where flexibility is externalized, that is where the production of components, workers' skills and other assets occur outside the organization. The latter is a common form of organization in Japan, where firms are frequently linked by long-term subcontracting rather than integrated ownership.[14] The contracting organization typically uses advanced technology, is large in the scale of its production, and employs highly paid, multiskilled, highly committed workers while subcontractors are smaller in scale and employ low-paid, frequently marginal labour.[15] The constellation of subcontracted firms cushions the core firm against market shock, especially where this requires labour redundancy.

Although the emergence of relatively large-scale flexible manufacturing is the primary transformation in the sphere of work, albeit in a downscaled, flatter and more humane form than under mass production, it would be remiss to ignore the less central but nonetheless significant developments occurring in smaller organizations. The most important such development the 'regional conglomeration' is described by Piore and Sabel (1984: 265–7). Here the core is not a single dominating firm but a group of approximately equal small enterprises. Relations between them are arranged by short-term contracts so that firms are both buyers and sellers of labour relative to other firms. There also exist in the region such integrating collective institutions as trade associations, guilds, unions, and purchasing and marketing co-operatives. Piore and Sabel stress the ascendancy and indeed the necessity of the bonds of community as a regulative mechanism, a pattern not unlike the processes of cultural as opposed to bureaucratic integration found in Japanese manufacturing enterprises. The picture that emerges is the familiar postmodernizing one of fluid shapelessness driven by shifting tastes on one hand and localized decision making on the other.

However unique the Italian case may be, it offers clear evidence that downscaling and increased petty entrepreneurialism of the sort described by Piore and Sabel is having an effect in wider contexts. Murray (1988: 264) reports that between 1971 and 1978 the proportion of the Italian labour force working in firms with less than 19 employees rose from 22 to 29 per cent. Between 1974 and 1978 employment in firms with over 500 employees fell by 52,000 while that in firms with fewer than 19 increased by

160,000. Between 1968 and 1980 the number of engineering firms in the Bologna district employing 15 employees or less increased by 43 per cent to over 9000. Murray attributes these developments to the putting-out and transfer of work previously aggregated in large firms to smaller firms, artisan workshops and domestic outworkers. Like Piore and Sabel he notes the rise of a 'dense network' of artisans, workshops and small firms. Solinas (1988) describes a similar situation in the Italian knitwear industry noting a pronounced gender division of labour between artisans (men) and production workers and homeworkers (women).

Flexible Labour

The picture painted in the previous two sections is of a new responsiveness on the part of the manufacturing sector to shifting markets. We have already seen that one of the main cost factors in manufacturing production, technology, has achieved economies of scope by its adaptability to a wide range of products in moderate quantities. We now examine patterns of increased flexibility for a second main cost factor in production, labour. In general there are two main ways in which labour can be made more flexible: external or numerical flexibility; and internal or functional flexibility (Pollert 1988: 283; Streeck 1987: 290). Numerical flexibility is the possibility of altering the amount of labour employed and its mix in terms of skills and qualifications according to market demand; functional flexibility means a high level of adaptability of workers both to a wide range of tasks and to the effort required to meet particular surges in demand. Figure 6.1 is a much cited diagram of a model of the maximally flexible firm in manpower terms produced by the British Institute of Management Studies (Evans and Bell 1986: 9; Harvey 1989: 151; Pollert 1988: 284). It shows a core group of lifetime employees on the Japanese model conceived to be functionally flexible. Surrounding them is an inner ring of peripheral employees able to be hired on a needs basis. Beyond them lie workers who are not participants in the firm. Peripheral and external workers provide numerical flexibility.[16] We now examine the patterns that each of the forms of labour flexibility follows.

Numerical Flexibility The chief object of numerical flexibility is the possibility of laying off labour in market downturns or periods of lack of market success and of taking it back on when demand rises. The traditional numerically flexible labour force is the secondary labour market (the first peripheral group in Figure 6.1) known in Marxist analysis as the 'reserve army of labour'. This usually consists disproportionately of ascriptively disadvantaged people including women, the young, the old, and members of minority racial and ethnic groups, who are forced to accept low pay and insecure conditions at least in part because of exclusionary practices on the part of members of the primary labour market. Because typically they are unprotected by unions and by social democratically inspired legislation

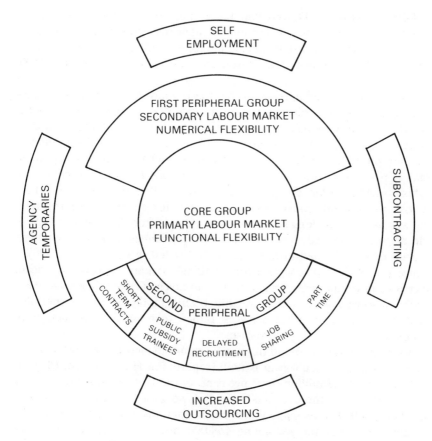

Figure 6.1 *Labour market differentiation in the flexible firm*
Source: Evans and Bell (1986: 9)

they can be taken on and laid off with relative freedom.

This is a longstanding form of numerical flexibility. Of greater interest are emerging forms of flexibility including part-time and temporary work but most especially outworking, homeworking and subcontracting. On the first two of these the data – and we rely mainly on data for Britain where interest in the issue is greatest – are a long way from offering conclusive evidence that a major change is in process. Certainly they are a major source of flexibility. Hakim (1988a: 439) reports that permanent part-time and temporary employees make up about 20 per cent of the workforce. However it must be stressed that the proportion in manufacturing is relatively small, at around 5 per cent, compared with 20 per cent or better in the arena of service production. Nevertheless the number of temporary workers increased by 70,000 between 1981 and 1985, and the number of part-time workers increased by one-third of a million between 1981 and 1986 while full-time employment fell by one million. Much of the increase is accounted for by female employment in the service sector (Pollert 1988:

287–8). So between 1981 and 1988 the proportion of employed workers in other than full-time, permanent employment rose from 30 to 36 per cent. Even among men, who traditionally monopolize the primary sector of the labour market, the proportion rose from 18 to 25 per cent (Hakim 1990: 165).

There is widespread agreement that the key development in the promotion of numerical flexibility is the use of subcontracted labour. Much of the growth in self-employment discussed in the previous main section is attributed to increased subcontracting (Hakim 1988a: 438–44; Steinmetz and Wright 1989: 1007). The Warwick Industrial Relations survey found that 37 per cent of the firms it questioned in 1984 reported an increase in subcontracting within the previous five years (Pollert 1988: 289–90). A British government report found that in most firms surveyed subcontracting was of relatively long standing – interestingly from the point of view of the argument offered in this book many companies reported that 'they started down this road in the early 1970s' (cited in Pollert 1988: 290).[17] Among a series of contradictory findings Pollert reports significant increases in components subcontracting in mechanical engineering (1988: 290). However, most subcontracting occurs in the arena of specialist professional and technical services rather than in the production of components as in the Japanese case.[18]

A similar pattern is found in homeworking, the most intensive study of which was also carried out in Britain (reported in Hakim 1988b: 613). In 1981 a total of 1.7 million, or 7 per cent, of the British labour force were homeworkers. Of these, 750,000 lived at work or had 'live-in' jobs and another 284,000 were manual service subcontractors (construction, road freight, etc.). For the remaining 658,000, four categories of work are significant: 43 per cent worked for clients on a fee-for-service basis; 44 per cent worked for a single employer; 9 per cent (mainly women) did manufacturing homework of the classical domestic outwork type; and 4 per cent were childminders. Hakim (1988b: 630) rejects the traditional image of the homeworker as low paid, with low skills, and engaged in manufacturing outwork; homeworkers are better qualified, in better health, own more property, and are more highly skilled, on average, than are other workers.

The above suggests that Toffler's evocative images of the 'electronic cottage' and of 'telecommuting' may well be emerging as a real force although probably not as a generalization (1980: 210–23). It may well be more important for flexible manufacturers to subcontract not the manufacturing itself, within which they will presumably seek to maximize returns on investment in expensive computerized machinery, but labour and skill-intensive services in which a long-term human investment would be far from worthwhile. If homework and subcontracting do indeed increase to significant dimensions then the separation of home from work which Marx found so dehumanizing may well be reversed.

Functional Flexibility Far better opportunities for a process of disalienation reside in increases in functional flexibility. Mathews (1989: 108–9) sums up the elements of increased functional flexibility:

- *Task integration* This takes two forms, horizontal integration in which job classifications widen and workers are able to rotate between a variety of tasks, and vertical integration in which manual workers take on some policy implementation and conceptualizing functions.
- *Multiskilling* The development of and credentializing of workers in broad-based skills including both quality control and maintenance functions as well as direct operation of manufacturing equipment.
- *Localized responsibility* The sharing of supervision responsibility on a collective basis between the members of a team. Middle management functions are reappropriated by workers.

Kern and Schumann's studies convince them of the widespread development of this flexible type of worker in West German industry (1984a: 59). They note in the car industry a general trend to the reintroduction of craftsmen to the assembly line especially in relation to the merging of such tasks as tool-setting, control, and inspection and maintenance procedures; they note the widespread introduction of an FMS in the chemical industry called 'total distributed control', which is accompanied by skill upgrading; and finally they note an overall increase in the number of skilled maintenance workers who are responsible for the functioning of automated technology.[19] Lane (1988) agrees with Kern and Schumann about such developments in the core industries but is less sanguine about change elsewhere. Nevertheless 'in the German industrial context there exist a number of distinctive features which make the Kern and Schumann scenario at least very likely if not inevitable' (1988: 154).[20]

Reprofessionalization of labour may emerge not only from reintegration of tasks within an existing industry but also from a shift in products relative to market demand. Alic and Harris (1988) report such a shift in the American electronics industry. Previously that industry had been based on consumer electronics (e.g. TV sets) produced under Fordist conditions. But the American industry proved unable to compete with Japanese organizations using high technology plant and their main competitive solution has been to send manufacturing offshore in order to use low-cost, third world labour. Meanwhile, the American industry has maintained a fragile competitive edge in microelectronics and in computer production. By mid-1985 there were over 800,000 workers in the industry, more than 4 per cent of the American manufacturing labour force. Each of the growth areas includes a high proportion of highly skilled, professional and technical labour. For example, skilled and professional jobs account for 60 per cent of the labour force in microelectronics but only 30 per cent in consumer electronics (1988: 670).

Kern and Schumann are convinced of the disalienating consequences of such a reprofessionalization of labour for the workers involved: 'work appears to have gained a new and attractive quality, opposing the tendency of an instrumental attitude, which counterbalances the urge to escape from it' (1984a: 62). Indeed work may contrast positively with commercialized leisure pursuits which are themselves vacuous and alienating. Yet Kern and Schumann are acutely aware that functional flexibility is not the condition of all workers, only those in the core group of leading technology industries. They predict a polarization process within the working class which will segment it into four groups: the winners in rationalization, the modern skilled production workers; the tolerators of rationalization, older primary sector workers whose protections stay in place; the losers, those made redundant by the rationalization process; and the long-term unemployed whose situation is made worse by demands for formal qualifications (1987: 165–6). Although there now exist prospects for long-term disalienation the term is very long indeed and the development will inevitably be uneven in character.

Conclusion

Under modern conditions of production Taylorism and Fordism represent model forms for the organization of production, an orthodoxy for the labour process. The emerging postmodern configuration of production is neither a simple continuation of the labour process nor a new orthodoxy in the form of either postindustrial services or flexible specialization. 'Flexibility' has recently become a managerial buzzword and a legitimizing ideology for managerial attacks on workers' control of jobs. The practical outcome of its institutionalization is that the emerging pattern is an absence of pattern, a chaotic mixture of forms of ownership, varieties of task organization, forms of relationship between owners and workers, and worker responses. In general terms then, economic life is experiencing structurally similar processes of change to those found in other arenas: an extreme level of substantive differentiation which, paradoxically, has the effect in many circumstances of the reintegration of economic and domestic arenas which had been separated by modernization; a corresponding decentralization so that the forms of economic life are progressively less determined by core mass production industries; and a level of differentiation of technology which significantly reduces material constraints on the organization of economic life so that it depends for its character far more on cultural flows of knowledge and information about preferred modes of organization than on technology itself.

The critical economic region in this process is the production of commodities. The general pattern of differentiation and decentralization which is *in statu nascendi* in this region as described above is summarized in Figure 6.2. The central element is the transfer of productive capacity out of

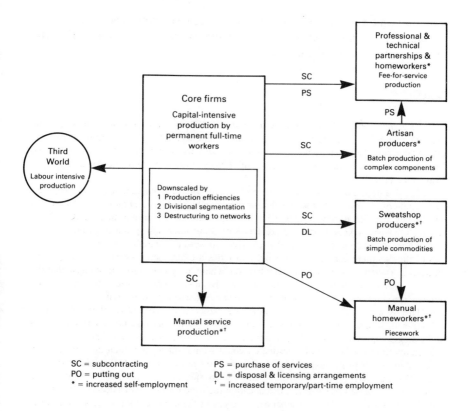

Figure 6.2   *The differentiation of production systems*

core firms as new production technology and flexible organization is introduced. Permanent full-time workers in this sector experience reprofessionalization as their personal skills and abilities assume increasing importance in relation to the maintenance of market share; middle management is released and specialized services contracted on a need basis; labour-intensive production requiring high levels of supervision is externalized; and in some instances the process of decentralization will go so far as a destructuring of the core firm into a looser arrangement. Around core firms are emerging networks of smaller-scale economic units with a variety of contractual arrangements with other firms and with their own employees: small 'postindustrial' professional and technical firms operating on a fee-for-service basis with a pronounced petty entrepreneurial character; specialist craftwork shops producing niche-market products or complex components supplied to core firms on a contractual basis; labour-intensive 'sweatshops' employing in the secondary labour market on a relatively insecure basis; entrepreneurial contract suppliers of such manual services as cleaning, catering, garbage disposal and waste recycling who also tend to employ in the secondary labour market; and beyond these manual homeworkers who as their name suggests experience the greatest measure of dedifferentiation of home from work but also conceivably the most insecure material rewards.

Notes

1. Blauner (1964: 91) estimates the level at about 5 per cent. Although this proportion appears small it must be remembered that assembly line technology defines both a mass form of capital accumulation and a more widely generalized organizational system. For a detailed analysis of the application of Taylorist and Fordist principles in white-collar work see Braverman (1974).

2. 'Hard' automation is the type which provides informatic linkages to a central computerized system of control by means of which workers can be continuously monitored and within which they provide purely routine labour. 'Soft' automation decentralizes and localizes control allowing workers *in situ* to make decisions about work flow, product quality, etc.

3. Although we concentrate almost exclusively on western capitalist societies, towards the end of the twentieth century state socialist societies are also being swept by developments indicating disalienation and debureaucratization. There are good reasons to suppose that the state socialist mode of production can only survive in a Fordist world where production defines consumption and material constraint defines industrial participation.

4. This is not markedly different, although rather more accessible, than Offe's own definition in terms of the functions of synthesizing, mediating and normalizing and thus 'defending and preserving the differentiated elements of social structure' (1985b: 105).

5. In an otherwise beautifully reasoned account Kumar makes the claim that much of the apparent growth in professional occupations is due to occupational relabelling and regrading, a 'sociological sleight of hand' (1978: 214–6). In this he fails to take account of the dramatically increased levels of formal education required for many such occupations.

6. There are in fact several independent sources of the argument for a general industrial transformation. These include, in addition to the two mentioned here, the French regulation school, long wave theory, diversified quality production arguments, and 'new management' literatures. For a survey see Badham and Mathews (1989).

7. It must be stressed that Piore and Sabel also refer to other instances of flexible specialization including the German and Japanese machine tool industries, American speciality steel mills, and American and European chemical production companies. The most common criticisms of the Piore–Sabel hypothesis are twofold: that flexible specialization is only occurring in a small minority of industrial contexts; and that where it is occurring there is very little general evidence of an emerging craft production paradigm (see Hyman 1988; Phillimore 1989; Pollert 1988; Smith 1989; Williams et al. 1987).

8. Kern and Schumann's major works, *Der Soziale Prozess bei technischen Umstellung* (1977) and *Das Ende der Arbeitsteilung?* (1984b) are not available in English. For this reason we rely on two short papers in *Economic and Industrial Democracy* (1984a, 1987), a summary of their work given by Schumann to the EEC (1987) and an excellent synthesis by Campbell (1989).

9. Dohse et al. (1985) point out that Japanese organizational practices are not necessarily post-Fordist because they are still oriented to mass production for mass markets. However they confirm that such practices are clearly post-Taylorist because they collapse the Taylorist separation of conceptualization and execution.

10. There is some variation in opinion about the extent of diffusion of QCCs. Swynge-douw (1987: 493) says that currently there are 100,000 operational in Japan, that is, in 71 per cent of all firms and in 91 per cent of firms with more than 10,000 workers. Mathews (1989: 81) says that there are about a million QCCs in Japan and that 100,000 had been formed in Southeast Asia during the previous ten years. Although the growth of QCCs is doubtless exponential it is unlikely to have increased tenfold in two years, even in Japan.

11. Wood (1988) is equivocal about the extent of flexible manufacturing in the US auto industry. It is clear that the newer plants are so organized but he argues that the overall commitment in the industry remains to mass production, as manifested, for example in the world car concept. Overall the response to the market crisis has been a complex of strategies but this certainly represents an increase in flexibility relative to a single-minded, mass production orientation.

If the small, machine tool company studied by Burawoy is in any way representative, the situation desribed by Wood is part of a general trend towards increased flexibility and disalienation in American production units. Noting first that the changes are independent of the introduction of CNC machines Burawoy describes the changes as wide-ranging between 1945 and 1975: 'the labour process underwent two sets of changes. The first is seen in the greater individualism promoted by the organization of work. Operators in 1975 had more autonomy as a result of the following: relaxed enforcement of certain managerial controls, such as inspection of pieces and rate-fixing; increased shop-floor bargaining between workers and foremen; and changes in the system of piece rates – changes that laid greater stress on individual performance, effort, and mobility and allowed more manipulations. The second type of change, related to the first, concerns the diminution of hierarchical conflict and its redistribution in a number of different directions. As regards the relaxation of conflict between workers and management, one notes a decline in the authority of the foreman and the reduction of tensions between those concerned with enforcement of quality in production and those primarily interested in quantity. The greater permissiveness towards chiselling, the improvement of tooling and machines, as well as easier rates, have all facilitated making out and in this way have reduced antagonism between worker and shop management. . . These changes do not seem to support theories of the intensification of the labor process or increase of managerial control through separation of conception and execution' (1988: 208–9).

12. Halal (1986: 130) estimates that 90 per cent of the top 100 firms have reorganized in such a way as to eliminate up to 40 per cent of middle management jobs.

13. Within such an organizational form, management takes on a new and reduced set of functions. Its job is no longer to control work and to ensure a given level of production but to set up an organizational framework of accountability and incentives which will allow the market to allocate resources and people to tasks (Halal 1986: 131; Mathews 1989: 82–3).

14. Fifty-four per cent of Japanese firms with less than 300 employees are subcontractors; 25 per cent of all such firms subcontract to only one core firm (Swyndgedouw 1987: 496).

15. Wages of workers in Japanese firms with less than 100 employees average 62 per cent of those in firms with more than 500 employees, while those in firms with 100–500 employees average 81 per cent of the wages of those in large firms (Swyngedouw 1987: 497).

16. Streeck (1987: 291–6) interprets the emergence of numerical and functional flexibility as a differentiation of status from contract in the relationship between the worker and the firm. Core, permanent, functionally flexible employees are protected by their status as members of the firm – the firm needs the secure commitment of such workers and establishes long-term and nontransferable, diffuse relationships with them. Contract workers provide only specific amounts of labour for a specific return over a specific period of time.

17. The same report claims that 'nine out of every 10 respondents had introduced changes to manning practices since 1980 designed to increase numerical flexibility', although many of these changes were to do with increased overtime rates for core employees (Pollert 1988: 294).

18. Because so many of the data come from the UK it is possible to overgeneralize the contradictory signs from a society which is scarcely at the leading edge of worldwide economic restructuring. Subcontracting has been well institutionalized in Japan for some thirty years and is increasing in the USA. What is interesting is that even in such a noncentral economy as that of Britain there are signs of increased numerical flexibility, however contradictory these signs may appear. In a comparison of Britain with Germany Lane (1988: 147) confirms some of the problems in the British situation: 'although Fordist employer practices have been widespread in the postwar period in both societies, their penetration has been more thoroughgoing in Britain'.

19. Recent empirical work at SOFI, Goettingen confirms the stabilization and extension of the pattern. Schumann (1990: 25) reports that: 'Unlike 1983/84 when we did '*The End of the Division of Labor?*' in these days the highly skilled systems' controllers are already a numerically important segment of the blue collar workforce. Once again, only after the crossing of the border toward comprehensive automation, i.e. after automatizing the key operations *and* the periphery of the manufacturing processes, can executive work be radically diminished and systems' control work gain the upper hand. This situation is realized now only in parts of the chemical industry, in the machine shops of the machine building industry, and in the stamping departments and the machine shops in the car industry. If one takes into account our further finding, that the new concepts of production are also spreading into the low-tech areas and generally stimulate the attempts at job enrichment and upskilling – as of now admittedly only in restricted forms – we can conclude that areas of skilled work have stabilized, and new areas of highly qualified, perhaps even quasi-professional work are going to be established. Even in a typical mass production industry like the automobile industry the critical mass for rising worker qualification currently seems to be present.'

20. Lane (1988) indicates a more piecemeal but nevertheless discernibly similar development in Britain. The impediments in the British case surround an unwillingness by management to invest in flexible technology which is a consequence of a commitment to cost control rather than quality control and market share. There nevertheless may be an unrecognized but widespread reprofessionalization or enskilling pattern in process in the UK, unrecognized because it lies outside the predictable arenas of technological development such as the machine tool industry and consists of pockets or islands of flexible manufacturing. For example the introduction of CNC machines in the paper and board industry has dramatically increased the proportion of skilled workers in the labour force and this without much compensatory deskilling (Penn and Scattergood 1985).

7

Science and technology: decomposition of the 'Grand Design'

The editor of the first (1665) volume of the *Philosophical Transactions* of the Royal Society exhorted his readers to 'contribute what they can to the Grand Design of improving Natural Knowledge, and perfecting all *Philosophical Arts* and *Sciences*' (Royal Society 1963: 2). This 'Grand Design' has since become central to the ways in which modern societies have understood their distinctiveness. Scientific understanding and technical mastery are believed to have shifted the human relation to the natural world onto a new plane. As Leiss (1974: xi) writes, linking the 'Grand Design' to the domination of nature:

> through a collective social enterprise, extending over many generations and paced by the march of science and technology, the human species would fulfil its destiny by gaining complete control over the forces of the natural world, appropriating to the full its resources for the satisfaction of human needs.

Faith in this enterprise supported a spectacular incremental growth in science during the modern period (see Price 1963: ch. 1). At the beginning of the final decade of the twentieth century, however, the gloss has faded on the Grand Design. Governments are increasingly reluctant to fund the indefinite expansion of 'pure' research, demanding that science produces 'practical' results. Among wider publics the view has become widespread that science and technology are responsible for many of the problems of contemporary civilization. Articulated with an increasing scepticism about science is a sense that the contingency of human society upon the natural order has not, after all, been transcended. The HIV/AIDS epidemic suggests uncomfortable analogies with pre- and early modern plagues, while a range of environmental problems from soil erosion and salinity to humanly induced climate change offer vivid icons of a natural order which is not indefinitely malleable to technical 'progress'.

In short, the spectacular historical growth of science has modulated into a rather less triumphalist prospect for the immediate future, and it is this modulation which is the focus of attention here. The trajectory of science and technology can be analysed in terms of the account of postmodernization outlined in Chapter 1 and developed in subsequent chapters. That is to say, the organized 'Big Science' of the mid-twentieth century is to be understood as a constitutive part of organized social modernity while its partial erosion over recent years is a symptom of disorganization. The dynamics of organization and disorganization shape the institutional reality of science, and there are clear analogies between the arguments to be developed here and those of Chapter 3 (on the state) and of Chapter 6 (on organizations). In each case the fundamental dynamic is one in which large-scale bureaucratic and corporatist structures emerge in response to the limitations of *laissez-faire* arrangements, only to decompose in a disorganizing realignment as their own limitations become visible. As was argued in Chapter 1, a major impetus for disorganization can be understood formally as an incompatibility between continuing centralization and continuing differentiation.

The first section of this chapter considers the modernization of science under the headings of professionalization and organization, differentiation, rationalization and commodification. The second section identifies processes which are currently promoting the disorganization of science, while the brief final section asks whether it is appropriate to think in terms of a postmodern 'postscience' on the model of postmodern postculture.

Science and Modernity

Professionalization and Organization

Price (1963: 2) took up the 'happy term "Big Science" ' to draw attention to 'the large-scale character of modern science, new and shining and all-powerful'. He saw Big Science as the outcome of a period of some 250 years of continual exponential growth, a period which was drawing to a close as he wrote. While Price's history of science focusses on the problems of modelling and measuring growth, it also acknowledges that Big Science is distinctive in terms of institutional relationships as well as size. He places considerable emphasis, for example (1963: ch. 3), on the role of 'invisible colleges' in modern collaborative science.[1] More formalized institutional structures cannot be ignored, however. Academic research scientists occupy precisely defined roles in highly differentiated institutions such as university departments and research institutes. They have qualified for these roles by meeting formal demands for credentials awarded by universities. Big Science is the product not only of a long period of growth, but a long period of progressive organization and professionalization. A brief review of this process of organization can give a purchase on the particular forms of institutional autonomy that modern science has enjoyed, and also on the disorganizing pressures that threaten that autonomy.

The insight that scientific institutions are pivotal in the development of science is not confined to recent sociology. Francis Bacon's utopian *New Atlantis* of 1627 elaborates his vision of a scientific society, 'Salomons House', dedicated to 'the knowledge of Causes and secret motions of things, and the enlarging of the bounds of Human Empire, to the effecting of all things possible' (Bacon 1978: 437, 447). The Royal Society of London for the Improvement of Natural Knowledge, founded some thirty-five years after the appearance of Bacon's text, is often regarded as the first modern scientific institution. It was conceived as a society to facilitate communication between gentlemen of 'philosophical' interests, and its limitations are set by its amateurism. As Ravetz (1977: 74) remarks, by the end of the seventeenth century, the Royal Society 'had lost the prophetic zeal of its earliest proponents, and indeed, in England at least, experimental philosophy came to be regarded as a gentleman's eccentricity'. Swift's satirical 'Academy of Lagado' is a Royal Society which has fallen into the hands of deranged 'projectors' attempting to extract sunshine from cucumbers, or to reconstitute food from faeces.

The development of the mature modern 'academic research system' in science (Gibbons 1985) required the overcoming of both the ethos and the organizational forms of amateurism in a thoroughgoing professionalization of science. Ben-David (1971), for example, traces a history in which scientific pre-eminence is strongly associated with institutional innovation. France in the early nineteenth century, Germany in the later nineteenth century and the USA in the twentieth century were pace-setters in scientific development because they developed institutions which promoted professionalization. In France the education system provided employment for career scientists. In Germany research laboratories developed as centres for professional scientific training, for an inter-institutional scientific community, and for government and industrial sponsorship of science. In the USA the competitive and professional research system comes to full flower in what Ben-David terms 'organized science'.

If the kind of autonomy enjoyed, if only temporarily, by modern science is to be understood it is essential to realize that the involvement of government and industry is not a twentieth-century innovation. Rothblatt (1985), for example, points to the critical role of government and commercial sponsorship in turning British science away from its decadent eighteenth-century amateurism and towards a serious professionalism. At the intellectual level this shift is carried by a struggle between materialistic, experimental science and idealistic 'natural philosophy', with the former tendency eventually victorious. Wynne's (1982) account of Cambridge physics at the turn of the century offers a case study in this struggle. The doctrine of the ether, a 'universal connecting medium which binds the universe together' (Lodge, cited in Wynne 1982: 215), is a rearguard action of the tradition of natural philosophy against the growing influence of 'professionalizers' who would reform the old universities and turn science towards a materialist and pragmatic engagement with the needs of state and industry .[2]

The history of science in the modern period is one of an institutional and professional evolution which culminates in an autonomous *system* of scientific research. The building-blocks of this system are those research establishments (both inside and outside universities) within which professional scientific 'roles' are performed, the professionalized role of 'scientist' itself, the university schools in which scientists are trained and accredited, and the networks of co-operative and competitive relations between research establishments which constitute the 'scientific community'. For the present argument, the most important defining characteristic of modern organized science is that it combines a systemic autonomy with close connections to the 'systems' of the polity and economy. That is, while government and industry provide resources for science, and thus have some capacity to shape research agendas, they do not directly intervene in the intra-systemic relations of science. One of the many pressures leading to a subsequent *dis*organization of science is a conviction that science is too important to be left to the scientists, which leads government and industry down the disorganizing track of increasing intervention in the intra-systemic relations of science itself. However, before turning to this question it is necessary to explore the structures and processes of organized science in a little more detail, under the heads of differentiation, rationalization and commodification.

Differentiation

As a principle of scientific development, differentiation invokes a paradox familiar from the discussion of culture in Chapter 2. If differentiation initially produces the institution and culture of a 'science' autonomous from other institutions, its operations within that institution and culture pose the threat of fragmentation and eventual disintegration as subdisciplines and research fronts proliferate. These processes operate at a number of different levels, including the cognitive (scientific ideas), the institutional (the organization of science) and the normative (science as a moral community). Durkheim recognizes the paradox. He argues (1964: Book 3 ch. 1) that the emergence of ever more specialized sciences can appear as an anomic threat to the overall 'unity' of science. Philosophy, the collective conscience of science, becomes less and less capable of articulating the solidary 'sameness' of the sciences. Durkheim sets little store by the capacity of a shared scientific method to override disciplinary difference and cites Schaeffle's warning against a fragmenting 'new Alexandrianism' which would destroy science (Durkheim 1964: 356–7). However, while he regards an anomic division of labour as a real, if transitional, problem for the youthful social sciences his overall thesis is upbeat. The decline of a 'mechanical' principle of the unity of science is compensated for by the rise of an 'organic' principle.

> The unity of science will . . . form itself not through the abstract unity of a formula, far too scanty for the multitude of things that it must embrace, but through the living unity of an organic whole. For science to be unitary, it is not necessary for it to be contained within the field of one and the same conscience – an impossible feat anyhow – but it is sufficient that all those who cultivate it feel that they are collaborating in the same work. (1964: 371)

Merton's celebrated (1973: ch. 13) account of the 'institutional imperatives' of science offers a model of science as a differentiated system of norms and values. It can be read as an attempt to spell out how it is possible for scientists to 'feel that they are collaborating in the same work'. Merton blurs the distinction between 'mechanical' and 'organic' solidarity. Formally, the imperatives of science (universalism, communism, disinterestedness and organized scepticism) have the binding, regulative, character of traditionally solidaristic norms. However, the community to which they give a moral character is pluralistic and competitive. Each of the norms serves to cancel the incompatibility between pluralism and competition on the one hand and communal solidarity on the other.[3]

Merton's account has a Weberian, as much as a Durkheimian, pedigree. It develops the insight that the differentiated autonomy of modern science is not simply cognitive and institutional but moral and cultural: science is a 'value sphere' and the occupation of scientist is a 'vocation'. Just as Merton implies that science can evade an anomic fragmentation, he calms fears of an alienating routinization: the ethos of science is, in effect, already routinized and institutionalized but in a way which preserves rather than threatens its moral and vocational character. Of course, it is not only the ethos of science which has become differentiated from wider patterns. Merton (1973: Part 4) devotes considerable attention to the peculiar stratification and reward systems of science. Science institutionalizes an intense competition for recognition which yields a sharply delineated hierarchy of merit, but in ways which reinforce, rather than threaten, its moral community.[4]

Considered as the emergence of ever more disciplines, subdisciplines and research fronts, differentiation is clearly an index of scientific development. This insight is given an important twist in Mulkay's (1975) model of development through 'branching'.[5] Many scientific discoveries 'reveal "new areas of ignorance" to be explored' while not revolutionizing the 'established conceptual and technical apparatus' (Mulkay 1975: 517). Their significance is that they open up new research areas. By way of example Mulkay (1975: 518) shows that the general problem of 'cosmic noise' which defined the then new research area of radio astronomy in 1930 had proliferated into seventeen problem areas, of variable vintage, by 1970.

Mulkay establishes, first, that differentiation is the key to scientific growth and not simply a *post hoc* response to growth. 'It seems probable that science has grown, not by the continued expansion and recurrent redefinition of a stable set of research areas, but by the cumulative efflorescence of new lines of investigation' (1975: 519). Two further implications of the thesis are consequential. First, a clear link is established between 'growth' in the sense of expansion and in the sense of progress. That flattening of the exponential growth-curve of science which Price regarded as inevitable, and which is currently being accomplished through restrictions on funding for science, threatens the modern expectation of continual scientific progress. Second, Mulkay points to the most intimate link between cognitive and institutional differentiation.

The conceptions of the institutional reality of science held by Ben-David and Merton share an assumption that institutional and cognitive development are, in some general way, articulated with each other. Ben-David has an eye for the happy accidents through which productive institutional innovations arise, while Merton draws attention to those normative dimensions of science which promote innovation. In Mulkay the connection is not only more direct, but also operates within the fine-grain of scientific practice as well as within the big picture of the history and systematicity of science. Branching is at the same time an organizational and a cognitive phenomenon, to be accounted for in terms of the material and cognitive 'interests' of scientists. New problem areas open up as researchers move out of adjacent areas in which significant results and, therefore, funding are dwindling. The consolidation of a new area depends on complex processes of competition and negotiation within research communities.

In the functionalist tradition, differentiation appears as an autonomous and spontaneous process of cognitive splitting which institutional arrangements merely advance or retard. The phenomenon of branching suggests an alternative account of differentiation cast in terms of the interests of scientists, an account which can also draw on Yearley's suggestion that science should be analysed as a social movement. The authority modern science enjoys is the outcome of a competitive struggle for recognition as a form of knowledge in which science has won an effective 'closure' (Yearley 1988: 45). This view confirms the commonplace observation that science does not merely 'split' from religious, metaphysical and commonsense knowledges, but seeks to displace them. The Mertonian vision of science as a moral community, along with philosophical models of the scientist as cognitive hero, effectively elaborates an 'ideology of science', an image which is at best partially correct. Taking this view a step further, the relations between organized science, industry and the state appear not as the functional interplay of subsystems but as the contingent and shifting outcome of a pragmatic convergence of interests, interests which are continually in movement within, as well as between, the 'subsystems'. In short, the model of a fundamentally benign and 'functional' differentiation which animates the work of Durkheim and Merton can be given a twist in which differentiation becomes a dynamic principle within a less benign economy of interest.[6]

Rationalization

For Weber, science is the instrument of that intellectualization of the relations between human beings and their environment which is the key to disenchantment and rationalization (see Weber 1970: 139, for example). The formality and abstraction of science transform the pragmatics of our relation to the world in the direction of control, or 'technical mastery'. To this extent, Weber echoes a theme of Durkheim's, whose distinction between ideology and science (1964: ch. 2) makes clear that the cognitive superiority of science generates a superior form of practice. However, while Durkheim has few doubts about the benefits of a scientized human practice, Weber is doubtful in the extreme. He cites Nietzsche's critique of the utilitarian 'last men' as having already exposed 'the naive optimism in which science . . . has been celebrated as the way to happiness' (Weber 1970: 143). The intellectualization which increases technical control is part of a process that erodes the rationality of values, and becomes increasingly disconnected from them.

> Natural science gives us the answer to the question of what we must do if we wish to master life technically. It leaves quite aside, or assumes for its purposes, whether we should and do wish to master life technically and whether it ultimately makes sense to do so. (1970: 145)

Durkheimian optimism and Weberian pessimism have set the boundaries for modern debates about the rationality of science and technology. While optimism has been dominant in popular presentations of science and has underpinned the development of science policy, a marked strain of pessimism has been present in social theory since Weber. It is developed within a tradition which runs from Adorno and Horkheimer (1979) to Habermas (1971) and Leiss (1974). The starting point of the tradition can be summed up in three theses:

• The purest science and the most applied technology are linked by a constitutive logic of control.
• While this drive to control begins as the servant of broader human purposes, it inflates to become an unchallenged end in itself which is either indifferent to, or subversive of, its original purpose.
• The model of technical control over natural processes is illicitly imposed on social processes, so that there comes to be 'an inextricable bond between the domination of nature and the domination of man' in Leiss' (1974: xiv) formula.

Advocates of this model can appeal to a number of features of organized science for confirmation, such as the dominant position of military research within the organized science of scientific superpowers. On OECD figures, in 1971 overtly defence-oriented projects took 53 per cent of all government R&D expenditure in the USA and 44 per cent in Britain (OECD 1975: 129). Of course, both of these indices can be argued to underestimate the level and proportion of support given to military science because of the potential for military application of research funded from non-defence budgets.

There are grounds here for a critique of the 'substantive irrationality' of a scientific establishment grotesquely skewed towards the refinement of death and destruction. There are also some clearly 'unintended' economic consequences of military science. Barnes (1985: 30) argues that as a result of the success of the military in dominating research budgets 'resources and manpower of rare quality become a burden to the rest of the economy rather than an asset to it'. The basic radical Weberian critique of science agrees with optimistic scientism that an instrumental logic of control links basic science to applied technology, but denies that this 'logic' serves humane objectives. The more interesting developments of the critique move some way, but perhaps not far enough, towards a rejection of the shared premise.

Leiss moves some way in this direction. He argues that science achieves its 'mastery' as 'its theoretical formulations achieve progressively greater generality and coherence – and thus greater rationality' (Leiss 1974: 118). In scientistic models, technology 'translates' these formulations into 'new possibilities for the satisfaction of human wants'. What is overlooked is that the rationality of scientific 'mastery' is not the rationality of a technological 'mastery' which turns on more concrete forms of manipulation and control. For Leiss, the substantive irrationality of modern science is the outcome not of a single unfolding logic, but of the concrete interaction of a scientific and a technical logic in specific social circumstances. Habermas, too, moves away from the basic critique. He allows that a 'technical' rationality of control has a legitimate place in human affairs, but suggests that it gives rise to two related problems. First, there is a tendency for technical rationality to move beyond its proper domain and to 'colonize' large areas of social and political life. Second, there is a gulf between the specialist discourses of the various forms of technical control and the ordinary language in which social and political issues are conventionally discussed. Without 'translation' between discourses democratic participation in technical decisions becomes impossible.[7]

Despite their undoubted insights, Leiss and Habermas remain committed to a mistaken view of the relations between science and technology. They do not challenge the 'traditional hierarchical model' according to which 'the production of new knowledge is the concern of science' while technology is 'the routine activity of working out and realizing the "implications" of scientific theories' (Barnes and Edge 1982: 148). There can be two major objections to this model. First, cases can be cited where the dependency is reversed. Whole fields of modern science are inconceivable without such technologies as electron microscopes, particle accelerators or computers. Second, a number of empirical studies of technology have made it clear that technology has a culture of its own, and that the development of new technology typically builds on old technology much more than on new science (see Price 1982). Barnes and Edge (1982: 150–2) urge a view of the science–technology relation in which the two are 'distinguishable subcultures, each with their own bodies of lore and competence', between which subsists a symmetrical relationship which allows 'two-way interactions'.

The salient point is that in studies of what Hughes (1988) has termed the 'seamless web' between science and technology the idea of a governing logic of control – whether benign or malign, unitary or dual – has been laid aside in favour of a more empirically sensitive approach in which the contingent, pragmatic and rhetorical dimensions of science and technology can emerge.[8] From such a perspective the issues of rationality and control in science and technology appear to be much more open ended and problematic. At issue in any particular case are questions about which groups are contesting for 'control' of and through a technology, for what purposes and with what outcomes. To close with an example from the field of military technology, Mackenzie and Spinardi (1988) show how the Fleet Ballistic Missile project unfolded within a contest for control in which interested parties included US Navy scientists, the US Navy command, the Department of Defense and the US Congress. The FBM was able to survive a series of spectacular and highly visible failures because US Navy interests had successfuly 'black-boxed' the project, insulating 'technical' issues from 'political' scrutiny. By contrast, the MX missile was never successfully black-boxed, and in consequence was subjected to continual oversight from the US Congress.

Commodification

The case has already been stated that the development of organized science proceeds in close relation to commercial, as well as political, interests. The point that the majority of scientific workers are situated within commercial and governmental laboratories has been made by Cotgrove and Box (1970), and linked by Ciccotti et al. (1976) to the integration of science into the capitalist system of commodity production. More recent collections such as Albury and Schwarz (1982) and Gibbons and Wittrock (1985) continue this 'political economy of science'. The point such arguments often miss is that while organized science is defined in important part by its systemic relations to government and commerce it cannot be collapsed into them. The question of the commodification of science is closely linked to the question of its autonomy.

Many attempts to account for the peculiarity of modern science do so in terms of a uniquely scientific 'economy'. Merton (1973) emphasizes the role that 'professional recognition' plays in the unique reward system of science. Storer (1966) offers a model of the 'social system' of science, where a social system is defined in terms of 'the exchange of a qualitatively unique commodity . . . guided by a set of norms that facilitate the continuing circulation of that commodity' (1966: 75). In the case of science the commodity is 'response to creativity', operationalized as the 'certified responses' of the scientific community. In alternative models Hagstrom (1982) has proposed that scientific work enacts a gift relationship in which knowledge is exchanged for recognition, an exchange which both embodies and reinforces scientific norms. Latour and Woolgar (1982) challenge the normative basis of the functionalist accounts of the exchange system of science, but preserve the idea of a distinct scientific economy in a model of the circulation, or 'cycle' of the commodity 'credibility'.

Modern science develops through its own unique process of 'commodification' which establishes a measure of systemic autonomy for organized science, although there may be tensions between the scientific and the capitalist economy. Commercial (as well as political and military) requirements for secret research may obstruct the circulation of the scientific commodity, and industrial researchers may feel torn between the normative and reward systems of the two economies they straddle. However, the principle of organized science is that the two-way exchanges of scientific knowledge for money and/or power take place at the boundaries between systems. It is in smoothing the way for such exchanges that what Weingart (1982) has termed 'hybrid communities' of scientists and politicians-administrators are so important.

So long as the core 'academic research system' constitutes its own economy, and so long as scientific training is tied to that system, the autonomy of science is not fundamentally threatened by the proliferation and growth of other research systems. The threat to autonomy comes not from the coexistence of a large industrial or government sector devoted to 'applied' research, but from more recent and disorganizing policy initiatives which effectively seek the abolition of any distinction between the economy of science and that of these sectors.

Postmodernizing Tensions in Contemporary Science

It will be clear by now that the autonomy which modern organized science enjoyed depended on a capacity to hold in check a number of constitutive tensions. Differentiation threatens to become fragmentation, control through technology threatens to become control by technology, co-operation with government and industry threatens to become colonization by them. The remainder of the chapter expands on the proposition that the tensions of organized science are leading to a postmodernizing disorganization. Three problems can serve as case-studies related to aspects of organization-commodification, rationalization and differentiation respectively.

- The contraction of growth threatens the modern pattern of continual 'unplanned' scientific progress.
- The effectiveness of the 'grand design' for control of nature comes under sustained challenge.
- Public support for science and science funding becomes both more volatile and more instrumental.

Science Policy: Hypercommodification and Disorganization

The contemporary form of national science policy has been powerfully influenced by OECD initiatives in the 1960s (see Ronayne 1984: 30–1). The OECD's regular publication of comparative R&D statistics, and its programme of reviews of specific national science policies, have brought the issue into sharp focus for governments and scientific administrators.[9] The idea and practice of national science policy comes to prominence in just the period (the 1970s on) when the stabilities of organized science begin to be eroded. To borrow a figure from Baudrillard, contemporary science policy in the advanced societies has the air of a 'panic production', a simulation of organization in a rapidly disorganizing world. The problem turns on the centrality of growth to organized science. It will be recalled that Mulkay's (1975) model of 'branching' links scientific progress to the growth of science. This model can be placed in the context of Price's (1963) analysis of the growth of science, which insists that the exponential growth of science must reach a point of saturation.

> The growth curve of science as a whole . . . has had an extraordinarily long life of purely exponential growth . . . [but] . . . at some time this must begin to break down and be followed by a generation-long interval of increasing restraint which may tauten its sinews for a jump either toward escalation or toward violent fluctuation. (Price 1963: 30)

Price goes on to assert (1963: 31) that the percentages of GDP given to science in the advanced societies in the late 1950s may already represent saturation. Barnes (1985: 4–5) has echoed Price's diagnosis, arguing that in the postwar period 'there was no way science could hope to maintain an exponential rate of expansion: it was pressing hard against external constraints'.

The problem of external constraints on scientific growth becomes more acute during the 1970s when the sponsors of organized science, government and industry themselves become subject to disorganizing pressures and fiscal crises. These questions are discussed at length in Chapters 3 and 6, and will not be explored any further here. The main point is that national science policy comes onto the agenda in response to increasingly apparent uncertainties and instabilities within and outside organized science. The push for science policy recognizes that the benefits of scientific and technological progress will no longer arrive regularly and spontaneously as a simple function of continuing growth in science and technology. The science policy agenda raises questions about the necessity for choice between research priorities, and about cost-effectiveness, which have a considerable disorganizing potential.

Of course, disputes about priorities and costs have always been present, but in times of economic and scientific growth they can be resolved with minimal fuss. When growth tapers off, however, the question of priorities threatens to disrupt the academic research system itself. To adapt Habermas' (1987a: 318–26) argument, the autonomy of science is threatened with 'colonization' by economy and state. To impose the priorities of government or commerce on the research agenda of academic science is effectively to displace the qualitatively unique commodification which has defined the system of science. To carry the process to its conclusion would be wholly to assimilate scientific research into the circuits of money or power.

The precise mix of policy problems and solutions will vary from nation to nation, of course. Quite clearly, the circumstances which science policy in the USA must address are very different from those of Australia. In the USA, where expenditure on R&D has recently run at just under 3 per cent of GNP, roughly 50 per cent of R&D expenditure has been by business enterprises and about 28 per cent has been for military purposes (compare 70 per cent and under 2 per cent respectively for Japan). In Australia, where R&D expenditure bounces along at around 1 per cent of GNP, only about 23 per cent of R&D has been funded by business (all figures from ASTEC 1985: 115). Clearly, Australia's expenditure will fall well short of the scientific superpowers. In 1987 the total government R&D outlay in Australia came to $US 738 million, compared to $US 2797 million in Britain and $US 14,905 million in the USA (ASTEC 1990: 31).

As a small advanced nation Australia faces the problem of selecting a few areas in which its science can reach 'world class' as well as the problem of funding economically relevant research in the face of business indifference. The Australian case brings to the forefront two common, and potentially fatal, problems for science policy. It is unclear on what kind of criteria and through what kinds of procedure scientific winners are to be picked in advance. It is equally uncertain how scientific and technical innovation are to be contained within national boundaries when research fronts are increasingly defined by transnational networks or 'invisible colleges'.

Despite these differences and difficulties there has been a common and disorganizing thrust to science policy in the advanced societies. A point of convergence has been those strategies which Offe (1984: ch. 4) has termed 'administrative recommodification', and which are linked in Chapter 2 with contemporary cultural policies. Offe (in collaboration with Ronge) sees recommodification as a response to the 'obsolescence of the commodity form' brought about by welfarist 'decommodification' (1984: 124). The principle is to direct state funding towards measures which will enable more and more areas of activity to operate as commodified markets.[10]

Science policy becomes implicated with recommodification in at least two senses:

- Science and technology are increasingly perceived as important instruments for enhancing the market position of strategically important national industries.
- Important as science and technology may be, they also represent a considerable cost to governments in times of fiscal crisis.

The recommodification of scientific and technological research is doubly attractive to governments, as it promises to reduce their direct outlays (at least in the long-term) and to enhance the sensitivity of research institutions to the 'needs of industry'. This priority causes particular concern within scientific communities. The not always unfounded fear is that 'serious' scientific research in universities and other publicly funded institutions will be displaced by what is, in effect, subsidized low-level R&D for private industry.

Recommodification was pursued particularly vigorously in Britain under the Thatcher administration. Webster (1988: 27) has documented the changing links between industry and public sector research science (PSRS) in Britain:

- The institutions of PSRS (academic departments and research institutes) are increasingly required to adopt commercial accounting practices, to balance budgets and to compensate for lower public subsidies by generating profits.
- As a corollary of this development PSRS has become 'increasingly self-exploitative of its own expertise'.
- Management styles in PSRS become more directive and professional while institute directorates become critical links between PSRS, government and industry.
- 'Socio-technical' networks linking PSRS to industry have begun to emerge while 'club' arrangements for pre-competitive research have been encouraged.
- 'Strategic' work in new technology areas such as biotechnology, IT and materials science have attracted an increasing proportion of funds from all sources.

Such developments represent an accelerating disorganization of organized science as the unique system-characteristics of the academic research system are eroded and colonized. The autonomy of science is squeezed between the hyperorganizing pressures of increasingly direct government priority-setting and the hypercommodifying pressures of commercialization. Among the implications of commercialization that Webster discusses, two in particular index its disorganizing potential. First, in currently favoured strategic areas the distinction between 'basic' and 'applied' research which is fundamental to organized science is eroded. A fundamental breakthrough in genetic engineering, or in IT, will often be almost immediately a *commercial* breakthrough (Webster 1988: 29). Research institutes become increasingly caught up in the race to patent and exploit their discoveries, a circumstance which partly explains the rushed announcement of the Pons–Fleischmann 'cold fusion' findings, and the resulting fiasco.

Second, it follows from this that the 'open' communication of results, which had been central to the academic research system as modelled by Merton and others, comes under threat (Webster 1988: 31). Once again, the consequential shift is from an 'organized' accommodation of commercial (or military) secrecy which operates in subsystems of research to a 'disorganizing' circumstance in which secrecy threatens the 'core' of the system itself. Taken together, these two developments suggest that scientific information increasingly circulates in the commodified financial and industrial economy, to the detriment of the peculiar form of commodification which characterized the autonomous 'economy' of organized science.

Paradoxes of a Rationality of 'Control'

The radical Weberian critique of science and technology is based on assumptions about a 'logic' of control which were queried earlier. The critique claims, in effect, that the Grand Design for the control of nature has been realized, but that its realization has brought unforeseen and terrible social costs. The rather different case that 'control' has always been problematic, and that a visible *failure* to deliver control is a disorganizing force in contemporary science, can be sketched here in relation to increasingly prominent concerns about the environment.

One impact of environmental concerns has been to alter the meaning of 'control' in claims about the 'control of nature'. Perhaps the most influential modern image of control has been that of 'harnessing' natural forces. Science discerns order in the protean unruliness of natural forces so that these forces can be tamed by technology and put to productive use. The paradigm here, and perhaps for all modern technology, is the development of energy sources: the forces which produce fire, lightning, flood, or even the forces which hold together matter itself, become the servants of human industry. A related image is that of 'transformation'. Not only are natural materials processed and shaped into objects of use, but modern science conjures up new materials from base elements, and turns them to new purposes.

The environmentalist critique of science and technology insists that pay-back time has arrived for the project of harnessing and transforming nature and for the industrial economy which is premised upon it. Of course, the argument that scientific-industrial civilization rests on an alienating human relationship with nature is familiar from the radical-Weberian critique and stretches back to Romanticism (see Leiss 1974: ch. 8). Two peculiarities, at least, mark out contemporary concerns from the established tradition. The first can be indicated by way of contrast. Campaigns such as those to prevent damming, logging and mining in the temperate rainforests of south-west Tasmania have a relatively traditional relationship to the 'lifeworlds' of campaigners. They invoke images of a 'special' region that embodies the virtues of a wilderness which can be experienced by visiting the region or intimated by way of films and photographs. Concerns about global warming and ozone depletion, on the other hand, are not related to the lifeworld in the same way: they exist *as* concerns only by virtue of scientific measurement and hypothesis. No particular value attaches to the ozone layer other than its role as a global sunscreen, and ozone depletion cannot be seen in the way that the desolate results of clear-felling in native Australian forests can be seen.

The second peculiarity of contemporary global concerns is that they are unsettling because they suggest the failure of the project for 'control' of nature understood as harnessing and transformation. As Newby (1991: 2) notes in relation to the shifting focus of British environmental concerns, 'there is now a greater emphasis on the finite nature of the earth's resources and a growing suspicion that we may, in ways which remain not yet fully understood, be irreversibly tampering with the habitability of our planet'. Two dimensions of failure can be distinguished. The theme of 'scarcity' surfaced in the 1970s. It challenges the idea that nature will furnish raw materials for an indefinite prolongation of harnessing and transformation. A twist in the more recent versions of the theme points to the second dimension. Scarcity is due not simply to the exhaustion of natural resources, but to their despoliation by the practices through which they are exploited. So, modern agriculture threatens long-term productivity by reducing biological diversity, promoting soil erosion and increasing salinity (see Brown 1990). The twist, and the second dimension of failure, is that the project for control of nature is self-defeating in the long term: attempts at control set in train unforeseen consequences (soil degradation, ozone depletion, warming) which subvert the original attempt.

Increasingly, science and technology are required to turn their attention to another kind of control: the 'damage control' of the unforeseen consequences of the project for the control of nature. This kind of control is not new. Medicine has always aimed at a control of nature which, while informed by theoretical knowledge, establishes pragmatic criteria of success in terms of a capacity to halt or reverse pathological processes. Science and technology, one might say, are required to become more like medicine, to diagnose and (more problematically) to cure the diseases that scientific-industrial civilization has induced in the planet.

This shift in emphasis carries a disorganizing, postmodernizing, potential. Most generally, the question mark it places over the 'Grand Design' challenges the most potent of meta-narratives of modern science. If they are no longer in the vanguard of a 'progress' understood as unalloyed benefit, science and technology can be subject to more pragmatic and piecemeal judgements of worth. Perhaps more fundamentally, the clear lines between 'natural', 'technical' and 'social' processes are eroded. When Brown et al. (1990) try to depict a sustainable society, for example, the issues they raise illustrate the complex and fine-grained interdependence of choices made at each of these levels. So to shift the advanced societies from their reliance on private petrol-driven automobiles requires the development of new transport and energy technologies, as well as the revival of old ones (bicycles), the transformation of the social geography of cities, and shifts in the relations between home and work. The traditional model, in which science and technology connect with social processes only at the points of 'application' or 'use' is not adequate to these complexities.

It is notable that a similar erosion of apparently stable system-boundaries is suggested by developments in areas of research where the old project for control lives on. The hyper-rationalized projects of biotechnology challenge the boundaries between natural and technical processes. Is a fly engineered to transmit sterility to its descendants and released into the wild to be considered as a part of 'nature' or as a pest-control 'technology'? In the area of human genetics, Suzuki and Knudtson (1988: ch. 7) prefigure the possibility of a total 'gene screen' whereby the genetically determined susceptibility of each individual to a range of disorders could be known in advance. Such knowledge could be used, in turn, to exclude susceptible individuals from employment that would expose them to the environmental factors (chemicals, radiation) that would trigger the disorders to which they were prone. Such screening could serve employers as a cheap alternative to stricter environmental controls. The gene screen might create an unemployable underclass of persons with genetic 'disorders'. Here, again, the boundaries between natural, technical and social processes are tangled in ways which modern paradigms find difficult to encompass.

Biotechnology is a field in which the traditional programme of control and contemporary preoccupations with damage control have become intertwined. A disorganizing complication lies in what Collingridge (1980) terms the 'dilemma of control'. The first horn of the dilemma is that when technologies are in their early stages of application, and could be controlled easily, 'the harmful social consequences of the fully developed technology cannot be predicted with sufficient confidence to justify the imposition of controls' (Collingridge 1980: 17). The second horn is that: 'by the time a technology is sufficiently well developed and diffused for its unwanted social consequences to become apparent, it is no longer easily controlled' (1980: 17–18). Collingridge reviews the ways in which the baleful logic of this dilemma has been played out in areas as diverse as the development of nuclear power and the addition of lead to petrol. Collingridge's solution is to advocate a model of 'decision making under ignorance'. Rather than aim for the impossible objective of removing all possibility of error in a once-and-for-all judgement about any given technology, we should accept the high probability of error and design processes of decision making which allow for the quickest and cheapest possible revision of wrong decisions. As Collingridge points out, 'an immediate consequence of this view is that a decision under ignorance cannot be seen as a point event, it must be seen as a process' (1980: 30). Collingridge's model has a clear relevance for science and technology conceived as instruments of environmental damage control, but its disorganizing implication is that, once again, clear boundaries and directionalities between the technical and the social give way to a much more complex, ongoing and two-way interaction.

To sum up, modern, organized, science and technology come under disorganizing pressure from the fragmentation of the unified 'logic of control' which defined the rationality of the Grand Design. In areas where the rationality of control is hyperextended, it produces results which transgress boundaries between the stable and autonomous registers of nature, technology and society. Where that rationality is challenged, and mutates from 'control' to 'damage control', as it does in the face of looming environmental catastrophe, the same boundaries are again eroded. In neither case can the modern paradigm of an autonomous 'science' mediated to an autonomous 'society' by way of a uniquely rational 'technology' be sustained.

The Problem of 'PUS'

One of the critical problems facing contemporary science is that of its relations with lay publics whose support for science may be required, but whose level of understanding of science will probably be low. Surveys of public attitudes to science and technology in advanced societies typically paint an ambiguous picture. A recent Australian study (Eckersley 1987: 3) finds that while roughly 60 per cent of respondents favour more emphasis on the development of new technology, a similar proportion agree with a series of gloomy propositions about the impact of science and technology.[11] Birke (1990: 33) cites a series of studies which find signs of widespread public ignorance about science.

It is not surprising that wide sections of the public in advanced societies have little understanding of science. The fact that modern science is highly differentiated, highly rationalized and subject to a unique commodification cuts it off from the 'lifeworlds' of most people. Indeed, as Collins (1987) points out in response to a 1985 Royal Society report on Public Understanding of Science (or 'PUS'), it is unclear what the idea of 'understanding' is to mean in this context. When scientists worry about PUS they have in mind a combination of ignorance (about basic 'scientific facts' and about 'scientific method'), credulity (regarding astrology as scientific, for example) and hostility (regarding science as pointless, or dangerous).[12] However, widespread ignorance, credulity and hostility have been quite compatible with broad public support for science and technology in the past. The interesting problem is whether the institutional and budgetary interests of science will be served by a better informed public.

As Birke (1990) noted, the Royal Society PUS report argued the cultural-social-political case for PUS: scientific literacy was necessary if citizens were to participate in policy decisions. She goes on to suggest that

> scientists have two more reasons to popularise their activities. As cuts in public spending bite deeper, scientists have come to realise the need to justify what they spend. But that need for greater public accountablity comes at a time of increasing disquiet about the activities of science in, for example, genetic engineering, experiments on embryos, or the use of animals in research. (Birke 1990: 32)

The recent interest in PUS can be compared with a wave of concern about 'anti-science' which swelled up in the late 1960s and early 1970s. Radical intellectual and political currents were widely perceived to be hostile to science and scientific rationality. One important response was to place this 'anti-science' in the context of a history of ideas which linked it to Blake, Goethe, Swift and Montaigne (Toulmin 1973), or even back to Aristophanes (Ravetz 1977). Another was to recognize that the institutions and imperatives of modern science had produced dangerous disconnections between the scientist and the wider society, the work of pure research and its far from pure social applications. So Bloch (1973: 6) urged that the goal of science policy should be 'to reintegrate science into our civilization'.[13] There are clear thematic continuities between these debates about 'anti-science' and the more recent sense of crisis. What was missing in the earlier formulations was a pressing concern with funding. Shils, for example (1973: 45) wrote reassuringly that the prospect of a 'slight decline' in budgets was 'not very dangerous' to science. In order to understand the implications of the present crisis in PUS and its relation to funding it is necessary to consider the roots of public enthusiasm for, as well as opposition to, science.

A critical factor here must be the ways in which science is reported in mass media: For many publics this will be the only source of information and assessment.[14] Analysis of television science has been greatly influenced by Gardner and Young's (1981) polemic. They argue that 'serious' science programmes (*Horizon* in Britain or *Quantum* in Australia) adopt the conventions of 'the informative lecture' (1981: 178) which discourages engagement or comment. 'Popular' programmes (*Tomorrow's World* or *Beyond 2000*) offer a 'shallow and flashy' advertisement for scientific and technical innovation. Bell and Boehringer (1989: 114) summarize the argument: 'Science . . . is seen as authoritative, non-controversial, positive and value free. . . . Science programs are almost invariably about "progress" (or the "fight" to overcome a natural obstacle) and thus optimistically ignore *real* social/historical determinations.' Collins (1987, 1988) argues that television coverage equates science with certainty: even 'serious' programmes portray uncertainty in science as a pathological and transient state of affairs asssociated with an unusually high degree of controversy. For example, coverage of the Pons–Fleischmann 'discovery' of cold fusion often insinuated that a high degree of disagreement about experimental procedures and findings was as peculiar a feature of the case as the announcement of the discovery by way of a press conference.

Gardner and Young (1981: 190–1) argue for an 'opening up' of television science. A real 'public understanding' of science would require attention to the (social) sources of the priorities of science, to the 'labour process' of science, and to the articulations between the products of science and their social context. Collins sets no such explicit agenda, but argues strongly against the idea that the purpose of an increased level of PUS can be to transform publics into quasi-expert judges of technical questions. He offers a critique of televised 'demonstrations' (of the safety of containers for transporting nuclear waste, for example) which masquerade as 'experiments'. For Collins (1987: 691): 'it is radically misleading to pretend that the citizen can judge between the competing views of technical experts even where the experts cannot agree'. He converges with Gardner and Young in his insistence that publics require to understand science as a 'cultural enterprise' rather than as a set of technical problems.

Research scientists appear to be deeply suspicious of *any* nontechnical reporting of their work. On the one hand, they seem to believe that their findings are almost wilfully distorted. As Nelkin (1987: 155) writes 'despite the generally friendly tone and positive, even promotional, images that characterize science and technology reporting, scientists complain of sensationalism and oversimplification'. On the other hand, working scientists are dismissive of the efforts of colleagues who produce 'popular' science (see Charlton 1990). Nelkin goes on to argue that scientists are caught between a sense that publicity about science is desirable and a recognition that it threatens the autonomy of science because 'it extends their accountability beyond the science community' (Nelkin 1987: 159). A high level of PUS may not be in the interests of science, precisely because it will threaten scientific autonomy. Scientific authority and cognitive closure are far better defended when publics hold science in high esteem but remain relatively ignorant of its inner workings. Television coverage of science promotes this outcome by endorsing two key ideologies of science: that science is 'impartial' and 'productive'. These would be undermined by the kind of 'sociological' public understanding that Gardner and Young or Collins advocate.

The media discovery of looming environmental catastrophes (global warming, ozone depletion) around 1988 accelerated a trend towards the association of science and technology with 'bad news' rather than 'good news' which has muddied the waters of PUS. In a sub-genre of environmental science programmes technological development is shown to carry heavy costs. The point is not that such programmes promote hostility to science. Indeed, such shows as the Australian ABC's series *Race to Save the Planet* are upbeat about the role of science in 'finding solutions' to environmental problems.

In relation to environmental matters scientists appear as assessors of risk and projectors of trends more frequently than as solvers of problems. Low assessments (of the risk of nuclear or toxic contamination, for example) invite a sceptical response, while high assessments associate science with gloom and doom. Further, environmental issues more than any other bring disagreements between scientists into the public eye. Collingridge and Reeve (1986: x) argue that the increasing involvement of scientists in policy making produces bad policy and bad science: 'science under these conditions leads not to agreement, but to endless technical bickering about an ever growing number of issues'. On any environmentally sensitive issue each side will be represented by experts who will disagree on the validity and interpretation of evidence. As Nelkin (1982: 278) argues, 'expertise is reduced to one more weapon in a political arsenal'. In the light of these trends, the finding that public attitudes to science and technology are confused is unsurprising.

However, the basic reason why PUS has become a problem in a time of contracting science budgets may not be that media coverage has changed, but that it has stayed so much the same. Despite the grumbles of scientists, media presentations of a *productive* science converge with the way in which science has sold itself to publics, governments and corporations throughout the modern period. The rhetoric of science policies which aim to cut and target research expenditure is, precisely, one of the need to increase the 'productivity' of scientific and technical research. Publics for whom science is defined by its technical products will not see such rhetoric as any kind of threat to science.

Science has never been wholeheartedly embraced by publics in the advanced societies. Overt 'anti-science' has had a continuing presence, but by and large publics tolerated organized science, used its products, but never 'assimilated' its culture (as Handlin 1972: 253 puts it). During periods of expansion this public response served perfectly well as a basis for further bids. The disorganizing potential of the public response lies in its indifference to the cherished 'autonomy' of science. Particularly if the authority of science is somewhat eroded, as it arguably has been by the rise of environmental concerns, publics will not be outraged by government and corporate challenges to its autonomy. Science is caught in a bind here. Present trends threaten its autonomy, so that the television image of science as no more than the producer of technical marvels may well come to correspond to the reality. The drive for an improved level of PUS is a two-edged sword in the fight against this trend: a greater awareness of science as a 'cultural enterprise' would itself be likely to intensify demands for scientific accountability.

A Postmodern Postscience?

No systematic attempt has been made here to characterize modern science in terms of its intellectual frameworks. The omission does not endorse the view that sociology can have nothing to say about the determinants of the 'internal', cognitive, concerns of science. The problem, rather, is that the 'sociology of scientific knowledge', as it has been termed (see, for example, Woolgar 1988: ch.3) works best with the fine-grained detail of the day-to-day practice of science. Attempts to link the development of scientific knowledge with wider cultural and social trends are usually more suggestive than convincing.[15] It follows that no systematic attempt will be made to define the themes of a 'postmodern' science at that level. The real point of interest in many characterizations of postmodern science is that they identify critical shifts in the way scientific knowledge is integrated with other knowledges and practices.

Lyotard's (1984) announcement of the 'postmodern condition' draws on Luhmann's functionalism to suggest that 'performativity' rather than 'truth' has become the criterion of scientific knowledge. The claim that contemporary science is subject to increasingly pragmatic judgements is frequently advanced, and not always as a criticism. Rorty urges a pragmatic acknowledgement that the unity and purpose of science is a function of human solidarity. For Rorty (1989: 11) 'the value of co-operative human enquiry has only an ethical base, not an epistemological or metaphysical one'. Toulmin (1982: 255) also pursues a pragmatic theme. 'In our . . . "postmodern" world, the pure scientist's traditional posture as *Theoros*, or spectator, can no longer be maintained: we are always – and inescapably – participants or agents as well.'

These suggestions echo a case which has been made above primarily in terms of institutional relations: that the qualitative distinctiveness of science is being eroded as scientific practices come to be inserted in other, more pervasive, economies and discourses. The idea of postscience suggests that the knowledges and practices which once constituted the autonomous sphere of 'science' have become so pervasive, so embedded in other knowledges and practices, that it no longer makes sense to use the term 'science' as if it distinguished one set of knowledges and practices from others.

Postscience has not yet completely displaced organized science. Formidably large scientific institutions continue to exist and prosper. Many billions of dollars continue to be spent on basic research in science, and some glamorous fields of research continue to grow and branch at a staggering rate. The modern project for ever more powerful forms of rational control continues to be pursued relentlessly in many of these fields. Nevertheless, the writing is on the wall of the monumental edifice of organized science. Disorganizing processes are under way whose arrest, or reversal, is not easy to imagine. Three points can sum up the challenge posed by these developments.

- The thesis of a movement towards postscience does not imply a decline in the importance of expert knowledges; quite the reverse.
- The thesis does mean that it will become increasingly difficult to maintain categorical distinctions between the 'technical' and the 'social' dimensions of any particular issue.
- It follows that the loss of autonomy of science and technology must have as its corollary an erosion of the autonomy of 'the social'.

The implications of a problem such as ozone depletion cannot be neatly subdivided into its 'social' and 'natural-technical' dimensions. Increasing rates of skin cancer are a 'social' as well as a 'natural' phenomenon, and no algorithm exists to establish commensurability between chemical and organic processes, potential technical fixes, and planned or unplanned social responses. Or at least, this is true if the attempt is made to maintain the categorical distinctions. The more appropriate response may be to follow the lead of Callon (1986), Latour (1989) and Law (1986) by bracketing distinctions between natural, technical and social processes.[16]

The dangers and possibilities for a disorganizing, postmodernizing, science are different from those of modern and organized science. In the latter case critical tensions concern the balance of power and prestige between the 'system' of science and the other 'systems' with which it is co-ordinated. In this context it makes sense to argue for the maximum autonomy of science, or for a science which is more responsive to demands of public welfare (however defined). Contemporary debates about science policy are often conducted as if relations between systems were still the issue. But if postmodernization and disorganization are in train, the terms of these debates are rapidly becoming anachronistic. In the long term the autonomy of science as traditionally understood is simply no longer on the agenda. All that is now at stake is the *manner* in which science will dissolve into, and transform, other economies and discourses: in the manner of the optimistic and humanistic pragmatism of a Rorty or a Toulmin, or that of the harder-edged pragmatism of administrative recommodification.

Notes

1. Invisible colleges, for Price (1963: 84–6), are elite groups of researchers whose cross-institutional ties are the primary focus of their professional identities. See also Crane's classic (1972) study of the phenomenon.

2. The class dimension of this conflict is stressed by Rothblatt (1985) and by Wynne (1982). Barnes (1985: 16–17) insists that the middle-class enthusiasm for science in the nineteenth century was not simply pragmatic or utilitarian: science was 'to be the cultural and intellectual basis for a form of life which would stand as a developed alternative to that of the old landed classes'.

3. So 'universalism' ensures the impersonality of scientific judgement, 'communism' permits competition for recognition while asserting the communal 'ownership' of scientific knowledge, 'disinterestedness' establishes institutional regulation of the diverse, even base, motives of individual scientists, and organized scepticism ensures that adherence to the two 'technical' imperatives of science (empirical confirmation and logical consistency) is required of all contributions to knowledge.

4. Cole and Cole (1973) elaborate on this functionalist thesis, arguing that science can be both highly stratified and highly consensual because rewards are matched to talent.

5. The model is offered, first, as an alternative to the Mertonian view that development occurs through the 'openness' of the scientific community to new knowledge. It also offers a corrective to the Kuhnian view of development as concentrated in intense periods of revolutionary change which punctuate long periods of orthodoxy.

6. Two qualifications should be noted. First, Durkheim and Merton are both aware that differentiation has potential dysfunctions: anomie for Durkheim, a problematic relation to wider value-systems and publics for Merton. Second, the 'Edinburgh' conception of interest has been effectively criticized by Woolgar (1981) on the ground that 'interests' are not independent explanatory variables, but are constructed within the fields which Edinburgh analysts seek to explain. A reflexive relation between an interest and the field within which it operates is quite compatible with the broad use of the term here.

7. This is an over-simplified synthesis of a developing argument. The translation problem is discussed in Habermas 1971: ch. 5. The distinction between technical and other rationalities is explored in the 'appendix' to Habermas 1972, while the 'colonization' argument is rehearsed in Habermas 1987a: ch. 8.

8. These themes are pursued in the tradition of 'social studies of technology' (see Bijker et al. 1989). A more traditionally 'political-economic' approach is well represented in Mackenzie and Wajcman (1985).

9. Ronayne (1984: 31) argues that the OECD reviews tend to favour a 'concerted action approach', based on an apparatus of ministers, committees and advisory councils.

10. Offe (1984: 124–5) cites three major concerns in economic policy as defining the strategy: improving the adaptability of labour power, using a variety of policy tools to enhance the saleability of capital and manufactured goods, and allowing 'lame duck' industries and regions to fall victim to market forces. This analysis dates from the mid-1970s, and is remarkably prescient. Offe (1984: 125) makes the point that recommodification is to be distinguished from both free-market and welfare-state strategies. With hindsight, however, it is clear that recommodification has very fuzzy boundaries with more aggressively free-market policies of recommodification such as overt privatization. The critical point may be that such policies (as in the sale of public utilities in Britain) require large and often hidden state subsidies if recommodification is to be effected.

11. That science and technology 'have unleashed powers beyond our control', that 'we are gradually being taken over by machines' and that 'these days everything is changing too fast'.

12. Functionalist sociology of science has reflected on both 'credulity' and 'hostility'. The latter is often explained in terms of affect and expressive needs (see the discussion in Barnes 1972). Merton (1973: ch. 12) regards credulity as the result of the prestige of science among public with little knowledge of science.

13. Bloch's argument resonates with a long history of claims that science should be, but has never become, an integral part of the public culture of the advanced societies. C.P. Snow's *The Two Cultures* is perhaps the best-known statement.

14. More accurately, mass media in a more general sense will be the only source of 'images' of science. Television fictions and advertisements may be as consequential as scientific news and current affairs broadcasting.

15. In one of the better-known and more successful, but still controversial, examples Forman (1980) links the emergence of quantum physics to cultural movements in Germany after the First World War (see also Hendry's [1980] critique). Ferguson's ambitious (1990) account of the trajectory of the 'bourgeois world view' links its collapse to the failure of the mechanistic vision of an all-encompassing system of knowledge. Twentieth-century physics led to the conclusion that 'the fundamental characteristics of matter and energy . . . were inexpressible through a single, logically uniform, and physically meaningful, system of concepts' (Ferguson 1990: 236).

16. Also the point here is Hill's phenomenologically and historically sensitive account of the ways in which technology, when viewed as a *cultural* phenomenon forges alignments with wider cultural meaning systems (Hill, 1988: 4).

8

The dialectics of postmodernization

Change, as Heraclitus was probably not the first to observe, is both pervasive and paradoxical. As soon as we attempt to acknowledge the rule of change by specifying its principal dimensions and fields of operation, we are left with only its empty husk: the phenomenon itself has moved on. Sociology is no more immune than any other discourse from a certain flat-footed awkwardness in the presence of change. Indeed, the image of lumbering social scientists attempting to capture change in traps fashioned from fourfold typologies or social surveys is the butt of many a parody. Nevertheless, the attempt has to be made, not least because of the manifest centrality of the experience and prospect of change in public discourses. If sociology at the threshold of the twenty-first century gives up thinking about change it might as well give up more generally, diminishing into a footnote in the history of ideas to be discussed in the same breath as, say, phrenology or the rational dress movement.

It is against this background that we have attempted to address the direction and scope of change in the contemporary advanced societies. Our general argument can be summarized as follows:

- Advanced societies are undergoing a long-term and multidimensional process of postmodernization, a process whose consequences will be as far-reaching as those of modernization.
- Postmodernization is best understood as a continuation of the processes of modernization, where those processes operate with increasing scope and intensity to erode what appears in retrospect as the regional stability of modernity.
- The transformational processes of organization and differentiation which present themselves in the peculiarly modern guise of rationalization and commodification become the postmodernizing processes of monocentric organization–disorganization, hyperdifferentiation–dedifferentiation, hyper-rationalization and hypercommodification.
- The shift from modernization to postmodernization is related to the convergence of modernizing processes on an 'impossible' combination of hyperdifferentiation with monocentric organization.
- In the face of this obstacle, postmodernizing change becomes multidirectional and unpredictable. Postmodernization erodes the boundaries of a specifically social-structural domain and promotes the effectivity of cultural processes.

The implications of this argument have been explored in six areas: culture, the state, inequality, politics, work organizations and science-technology. The basic conclusions for each area can also be summarized.

Culture

- Cultural modernity is a regional stability in which processes of differentiation, rationalization and commodification have produced autonomous value-spheres which cluster around their intrinsic 'logics' of development and which are already implicated in commodity relations.
- Cultural modernity generates a series of tensions: between differentiation and dedifferentiation, between rationalization and the nonrational moment in art, between commodification and its denial.
- Postmodernization of culture proceeds through a hypercommodification which finally erodes the distinction between commodified and non-commodified regions, through a hyper-rationalization which fragments the 'problem-solving' thrust of modernism, and through a hyperdifferentiation in which cultural fragments transcend categorical boundaries and produce the effect of dedifferentiation.
- Postmodernization issues in a postculture characterized by the consumerism of packaged 'lifestyles', the collapse of cultural tradition into an archive of styles, and the collapse of boundaries between 'culture' and 'society'.

State

- Processes of modernization produce the state as a container of rationalized power based on claims to sovereignty, and as the creator and protector of citizenship rights.
- The modern state becomes a corporate manager, securing a 'grand armistice' between warring socio-economic interests. Its functions include internal and external stabilization, economic regulation, infrastructural development, the amelioration of social problems and social-political legitimation.
- Processes of postmodernization 'shrink' the corporatist state, causing a shift from centralized to decentralized apparatuses and from authoritative to manipulative forms of control.
- Postmodern conditions challenge the idea of the state as an autonomous entity enjoying privileged links with politics and the public sphere.

Inequality

- In liberal capitalism inequalities of class and gender are determined by processes of production, accumulation and social reproduction which respectively define three categories of inequality: male capitalists, male workers and women.

- Processes within organized capitalism subject these categories to progressive elaboration and ultimately to decomposition. The capitalist class is displaced by a service class; the working class fragments, each fragment oriented to securing its place in the distributive system; and women are drawn out of domestic reproduction and into reproduction-oriented occupations in the public sphere.
- In the later stages of organized capitalism inequalities begin to be structured by patterns of consumption rather than production, a development which in turn promotes further and more intensive differentiation of class-gender positions. This is expressed as a hypercommodification of products in which they are consumed not in terms of use value but in terms of their semiotic capacity to establish unequal relationships.
- Under conditions of postmodernity mass media play a crucial role in the simulation of multiple and cross-cutting identities which are situated in equally multiple 'imagined communities' or 'simulated power blocs'. Membership of these is a function of taste, choice and commitment, and the categories are therefore fluid in relation to one another and indeterminate at the boundaries.

Politics

- Modern politics has been increasingly organized, formalized and instrumentalized; it centres on the state, involves extension of formalized citizenship status, and promotes orderly representation of interests.
- Socio-political turbulences of the first half of the twentieth century prompted further organization of politics, and further bureaucratization and corporatization of the political idiom.
- New developments arrest and reverse these trends: the new politics is decoupled from structural (class) divisions and anti-bureaucratic in its idiom (orientations and form). It takes the form of civic initiatives and mass social movements; it affects the young and educated sections of the the postwar generation; and its diffusion occurs through the mass media.
- Postmodern change marks a shift from structurally based to more contingent and diverse divisions; from economic to socio-cultural concerns; and from 'interest politics' to politics of universalistic concerns.

Work Organization

- Modern forms of production are highly rationalized and alienating. In organized capitalism, dominant 'Fordist' assembly line production systems are characterized by standardization, continuity, constraint and task-simplicity. Such systems are articulated with the requirements of mass production for mass markets.
- Fordist, and then neo-Fordist, production strategies are subverted by crises of demand as mass markets become saturated. These crises led to

major industrial and organizational realignments in the 1970s and 1980s.

- The three main forms of realignment lead to the decomposition of Fordist production strategies. Postindustrialism promotes the development of professional, collegial, forms of work organization; petty entrepreneurialism promotes self-employment; and flexible specialization promotes a bewildering variety of work practices.
- Flexible specialization is the cutting edge of the postmodernization of production, manifesting itself as: computer-controlled production technologies which can respond rapidly to changes in demand; decentralized and dehierarchized management systems; and numerically and functionally flexible labour markets.

Science and Technology

- Modern organized science is the outcome of a long-term process of institutionalization and professionalization unified under the aegis of the 'Grand Design' for human control of nature.
- Organized science is an autonomous system, an economy in which a qualitatively unique commodity circulates. Under conditions of growth this system spontaneously produces new and useful knowledge which it exchanges for political and financial support from government and industry.
- Modern science faces postmodernizing pressures from the contraction of growth in response to fiscal crises, from increasingly visible failures of the project for control which create the need for 'damage control', and from ambiguities in the public understanding of science.
- A postscience would entail the final erosion of boundaries between the knowledges and practices of science and those of other domains. It remains unclear whether postscience will enjoy an open and pragmatic integration with public interests, or whether it will be subject to a commercially dominated hypercommodification.

It would be possible to end the book here, after this summary of its substantive argument. However, that argument raises important and difficult questions about the general dynamics of postmodernizing change and about the tasks and resources of a postmodernizing sociology. The rest of the chapter offers a sketch of the ways in which these questions arise and of the general directions in which appropriate answers may lie. The first of three sections considers the dynamics of postmodernizing change in relation to the limitations under which any analysis of change must operate. The second examines the pathologies which are generated by change in advanced societies, and poses the question of whether there can be any general and synthetic 'crisis theory' of postmodernization which matches the ambition and scope of the modernisms of a Marx or a Durkheim. A brief final section sketches a provisional and general agenda for a sociology of postmodernization.

The Dynamics of Change

Theorizing Change

The idea of a 'dialectic of enlightenment' developed by Adorno and Horkheimer (1979) forms a useful starting point for a discussion of the limits to thinking about change, positioned as it is on the line between two potent images of change. Roughly, the process of 'enlightenment' begins as an escape from a mythic cosmos in which fear of nature is held at bay in a calculus of ritual and sacrifice to the gods. Adorno and Horkheimer (1979: 43) see Homer's Odysseus as 'a prototype of the bourgeois individual', an Attic trickster who tests, and breaches, the limits of the *mythos* and of self by using nominal observance of ritual requirements as a cover for manipulation in the pursuit of self-interest. Enlightenment demystifies the mythic balance between fear and sacrifice, putting in its place a programme for a knowledge-based human control over nature. It is in something like this sense that Lyotard (1984) takes the idea of 'enlightenment' (along with 'emancipation') as one of the 'grand narratives' in terms of which modernity has understood its historical task and specificity.

Notoriously, Adorno and Horkheimer do not end their account on any triumphalist note. The dialectic, or irony, of enlightenment is that as it gathers pace and expands in scope it effectively reverses itself. In a thoroughly Weberian manner, disenchantment consumes not only the mythic universe but all religion, not only religion but metaphysics, not only metaphysics but any claim to rational reflection. All that is left intact by the 'dissolvent rationality' of enlightenment (Adorno and Horkheimer 1979: 6) is a drive to control which is subject to no rational accountability, a principle of 'blind domination' (1979: 42). This process reduces thinking itself to a ritual, so that the alienated products of enlightenment domination, such as nuclear weaponry, become a new source of fear. In the famous chiasmus: 'myth is already enlightenment; and enlightenment reverts to mythology' (1979: xvi).

The interest of this argument, for present purposes, lies more in some of its formal characteristics than in its overall diagnosis. It can suggest both an important insight for, and an important limitation on, the study of change. The limitation, which carries the label 'relationalism', will be considered shortly. The insight is that a single dynamic principle can produce very different effects according to the stage, or pace or scope of its operation. One of the chronic problems in attempting to account for alleged ruptures in social development, as between 'industrial' and 'post-industrial' or 'modern' and 'postmodern', is that of deciding whether the same dynamic principles are operative on both sides of the gulf or, to put it another way, whether the principles of change are themselves changeable. So, it can be debated whether the processes of capital accumulation identified by Marx, or of rationalization as specified by Weber, or of functional differentiation elaborated by Durkheim explain not only the emergence of capitalism/

modernity/ industrialism but also any or all later ruptures.[1] The alternative is to argue that the rupture can only be accounted for by the emergence of some new dynamic principle, such as might be set free by new information technologies or electronic media.

The advantage of Adorno and Horkheimer's position is that it allows something of an each-way bet: single dynamic principles need not unfold in a steady, incremental way producing steady, incremental and predictable effects. They may speed up, slow down, switch fields of operation in ways which produce a bewildering array of seemingly contradictory effects. The core of good sense in Baudrillard's (1983b: 23) exorbitant metaphor of a principle of expansion of the social (nuclear explosion) which mutates, or switches, into contraction and 'invisibility' of the social (nuclear implosion) is its echo of Adorno and Horkheimer's conception of social dynamics. A first thesis can be extracted from the idea of a 'dialectic of enlightenment', then:

- Any dynamic principle will operate so as to produce different, and even contradictory, effects at different stages and paces of operation and in different fields of operation.

This thesis holds for 'differentiation', so widely identified as the fundamental dynamic principle of modernization.[2] Kant (1952: Introduction) announces differentiation of culture as the principle of modernity in the doctrine of the three spheres (of knowledge, morality and aesthetics), and the doctrine is given a sociological twist in Weber's (1970) treatment of 'value-spheres'. As cultural differentiation intensifies, it sets to work within the 'value-spheres' as well as between them. Not only is science differentiated from art, but physics is differentiated from the other sciences. Of course, it does not stop there: astrophysics becomes differentiated from subatomic physics, and within these fields different research fronts proliferate through 'branching' (Mulkay 1975). The result of this hyperdifferentiation is that not only are experts unable to communicate with laity in that 'elitist splitting off' which Habermas laments (1987a: 326–31), they are more often than not unable to communicate with each other outside a tightly circumscribed community of interest. However, when physicists can no longer talk to other physicists they might as well talk to chemists, or classicists or mathematicians or musicians: looked at from a certain angle, hyperdifferentiation appears as dedifferentiation.

Lash offers one way of grasping this cultural transformation: 'if modernization is a process of cultural differentiation . . . then *post*modernization is a process of dedifferentiation' (Lash 1990: 5). Tidy as this solution is, it merely displaces the problem of change, since the question now arises of why a process of differentiation should suddenly give way to a process of dedifferentiation.[3] The 'dialectic of differentiation' proposed here begins from a relatively undifferentiated premodern culture which becomes modern in the establishment of clearly differentiated spheres of value, each with its own inner logic. As differentiation accelerates into hyperdifferentiation the autonomous spheres of modern culture dissolve into fragments which achieve only a kaleidoscopic unity in a dedifferentiated postculture. The *same* dynamic principle has both produced and destroyed modern culture.

Looked at in this way, the process of differentiation, like that of enlightenment, takes on an ironic quality which places it between two conceptions of the 'meaning' of change. In the first, powerfully seductive, conception the analyst is positioned as if within some inherently meaningful process. It is difficult to think about history, as it is to think about one's own life, without imagining it as a narrative with a beginning, middle and projected end. The most sophisticated version of this teleological conception of change is Hegel's account of world history, in which the lost unity of classical Greek culture is recovered at a 'higher' level in the modern Prussian state. A crucial Hegelian insight is that such global history can only be written on the assumption that the writing is placed at the end (the terminus and the fulfilment) of the history in question.

Perhaps the most potent anti-Hegelian image of history and change remains Benjamin's (1973a: 259–60) commentary on Klee's *Angelus Novus*. The angel of history is blown backwards into the future by the wind of progress, able to glimpse only the rubble left by his passing. Benjamin's insight is that Hegel's assumption can never be satisfied: the 'end' is never reached, and the only materials for the study of change are its disordered and fragmentary traces. The image of change as an ironic dialectic can evade both the Scylla of an Hegelian conception which is overly full of meaning and the Charybdis of a conception which evacuates all meaning.[4] It can do so to the extent that it implies a 'relational' account of the constitution of meaningful analytic objects.[5]

Adorno and Horkheimer follow Weber in offering a reconstruction of processes of change whose principle of unity cannot be separated from a 'point of view'. The dialectic of enlightenment is constituted as a phenomenon, and by the same token given its ironic or tragic quality, only from the point of view of an interest in human emancipation. That is to say, change is neither salient nor meaningful independent of any point of view, but neither is it entirely meaningless. This claim can be formulated as a second thesis:

- Processes of change are constituted as salient objects of analysis only in relation to the 'interest' or 'point of view' of the analyst.

This thesis has a corollary:

- The reversals and ironies generated by dynamic principles are also conditioned by the relationalism of the 'interest' or 'point of view'.[6]

Any study of social change operates under the auspices of an interest which selects and conditions topics for scrutiny, yet is itself conditioned by its own time and place. As will be argued shortly, the present study is not exempt. Any study takes from branches of the sociological tradition and from other regions of public discourse a sense of which institutional arenas are the most important foci of experience and action, arenas such as culture, science and technology, state, gender relations, economic enterprises, social movements. Any assessment of the salience of arenas such as these will be informed by an evaluative complex which directs attention to a selection from a wide range of possible desiderata, from material prosperity to environmental rehabilitation, from social order to self-realization, or from cultural enrichment to humane working conditions. The relationalist thesis denies that the study of social change can achieve total objectivity in the Hegelian sense (by standing at the 'end' of change), or in the more familiar sense of independence from context. But this need be neither a debunking critique nor a counsel of despair. A view of change which is alive to the multifaceted possibilities of irony and reversal need not be paralysed by metaphysical doubts about the appearance of change in relation to its reality, or about the possibility of a view of process 'from the perspective of eternity'. An open and pragmatic 'relationalism' is the best defence against metaphysical doubts and entanglements.

Moving out of Modernity

With these complications and reservations in mind, it is possible to pass to a more dogmatic statement of the dynamics of change in advanced societies. The basic figure is provided by the model of a 'dialectic of differentiation':

- differentiation > hyperdifferentiation > dedifferentiation.

The way in which this dialectic plays out in the dynamics of culture has been rehearsed in outline above: as differentiation becomes hyperdifferentiation the stable 'value-spheres' of cultural modernity are eroded. In the field of work organization, to take another case, specifically modern differentiations between, say, 'mental' and 'manual' labour, or the 'functions of capital' and the 'functions of labour' are subjected to a hyperdifferentiation which permits, or even requires, dedifferentiation across the original boundaries. A particular nuance here is the way in which technical developments which allow the (hyper)automation of many tasks become the bearers of a hyperdifferentiation which allows dedifferentiation among the remaining human bearers. So, when an automobile production line becomes a set of hyperdifferentiated and automated tasks, the human tasks of oversight and co-ordination can be dedifferentiated. The many complexities of 'flexible specialization' are usefully considered as aspects of a dialectic of differentiation. To take another field, it is arguable on a variety of grounds that 'gender' under conditions of modernity is no more differentiated than in premodernity. Perhaps modernity simply reinscribes the traditional dichotomy in the institutions of a public–private split. However, the possibility now arises of a proliferation of gender-like divisions based, for example, on sexual orientation, which accompanies a blurring of the traditional–modern principles of gender differentiation. Connell argues that an abolition of gender (dedifferentiation) would produce a profuse and 'open-ended variety' of identities (a hyperdifferentiation) (Connell 1987: 288).

These rather diverse examples make it clear that the 'dialectic of differentiation' should not be understood as a mechanistic law of three stages which must be played out in the same order and relation in all fields. The consistent principle is simply that things are not always what they seem, that processes whose effects we have come to regard as predictable and unidirectional may have a twist in the tail. A rough parallel can be drawn between our predicament in the face of the onset of postmodernization and that of early students of modernization. Berman's widely praised (1982) study of Marx draws a distinction between his 'melting' and 'stable' visions of bourgeois society which can be hijacked here. From the point of view of a premodernity in which stasis is the norm, capitalist modernity can only appear as a maelstrom in which 'all that is solid melts into air'. A stable vision of modernity is only possible once the permanence of change is acknowledged and its basic 'laws' have been identified. The classics of nineteenth- and early twentieth-century social theory attempt to tame the melting vision by specifying the laws of change. For a period around the middle of the twentieth century, and perhaps then only in the United States, it became possible to elaborate a 'vision' of modernity in which a predictable, progressive and fundamentally benign process of 'modernization' would become diffused throughout the world.[7] But this vision became untenable remarkably quickly. What came under challenge was not the permanence of change, but its predictability and benignity: once again, 'all that is solid melts into air'. And that is where the present modest attempt to tame the return of the melting vision comes in. What must be understood is how processes which once seemed predictable and unidirectional now have a different aspect. Looked at in that way, the idea of a dialectic of differentiation simply formulates the problem but, given the complications discussed above, perhaps such a formulation is the most it is given to our 'point of view' to achieve.

The accelerations and reversals of differentiation are linked to the dynamics of 'organization', considered somewhat in the manner of Lash and Urry (1987) as a process of concentration and centralization. The dialectic of differentiation is paralleled by a dialectic of organization:

- organization > hyperorganization > disorganization.

In modernity, production concentrates in the factory, intellectual and technical innovation concentrates in 'Big Science', population concentrates in the city, wealth concentrates in the corporation, political power concentrates in the bourgeois state. Of course, these concentrations are also deconcentrations, or differentiations, of the power structures of premodernity. The bewildering spectacle offered by contemporary processes of change is one in which hyperconcentration and deconcentration appear to march arm in arm. So, in Australia and the United Kingdom at least, programmes of 'deregulation' ostensibly aimed at rolling back the boundaries of the state are accompanied by efforts to concentrate powers in the central government authority.[8] But of course, as the state 'rolls back', quasi-political decisions must be farmed out to parts of the private sector. The privatizations of water and electricity supply in Britain point in this direction, as do the various schemes floated by the Federal Coalition in Australia for the privatization of welfare. One paradoxical effect of rolling back the state is to blur the distinction between state and civil society.

In the sphere of economic power, industrial production is deconcentrated from cities (and, indeed, from the 'core' national economies of modernity). In some occupations the workforce may become deconcentrated from the workplace, or, to put it another way, 'workplaces' may cease to be single unified sites in space/time and become networks. At the same time, these manifest deconcentrations are accompanied by the hyperconcentration of economic power in transnational corporations which are themselves more like networks unified in a space and time which is not that of mundane experience. The paradoxes of science policy follow the same logic: attempts by government and industry to hyperorganize scientific research promote the disorganization of the 'academic research system'. These examples suggest that just as 'dedifferentiation' must be understood as operating in a field whose other pole is 'differentiation', so 'disorganization' requires to be placed in a constitutive relation of tension with 'organization'.

To summarize the argument, the basic processes of postmodernization operate on two axes: differentiation (which is also serving here as an umbrella for rationalization and commodification) and organization. Each principle puts in train a dialectic of hyper-extension and reversal. Two more specific processes, which can be labelled 'the increasing effectivity of culture' and 'the return of nature', are critical in the passage out of social modernity. Each can be linked to the problem of differentiation, and each poses difficult questions about the future of sociology. The idea of an increasing effectivity of culture is perhaps the more straightforward, and breaks into three theses.

- Models in which cultural processes appear as functions of 'deeper' economic or social dynamics cease to apply, if they ever did.
- Freed from their subordination, cultural components proliferate, split off and recombine in ways which do not correspond to any supposed 'logic' of modernity.
- Putting these two theses together, cultural dynamics not only reverse conventional hierarchies of material and ideal determination, but play a crucial role in disrupting the autonomous and predictable developmental logics of economy, polity and society.

This process connects with the dynamics of differentiation at every point, and particularly with that hyperdifferentiation which presents itself

as dedifferentiation. When the stable unities of modernity have fragmented, the possibility arises of the recombination of fragments across the
old boundaries. This possibility arises both within the field of culture and
between culture and other fields. So, to take a fashionable example,
considered in Chapters 2 and 6 above, 'consumption' can be understood
less and less as a purely economic function. As Featherstone (1990: 5)
urges, 'it is important to focus on the growing prominence of the *culture* of
consumption and not merely regard consumption as derived unproblemat-
ically from production'. Semiosis released from the hierarchies of modernity has a peculiar productive potency, enabling, for example, the rise of
the politics of new social movements as well as the triumph of consumerism
and 'lifestyle'. Ewan echoes both Marcuse and Baudrillard when he notes
the ubiquity of 'style'.

> The ability to stylize anything: toothpaste, roach spray, food, violence, other
> cultures around the world, ideas etc., provokes a comprehension of the world
> which focuses on its easily manipulated surfaces. Most notably, as the evanes-
> cent becomes increasingly 'real', reality becomes increasingly evanescent. (Ewan
> 1990: 52)

Meanings are increasingly constituted across previously firm categorial
boundaries between culture, economy, polity and society and across
previously firm social boundaries of class and nationality. Katz and Liebes'
(1986) study of the way in which Europeans and North Africans, Muslims
and Jews can 'makesense' of *Dallas* illustrates this protean quality. One
might say that the sign-system of *Dallas* is open to a range of second-order
semioses which relate it to almost any culture. Of course, what modernity
means by 'culture' is certainly not this kind of promiscuous productivity. If
an autonomous culture is a peculiarly modern phenomenon, it is a paradox
of the increased effectivity of culture is that what becomes 'effective' is
better seen as a 'postculture'.[9]

The question of the 'return of nature' requires particularly careful
treatment if relapses into metaphysical and theological thinking are to be
evaded. It is tempting, for example, to regard pollution and humanly
induced climate change, to say nothing of HIV/AIDS, as a richly deserved
chastisement for the sins of modernity.[10] The question is important here
primarily at a meta-analytic level, and involves no presumption to usurp
the first-order tasks of natural science. The great achievement of the
nineteenth- and early twentieth-century founders of sociology was to mark
out the terrain of an autonomous social reality which was to be the analytic
object of a specific, and equally autonomous, science. The strategy is at its
most transparent in Durkheim's social realism. The discovery of the reality
of society was never merely an academic matter, of course. Sociology drew
credit from its promise to redefine and to resolve the complex 'social
question' which preoccupied Europe, the question of the masses of
proletarians excluded from the institutions of contemporary civil society
and concentrated in vast insanitary industrial cities.

Over a long period, sociology's claim to academic and public legitimacy has turned on its capacity to convince an audience that there are urgent intellectual and practical problems which are peculiarly and exclusively 'social'. The phenomenon of the return of nature is a threat to the temporary, regional, autonomy of social reality and, *ipso facto*, to the autonomy and utility of sociology. It is particularly telling to the extent that theories of the autonomy of the social such as Marx's are explicitly linked to a theme of the 'overcoming' of (merely) natural constraint. The threat comes, most obviously, from a growing sense that the contingency of 'social' upon 'natural' processes has not been neutralized by modernity and enlightenment. Adorno and Horkheimer would surely enjoy a moment of gloomy satisfaction from the prospect of climate change, finding confirmation of their view that the attempt to evade fear and uncertainty through a programme of domination can only issue in more fear and uncertainty. In any event, the contemporary salience of environmental problems of all kinds, of the HIV/AIDS phenomenon, or of controversies in biotechnology and bioethics can only impress upon publics that the urgent issues of the day are not primarily, or even significantly, 'social'.

At the same time, publics and decision makers have wearied of the intractability of the traditional social problems of poverty, unemployment, crime and the rest. Two responses are typical. First, social problems are normalized so that certain levels of poverty or unemployment are accepted as part of the order of things. Second, problems are increasingly, and often stridently, desocialized so that crime becomes a moral, psychological or legal phenomenon. The 'return of nature' thus gives a double impetus to the disintegration of modern conceptions of the social.

- Social processes are increasingly seen to have 'natural' conditions of existence and natural processes are seen to have social consequences.

In this context the salience of sociology is eroded:

- by the normalization and desocialization of social problems noted above;
- by the growing public and state concern with the 'new' quasi-natural problems of the environment.

On both counts sociology is left behind as the major sites of complexity and uncertainty shift. A sociology which does not face up to these uncomfortable developments has very little future.

Postmodernization and the Tasks of Sociology

Sociology and the Postmodern

Sociology came into being as a set of responses to the emergence of cultural and social modernity. It follows that if the advanced societies are embarked on a passage out of modernity, the standing of sociology itself must come under question. An influential and reassuring response to the question has come from Bauman (1988a, 1988b), whose strategy closely parallels Bürger's earlier attempt to resolve the stand-off between modernism and postmodernism in aesthetics. For Bürger (1984–5: 127) an appropriate contemporary aesthetic would 'strive to affirm essential categories of modernism, but at the same time to free them from their modernist rigidities and bring them back to life'. For Bauman (1988a: 231) the task for a critically oriented sociology must be 'to preserve the hopes and ambitions of modernity in the age of postmodernity'. The break with sociological modernism, which in Bauman's view renders his strategy appropriately postmodern, lies in 'the bluntness with which its premises are recognised as assumptions'. Assumptions and values replace foundations and laws as the basis of sociological practice (1988a: 231–2).

Once this adjustment is made, sociology can carry on about its usual business, with a focus 'on making the opaque transparent, on exposing the ties linking visible to invisible social processes, on understanding what makes society tick, to make it tick, if possible, in a more "emancipatory" way' (Bauman 1988a: 234). The barely ruffled continuity of sociological practice is evident in Bauman's claim that '(p)ost modernity is an aspect of a fully fledged, viable social system which has come to replace the "classical" modern capitalist society and thus needs to be theorised according to its own terms' (Bauman 1988b: 811).

On the argument advanced here, this claim betrays the inadequacy of Bauman's response to postmodernization. Minimally, the claim is radically premature: the passage out of modernity has simply not reached a stage, nor made available a 'point of view', from which it could be advanced with any confidence. In a stronger sense, Bauman fails to consider that the movement beyond modernity may not be just a movement from one 'social system' to another, but a movement away from the reassuring stabilities of 'social systems' as such. Just such a movement is implied in the figures of the 'increasing effectivity of culture' and the 'return of nature' discussed above.

Bauman's strategy endorses Featherstone's call for a 'sociology of the postmodern' rather than a 'postmodern sociology'. The latter enterprise, embodying the anti-totalizing, anti-realist, thrust of postmodernism 'would abandon its generalizing social science ambitions and instead parasitically play off the ironies, inconsistencies and intertextuality of sociological writings' (Featherstone 1988: 127). Leaving aside, for a moment, this rather tendentious characterization, Smart is correct to question the viability of a 'sociology of the postmodern' which proceeds as if it were itself immune to wider cultural transformations. 'To what extent can any (modern) sociology remain undisturbed or unchanged by the problematization of representation, the "critique of grand narratives" and associated "crisis of the foundations" . . . ?' (Smart 1990a: 26). Bauman's version of the project surely suggests that a 'sociology of the postmodern' could all too easily resolve into the anachronistic and nostalgic projection of the defining figures of modernity onto any and all possible futures. Despite the rhetoric of relevance and engagement which Bauman and Featherstone deploy, any such project is doomed to intellectual sterility and practical impotence. Why should a 'modern' account of postmodernity deserve any more attention than a 'premodern' account of modernity?

On this account, neither a 'postmodern sociology' as characterized by Featherstone nor a 'sociology of the postmodern' as practised by Bauman offer much chance of a serious engagement with postmodernization. Each threatens to undermine the project we have attempted here by restricting the 'point of view' which is available to us. If we are to practise a 'sociology of the postmodern', we can only 'see' change as an extension of modernity because we cannot remove the spectacles of modern sociology. If we are plunged into a 'postmodern sociology' we cannot 'see' those processes within modernity which generated postmodernizing change. Fortunately, there is no reason to regard these alternatives as exhaustive. A sociology which achieved a relational sensitivity to its place within the passage out of modernity could generate analyses of change which would be neither anachronistic nor parasitic.

In one sense, the point of view from which we have approached postmodernization is, indeed, inescapably modern. The 'post-' in postmodernization requires that we understand the process in its relation to modernization and modernity. In the absence of an Hegelian point of view at the end of postmodernization, we can only project forward from modernity, as it were, using the resources of modern sociology. In another sense, however, we hope we have been able to use those resources to make visible their own limits and those of the syndrome of modernity. The suggestion, first aired in Chapter 1, that the space of the postmodern appears as the impossible simultaneous hyperextension of differentiation and organization can be understood in this light. Sociology, like society, is entering a period of transition whose outcome cannot be specified in advance. In such circumstances sociology will continue to work with modern models, concepts and metaphors at the same time as new ones begin to emerge. An appropriate sociological response to postmodernization must try to avoid two forms of anachronism: nostalgia for modernity and premature systematizations of postmodernity. Two forms of adjustment can assist the transition. First, sociological tradition requires interrogation and revision to enable the identification and replacement of analytic figures whose horizons are those of social modernity. Second, the sociological agenda requires revision in a pragmatic reorientation away from some traditional concerns and towards emerging sites of complexity and uncertainty.

System and Crisis

The figures of 'system' and 'system crisis' have been fundamental to the diagnostic and critical claims of modern sociology. They have helped to hold together the volatile amalgam of stability and change which defines social modernity. This is most clearly the case in Marx, where the limits of capitalist development are drawn in a theory of crisis which also points to a new order beyond those limits, beyond the system contradictions which produce crisis. Durkheim's theory of modernity is also a theory of system and crisis, but one in which the crisis-potential of egoism and anomie, spawned by the process of modernization, can be defused within that process itself. In each of these cases the theory of crisis, historical materialism or sociology, is decisive to the resolution of crisis itself. Social modernity is defined in terms of a double 'great divide' in which a new social order can only be comprehended, and thereby brought to completion, in a new form of knowledge. We have used some of the vocabulary of crisis theory ourselves in an ad hoc way in earlier chapters. The question prompted by that occasional use is whether a sociological account of postmodernization can take the form of a crisis theory proper, or whether the figures of system and crisis are peculiarly modern. A suspicion that 'system' and 'crisis' are definitionally tied to modernity is fuelled by their centrality to Habermas' modernism.[11] In *Legitimation Crisis* (1976) Habermas argues that the crisis potential of capitalism which Marx diagnosed did not have the consequences predicted because he underestimated the capacity of capitalist modernity to displace, and thereby postpone, its crises. In advanced capitalism this process of displacement originates in increasing state activity which supplements market mechanisms in the attempt to preserve the value-form. But this attempt cannot succeed, and the real consequence of state activity is that economic crisis now appears as political crisis. The state's failure to meet the contradictory demands placed on it by the economy generates crises of administrative rationality and of mass loyalty or legitimation. Eventually, crises of legitimation generate deficiencies of motivation which strike at the roots of social integration. The liability of advanced capitalism to its four 'crisis-tendencies' remains a function of 'the fundamental contradiction of the capitalist system' (Habermas 1976: 49), and the figure of system crisis ties contemporary pathologies to the matrix of social modernity.

The Theory of Communicative Action works with functionalist and Weberian, as well as Marxist, resources to redraw the analytic map of advanced societies and to redraft the theory of crisis. Weber's account of societal rationalization offers a starting point for Habermas, but he is reluctant to allow the paradoxes of rationalization to warrant a pessimistic conclusion that modernity as such has become pathological. In a reworking of the system/social integration theme, the social world is divided into 'systems' and 'lifeworlds'. Systems emerge out of communicatively based lifeworlds through a process of rationalization which 'makes it possible to convert societal integration over to language-independent steering media and thus to separate off formally organised domains of action' (Habermas 1987a: 318). Two media are crucial in this mediatization: money and power, which become the organizing principles of the subsystems of economy and polity respectively. The development of mechanisms of system integration which are independent of social integration is a prerequisite of social and cultural modernity which should not be regarded as inherently pathological. It becomes so only when subsystems turn back on the lifeworld and erode its communicative basis in a process of 'colonization'. Typically, the private sphere is eroded by the economic system and the public sphere by the administrative system (see Habermas 1987a: 325). Habermas' systems theorizing once more brings to bear an analytic matrix which cannot display contemporary pathologies as other than pathologies of modernity. Further, his view of the rights and duties of analysis itself recapitulates the 'modernist radicalism' of a Marx or Durkheim: analysis can determine objectively the point at which social pathologies set in,[12] and can determine equally objectively the measures required to correct the imbalances of a pathological modernity. On this basis, critical analysis serves as a midwife to the completion of modernity.

Each of Habermas' models allows contemporary advanced societies to be understood only in a direct line of continuity with early modernity. Each asserts that the fundamental 'logic' of modernity continues to operate. Each offers an image of late modernity as a system built around defining contradictions or crisis-tendencies. Those images, in turn, warrant theories of late modernity which are 'critical' in the strict sense of programmes oriented to the diagnosis and resolution of crisis. The point here is not that Habermas is wrong to draw attention to processes of displacement or mediatization. Indeed, they are significant elements of postmodernization to which we have drawn attention above. The point is, rather, that by locking these processes into an inescapably modernist grid of system and crisis, Habermas erodes his ability to consider the possibility that they point *beyond* modernity. His point of view is overly Hegelian, in the terms discussed above: the defence of modernity as both a project and a frame of reference for sociological analysis turns on the projection of a site from which it is possible to comprehend the completion of modernity, and to identify its core contradictions. On the argument here, no such site is available: to understand processes of change through the grid of a logic of contradiction and resolution is both anachronistic and question-begging.

A similar case can be urged even more forcefully against Harvey's much praised *The Condition of Postmodernity*. Harvey is impressed by the pace and variety of change in the advanced societies, and accepts a version of the modernity–postmodernity distinction. He concludes, however, that recent transformations are 'certainly within the grasp of historical materialist enquiry, even capable of theorization by way of the meta-narrative of capitalist development that Marx proposed' (Harvey 1989: 328). In Harvey as in Habermas, the problem lies in the repression of a great effort to make the phenomenon fit the framework, capped by the announcement that the framework fits the phenomenon. Sociology requires a much more agnostic position on the outcome of postmodernization. It should leave open the question of how the balance of continuity and discontinuity between modernity and postmodernity will look to the historians of the future who will be able, as we are not, to formulate the latter phenomenon.

One consequence of Habermas' commitment to a modernist framework which will recognize change only as the continuation of modernity is that he cannot register that contraction of the space and the salience of the social which is the consequence of pressure from the increasing effectivity of (post-) culture on one side and the return of nature on the other. One formulation of crisis which seems at least open to the effectivity of culture is Bell's (1976) account of the growing strain between a modernist culture and socio-economic modernity. Here, an accelerating 'logic' of cultural development based on the principle of gratification splits off from an instrumentally based process of social development. Culture comes to elaborate 'an ideology of self-fulfilment, spontaneity and experiential richness' as Martin (1981: 18) puts it, and this ideology comes to oppose the priorities of socio-economic modernity, witness the phenomenon of the sixties 'counter-culture'. The problem with Bell's theory of crisis is its analytic, rather than political, conservatism.[13] His account of cultural development may be quite astute, but it is counterposed to an anachronistic model of a stable and autonomous socio-economic structure. The increasing effectivity of culture fills the gap left by the hyper- and dedifferentiation of social structures, as the chameleon-like phenomenon of consumption illustrates.[14]

Modernist figures of social structure, contradiction and crisis are disqualified from considering the possibility that they represent not an eternal analytic template, valid for all times and places, but a reflection of the merely regional stabilities of modernity. Perhaps neither premodern nor postmodern constellations are based on social structure, contradiction and crisis in quite the modern manner. If this possibility is even to be considered in the analysis of contemporary patterns of change, it will not do to follow the path of Habermas, Harvey or Bell. What the study of change requires is a way of handling process which does not invoke the teleology of an Hegelian 'end' and a way of handling pathology which is independent of the figures of contradiction and crisis. The figures suggested here, summed up in the image of a dialectic of differentiation which produces ironic reversals, meet this requirement at least to the extent that they are compatible with a relationalism which acknowledges the contingency of the non-Hegelian point-of-view from which some changes appear to be particularly significant and some developments are judged to be pathological. It is entirely appropriate that sociological theorizing about postmodernization should carry a relationally conditioned sense of being provisional, incomplete and always revisable: the sociology of postmodernization must be a sociology which is itself in transition. A failure to recognize these contingencies can only produce anachronism in the form of either a nostalgic recapitulation of the categories of modernity, or a premature systematization of a not-yet-complete postmodernity.[15]

Sociological Agenda

A sense that its continuing salience is far from assured has exerted powerful pressures towards nostalgia on sociology. Reaction against what are perceived as the relativistic excesses of the recent past has produced a rather desperate flight towards the reassuring solidities of, for example, 'new realism', 'neofunctionalism' and the 'modernist radicalism' of Habermas. It becomes all too tempting to succumb to myths of some golden age in which the relevance of sociology was unproblematic, and to urge sociology to renew itself in a return to the concerns of that age.[16] On the analysis advanced here, this kind of nostalgia can only be fatal for sociology, tying it ever more firmly to the problems of the past. The peculiarly delicate task sociology faces is that of disentangling itself from the concerns and analytic figures of modernity without simply dissolving itself. In a refusal of the stark opposition between a 'postmodern sociology' and a 'sociology of postmodernity', it is critical that a 'sociology of postmodernization' should also be a 'postmodernizing sociology'.

At one level this simply means that sociology is subject to the same shaping principles as other elements of culture. The profusion of sociological paradigms and research fronts is evidence of hyperdifferentiation, and their incommensurability and inaccessibilty to all but initiates bears witness to hyper-rationalization. The 'niche marketing' of particular sociological practices and discourses (for trainee managers, nurses and teachers) might signal hypercommodification. Equally, the complex and ambiguous relations between sociologists and state or commercial agencies in different national societies are caught in the paradoxes of organization and disorganization. Clearly, the unity of a sociology subject to these processes is not usefully conceived as that of an integrated body of theory, or that of a single project legitimized by some overarching meta-narrative. A somewhat misplaced argument of Kellner's on this latter point can help to point the implications of sociology's inescapable place within a postmodernizing culture.

Kellner runs a version of the by now familiar Bauman–Featherstone–Harvey line on sociology and postmodernity, which Smart (1990b: 413) has termed 'a return to "business as usual"'. He takes issue with Lyotard's rejection of modernist 'meta-narratives' in order to defend the continuing salience of a generalizing social theory.

> Against Lyotard, we may want to distinguish between metanarratives that tell a . . . story about the foundation of knowledge contrasted to the narratives of macro social theory that attempt to conceptualize and interpret a complex diversity of phenomena within a global or totalizing context. (Kellner 1990: 272)

This suggestion misses the point that the difference between narrative andmeta-narrative is not simply one of degrees of generality: we can tell narrative 'stories' about the entire course of creation. Meta-narrative is

defined by its second-order, legitimizing, function, by 'the modern procliv-
ity to define the conditions of a discourse in a discourse on those
conditions' (Lyotard 1984: 30). This function extends well beyond founda-
tionalist theory of knowledge, and Lyotard explicitly draws attention to
meta-narratives which have been influential in the human sciences:
progress, enlightenment and emancipation. Further, Kellner forgets that
while Lyotard regards *meta*-narratives as victims of the crisis of metaphysics, he is entirely in favour of narrative. It follows that the limitation placed
on a postmodernizing sociology which seeks to evade meta-narrative is not,
directly, that it cannot make general claims but, rather, that its claims
enjoy no guaranteed salience or guaranteed cognitive privilege. Sociology
is not the discourse which will complete modernity, or realize reason, or
generalize liberty. It also follows that sociology is quite free to tell what
stories it likes about change or any other matter, but that these stories are
part of a more general economy of discourse in which they must fight to
find an audience and establish a salience in competition with other stories,
and in the absence of guarantees.

Within this economy of narratives, sociology is under threat from the
'end of the social', partly in the light of arguments such as Baudrillard's but
more significantly through that displacement of major sources of uncertainty noted above. It follows that no agenda for sociology is likely to
succeed which is based on realist claims for the autonomy and causal
powers of the social. On the contrary, sociology needs to shift its attention
to the boundaries between the once-autonomous spheres of modernity in
order to gain some purchase on postmodernity. For this reason, if classical
models for contemporary sociology are required, Simmel and Weber have
more to offer a postmodernizing sociology than do Marx and Durkheim.
Simmelian and Weberian conceptions of social action are left relatively
unscathed by 'end of the social' critiques which subvert the modernist
radicalisms and social realisms of Marx and Durkheim.[17] The terrain of a
sociology of postmodernization might be 'social action' considered as a
principle which intersects with natural, technical, signifying and psychic
processes. 'Society' would be conceived less as an ontologically specific
region of reality than as a way of looking at, and acting in, reality. On that
basis, the intellectual and pragmatic tasks of a sociology of postmodernization might be specified provisionally as follows:

- to identify the emerging/shifting foci of uncertainty in the processes of
  postmodernization;
- to study the ways in which principles of uncertainty in any register
  become implicated in social action;
- to alert publics and decision makers to the rich possibilities for irony and
  reversal in any attempts to plan and manage change.

Postmodernization does not directly void the traditional practices and
concerns of sociology. Rather, it transforms the field within which they
operate, removes the guarantees of their salience furnished by the meta-

narratives of modern social theory and renders sociology accountable for its preoccupations and procedures in relation to other discourses and practices.[18] The position of established sociological themes and methods is analogous to that of a modernist architecture which continues to operate within, and therefore has its meaning transformed by, postmodernity. A sociology which was able to meet the challenge of accountability would not be that apex of the hierarchy of the sciences which Comte envisaged and which Marx and Durkheim pursued. It would have no power to legislate 'scientific' solutions to complex and ever-changing problems, nor to predict the future. But it would retain a claim to relevance in the endless pragmatic task of responding to uncertainty and change.

Notes

1. So, for example, the burden of Kumar's (1978, 1988) critique of theories of postindustrialism is that the phenomenon that Bell and others identify can be understood as the outcome of established processes in industrial society. In consequence, he prefers the term 'hyper-industrialism'.

2. We have argued in Chapter 1 and throughout that the principle of differentiation is closely related to rationalization and commodification. Here, precision is sacrificed to generality and 'differentiation' serves as an umbrella term for all three processes.

3. Other problems also arise. Lash's somewhat formalist alignment of the modern with differentiation and the postmodern with dedifferentiation dissolves by a definitional fiat the problem of understanding cultural modernity and postmodernity as distinct fields of tension and conflict between differentiating and dedifferentiating trends.

4. Of course, Benjamin himself does not accept this as the final implication of Klee's image. His anti-historicism mingles with Jewish theology to produce a conception 'of the present as the time of the now (*Jetztzeit*) which is shot through with chips of Messianic time' (Benjamin 1973a: 265).

5. Relational in something like the sense implied in Mannheim's 'relationism', for which '(w)hat is intelligible in history can be formulated only with reference to problems and conceptual constructions which themselves arise in the flux of historical experience' (Mannheim 1960: 71). Weber's (1949) critique of Eduard Meyer offers an eminently 'relational' account of the constitution of objects of historical analysis. Crook (1991: ch. 2) assesses the relationalism of Weber and Simmel as a resource for contemporary social theory.

6. In this context 'interest' does not equate with 'material interest': we are not offering a reductionist 'sociology of sociological knowledge' here. Indeed, the problem with Mannheim's (1960) 'relationism' is that it assumes a categorial distinction between social and cognitive dimensions of knowledge. More appropriate models for 'interest' can be found in the sociology of science. Pickering (1982), for example, draws cognitive and social dimensions together in the figure of the 'exemplars' around which scientists develop their expertise and in which they acquire a considerable investment. A cautionary note is sounded in Woolgar's (1981) insistence that 'interests' are not independent variables external to the practice of science. They are contingent and context-bound accomplishments which are managed by scientists and attributed by them to each other. Woolgar's argument is most usefully read not as a 'debunking' of interest-based explanations (although it is that, too), but as an insight into the ways in which social-cum-cognitive interests are woven into the fabric of all science, including social science, as an ineradicable topic and resource.

7. A useful selection of classic 'modernization' texts can be found in Part 4 of Etzioni and Etzioni-Halevy (1973). Parsons (1977) represents the high point of the tradition.

8. British examples of concentration include the recent design and imposition of a National

Curriculum in education and, notoriously, the community charge or 'poll tax', which was specifically designed to erode the autonomy of local authorities. In Australia the drive to root out organized crime and to control abuse of the taxation and welfare systems has led to an extraordinary extension of Commonwealth powers to obtain, store and cross-match information on citizens. The Prime Minister's drive for a 'new federalism' is likely to see a concentration of powers over infrastructure policy in the hands of the Commonwealth.

9. This line of argument finds its quintessential (over-?) statement in Baudrillard's (1988) insight that the productivity of hypersimulation and the hyperreal has displaced articulations between image/reality or culture/society. Slater (1987) is among those to attempt a Marxist 'taming' of the argument.

10. The ground for such a view is well prepared in the German critical tradition. As Habermas (1971: 86) notes, the theme of a 'resurrection of fallen nature' runs from Schelling through the young Marx to Bloch, Benjamin and Marcuse.

11. The defence of the uncompleted 'project of modernity' is central to Habermas' work in the early 1980s, culminating in his (1987b) critique of postmodernist theory. Chapter 4 of Crook (1991) develops the argument that Habermas remains tied to the defining themes of modernist radicalism.

12. In this model, where the expanding principle of mediatized 'system integration' threatens the communicatively based principle of 'social integration' and thereby becomes 'dysfunctional', a term which Habermas (1987a: 373) specifically uses in relation to 'juridification' (increasing legal regulation of lifeworld relations).

13. Habermas offers a critique of Bell's neo-conservative stance which emphasizes his own analytic modernism in its insistence on a line of causality from 'society' to 'culture'. 'The neo-conservative does not uncover the economic and social causes for the altered attitudes towards work, consumption, achievement and leisure' (Habermas 1981a: 7).

14. Even when viewed historically, Bell's account of a mis-match between culture and society may be mistaken. Campbell (1987) has argued persuasively that the tension between a work ethic and a consumption-based culture is more apparent than real, and that any tenable account of the emergence of socio-economic modernity must grant a significant place to the development of modern consumption patterns.

15. In fact, as the cases of Bauman and Harvey considered above illustrate, the second form of anachronism can only be a slightly displaced version of the first.

16. The sharp diagnosis of the 'dissolution of the classical project' in sociology advanced by Wardell and Turner (1986) identifies the grounds of such golden age myths, but arguably succumbs itself, in the end.

17. So, Foucault (1970: 261, e.g.) repeatedly insists that Marxism is a direct continuation of early modern metaphysics, while Baudrillard's (1983b: 34) image of a 'pataphysics of the social' as the only response to hypersimulation is a direct parody and critique of Durkheim.

18. To take an example, IVF technology might serve as a case study of the intersection of different registers: nature (reproductive biology), culture (the desire for children, ethical dilemmas) and technique (IVF procedures). Social action becomes the red thread that draws these registers together in what becomes an identifiable and problematic phenomenon in a number of different lay and professional discourses. The field is rich in ironies and reversals. Women appear in the discourses of IVF now as clients, now as experimental subjects. Funding growth, that 'selfish gene' of research programmes, becomes a self-perpetuating imperative. The push for IVF programmes from professionals and 'clients' pre-empts any rational discussion of priorities in health budgets.

References

Abercrombie, Nicholas and Urry, John (1983) *Capital, Labour and the Middle Classes*. London: Allen & Unwin.

Abercrombie, Nicholas, Hill, Stephen and Turner, Bryan S. (1980) *The Dominant Ideology Thesis*. London: Allen & Unwin.

Adorno, T.W. (1981) *In Search of Wagner*. London: New Left Books.

Adorno, T.W. (1984) *Aesthetic Theory*. London: Routledge & Kegan Paul.

Adorno, T.W. and Horkheimer, M. (1979) *The Dialectic of Enlightenment*. London: Verso.

Adorno, T.W., Frenkel-Brunswik, E., Levinson, D. and Sanford, R. (1975) 'Studies in the Authoritarian Personality', in T.W. Adorno, *Gesammelte Schriften*, Band 9.1. Frankfurt: Suhrkamp.

Albury, D. and Schwarz, J. (eds) (1982) *Partial Progress: The Politics of Science and Technology*. London: Pluto.

Alexander, Jeffrey C. (1990) 'Differentiation Theory: Problems and Prospects', in Jeffrey Alexander and Paul Colomy (eds), *Differentiation Theory and Social Change*. New York: Columbia University Press.

Alexander, Jeffrey C. and Colomy, Paul (eds) (1990) *Differentiation Theory and Social Change*. New York: Columbia University Press.

Alic, John A. and Caldwell Harris, Martha (1988) 'Employment Lessons from the US Electronics Industry', in R.E. Pahl (ed.), *On Work*. Oxford: Blackwell, pp. 670–83.

Amin, Samir (1976) *Unequal Development*. London and New York: Harvester.

Anderson, B. (1983) *Imagined Communities*. London: NLB (Verso).

Anderson, Perry (1979) *Lineages of the Absolutist State*. London: Verso.

Anderson, Perry (1984) *In The Tracks of Historical Materialism*. Chicago: Chicago University Press.

Arendt, Hannah (1966) *The Origins of Totalitarianism*. Glencoe, Illinois: Free Press.

Ash, T.G. (1989) *The Uses of Adversity: Essays on the Fate of Central Europe*. New York: Random House.

Ash, T.G. (1990) *We the People*. London: Frances Pinter.

ASTEC (1985) *Public Investment in Research and Development in Australia*. Canberra: AGPS.

ASTEC (1990) *Government Funding of Academic and Related Research in Australia*. Canberra: AGPS.

Bacon, F. (1978) *Francis Bacon: A Selection of his Works*, ed. S. Warhaft. Indianapolis: Odyssey Press.

Badham, Richard and Mathews, John (1989) 'The New Production Systems Debate', *Labour & Industry*, 2(2): 194–246.

Baglioni, G. (1990) 'Industrial Relations in Europe in the 1980s', in G. Baglioni and C. Crouch (eds), *European Industrial Relations*. London: Sage, pp. 1–41.

Baker, Kendall, Dalton, Russell and Hildebrandt, Kay (1981) *Germany Transformed*. Cambridge, Mass.: Harvard University Press.

Bakhtin, M. (1984) *Rabelais and his World*. Bloomington: Indiana University Press.

Baran, P. and Sweezey, P. (1966) *Monopoly Capital: an Essay on the American Economic and Social Order*. New York: Monthly Review Press.

Barnes, Barry (1985) *About Science*. Oxford: Blackwell.

Barnes, B. and Edge, D. (eds) (1982) *Science in Context: Readings in the Sociology of Science*. Milton Keynes: Open University Press.

Barnes, S.B. (1972) 'On the Reception of Scientific Beliefs', in B. Barnes (ed.), *Sociology of*

Science: Selected Readings. Harmondsworth: Penguin.

Barnes, S.H. and Kaase, M. (1979) *Political Action: Mass Participation in Five Western Democracies*. Beverly Hills: Sage.

Baudrillard, Jean (1981) *For a Critique of the Political Economy of the Sign*. St Louis: Telos Press.

Baudrillard, Jean (1983a) 'The Ecstacy of Communication', in H. Foster (ed.), *The Anti-Aesthetic*. Port Townsend, Wash.: Bay Press.

Baudrillard, Jean (1983b) *In the Shadow of Silent Majorities . . . or the End of the Social and Other Essays*. New York: Semiotext(e).

Baudrillard, Jean (1988) *Selected Writings*. Stanford, Cal.: Stanford University Press.

Bauman, Zygmunt (1988a) 'Is There a Postmodern Sociology?', *Theory, Culture & Society*, 5: 217–37.

Bauman, Zygmunt (1988b) 'Sociology and Postmodernity', *Sociological Review*, 36: 790–813.

Bauman, Zygmunt (1991) 'A Postmodern Revolution?', in J. Frenzel-Zagorska (ed.), *From a One-party State to Democracy: Post-communist Change in Eastern Europe*, forthcoming.

Beer, S.H. (1982) *Britain against Herself: The Political Contradictions of Collectivism*. New York: W.W. Norton.

Bell, Daniel (1973) *The Coming of Post-Industrial Society*. New York: Basic Books.

Bell, Daniel (1976) *The Cultural Contradictions of Capitalism*. London: Heinemann.

Bell, P. and Boehringer, K. (1989) 'Publicising Progress: Science on Australian Television', in J. Tulloch and G. Turner (eds), *Australian Television*. Sydney: Allen & Unwin.

Ben-David, Joseph (1971) *The Scientist's Role in Society: A Comparative Study*. Englewood Cliffs, NJ: Prentice-Hall.

Benjamin, W. (1973a) 'Theses on the Philosophy of History', in W. Benjamin, *Illuminations*, ed. H. Arendt. London: Fontana.

Benjamin, W. (1973b) 'The Work of Art in an Age of Mechanical Reproduction', in W. Benjamin, *Illuminations* (ed. H. Arendt). London: Fontana.

Bennett, R.J. (1989) *Territorial and Administrative Decentralisation in Europe*. London: Frances Pinter.

Bennett, R.J. (ed.) (1990) *Decentralisation, Local Governments and Markets*. Oxford: Clarendon Press.

Bennett, T. (1986) 'The Politics of the Popular and Popular Culture', in T. Bennett, C. Mercer and J. Woolacott (eds), *Poplar Culture and Social Relations*. Milton Keynes: Open University Press.

Berger, Peter (1987) *The Capitalist Revolution*. New York: Gower.

Berger, S. (1979) 'Politics and Anti-Politics in Western Europe in the Seventies', *Daedalus*, 108: 27–50.

Berger, S. (ed.) (1981) *Organizing Interests in Western Europe*. Cambridge: Cambridge University Press.

Berle, Adolph, Jr and Means, Gardiner C. (1967) *The Modern Corporation and Private Property*. New York: Harcourt. First published 1932.

Berman, M. (1982) *All That is Solid Melts into Air: the Experience of Modernity*. New York: Simon & Schuster.

Bijker, W., Hughes, T. and Pinch, T. (eds) (1989) *The Social Construction of Technological Systems*. Cambridge, Mass.: MIT Press.

Birch, A. (1984) 'Overload, Ungovernability and De-legitimation', *British Journal of Political Science*, 14: 135–60.

Birke, L. (1990) 'Selling Science to the Public', *New Scientist*, 1730 (18 August): 32–6.

Blauner, Robert (1964) *Alienation and Freedom*. Chicago: University of Chicago Press.

Bloch, H. (1973) 'The Problem Defined', introduction to Ciba Foundation Symposium, *Civilization and Science: in Conflict or Collaboration?* Amsterdam: Elsevier.

Blondel, Jean (1978) *Political Parties: A Genuine Case for Discontent?* London: Wildwood.

Bourassa, S. (1989) 'Postmodernism in Architecture and Planning: What Kind of Style?', *Urban Research Unit Working Paper 12*, Australian National University.

Bourdieu, Pierre (1984) *Distinction: a Social Critique of the Judgement of Taste*. London: Routledge.

Brand, K-W. (1990) 'Cyclical Aspects of New Social Movements', in R.J. Dalton and M. Kuechler (eds), *Challenging the Political Order*. Cambridge: Polity, pp. 23–42.

Braverman, Harry (1974) *Labor and Monopoly Capital*. New York: Monthly Review Press.

Brenner, Johanna and Ramos, Maria (1984) 'Rethinking Women's Oppression', *New Left Review*, 144: 33–71.

Brittan, Arthur (1989) *Masculinity and Power*. Oxford: Blackwell.

Brittan, S. (1975) 'The Economic Contradictions of Democracy', *British Journal of Political Science*, 5: 129–59.

Brown, L. (1990) 'The Illusion of Progress', in L. Brown et al., *State of the World 1990*. Sydney: Allen & Unwin.

Brown, L., Flavin, C. and Postel, S. (1990) 'Picturing a Sustainable Society', in L. Brown et al., *State of the World 1990*. Sydney: Allen & Unwin.

Brubaker, Rogers (1984) *The Limits of Rationality: An Essay on the Social and Moral Thought of Max Weber*. London: Allen & Unwin.

Brus, W. and Laski, K. (eds) (1990) *From Marx to Market*. Oxford: Clarendon Press.

Brym, R.J. (1980) *Intellectuals and Politics*. London: Allen & Unwin.

Burawoy, Michael (1988) 'Thirty Years of Making Out', in R.E. Pahl (ed.), *On Work*. Oxford: Blackwell, pp. 190–211.

Bürger, P. (1984) *Theory of the Avant Garde*. Minneapolis: University of Minnesota Press.

Bürger, P. (1984–5) 'The Decline of the Modern Age', *Telos*, 62: 117–30.

Burke, P. (1978) *Popular Culture in Early Modern Europe*. London: Temple-Smith.

Bürklin, W. (1985) 'The Greens: Ecology and the New Left', in G. Romoser and P. Wallach (eds), *West German Politics in the Mid Eighties*. New York: Praeger.

Burnham, James (1941) *The Managerial Revolution*. New York: Doubleday.

Burris, Beverly H. (1989) 'Technocratic Organization and Control', *Organization Studies*, 10(1): 1–22.

Calhoun, Craig (1989) 'Imagined Communities, Indirect Relationships and Postmodernism: Large Scale Social Integration and the Transformation of Everyday Life'. Working Paper No. 2, Program in Social Theory and Cross-Cultural Studies, University of North Carolina, Chapel Hill.

Calhoun, Craig (1990) 'Postmodernism as Pseudohistory', paper presented at the World Congress of Sociology, Madrid, 9–14 July.

Callon, M. (1986) 'Some Elements of a Sociology of Translation: Domestication of the Scallops and Fishermen of St Brieuc Bay', in J. Law (ed.), *Power, Action and Belief* (Sociological Review Monograph 32). London: Routledge & Kegan Paul.

Campbell, Colin (1987) *The Romantic Ethic and the Spirit of Modern Consumerism*. Oxford: Blackwell.

Campbell, Iain (1989) 'New Production Concepts? The West German Debates on Restructuring', *Labour & Industry*, 2(2): 247–80.

Carr, E.H. (1968) *Nationalism and After*. London: Macmillan. First published 1945.

Carrigan, Tim, Connell, Bob and Lee, John (1985) 'Toward a New Sociology of Masculinity', *Theory and Society*, 14(5): 551–604.

Cawson, A. (1986) *Corporatism and Political Theory*. Oxford: Blackwell.

Chambers, I. (1986) *Popular Culture: The Metropolitan Experience*. London: Methuen.

Charlton, B. (1990) 'The Perils of Popular Science', *New Scientist*, 1730 (18 August): 28–32.

Ciccotti, G., Cini, M. and De Maria, M. (1976) 'The Production of Science in Advanced Capitalist Society', in H. Rose and S. Rose (eds), *The Political Economy of Science: Ideology of/in the Natural Sciences*. London: Macmillan.

Clarke, J. (1975) 'Skinheads and the Magical Recovery of Community', in S. Hall and T. Jefferson (eds), *Resistance through Rituals*. London: Hutchinson.

Claygill, H. (1990) 'Architectural Postmodernism: The Retreat of an Avant Garde?', in R. Boyne and A. Rattansi (eds), *Postmodernism and Society*. London: Macmillan.

Cole, J. and Cole, S. (1973) *Social Stratification in Science*. Chicago: University of Chicago Press.

Collingridge, D. (1980) *The Social Control of Technology*. Milton Keynes: Open University Press.

Collingridge, D. and Reeve, C. (1986) *Science Speaks to Power*. London: Frances Pinter.

Collins, H. (1987) 'Certainty and the Public Understanding of Science: Science on TV', *Social Studies of Science*, 17: 689–713.

Collins, H. (1988) 'Public Experiments and Displays of Virtuosity: the Core Set Revisited', *Social Studies of Science*, 18: 725–48.

Connell, R.W. (1987) *Gender and Power*. Sydney: Allen & Unwin.

Cornford, J. (1975) 'Introduction', in J. Cornford (ed.), *The Failure of the State*. London: Croom Helm, pp. 7–14.

Cotgrove, S. (1982) *Catastrophe or Cornucopia*. New York: Wiley.

Cotgrove, S. and Box, S. (1970) *Science, Industry and Society*. London: Allen & Unwin.

Cotgrove, S. and Duff, A. (1981) 'Environmentalism, Values and Social Change', *British Journal of Sociology*, 32: 92–110.

Crane, D. (1972) *Invisible Colleges*. Chicago: University of Chicago Press.

Crook, Stephen (1991) *Modernist Radicalism and its Aftermath: Foundationalism and Anti-Foundationalism in Radical Society Theory*. London: Routledge.

Crouch, C. (1977) *Class Conflict and the Industrial Relations Crisis*. London: Heineman.

Crouch, C. (1983) 'The State, Capital and Liberal Democracy', in D. Held et al. (eds), *States and Societies*. New York: New York University Press, pp. 320–9.

Crozier, M., Huntington, S. and Watanuki, J. (1975) *Crisis of Democracy*. New York: New York University Press.

Cultural Ministers Council Statistical Advisory Group (1990) *The Australian Culture Industry: Available Data and Sources*, 2nd edn. Canberra: Australian Government Publishing Service.

Dahrendorf, Ralf (1959) *Class and Class Conflict in Industrial Society*. London: Routledge & Kegan Paul.

Dahrendorf, Ralf (1988) *The Modern Social Conflict*. London: Weidenfeld & Nicholson.

Dalton, R.J. (1988) *Citizen Politics in Western Democracies*. Chatham, NJ: Chatham Publishers.

Dalton, R.J., Flanagan, S.C. and Beck, P.A. (1984a) 'Electoral Change in Advanced Industrial Societies', in R.J. Dalton, S.C. Flanagan and P.A. Beck (eds) *Electoral Change in Advanced Industrial Democracies*. Princeton, NJ: Princeton University Press, pp. 3–24.

Dalton, R.J., Flanagan, S.C. and Beck, P.A. (1984b) 'Political Forces and Partisan Change', in R.J. Dalton, S.C. Flanagan and P.A. Beck (eds), *Electoral Change in Advanced Industrial Democracies*. Princeton, NJ: Princeton University Press, pp. 451–76.

Dalton, R.J., Kuechler, M. and Bürklin, W. (1990) 'The Challenge of New Movements', in R.J. Dalton and M. Kuechler (eds), *Challenging the Political Order: New Social and Political Movements in Western Democracies*. Cambridge: Polity, pp. 3–22.

Davies, James A. (1962) 'Towards a Theory of Revolution', *American Sociological Review*, 27: 5–19.

Dobb, Maurice (1964) *Studies in the Development of Capitalism*, revised edn. New York: International Publishers.

Dodgson, M. (1987) 'Small Firms' Investment in, and Use of, CNC Machine Tools: Lessons for Flexible Use', in W. Wobbe (ed.), *Flexible Manufacturing in Europe*. Brussels: FAST (Commission of the European Communities), pp. 259–70.

Dohse, Knut, Jürgens, Ulrich and Malsch, Thomas (1985) 'From "Fordism" to "Toyotism"? The Social Organization of the Japanese Automobile Industry', *Politics & Society*, 14(2): 115–46.

Dore, Ronald (1989) 'Where We Are Now: Musings of an Evolutionist', *Work, Employment and Society*, 3(4): 425–46.

Durkheim, E. (1964) *The Division of Labor in Society*. New York: Free Press.

Eckersley, Robyn (1987) *Australian Attitudes to Science & Technology and the Future*. Canberra: Commission for the Future.

Eckersley, Richard (1989) 'Green Politics and the New Class', *Political Studies*, 37(2): 205–23.

Eder, K. (1990) 'The Rise of Counterculture Movements against Modernity', paper presented at the World Congress of Sociology, Madrid, Spain, 9–12 July.

Ehrenreich, Barbara and Ehrenreich, John (1979) 'The Professional-Managerial Class', in P. Walmer (ed.), *Between Labor and Capital*. Boston: South End, pp. 5–45.

Elias, N. (1978) *The Civilising Process Volume One: The History of Manners*. Oxford: Blackwell.

Elias, N. (1982) *The Civilising Process Volume Two: State Formation and Civilisation*. Oxford: Blackwell.

Enzensberger, H.M. (1976) 'Constituents of a Theory of the Media', in H.M. Enzensberger, *Raids and Reconstructions*. London: Pluto Press.

Erikson, R., Goldthorpe, J.H. and Portacarero, L. (1982) 'Social Fluidity in Industrial Nations: England, France and Sweden', *British Journal of Sociology*, 33(1): 1–34.

Etzioni, A. and Etzioni-Halevy, E. (eds) (1973) *Social Change: Sources, Patterns, Consequences*. New York: Basic Books.

Evans, Alastair and Bell, Jenny (1986) 'Emerging Themes in Flexible Work Patterns', in C. Curson (ed.), *Flexible Patterns of Work*. London: Institute of Personnel Management.

Evans, P.B., Rueschemeyer, D. and Skocpol, T. (eds) (1985) *Bringing the State Back In*. Cambridge: Cambridge University Press.

Ewan, S. (1990) 'Marketing Dreams: the Political Elements of Style', in A. Tomlinson (ed.), *Consumption, Identity & Style*. London: Routledge.

Featherstone, M. (1987) 'Lifestyle and Consumer Culture', *Theory, Culture & Society*, 4(1): 54–70.

Featherstone, M. (1988) 'In Pursuit of the Postmodern', *Theory, Culture & Society*, 5: 195–215.

Featherstone, M. (1990) 'Perspectives on Consumer Culture', *Sociology*, 24(1): 5–22.

Feher, F. and Heller, A. (1983) 'From Red to Green', *Telos*, 4 (Sept.): 35–45.

Feist, A. and Hutchison, R. (1990) *Cultural Trends in the Eighties*. London: Policy Studies Institute.

Ferguson, H. (1990) *The Science of Pleasure: Cosmos and Psyche in the Bourgeois World View*. London: Routledge.

Fiske, J. (1987) *Television Culture*. London: Routledge.

Fiske, J. (1989) *Understanding Popular Culture*. Boston: Unwin-Hyman.

Fix-Sterz, J. and Lay, G. (1987) 'The Role of Flexible Manufacturing Systems in the Framework of New Developments in Production Engineering', in W. Wobbe (ed.), *Flexible Manufacturing in Europe*. Brussels: FAST (Commission of the European Communities), pp. 83–115.

Forman, P. (1980) 'Weimar Culture, Causality and Quantum Theory, 1918–1927', in C. Chant and J. Fauvel (eds), *Darwin to Einstein: Historical Studies on Science and Belief*. Harlow, Essex: Longman.

Foster, H. (1983) 'Post Modernism: a Preface', in H. Foster (ed.), *The Anti-Aesthetic*. Port Townsend, Wash.: Bay Press.

Foucault, M. (1970) *The Order of Things*. London: Tavistock.

Frank, A.G. (1975) *On Capitalist Underdevelopment*. Oxford: Oxford University Press.

Frankel, Boris (1987) *The Post-Industrial Utopians*. Cambridge: Polity.

Gans, H. (1975) *Popular Culture and High Culture*. New York: Basic Books.

Gardner, C. and Young, R. (1981) 'Science on TV: a Critique', in T. Bennett et al. (eds), *Popular Television and Film*. London: BFI/Open University Press.

Gerlach, L. and Hine, V. (1970) *People, Power Change*. Indianapolis: Bobbs-Merrill.

Gershuny, J.I. and Pahl, R.E. (1979) 'Work outside Employment', *New Universities Quarterly*, 34(1): 120–35.

Gibbins, J.R. (1989) 'Contemporary Political Culture: An Introduction', in J.R. Gibbins (ed.), *Contemporary Political Culture*. London: Sage, pp. 1–30.

Gibbons, M. (1985) 'The Changing Role of Academic Research Systems' in M. Gibbons and B. Wittrock (eds), *Science as a Commodity*. Harlow, Essex: Longman.

Gibbons, M. and Wittrock, B. (eds) (1985) *Science as a Commodity*. Harlow, Essex: Longman.

Giddens, Anthony (1981) *A Contemporary Critique of Historical Materialism. Vol. 1 Power, Property and the State*. Berkeley: University of California Press.

Giddens, Anthony (1985) *Nation-State and Violence. Volume Two of a Contemporary Critique of Historical Materialism*. Berkeley: University of California Press.

Giner, S. (1976) *Mass Society*. Oxford: Martin Robertson.

Goldthorpe, John H. (1980) *Social Mobility and Class Structure in Modern Britain*. Oxford: Clarendon.

Goldthorpe, John H. (1982) 'On the Service Class, its Formation and Future', in Anthony Giddens and Gavin Mackenzie (eds), *Social Class and the Division of Labour*. Cambridge: Cambridge University Press, pp. 162–85.

Goldthorpe, J.H., Bechhofer, F. and Platt, J. (1968) *The Affluent Worker: Industrial Attitudes and Behaviour*. Cambridge: Cambridge University Press.

Gorz, André (1982) *Farewell to the Working Class*. London: Pluto.

Gouldner, A.W. (1975) *For Sociology*. Harmondsworth: Penguin.

Gouldner, A.W. (1979) *The Failure of Intellectuals and the Rise of the New Class*. New York: Seabury.

Grew, R. (1984) 'The 19th Century European State', in C. Bright and S. Harding (eds), *Statemaking and Social Movements*. Ann Arbor: University of Michigan Press, pp. 83–120.

Gunderlach, P. (1984) 'Social Transformation and the New Forms of Voluntary Associations', *Social Science Information*, 23: 1049–81.

Gurevich, A.J. (1985) *Categories of Medieval Culture*. London: Routledge & Kegan Paul.

Habermas, Jürgen (1971) *Toward a Rational Society*. London: Heinemann.

Habermas, Jürgen (1972) *Knowledge and Human Interests*. London: Heinemann.

Habermas, Jürgen (1976) *Legitimation Crisis*. Boston: Beacon.

Habermas, Jürgen (1981a) 'Modernity versus Postmodernity', *New German Critique*, 22 (Winter): 3–14.

Habermas, Jürgen (1981b) 'New Social Movements', *Telos*, 49 (Fall): 33–8.

Habermas, Jürgen (1984) *The Theory of Communicative Action*, Vol. I: *Reason and the Rationalization of Society*. Boston: Beacon.

Habermas, Jürgen (1985) 'Neoconservative Culture Criticism in the United States and West Germany: An Intellectual Movement in Two Political Cultures', in R. Bernstein (ed.), *Habermas and Modernity*. Cambridge: Polity.

Habermas, Jürgen (1987a) *The Theory of Communicative Action*, Vol. 2: *The Critique of Functionalist Reason*. Cambridge: Polity.

Habermas, Jürgen (1987b) *The Philosophical Discourse of Modernity*. Cambridge: Polity.

Hadley, R. and Hatch, S. (1981) *Social Welfare and the Failure of the State*. London: Allen & Unwin.

Hagstrom, W. (1982) 'Gift Giving as an Organizing Principle in Science', in B. Barnes and D. Edge (eds), *Science in Context: Readings in the Sociology of Science*. Milton Keynes: Open University Press.

Hakim, Catherine (1988a) 'Self-employment in Britain', *Work, Employment and Society*, 2(4): 421–50.

Hakim, Catherine (1988b) 'Homeworking in Britain', in R.E. Pahl (ed.), *On Work*. Oxford: Blackwell, pp. 609–32.

Hakim, Catherine (1990) 'Core and Periphery in Employers' Workforce Strategies', *Work, Employment and Society*, 4(2): 157–88.

Halal, William E. (1986) *The New Capitalism*. New York: Wiley.

Hall, S. and Jefferson, T. (1975) *Resistance through Rituals*. London: Hutchinson.

Handlin, O. (1972) 'Ambivalence in the Public Response to Science', in B. Barnes (ed.), *Sociology of Science: Selected Readings*. Harmondsworth: Penguin.

Harris, H. and Lipman, A. (1986) 'A Culture of Despair: Reflections on "Post-modern" Architecture', *Sociological Review*, 34: 837–54.

Harvey, David (1989) *The Condition of Postmodernity*. Oxford: Blackwell.

Hassan, I. (1985) 'The Culture of Postmodernism', *Theory, Culture & Society*, 2: 119–31.

Held, D. (1989) *Political Theory and the Modern State*. Cambridge: Polity.

Held, D. and Pollitt, C. (1986) *New Forms of Democracy*. London: Sage.

Hendry, J. (1980) 'Weimar Culture and Quantum Causality', in C. Chant and J. Fauvel (eds), *Darwin to Einstein: Historical Studies on Science and Belief*. Harlow, Essex: Longman.

Hernes, Helga Maria (1984) 'Women and the Welfare State. The Transition from Private to Public Dependence', in H. Holter (ed.), *Patriarchy in a Welfare State*. Oslo: Universitetsforlaget.

Hilferding, Rudolph (1981) *Finance Capital*. London: Routledge. First published 1910.

Hill, S. (1988) *The Tragedy of Technology*. London: Pluto Press.

Hirschhorn, Larry (1986) *Beyond Mechanization*. Cambridge: MIT Press.

Holloway, Geoffrey (1990) 'The Organisational Structure of the Wilderness and Anti-nuclear Movement in Australia', PhD thesis, Department of Sociology, University of Tasmania.

Holter, Harriet (1984) 'Women's Research and Social Theory', in *Patriarchy in a Welfare State*. Oslo: Universitetsforlaget, pp. 9–25.

Horkheimer, M. (1974) *The Eclipse of Reason*. New York: Seabury.

Hughes, T. (1988) 'The Seamless Web: Technology, Science Etcetera Etcetera', *Social Studies of Science*, 16: 281–92.

Hülsberg, W. (1988) *The German Greens: A Social and Political Profile*. London: Verso.

Hume, D. (1964) 'Of the Standard of Taste', in D. Hume, *The Philosophical Works Volume Three*, ed. T.H. Green and T.H. Gross. Aalen: Scientia Verlag.

Huntington, S. (1973) 'Political Modernization: America vs. Europe', in R. Bendix (ed.), *State and Society*. Berkeley and London: University of California Press, pp. 170–200.

Huyssen, A. (1986) *After the Great Divide*. Bloomington: Indiana University Press.

Hyman, Richard (1988) 'Flexible Specialization: Miracle or Myth?', in R. Hyman and W. Streeck (eds), *New Technology and Industrial Relations*. Oxford: Blackwell, pp. 48–60.

Inglehart, R. (1977) *The Silent Revolution: Changing Values and Political Styles among Western Publics*. Princeton, NJ: Princeton University Press.

Inglehart, R. (1981) 'Post-Materialism in an Environment of Insecurity', *American Political Science Review*, 75: 880–90.

Inglehart, R. (1984) 'The Changing Structure of Industrial Cleavages in Western Societies', in R.J. Dalton, S.C. Flanagan and P.A. Beck (eds), *Electoral Change in Advanced Industrial Democracies*. Princeton, NJ: Princeton University Press, pp. 25–69.

Inglehart, R. (1990) 'Values, Ideology and Cognitive Mobilisation in New Social Movements', in R.J. Dalton and M. Kuechler (eds), *Challenging the Political Order: New Social and Political Movements in Western Democracies*. Cambridge: Polity, pp. 43–66.

Inglehart, R. and Flanagan, S.C. (1989) 'Value Change in Industrial Societies', *American Political Science Review*, 81(4): 1289–319.

Jameson, Fredric (1984) 'Postmodernism: Or the Cultural Logic of Late Capitalism', *New Left Review*, 146: 53–92.

Janicke, M. (1990) *State Failure*. Cambridge: Polity.

Jasnay, A. de (1985) *The State*. Oxford: Blackwell.

Jencks, Charles (1987) *What is Post-Modernism?* (2nd edn) London: Academy.

Jessop, Bob (1978) 'Corporatism and Liberal Democracy', in G. Littlejohn et al. (eds), *Power and the State*. London: Croom Helm. pp. 10–51.

Jessop, Bob (1982) *The Capitalist State*. New York: New York University Press.

Johnson, Terence (1977) 'The Professions and the Class Structure', in Richard Scase (ed.), *Industrial Society*. London: Allen & Unwin.

Jones, Barry (1983) *Sleepers, Wake!* (new edn). Melbourne: Oxford University Press.

Jones, F.L. and Davis, Peter (1988) 'Class Structuration and Patterns of Social Closure in Australia and New Zealand', *Sociology*, 22(2): 271–91.

Jones, Peter d'A. (1965) *The Consumer Society*. Harmondsworth: Penguin.

Kaase, M. (1984) 'The Challenge of the "Participatory Revolution" in Pluralist Democracies', *International Political Science Review*, 5: 299–318.

Kaase, M. (1990) 'Social Movements and Political Innovation', in R.J. Dalton and M. Keuchler (eds), *Challenging the Political Order*. Cambridge: Polity, pp. 84–104.

Kant, I. (1952) *The Critique of Judgement*. Oxford: Oxford University Press.

Kant, I. (1956) *Critique of Practical Reason*. Indianapolis: Bobbs-Merrill.

Katz, E. and Liebes, T. (1986) 'Decoding Dallas: Notes from a Cross-Cultural Study', in G. Gumpert and R. Cathcart (eds), *Inter/Media: Interpersonal Communication in a Media World*. New York: Oxford University Press.

Kellner, Douglas (1990) 'The Postmodern Turn: Positions, Problems and Prospects', in G. Ritzer (ed.), *Frontiers of Social Theory*. New York: Columbia University Press, pp. 255–86.

Kelly, Jeffrey A. and Worrell, Judith (1977) 'New Formulations of Sex Roles and Androgyny', *Journal of Consulting and Clinical Psychology*, 45(6): 1101–15.

Kerckhoff, Alan C., Campbell, Richard T. and Winfield-Laird, Idee (1985) 'Social Mobility in Great Britain and the United States', *American Journal of Sociology*, 91(2): 281–308.

Kern, Horst, and Schumann, Michael (1984a) 'Work and Social Character', *Economic and Industrial Democracy*, 5: 51–71.

Kern, Horst and Schumann, Michael (1984b) *Das Ende der Arbeitsteilung?* Munich: Verlag C.H. Beck.

Kern, Horst and Schumann, Michael (1987) 'Limits of the Division of Labour. New Production Concepts in West German Industry', *Economic and Industrial Democracy*, 8: 151–71.

Kitchelt, H. (1986) 'Political Opportunity Structure and Political Protest', *British Journal of Political Science*, 16: 58–95.

Kitchelt, H. (1990) 'New Social Movements and the Decline of Party Organisation', in R.J. Dalton and M. Kuechler (eds), *Challenging the Political Order*. Cambridge: Polity, pp. 179–208.

Konrad, G. and Szelenyi, I. (1979) *The Intellectuals on the Road to Class Power*. New York: Harcourt.

Kornhauser, William (1959) *The Politics of Mass Society*. Glencoe, Illinois: Free Press.

Koselleck, Reinhart (1988) *Critique and Crisis*. Oxford: Berg. First published 1959.

Kriesi, H.P. (1989) 'New Social Movements and the New Class in the Netherlands', *American Journal of Sociology*, 94(5): 1078–116.

Kristol, I. (1979) *Two Cheers for Capitalism*. New York: Basic Books.

Kroker, A. and Cook, D. (1988) *The Postmodern Scene: Excremental Culture and Hyper-Aesthetics* 2nd edn. London: Macmillan.

Kumar, Krishnan (1978) *Prophecy and Progress*. Harmondsworth: Penguin.

Kumar, Krishnan (1988) *The Rise of Modern Society*. Oxford: Blackwell.

Ladurie, E. Le Roy (1978) *Montaillou*. New York: Braziller.

Lane, Christel (1988) 'Industrial Change in Europe: The Pursuit of Flexible Specialisation in Britain and West Germany', *Work, Employment and Society*, 2(2): 141–68.

Lash, Scott (1990) *Sociology of Postmodernism*. London: Routledge.

Lash, Scott, and Urry, John (1987) *The End of Organized Capitalism*. Cambridge: Polity.

Laslett, Barbara and Brenner, Johanna (1989) 'Gender and Social Reproduction: Historical Perspectives', *Annual Review of Sociology*, 15: 381–430.

Latour, B. (1989) 'Clothing the Naked Truth', in H. Lawson and L. Appignanesi (eds), *Dismantling Truth: Reality in the Post-Modern World*. New York: St Martin's Press.

Latour, B. and Woolgar, S. (1982) 'The Cycle of Credibility', in B. Barnes and D. Edge (eds), *Science in Context: Readings in the Sociology of Science*. Milton Keynes: Open University Press.

Law, J. (1986) 'On the Methods of Long Distance Control: Vessels, Navigation and the Portuguese Route to India', in J. Law (ed.), *Power, Action and Belief* (Sociological Review Monograph 32). London: Routledge & Kegan Paul.

Lechner, F. (1990) 'Fundamentalism and Sociocultural Revitalization: On the Logic of

De-differentiation', in J. Alexander and P. Colomy (eds), *Differentiation Theory and Social Change*. New York: Columbia University Press.

Leff, G. (1958) *Medieval Thought: St Augustine to Ockham*. Harmondsworth: Penguin.

Lehmbruch, G. (1977) 'Liberal Corporatism and Party Government', *Comparative Political Studies*, 10: 91–126.

Lehmbruch, G. and Schmitter, P.C. (eds) (1982) *Patterns of Corporatist Policy-Making*. London: Sage.

Leiss, W. (1974) *The Domination of Nature*. Boston: Beacon Press.

Lengermann, Patricia Madoo and Wallace, Ruth A. (1985) *Gender in America*. Englewood Cliffs, NJ: Prentice-Hall.

Levine, D.N. (1981) 'Rationality and Freedom: Weber and Beyond', *Social Inquiry*, 51(1): 5–25.

Levitt, T. (1973) *The Third Sector: New Tactics for a Responsive Society*. New York: Amacom.

Levy, Marion J., Jr (1966) *Modernization and the Structure of Societies*. Princeton, NJ: Princeton University Press.

Lewis, G. (1981) 'Taste Cultures and Their Composition', in E. Katz and T. Szecsko, *Mass Media and Social Change*. Beverly Hills: Sage.

Lipset, S.M. (1960) *Political Man, The Social Bases of Politics*. New York: Doubleday.

Lipset, S.M. (1981) *Political Man*, 2nd edn. Baltimore: Johns Hopkins University Press.

Lowe, P.D. and Rudig, W. (1986) *Political Ecology and the Social Sciences*. IUUG reprint. Berlin: IIES.

Luard, E. (1977) *International Agencies: The Emerging Framework of Interdependence*. London: Macmillan.

Luard, E. (1990a) *International Society*. London: Macmillan.

Luard, E. (1990b) *The Globalisation of Politics*. London: Macmillan.

Lyotard, Jean-François (1984) *The Postmodern Condition: A Report on Knowledge*. Manchester: Manchester University Press. First published 1979.

Lyotard, J.-F. (1988) *The Differend: Phrases in Dispute*. Manchester: Manchester University Press

Mackenzie, D. and Spinardi, G. (1988) 'The Shaping of Nuclear Weapon System Technology', *Social Studies of Science*, 18: 419–63, 581–624.

Mackenzie, D. and Wajcman, J. (eds) (1985) *The Social Shaping of Technology*. Milton Keynes: Open University Press.

Magirier, G. (1987) 'Flexible Automation and Machining in France: Results of a Survey', in W. Wobbe (ed.), *Flexible Manufacturing in Europe*. Brussels: FAST (Commission of the European Communities), pp. 41–61.

Mallet, Serge (1975) *The New Working Class*. Nottingham: Spokesman.

Mann, Michael (1986) *The Sources of Social Power Vol. 1*. Cambridge: Cambridge University Press.

Mann, Michael (1987) 'Ruling Class Strategies and Citizenship', *Sociology* 21(3): 339–54.

Mannheim, K. (1952) 'The Problem of Generations', in P. Kecskemeti (ed.), *Essays on the Sociology of Knowledge*. Oxford: Oxford University Press, pp. 276–422.

Mannheim, K. (1960) *Ideology and Utopia*. London: Routledge & Kegan Paul.

Marcuse, H. (1964) *One Dimensional Man*. Boston: Beacon Press.

Marshall, Gordon, Rose, David, Vogler, Carolyn and Newby, Howard (1985) 'Class, Citizenship and Distributional Conflicts in Modern Britain', *British Journal of Sociology*, 36(2): 259–84.

Marshall, Gordon, Rose, David, Vogler, Carolyn and Newby, Howard (1987) 'Distributional Struggle and Moral Order in a Market Society', *Sociology*, 21(1): 55–73.

Marshall, T.H. (1973) *Class, Citizenship and Social Development*. Westport: Greenwood. First published 1949.

Martin, B. (1981) *A Sociology of Contemporary Cultural Change*. Oxford: Blackwell.

Marx, K. (1954) *Capital*, Volume 1. London: Lawrence and Wishart.

Marx, Karl (1967) 'Alienated Labor', in Loyd D. Easton and Kurt H. Guddat, *Writings of the*

Young Marx on Philosophy and Society. Garden City: Anchor Doubleday, pp. 287–300. First published 1844.

Marx, Karl (1971) *Marx's Grundrisse*, ed. David McLellan. St Alban's: Paladin.

Marx, K. (1977) 'Preface to a"Contribution to the Critique of Political Economy"', in K. Marx, *Selected Works*, (ed. D. McLellan). Oxford: Oxford University Press.

Mathews, John (1989) *Tools of Change*. Sydney: Pluto.

McCracken, G. (1988) *Culture and Consumption*. Bloomington: Indiana University Press.

McEachern, D. (1990) *The Expanding State: Class and Economics since 1945*. London: Harvester.

McLuhan, M. (1967a) *The Mechanical Bride: Folklore of Industrial Man*. Boston: Beacon Press.

McLuhan, M. (1967b) *Understanding Media*. Harmondsworth: Penguin.

Melucci, A. (1985) 'The Symbolic Challenge of Contemporary Movements', *Social Research*, 52: 789–815.

Melucci, A. (1988) 'Getting Involved', in B. Kladermans, H. Kriesi and S. Tarrow (eds), *From Structure to Action*. Greenwich, CT: JAI Press.

Mennell, S. (1990) 'Decivilising Processes: Theoretical Significance and Some Lines of Research', *International Sociology*, 3: 205–23.

Merton, Robert K. (1973) *The Sociology of Science: Theoretical and Empirical Investigations*, ed. N.W. Storer. Chicago: University of Chicago Press.

Michels, Robert (1962) *Political Parties*. Glencoe, Illinois: Free Press.

Middlemas, K. (1979) *Politics in Industrial Society*. New York: Rowman.

Miliband, Ralph (1973) *The State in Capitalist Society*. London: Weidenfeld & Nicolson.

Miller, W.L. (1990) 'Party Politics', in P. Dunleavy et al. (eds), *Developments in British Politics*. London: Macmillan.

Mills, C. Wright (1970) *The Sociological Imagination*. Harmondsworth: Penguin. First published 1959.

Minkenberg, M. and Inglehart, R. (1989) 'Neo-Conservatism and Value Change in the USA', in J.R. Gibbins (ed.), *Contemporary Political Culture*. London: Sage, pp. 81–109.

Misztal, B. (1985) 'Social Movements against the State', in B. Misztal (ed.), *Poland after Solidarity*. London: Transaction, pp. 143–64.

Moorehouse, H.F. (1983) 'American Automobiles and Workers' Dreams', *Sociological Review*, 31: 403–26.

Moriarty, M. (1988) *Taste and Ideology in Seventeenth Century France*. Cambridge: Cambridge University Press.

Morley, D. (1987) *Family Television: Cultural Power and Domestic Leisure*. London: Comedia.

Morrison, D.E. and Dunlap, R.E. (1986) 'Environmentalism and Elitism: A Conceptual and Political Analysis', *Environmental Management*, 10(5): 581–9.

Mosse, G.L. (ed.) (1979) *International Fascism: New Thoughts and New Approaches*. London: Sage.

Mowlana, H. and Wilson, C. (1990) *The Passing of Modernity*. White Plains, NY: Longman.

Mulkay, M. (1975) 'Three Models of Scientific Development', *Sociological Review*, 23: 509–26.

Müller-Rommel, F. (1990) 'New Political Movements and "New Politics" Parties in Western Europe', in R.J. Dalton and M. Kuechler (eds), *Challenging the Political Order: New Social and Political Movements in Western Democracies*. Cambridge: Polity, pp. 209–31.

Müller-Rommel, F. and Poguntke, T. (1989) 'The Unharmonious Family: Green Parties in Western Europe', in E. Kolinsky (ed.), *Greens in West Germany: Organisation and Policy Making*. Oxford: Berg, pp. 11–30.

Murray, Fergus (1988) 'The Decentralization of Production – The Decline of the Mass-Collective Worker?', in R.E. Pahl (ed.), *On Work*. Oxford: Blackwell, pp. 258–78.

Naisbitt, Jeffrey and Aburdene, Patricia (1990) *Megatrends 2000*. London: Sidgwick & Jackson.

Nelkin, D. (1982) 'Controversy as a Political Challenge', in B. Barnes and D. Edge (eds),

Science in Context: Readings in the Sociology of Science. Milton Keynes: Open University Press.

Nelkin, D. (1987) *Selling Science*. New York: W.H. Freeman.

Nettl, J.P. (1968) 'The State as a Conceptual Variable', *World Politics*, 20: 559–92.

Netzer, D. (1978) *The Subsidized Muse: Policy Support for the Arts in the United States*. Cambridge: Cambridge University Press.

Newby, H. (1991) 'One World, Two Cultures: Sociology and the Environment', lecture to mark the fortieth anniversary of the British Sociological Association, *Network*, 50.

O'Connor, J. (1973) *The Fiscal Crisis of the State*. New York: St Martin's Press.

OECD (1975) *Changing Priorities for Government Research and Development*. Paris: OECD.

Offe, C. (1984) *Contradictions of the Welfare State*, ed. J. Keane. London: Hutchinson.

Offe, C. (1985a) 'New Social Movements: Challenging the Boundaries of Institutional Politics', *Social Research*, 52(4): 817–68.

Offe, C. (1985b) *Disorganised Capitalism*. Cambridge: Polity.

Offe, C. (1990) 'Reflections on the Institutional Self-transformation of Movement Politics: A Tentative Stage Model', in R.J. Dalton and M. Kuechler (eds), *Challenging the Political Order*. Cambridge: Polity, pp. 232–50.

Offe, C. and Ronge, V. (1984) 'Theses on the Theory of the State', in C. Offe (ed.) *Contradictions of the Welfare State*. London: Hutchinson.

Pakulski, Jan (1986) 'Legitimacy and Mass Compliance', *British Journal of Political Science*, 16: 43–59.

Pakulski, Jan (1990) 'Social Movement and Class', paper presented at the World Congress of Sociology, Madrid, 9–11 July.

Pakulski, Jan (1991) *Social Movements: The Politics of Moral Protest*. Melbourne: Longman Cheshire.

Papadakis, Elim (1984) *The Green Movement in West Germany*. New York: St Martin's Press.

Papadakis, Elim (1989) 'Green Issues and Other Parties', in E. Kolinsky (ed.), *Greens in West Germany: Organisation and Policy Making*. Oxford: Berg, pp. 61–86.

Parkin, Frank (1968) *Middle Class Radicalism*. Manchester: Manchester University Press.

Parkin, Frank (1979) *Marxism and Class Theory*. London: Tavistock.

Parkin, Susan (1989) *Green Parties: An International Guide*. London: Heretic.

Parsons, T. (1977) *The Evolution of Societies*, ed. J. Toby. Englewood Cliffs, NJ: Prentice-Hall.

Parsons, T. and Smelser, N. (1984) *Economy and Society: a Study in the Integration of Economic and Social Theory*. London: Routledge and Kegan Paul.

Parsons, T., Bales, R. and Shils, E. (1953) *Working Papers in the Theory of Action*. New York: Free Press.

Penn, Roger and Scattergood, Hilda (1985) 'Deskilling or Enskilling? An Empirical Investigation of Recent Theories of the Labour Process', *British Journal of Sociology*, 36(4): 611–30.

Phillimore, A.J. (1989) 'Flexible Specialisation, Work Organisation and Skills: Approaching the "Second Industrial Divide" ', *New Technology, Work and Employment*, 4(2): 79–91.

Pickering, A. (1982) 'Interests and Analogies', in B. Barnes and D. Edge (eds), *Science in Context: Readings in the Sociology of Science*. Milton Keynes: Open University Press.

Piore, Michael J. and Sabel, Charles F. (1984) *The Second Industrial Divide*. New York: Basic Books.

Pizzorno A. (1981) 'Interests and Parties in Pluralism', in S. Berger (ed.), *Organizing Interests in Western Europe*. Cambridge: Cambridge University Press.

Poggi, Gianfranco (1978) *The Development of Modern State*. London: Hutchinson.

Poggi, Gianfranco (1990) *The State*. Cambridge: Polity.

Pollert, Anna (1988) 'The "Flexible Firm": Fixation or Fact?', *Work, Employment and Society*, 2(3): 281–316.

Poulantzas, Nicos (1978) *State, Power, Socialism*. London: Verso.

Poulantzas, Nicos (1982) 'On Social Classes', in Anthony Giddens and David Held (eds),

Classes, Power, and Conflict. Berkeley: University of California Press.

Price, D.J. de Solla (1963) *Little Science, Big Science.* New York: Columbia University Press.

Price, D.J. de Solla (1982) 'The Parallel Structures of Science and Technology', in B. Barnes and D. Edge (eds), *Science in Context: Readings in the Sociology of Science.* Milton Keynes: Open University Press.

Ravetz, J. (1977) 'Criticisms of Science', in D. de Solla Price and I. Spiegel-Rösing (eds), *Science, Technology and Society.* London: Sage.

Reimer, B. (1989) 'Postmodern Structure of Feeling', in J.R. Gibbins (ed.), *Contemporary Political Culture.* London: Sage, pp. 110–26.

Renner, Karl (1978) 'The Service Class', in T.B. Bottomore and P. Goode (eds), *Austro-Marxism.* Oxford: Clarendon, pp. 249–52. First published 1953.

Rocher, G. (1974) *Talcott Parsons and American Sociology.* London: Nelson.

Rodgers, P. (1989) *The Work of Art.* London: Policy Studies Institute.

Ronayne, J. (1984) *Science in Government.* Melbourne: Edward Arnold.

Rootes, C.A. (1980) 'Student Radicalism: the Politics of Moral Protest and the Legitimation Problems of the Modern Capitalist State', *Theory and Society*, 9(3): 473–502.

Rorty, R. (1989) 'Science as Solidarity', in H. Lawson and L. Appignanesi (eds), *Dismantling Truth: Reality in the Post-Modern World.* New York: St Martin's Press.

Rose, David, Marshall, Gordon, Newby, Howard and Vogler, Carolyn (1984) 'Economic Restructuring: The British Experience', *Annals AAPSS*, 475: 137–58.

Rothblatt, S. (1985) 'The Norm of an Open Scientific Community in Historical Perspective', in M. Gibbons and B. Wittrock (eds), *Science as a Commodity.* Harlow, Essex: Longman.

Rothschild-Whitt, Joyce (1979) 'Conditions Facilitating Participatory-democratic Organizations', *Social Inquiry*, 46(2): 75–86.

Royal Society of London (1963) *Philosophical Transactions I: 1665–66.* New York: Johnson Reprint Company.

Saarlvik, B. and Crewe, I. (1983) *Decade of Dealignment.* Cambridge: Cambridge University Press.

Salisbury, R.H. (1979) 'Why No Corporatism in America?', in P.C. Schmitter and G. Lehmbruch (eds), *Corporatist Interest Intermediation.* London: Sage, pp. 213–30.

Schefter, M. (1977) 'Party and Patronage: Germany, England and Italy', *Politics and Society*, 7: 403–51.

Schefter, M. (1979) 'Party, Bureaucracy and Political Change in the United States', in L. Maisel and J. Cooper (eds), *The Development of Political Parties.* Beverly Hills: Sage Electoral Studies Yearbook Vol. 4, pp. 211–65.

Schmitt, R. (1989) 'From "Old Politics" to "New Politics" ', in J.R. Gibbins (ed.), *Contemporary Political Culture.* London: Sage, pp. 174–98.

Schmitter, P.C. (1974) 'Still the Century of Corporatism?', *Review of Politics*, 36: 85–131.

Schmitter, P.C. and Lembruch, G. (eds) (1979) *Trends Towards Corporatist Inter-Mediation.* London: Sage.

Schumann, Michael (1987) 'The Future of Work, Training and Innovation', in W. Wobbe (ed.), *Flexible Manufacturing in Europe.* Brussels: FAST (Commission of the European Communities). pp. 41–61.

Schumann, Michael (1990) 'New Forms of Work Organization in West German Industrial Enterprises', paper presented at the World Congress of Sociology, Madrid, 9–14 July [also published in German in M. Schumann, V. Baethge, U. Neumann, and R. Springer, *Breite Diffusion der Neuen Produktionskonzepte – Zögerlicher Wandel der Arbeitsstrukturen*, Soziale Welt Nr. 1. SOFI: Göttingen].

Scott, A.J. (1988) *New Industrial Spaces.* London: Pion.

Shils, E. (1973) 'Anti-Science: Observations on the Recent "Crisis" in Science', in Ciba Foundation Symposium, *Civilization and Science: in Conflict or Collaboration?* Amsterdam: Elsevier.

Sklair, L. (1973) *Organised Knowledge: A Sociological View of Science and Technology.* London: Hart-Davis.

Skocpol, Theda (1985) 'Bringing the State Back In: Strategies of Analysis in Current

Research', in P.B. Evans, D. Reuschemeyer, and T. Skocpol, (eds), *Bringing the State Back In*. Cambridge: Cambridge University Press, pp. 3–43.

Slater, D. (1987) 'On the Wings of the Sign: Commodity Culture and Social Practice', *Media, Culture & Society*, 9: 457–80.

Smart, Barry (1983) *Foucault, Marxism and Critique*. London: Routledge.

Smart, Barry (1990a) 'Modernity, Postmodernity and the Present', in B.S. Turner (ed.), *Theories of Modernity and Postmodernity*. London: Sage.

Smart, Barry (1990b) 'On the Disorder of Things: Sociology, Postmodernity and the "End of the Social" ', *Sociology*, 24(3): 397–416.

Smelser, Neil J. (1968) 'Towards a Theory of Modernization', in *Essays in Sociological Explanation*. Englewood Cliffs, NJ: Prentice-Hall, pp. 125–46.

Smith, Chris (1989) 'Flexible Specialisation, Automation and Mass Production', *Work, Employment and Society*, 3(2): 203–20.

Solinas, Giovanni (1988) 'Labour Market Segmentation and Workers' Careers: the Case of the Italian Knitwear Industry', in R.E. Pahl (ed.), *On Work*. Oxford: Blackwell, pp. 279–304.

Sorge, Arndt and Streeck, Wolfgang (1988) 'Industrial Relations and Technical Change', in R. Hyman and W. Streeck (eds), *New Technology and Industrial Relations*. Oxford: Blackwell, pp. 19–47.

Spencer, H. (1972) *On Social Evolution*. (ed. J. Peel). Chicago: University of Chicago Press.

Staniszkis, J. (1982) *Poland's Self-Limiting Revolution*. Princeton, NJ: Princeton University Press.

Steinmetz, George and Wright, Erik Olin (1989) 'The Fall and Rise of the Petty Bourgeoisie: Changing Patterns of Self-Employment in the Postwar United States', *American Journal of Sociology*, 94(5): 973–1018.

Storer, N. (1966) *The Social System of Science*. New York: Holt, Rinehart & Winston.

Streeck, Wolfgang (1987) 'The Uncertainties of Management and the Management of Uncertainty', *Work, Employment and Society*, 1(3): 281–308.

Suzuki, D. and Knudston, P. (1988) *Genethics*. Sydney: Allen & Unwin.

Swingewood, A. (1977) *The Myth of Mass Culture*. London: Macmillan.

Swyngedouw, Erik A. (1987) 'Social Innovation, Production Organization and Spatial Development. The Case of Japanese Style Manufacturing', *Revue d'Economie Régionale et Urbaine*, 3: 487–510.

Taylor, F.W. (1971) 'Scientific Management', in D.S. Pugh (ed.), *Organization Theory*. Harmondsworth: Penguin.

Thompson, G. (1989) 'The Way We Are', *The Bulletin* (Sydney), 10 January.

Tijssen, Lieteke van Vucht (1990) 'Women between Modernity and Postmodernity', in B.S. Turner (ed.), *Theories of Modernity and Postmodernity*. London: Sage, pp. 147–63.

Tilly, Charles (1978) *From Mobilisation to Revolution*. Reading, Mass.: Addison-Wesley.

Tilly, Charles (1988) 'Social Movements, Old and New', *Research in Social Movements, Conflict and Change*, 10: 1–18.

Toffler, Alvin (1980) *The Third Wave*. New York: Morrow.

Tomlinson, A. (1990) 'Consumer Culture and the Aura of the Commodity', in A. Tomlinson (ed.), *Consumption, Identity & Style*. London: Routledge.

Tomlinson, A. and Walker, H. (1990) 'Holidays for All: Popular Movements, Collective Leisure and the Pleasure Industry', in A. Tomlinson (ed.), *Consumption, Identity & Style*. London: Routledge.

Toulmin, S. (1973) 'The Historical Background to the Anti-Science Movement', in Ciba Foundation Symposium, *Civilization and Science: in Conflict or Collaboration?* Amsterdam: Elsevier.

Toulmin, S. (1982) *The Return to Cosmology: Postmodern Science and the Theology of Nature*. Berkeley: University of California Press.

Touraine, Alain (1985) 'An Introduction to the Study of Social Movements', *Social Research*, 52(4): 749–88.

Touraine, Alain (1986) 'Unionism as a Social Movement', in S.M. Lipset (ed.), *Unions in Transition*. San Francisco: ICS Press, pp. 151–73.

Toynbee, Arnold J. (1954) *A Study of History*, Vol. XIII. London: Oxford University Press. First published 1937.

Tunstall, J. (1983) *The Media in Britain*. London: Constable.

Turner, Bryan S. (1988) *Status*. Milton Keynes: Open University Press.

Turner, Bryan S. (1989) 'From Post-Industrial Society to Postmodern Politics', in J.R. Gibbins (ed.), *Contemporary Political Culture*. London: Sage, pp. 199–217.

Turner, Bryan S. (ed.) (1990) *Theories of Modernity and Postmodernity*. London: Sage.

Turner, S. and Factor, R. (1984) *Max Weber and the Dispute over Reason and Value*. London: Routledge & Kegan Paul.

Van Liere, K.D. and Dunlap, R.E. (1980) 'The Social Bases of Environmental Concerns', *Public Opinion Quarterly*, 44: 181–97.

Veen, H-J. (1989) 'The Greens as a Milieu Party', in E. Kolinsky (ed.), *Greens in West Germany*. Oxford: Berg, pp. 31–60.

Wallerstein, Immanuel (1974) *The Modern World System*. New York: Academic.

Wardell, Mark S. and Turner, Stephen P. (1986) 'Introduction: Dissolution of the Classical Project', in M. Wardell and S. Turner (eds), *Sociological Theory in Transition*. Boston: Allen & Unwin.

Waters, Malcolm (1982) *Strikes in Australia*. Sydney: Allen & Unwin.

Waters, Malcolm (1989a) 'Collegiality, Bureaucratization and Professionalization', *American Journal of Sociology*, 94(5): 945–72.

Waters, Malcolm (1989b) 'Pariarchy and Viriarchy: An Exploration and Reconstruction of Concepts of Masculine Domination', *Sociology* 23(2): 193–211.

Waters, Malcolm (1990a) 'Citizenship and the Constitution of Structured Social Inequality', *International Journal of Comparative Sociology*, 30(1–2): 159–80.

Waters, Malcolm (1990b) *Class and Stratification: Arrangements for Socioeconomic Inequality under Capitalism*. Melbourne: Longman Cheshire.

Weber, E. (1960) *Paths to the Present*. New York: Dodd, Mead.

Weber, Max (1949) *The Methodology of the Social Sciences*. New York: Free Press.

Weber, Max (1958) *The Rational and Social Foundations of Music*. Carbondale: Southern Illinois University Press.

Weber, Max (1970) 'Science as a Vocation', and 'Politics as a Vocation', in H. Gerth and C.W. Mills (eds), *From Max Weber*. London: Routledge & Kegan Paul.

Weber, M. (1976) *The Protestant Ethic and the Spirit of Capitalism*. Allen & Unwin.

Weber, Max (1978) *Economy and Society*, ed. G. Roth and C. Wittich. Berkeley: University of California Press.

Webster, A. (1988) 'The Changing Structural Relationship between Public Sector Science and Commercial Enterprise', *Science Policy Support Group Concept Paper No. 4*. Cambridge: Cambridge College of Arts and Technology.

Weingart, P. (1982) 'The Scientific Power Elite: a Chimera', in N. Elias, H. Martins and R. Whitley (eds), *Scientific Establishments and Hierarchies*. Dordrecht: Reidel.

Wilensky, H.L. (1981) 'Democratic Corporatism, Consensus and Social Policy', in *The Welfare State in Crisis*. Paris: OECD.

Williams, Karel, Cutler, Tony, Williams, John and Haslam, Colin (1987) 'The End of Mass Production?', *Economy and Society*, 16(3): 405–39.

Williams, R. (1981) *Culture*. London: Fontana.

Wilson, F.L. (1990) 'Neo-corporatism and the Rise of New Social Movements', in R.J. Dalton and M. Kuechler (eds), *Challenging the Political Order*. Cambridge: Polity, pp. 67–83.

Wilson, G.K. (1982) 'Why Is There No Corporatism in the United States?', in G. Lehmbruch and P.C. Schmitter (eds), *Patterns of Corporatist Policy-Making*. London: Sage, pp. 219–36.

Wilson, Julius William (1987) *The Truly Disadvantaged*. Chicago, Ill: University of Chicago Press.

Windschuttle, K. (1988) *The Media: A New Analysis of the Press, Television, Radio and Advertising in Australia*. Ringwood Vic.: Penguin.

Winkler, J.T. (1976) 'Corporatism', *European Journal of Sociology*, 17: 100–36.

Wolin, R. (1984) 'Modernism versus Post Modernism', *Telos*, 62: 90–130.

Wood, Stephen (1988) 'Between Fordism and Flexibility? The US Car Industry', in R. Hyman and W. Streeck (eds), *New Technology and Industrial Relations*. Oxford: Blackwell, pp. 101–27.

Woolf, S.J. (ed.) (1968) *European Fascism*. London: Weidenfeld & Nicolson.

Woolgar, S. (1981) 'Interests and Explanation in the Social Study of Science', *Social Studies of Science*, 11: 365–94.

Woolgar, S. (1988) *Science: the Very Idea*. Chichester: Ellis Horwood.

Wright, Erik Olin (1978) *Class, Crisis and the State*. London: New Left Books.

Wynne, B. (1982) 'Natural Knowledge and Social Context: Cambridge Physicists and the Luminiferous Ether', in B. Barnes and D. Edge (eds), *Science in Context: Readings in the Sociology of Science*. Milton Keynes: Open University Press.

Yearley, S. (1988) *Science, Technology and Social Change*. London: Unwin Hyman.

Name index

Abercrombie, N., Hill, S. and Turner, B.S. 6
Abercrombie, N. and Urry, J. 112, 113, 115, 174
Adorno, T.W. 7–8, 25, 47, 50–1, 54, 62, 67
Adorno, T.W. and Horkheimer, M. 53–4, 61, 75n, 78n, 203, 224–6, 231
Albury, D. and Schwartz, J. 205
Alexander, J.C. 42n
Alexander, J.C. and Colomy, P. 76n
Alic, J.A., and Caldwell Harris, M. 191
Amin, S. 105n
Anderson, P. 18–19, 69, 132
Arendt, H. 164n
Ash, T.G. 96, 158, 166n
ASTEC 208

Bacon, F. 198–9
Badham, R. and Mathews, J. 194n
Baglioni, G. 98
Baker, K., Dalton, R. and Hildebrandt, K. 164n
Bakhtin, M. 16
Baran, P. and Sweezy, P. 108
Barnes, S.H. and Kaase, M. 164n, 165n
Barnes, B. 41, 203, 207, 218n, 219n
Barnes, B. and Edge, D. 204
Baudrillard, J. 31–2, 44n, 45n, 67–8, 73, 78n, 124, 125, 130–2, 135n, 207, 225, 230, 238, 240n
Bauman, Z. 2, 23, 74, 138, 232, 233, 237, 240n
Beer, S.H. 105n
Bell, D. 30–1, 63, 77n, 78n, 113, 115, 164n, 174, 236, 239n, 240n
Bell, P. and Boehringer, K. 214
Ben-David, J. 25, 199, 202
Benjamin, W. 44n, 52, 67, 69, 78n, 226, 239n, 240n
Bennett, R.J. 100, 105n
Bennett, T. 78n
Berger, P. 86, 165n
Berger, S. 105n, 151, 164n, 165n
Berle, A. Jr. and Means, G.C. 111
Berman, M. 228
Bijker, W., Hughes, T. and Pinch, T. 218n
Birch, A. 105n
Birke, L. 213

Blauner, R. 194n
Bloch, H. 214, 219n, 240n
Blondel, J. 139
Bourassa, S. 64
Bourdieu, P. 21, 45n, 59, 78n, 131, 133
Boyne, R. and Rattansi, A. 219n
Brand, K.-W. 141
Braverman, H. 5, 112, 194n
Brenner, J. and Ramos, M. 22, 110, 125, 127
Brittan, A. 129
Brittan, S. 139
Brown, L. 211
Brown, L., Flavin, C. and Postel, S. 211
Brubaker, R. 8–9, 43n, 76n, 81, 137
Brus, W. and Laski, K. 166n
Brym, R.J. 164n
Burawoy, M. 195n
Bürger, P. 36, 51, 62, 77n, 232
Burke, P. 56, 77n
Burklin, W. 144
Burnham, J. 111, 115
Burris, B.H. 176

Calhoun, C. 42n, 132
Callon, M. 217
Campbell, C. 44n, 55, 60, 240n
Campbell, I. 194n
Carr, E.H. 44n
Carrigan, T., Connell, R.W. and Lee, J. 129
Cawson, A. 104n
Ceausescu, N. 158
Chambers, I. 71–2
Charlton, B. 215
Ciccotti, G., Cini, M. and De Maria, M. 205
Clarke, J. 74
Claygill, H. 64
Cole, J. and Cole, S. 218n
Collins, H. 213–15
Collingridge, D. 212
Collingridge, D. and Reeve, C. 215
Comte, A. 239
Connell, R.W. 15, 129, 228
Cornford, J. 105n
Cotgrove, S. 105n, 145, 164n, 165n
Cotgrove, S. and Box, S. 205

Cotgrove, S. and Duff, A. 144
Crane, D. 218n
Crook, S. 27, 76n, 239n, 240n
Crouch, C. 84, 105n
Crozier, M., Huntington, S. and
    Watanuki, J. 105n
Cultural Ministers Council Statistical
    Advisory Group 77n

Dahrendorf, R. 134n, 95, 104n, 105n, 143
Dalton, R.J. 105n, 139, 148, 164n, 165n
Dalton, R.J., Kuechler, M. and Burklin, W.
    144, 164n
Dalton, R.J., Flanagan, S.C. and
    Beck, P.A. 105n, 139, 164n
Davies, J.A. 146
Derrida, J. 133
Dobb, M. 24
Dodgson, M. 182
Dohse, K., Jürgens, U. and Malsch, T. 194n
Dore, R. 184
Durkheim, E. 3–5, 47, 200, 202, 218n,
    223–4, 230, 235, 248–9, 240n

Eckersley, R. 46, 144, 213
Edder, K. 165n
Edge, S. 204
Ehrenreich, B. and Ehrenreich, J. 112
Elias, N. 63
Engels, F. 91
Enzensberger, H.M. 75, 78n
Erikson, R., Goldthorpe, J.H. and
    Portacarero, L. 116
Etzioni, A. and Etzioni-Halevy, E. 239n
Evans, A. and Bell, J. 188–9
Evans, P.B., Rueschmeyer, D. and
    Skocpol, T. 104n
Ewan, S. 60, 230

Featherstone, M. 144, 230, 232–3
Feher, F. and Heller, A. 166n
Feist, A. and Hutchison, R. 78n
Ferguson, H. 16, 44n, 219n
Flanagan, S. 164n
Fiske, J. 44n, 59, 61, 71–2, 78n
Fix-Sterz, J. and Lay, G. 181–3, 185
Forman, P. 219n
Foster, H. 64–5, 69
Foucault, M. 134n, 240n
Frank, A.G. 105n
Frankel, B. 31, 170

Gans, H. 59
Gardner, C. and Young, R. 214–15
Gerlach, L. and Hine, V. 152

Gershuny, J.I. and Pahl, R.E. 173
Gibbins, J.R. 165n
Gibbons, M. 199
Gibbons, M. and Wittrock, B. 205
Giddens, A. 20, 119
Giner, S. 77n
Goldthorpe, J.H. 113, 115, 116, 164n
Goldthorpe, J.H., Bechhofer, F. and
    Platt, J. 115, 121, 164n
Gorz, A. 121
Gouldner, A.W. 50, 76n, 164n, 165n
Grew, R. 44n
Gunderlach, P. 151
Gurevich, A.J. 16

Habermas, J. 25–8, 30–1, 33, 36, 42n, 43n,
    44n, 47, 51, 62, 69, 75, 78n, 95, 105n,
    127, 130, 134n, 169, 203–4, 207, 218n,
    225, 233–6, 240n
Hadley, R. and Hatch, S. 105n
Hagstrom, W. 205
Hakim, C. 177–8, 189–90
Halal, W.E. 175–6, 186, 195n
Hall, S. and Jefferson, T. 72, 77n
Handlin, O. 216
Harris, H. and Lipman, A. 63–4
Harvey, D. 2, 29–30, 40, 69, 78n, 172–3,
    180, 188, 235–7, 240n
Hassan, I. 58, 77n
Held, D. 104n
Hendry, J. 219n
Hernes, H.M. 127
Hilferding, R. 169
Hill, S. 219n
Hirschhorn, L. 171–2
Holloway, G. 151
Holter, H. 126
Horkheimer, M. 7, 25, 53
Hughes, T. 204
Hulsberg, W. 151, 165n
Hume, D. 55, 77n
Huntington, S. 164n, 166n
Huyssen, A. 53, 62, 76n
Hyman, R. 194n

Inglehart, R. 94, 105n, 141, 145
Inglehart, R. and Flanagan, S.C. 105n

Jameson, F. 64–5, 69
Janicke, M. 105n
Jasnay, A. de 105n
Jencks, C. 62–3, 65–6, 70, 74
Jessop, B. 115, 83
Johnson, T. 112
Jones, B. 175

Jones, F.L. and Davis, P. 116

Kaase, M. 160, 165n
Kant, I. 47–8, 69, 225
Katz, E. and Liebes, T. 230
Kellner, D. 237–8
Kelly, J.A. and Worrell, J. 129
Kerckhoff, A.C., Campbell, R.T. and
    Winfield-Laird, I. 116
Kern, H. and Schumann, M. 179, 180,
    191–2, 194n
Kitchelt, H. 140, 141, 160–1, 163, 165n,
    166n
Konrad, G. and Szelenyi, I. 23, 138
Kornhauser, W. 164n
Kosselleck, R. 18, 45n
Kriesi, H.P. 86, 141, 164n, 165n
Kristol, I. 165n
Kroker, A. and Cook, D. 67–8
Kumar, K. 31, 42n, 170, 174, 176, 194n,
    239n

Lane, C. 191, 195n, 196n
Lash, S. 29, 36, 44n, 47, 50–1, 59, 61,
    69–70, 73, 76n, 78n, 117, 121, 164n,
    165n, 225, 239n
Lash, S. and Urry, J. 29–30, 42n, 44n, 58,
    112, 113, 164n, 165n, 171, 228
Laslett, B. and Brenner, J. 21–2, 127
Latour, B. 217
Latour, B. and Woolgar, S. 205
Law, J. 217
Lechner, F. 63, 76n
Leff, G. 16
Lehmbruch, G. 104n
Lehmbruch, G. and Schmitter, P.C. 104n,
    165n
Leiss, W. 197, 203–4, 210
Lengermann, P.M. and Wallace, R.A.
    128–9
Lenin, V.I. 91
Levine, D.N. 81
Levitt, T. 151
Levy, M.J. Jr. 4
Lewis, G. 72
Lipset, S.M. 139
Lowe, P.D. and Rudig, W. 166n
Luard, E. 101, 105n
Lyotard, J.-F. 31, 42n, 44n, 62, 65, 68, 170,
    216, 224, 237–8

Mackenzie, D. and Spinardi, G. 205
Mackenzie, D. and Wajcman, J. 218n
Magirier, G. 182
Mallet, S. 112

Mann, M. 10, 18, 19, 119
Mannheim, K. 82, 239
Marcùse, H. 8, 230, 240n
Marshall, G., Rose, D., Vogler, C. and
    Newby, H. 120
Marshall, T.H. 118, 119
Martin, B. 236
Marx, K. 5, 7, 9, 10, 29, 42n, 43n, 54, 75,
    108, 112, 115, 118, 142, 167–71, 173,
    181, 190, 223–4, 228, 234–5, 238–9,
    240n
Mathews, J. 171–3, 181, 183, 185, 186, 191,
    194n, 195n
McCracken, G. 61, 77n
McEachern, D. 104n
McLuhan, M. 67–8, 73, 78n
Melucci, A. 148, 151
Mennell, S. 63
Merton, R.K. 9, 25, 44n, 200–2, 205, 209,
    218n, 219n
Michels, R. 82, 150
Middlemas, K. 104n
Miliband, R. 104n
Miller, W.L. 139
Mills, C.W. 42n
Minkenberg, M. and Inglehart, R. 141
Misztal, B. 148, 151
Moorehouse, H.F. 120
Moriarty, M. 55
Morley, D. 67
Morrison, D.E. and Dunlap, R.E. 165n
Mosse, G.L. 105n
Mowlana, H. and Wilson, C. 56
Mulkay, M. 201–2, 207, 225
Müller-Rommel, F. 140, 141, 166n
Müller-Rommel, F. and Poguntke, T. 141,
    166n
Murray, F. 187

Nagy, I. 158
Naisbitt, J. and Aburdene, P. 105n
Nelkin, D. 215
Nettl, J.P. 166n
Netzer, D. 59
Newby, H. 211

O'Connor, J. 105n, 139
Offe, C. 28, 30, 42n, 58, 95, 109, 145,
    150–3, 164n, 165n, 166n, 173–7, 194n,
    208, 219n
Offe, C. and Ronge, V. 43n, 106

Pakulski, J. 105n, 141, 147, 164n, 165n,
    166n
Papadakis, E. 161, 164n

Parkin, F. 145, 164n, 166n
Parkin, S. 141, 166n
Parsons, T. 4, 5, 27, 42n, 47, 239n
Penn, R. and Scattergood, H. 196n
Phillimore, A.J. 194n
Pickering, A. 239n
Piore, M.J. and Sabel, C.F. 40, 172–3, 179, 180, 183–4, 187–8, 194n
Pizzorno, A. 166n
Poggi, G. 19, 20, 86, 104n, 105n
Pollert, A. 177–8, 188–90, 194n, 195n
Poulantzas, N. 24, 112, 114, 104n
Price, D.J. de Solla 25, 197–8, 201, 204, 207, 218n

Ravetz, J. 199, 214
Reimer, B. 166n
Renner, K. 112, 113, 115
Rocher, G. 42n
Rodgers, P. 208
Ronayne, J. 207, 219n
Rootes, C.A. 165n
Rorty, R. 217
Rose, D., Marshall, G., Newby, H. and Vogler, C. 120
Rothblatt, S. 26, 199, 218n
Rothschild-Whitt, J. 152

Saarlvik, B. and Crewe, I. 139
Salisbury, R.H. 90, 104n, 166n
Schefter, M. 166n
Schmitt, R. 148, 164n, 165n, 166n
Schmitter, P.C. 104n, 166n
Schmitter, P.C. and Lembruch, G. 104n, 164n, 165n
Schumann, M. 180, 194n, 196n
Scott, A.J. 40, 179
Shils, E. 214
Sklair, L. 26
Skocpol, T. 166n
Slater, D. 59, 240n
Smart, B. 232, 237
Smelser, N.J. 4
Smith, C. 195n
Solinas, G. 188
Sorge, A. and Streeck, W. 173
Spencer, H. 3, 4, 47
Stalin, J.V. 91
Staniszkis, J. 138
Steinmetz, G. and Wright, E.O. 177–8, 190
Storer, N. 205

Streeck, W. 188, 195n
Suzuki, D. and Knudtson, P. 212
Swyngedouw, E.A. 184–5, 194n, 195n

Taylor, F.W. 171
Thompson, G. 73
Tijssen, L. and van Vucht, L. 131
Tilly, C. 39
Toffler, A. 176, 190
Tomlinson, A. 61
Tomlinson, A. and Walker, H. 56
Tonnies, F. 42n
Toulmin, S. 214, 217
Touraine, A. 164n
Toynbee, A.J. 44n
Tunstall, J. 77n
Turner, B.S. 95, 120, 123, 124, 132, 134n, 144, 164n
Turner, S. and Factor, R. 76n

Van Liere, K.D. and Dunlap, R.E. 164n
Veen, H.-J. 105n, 144, 145, 163, 165n

Wallerstein, I. 43n, 105n
Wardell, M.S. and Turner, S.P. 240n
Waters, M. 22, 110, 119, 121, 122, 125, 127, 175
Weber, E. 49
Weber, M. 8–10, 22, 25, 43n, 44n, 49, 50, 541, 76n, 81–2, 84, 134n, 142, 150, 168–170, 175, 201–3, 224–6, 238, 239n
Webster, A. 209
Weingart, P. 206
Wilensky, H.L. 105n
Williams, K., Cutler, T., Williams, J. and Haslam, C. 194n
Williams, R. 54, 58, 76n, 77n
Wilson, F.L. 160, 166n
Wilson, G.K. 104n, 165n, 166n
Wilson, J.W. 121
Windschuttle, K. 60
Winkler, J.T. 83
Wolin, R. 68
Wood, S. 186, 195n
Woolf, S.J. 104n
Woolgar, S. 216, 218n, 239n
Wright, E.O. 112
Wynne, B. 199, 218n

Yearley, S. 202

Subject index

AIDS 96, 197, 230–1
American politics 23, 90–1, 137, 159–60, 166n
androgyny *see* viriarchy
anti-bureaucratic movements *see* new social movements
anti-partocratic movements 158–60, 165n
architecture 63–5
Australia 45n, 46n, 59, 73, 77n, 80, 99, 116, 139–40, 159, 208, 211, 214, 229, 240n
avant-garde 51–2, 62–3, 70

Britain *see* UK
bureaucratization 80–3, 136–7, 149–50; *see also* rationalization

CAD (computer-aided design) 181–3
CAI (computer-aided industry) 181–3
Canada 45n, 168
CAP (computer-aided planning) 181–3
capitalism and modernization 6–8, 10, 15, 10–21, 23–6, 30, 109–24
  disorganized 30, 32, 174–5, 223
  neo-, late, liberal, organized, corporate 26–30, 43n, 107–9, 124, 167, 169, 222–3
China 19, 105n
CIM (computer-integrated manufacturing) 181–3
citizenship 38, 118–20, 122–3, 137
'citizen politics' *see* new politics
civic initiatives 38, 138–40, 158
civil rights movements *see* new social movements
class 20–2, 35, 38–9, 109–25, 131–3, 134n, 139–47, 142–7, 165n, 218n, 221–2
  and status categories 123–5, 133
  'class voting index' 39
  new class 144–5, 165n
  new middle class 21, 110–12, 131, 134n, 144–5, 165n
  new petty bourgeoisie 112, 177–8
  new working class 112, 134n
  old and new class system 20–2, 38–9, 109–10, 114–18, 131–3, 144, 165n
  politics of class 162–4, 165n
  service class 112–18

underclass 121
  see also dealignment, decomposition of class, decoupling of social conflicts
closure processes 110, 117
CNC (computer numerically controlled) machines 181–3, 195–6n
Cold War 89
commodification 6–8, 23–5, 32, 43n, 47, 53–8, 73, 200, 205–6, 207, 220–1, 239n
  and decommodification 58, 208–9
  and hypercommodification 36, 47, 58–61, 68–74, 206–10, 220–1, 237
  and recommodification 58, 208–9
  defined 7, 53
  of art 18, 43n, 53–7
  of culture 7–8, 17–18, 53–8, 73, 221
  of science 25–6, 198, 200, 205–6, 208
  see also modernization, rationalization
consumption and consumerism 118–25, 131–3, 134n
control of nature 197, 202–5, 210–13
corporate capitalism 108–10; *see also* capitalism
corporatism 37–8, 80, 83–97, 136–8, 149–52, 157–9, 165n, 221
  communist (socialist) 86–7, 91–2, 137–8, 157–8
  fascist 86–7, 165n
  liberal (bureaucratic) 86–92
corporatist dysfunctions 92–7, 157–60
corporatist state 83–96, 157–8, 165n, 221
credentialization and credentialism 108, 110, 114, 117
cultural tradition 52–3, 65–6
culture industry 8, 15–16, 36, 53

dealignment 123, 139, 143–4
decentralization of state authority 97–8
deconstruction 111–17, 118–24, 125–31
  of capital 111–17
  of labour 118–24
  of patriarchy 125–31
  see also differentiation
decomposition of class 111–25, 131–3, 134n, 142–5
decoupling of social conflicts 39, 138, 143–5

Denmark 127, 177
deregulation 99–100
desocialization 230–1
devolution of state power 80, 97–9
dialectic of enlightenment 224–6
differentiation 3–6, 10–26, 32–3, 47–57, 63,
    110, 131–3, 192, 198, 200, 206, 225,
    227, 239n
    and dedifferentiation 32–3, 49, 51, 68,
        70–4, 106, 133–4, 193–4, 220, 225, 227
    dialectic of 225–6, 227–8
    and hyperdifferentiation 33–7, 41, 47, 57,
        61, 68–74, 106, 132, 134, 220–1, 225,
        227–9, 237
    and secularization 14–15
    of science 198, 200–2, 206
    structural 4–5, 32–3, 110
    and organization 10–11, 192, 227
    see also modernization

Eastern Europe 19, 80, 83, 89–92, 96, 103,
    105n, 119, 138–9, 147, 157–9
ecopax movements 138, 142; see also new
    social movements
electoral cycle 163
'end of the social' thesis 238
England 18–19, 24, 43n, 45n, 60, 63; see also
    UK
environmental critique of science 210–11
environmental movements see new social
    movements, ecopax movements
etatist projects 86–9

feminist movements see new social
    movements
feudal society 12–13
feudal state 18
First World War 84, 89, 91, 163, 219n
flexible specialization, manufacturing,
    technology, organization and labour 40,
    178–93, 194–5n, 227–8
Fordism 40, 42n, 170, 172–3, 178–9, 182,
    184–5, 192, 194, 222
France 42n, 45n, 55, 60, 78n, 98, 116, 119,
    134n, 177, 182, 199
Frankfurt School 7, 26–8, 78n, 83, 134n
functional flexibility 191–2

gender and sex differences 21–2, 35, 38–9,
    108–11, 117, 122–3, 125–34, 161, 189,
    221
    in occupational structure 21–2, 38–9,
        122–3, 125–34, 161, 189, 221
    in politics 21, 161
    see also patriarchy, viriarchy,

deconstruction of patriarchy
    generations 39, 146–7, 163–4
Germany 45n, 99, 134n, 162, 173, 177–9,
    182–3, 191, 194–5n, 199, 219n
globalization 101–2, 210–11
Great Depression 84, 86, 96, 146
green movements see new social
    movements, ecopax movements
green parties see Left-libertarian parties
Greenpeace 101, 153

Holland 18–19, 43n, 134n, 177

imagined communities 132–3
Italy 98, 177–8, 187–8
IVF 240n

Japan 45n, 182–7, 190–1, 194, 208
JIT (just-in-time) system 185–6

Left-libertarian parties 140–2, 151–2, 160–1,
    163
liberal society 13–14, 106–7
lifestyle 58–61, 73

managerial decentralization 186–8
marketization 38, 99–100
mass culture 53, 55–6
mass media 56, 67–8, 73, 111, 142, 154–9
    and diffusion of new social movements
        158–9
    and new social movements 154–7
mass production 171–3
mass society theories 26
medieval society 20
meta-narratives in sociology 237–9
milieu parties 39, 88–9, 136, 138–9, 142,
    164n
modernism 10, 51, 62–5, 74, 76n
    and sociology 233–6
modernization 3, 10–26, 33–41, 47–9, 56–7,
    63–5, 102, 107–9, 136–8, 157, 167–9
    compared with postmodernization 33–41,
        63–5, 74, 169–70, 233–6
    defined as differentiation,
        commodification and rationalization 3,
        10, 32–3
    of culture 16–18, 36, 48, 50–2, 56–7, 63–5
    of inequality 20–22, 38
    of organization, work and production
        23–5, 40, 108–9
    of politics 22–3, 39, 80–90, 136–8
    of science 25–6, 40, 197–206
    of the state 18–20, 37, 80–90, 102–3
    Soviet-type 91–2, 157

see also commodification, differentiation,
    rationalization

new politics 39–40, 138–64, 165–6n, 222
    and new elites 161
    characteristics 139–41, 148
    compared with conventional (power)
        politics 139, 149
    impact on the conventional parties 161–2
    in Eastern Europe 157–60, 164n
    rise in Western Europe 142–7
    transient nature of 162–3
    see also new social movements
New Right 146, 161
new social movements 39, 98–9, 138, 140–2,
    144–63;
    and the mass media 154–7
    assessment of strength 141
    compared with 'old' movements 140
    in the USA 159–60
    orientations and styles of 147–54
    structure of 151–4
    supporters of 146–7
    see also anti-partocratic movements,
        ecopax movements
new values 93–4, 105n, 141, 146
New Zealand 80, 99, 116, 119, 139–40, 160

OECD 203, 206
organization 10–16, 108–11, 167–70, 175–6,
    183–8, 192–3, 198–200, 220–2, 228–9,
    233, 237
    defined 10
    dialectic of 228–9
    and disorganization 28–30, 42n, 80, 106,
        175, 207–11, 216–7, 228–9, 237
    and hyperorganization 41, 228–9, 237
    and self-organization 148–51
organizational man 82–3
organized society 15–26

patriarchy 108, 125–6
peace movements *see* ecopax movements,
    new social movements
petty enterpreneurialism 177–8
Polish Solidarity 23, 138, 147, 157, 165n
popular music 56, 70–1
postculture 37, 57–8, 61, 74, 198
postindustrial society 30–2, 121, 170, 173–7,
    192
postmaterialist values *see* new values
postmodern 2, 31, 36–7, 41, 192, 217, 220–4,
    229
    age 41n, 232
    culture 31, 36–7, 37–9, 69–74, 221

meaning and application 2, 32–3
science and technology 216–18, 223
postmodernism 29, 32, 217
    and sociology 231–3, 237–9
postmodernization 2, 32–41, 47, 54, 63–5,
    74, 167, 211–12, 220–4, 225, 229, 231–3
    and sociology 231–9
    contrasted with modernization 32–41, 47,
        74
    defined as hyper- and de- differentiation,
        rationalization, organization and
        commodification 36, 47, 57, 167, 220–1,
        229
    general processes of 31–41, 220–1, 227–31
    of culture and art 36–7, 47–75, 221
    of inequalities 139–47, 221–2
    of organization, work and production 40,
        167, 192–4, 222–3
    of politics 37, 39–40, 222
    of popular culture 70–2, 221
    of science and technology 40–1, 206–11,
        216–18, 223
    of the state 37–8, 221
postscience 198, 216–18
post-Stalinist societies 43n, 92, 157–8
post-Stalinist generation 92, 147, 158
postwar generation 94–5
'power politics' 81, 89
privatization 38, 99–100
Public Understanding of Science 213–16

rationalization 8–10, 32, 47, 50–3, 57, 63,
    66, 136–8, 168, 192, 198, 200, 206, 239n
    and hyper-rationalization 36–7, 41, 47,
        61–5, 67–8, 70–4, 212, 220–1, 237
    defined 8–9
    formal 81–2
    of culture 50–7, 63, 66–7
    of inequality, production, work and
        science, and the state 16–26, 168–73,
        192
    of politics 16–26, 80–6, 136–8
    of science 198, 200, 202–6, 213
    see also modernization, commodification
Reformation 63
relational conception of knowledge 226–7
Romanticism 49, 63, 70
Royal Society 197

science policy 206–10
Second World War 91, 146
skinheads 73–4
societal types: absolutist, corporatist,
    feudal, forager-tribal, liberal,

organized, statist, technocratic 11–12, 34–5
Soviet Union 19, 91–2, 157–8
Spain 97–8
strategic management 184–5

Tasmania 162, 211
taste 55–6, 58–61
Taylorism 170–1, 179, 192, 194n

UK 18–19, 24, 60, 63, 116, 119, 134n, 173, 177, 182, 190, 195, 199, 219n, 229
UN 46n, 101, 103

USA 42n, 43n, 45n, 46n, 49, 53, 59–60, 77n, 78n, 80, 89–91, 105n, 121–2, 137, 157–60, 165–6n, 172–4, 177, 182–3, 194–5n, 199, 203, 205, 208

Vienna Conference 85
Vienna Congress 136–7
viriarchy 110, 126–9

women *see* gender and sex divisions, viriarchy

Yalta Conference 85